CRITICAL DIRECTIONS

A series of criticism selected and edited by
J.R. (Tim) Struthers
Department of English, University of Guelph

The volumes chosen for this series explore directions through which criticism can uphold its most urgent responsibilities: to the honouring of literature and language, to the cultivation of a more profound, more valuable experience of art and life, and to the building of a more enlightened society.

1. *Volleys*, Sam Solecki, John Metcalf and W.J. Keith

2. *An Independent Stance:*
Essays on English-Canadian Criticism and Fiction, W.J. Keith

3. *How Stories Mean*, ed. John Metcalf and J.R. (Tim) Struthers

How Stories Mean

EDITED BY JOHN METCALF
AND J.R. (TIM) STRUTHERS

The Porcupine's Quill

CANADIAN CATALOGUING IN PUBLICATION DATA

How stories mean

(Critical directions)
ISBN 0-88984-127-6

1. Short stories, Canadian (English) – History and criticism.*
2. Canadian fiction (English) – 20th century – History and criticism.*
3. Fiction – Technique. 4. Fiction - Authorship.
I. Metcalf, John, 1938- . II. Struthers, J.R. Tim, 1950- .
III. Series.

PS8191.S5H68 1993   C813'.0109054   C92-093115-4
PR91992.52.H68 1993

Published by The Porcupine's Quill, Inc., 68 Main Street, Erin, Ontario
NOB 1TO with financial assistance from The Canada Council and the
Ontario Arts Council. The support of the Government of Ontario through
the Ministry of Culture, Tourism and Recreation is also gratefully acknowledged.

Distributed by General Publishing, 30 Lesmill Road,
Don Mills, Ontario M3B 2T6.

Edited for the press by John Metcalf and J.R. (Tim) Struthers.
Assisted by Doris Cowan.

Cover is after a photograph by Blair Sharpe.

Contents

FOR MYRNA METCALF AND MARIANNE MICROS

J.R. (Tim) Struthers

METCALF & CO.

AS A STUDENT OF LITERATURE and as a university professor, I have benefited significantly from the lessons which the more imaginative literary critics (Northrop Frye and Balachandra Rajan, to name two) can teach us about literature. But in the years since I completed my formal academic training, I have found that my interests as a critic have shifted, and have been invigorated, as a result of a unique education gained by listening to creative writers. Some of my university colleagues find what I have to say on this subject a little surprising. They understand my enduring concern with literary form, but are a little bewildered by my more recent fascination with the possibilities of style.

How did I become interested in such and such? Through editing my collection *The Montreal Story Tellers*, I reply; in particular by studying the memoir-essays by Hugh Hood, John Metcalf, Ray Smith, Raymond Fraser, and Clark Blaise which open that volume. Or through interviewing writers, I say. Hearing how they resist most of my academically-based formulations. More recently, I continue, as a result of many, many conversations that I have enjoyed with John Metcalf as publisher of two books of his criticism through Red Kite Press and as co-conspirator with him as acquisitions editors for The Porcupine's Quill.

The formal training that I acquired in the process of obtaining three academic degrees in English has not been sufficient to teach me to read the way I want to read now. Nor has the huge body of literary theory that absorbs many critics of my generation been equal to this task. Narrowly academic obsessions have led many critics to lose sight of our principal responsibilities – to literature and language, to the experience of life, to the reading public – and to vanish into a haze of intellection and semantics. In contrast, many Canadian writers have succeeded in speaking passionately and lucidly and perceptively about the artistry of their own and other individuals' work.

By casting light upon the nature of their writing, the inside story, writers like John Metcalf provide the means to enhance our analytic understanding of literature and our sense of wonder about literature.

If I had not read essays like John Metcalf's 'Editing the Best', 'Punctuation as Score', and 'That Damn Clock Again', I doubt that I would have started to investigate the possibilities of style. Call this the music of prose: it is what generates, at some intuitive level, our sense of a story's power the first and every other time that we read the story. I would not have become so finely aware of this music, I would not have thought to comment on it, and I would not have begun to grasp how I might go about analysing it, if I had not kept listening to John Metcalf and his contemporaries talk about literature — about their craft.

For more than two decades, John Metcalf has laboured tirelessly to produce his own illuminating assessments of the art of fiction. He has also encouraged many other Canadian writers to discuss the making of their stories. Through his anthologies of stories and commentaries, John Metcalf has introduced generations of readers to exciting new possibilities of form, technique, style, and language found in contemporary writing. The present collaboration is even wider in scope, reprinting various seminal commentaries from John's earlier anthologies, gathering other intriguing items from relatively obscure sources, and including several more pieces newly commissioned by John. This book is a spirited testimonial by fifteen distinguished artists to the development of short story writing in Canada. It pleases me to have the opportunity to emphasize how indispensable the role played by John Metcalf in this ongoing history has been, how much enthusiasm and rigour he has contributed to the advancement of the short story in Canada.

John Metcalf

A WINE-DRENCHED SHOUT

IN THE LATE 1960s and early '70s there occurred what has often been called an 'explosion' of new writing in Canada. Those years were particularly fruitful for the short story. In 1967 Audrey Thomas published *Ten Green Bottles* (in the USA) and Hugh Hood published *Around the Mountain: Scenes from Montreal Life* and Dave Godfrey published *Death Goes Better with Coca-Cola*. In 1968 Alice Munro published *Dance of the Happy Shades* and Clark Blaise published a group of stories in *New Canadian Writing, 1968*. In 1969 Ray Smith published *Cape Breton is the Thought-Control Centre of Canada* and I published a clutch of stories in *New Canadian Writing, 1969*. In 1970 I published *The Lady Who Sold Furniture* and Margaret Laurence published *A Bird in the House*. In 1971 Hugh Hood published *The Fruit Man, the Meat Man and the Manager* and Norman Levine published *I Don't Want To Know Anyone Too Well*. In 1972 Terrence Heath published *the truth & other stories*. In 1973 Clark Blaise published *A North American Education* and in 1974 *Tribal Justice*. Also in 1974 Alice Munro published *Something I've Been Meaning To Tell You* and Ray Smith published *Lord Nelson Tavern*. In 1976 Jack Hodgins published *Spit Delaney's Island*.

What accounts for this surge of writing of such high quality in a period of just a few years, a surge of writing which was the consolidating and extending of the modern story in Canada? An explanation popularly held is that the 'explosion' was related to the founding of such nationalist small presses as Oberon, Coach House, and Anansi. Robert Weaver in the entry 'Short Stories in English' in *The Oxford Companion to Canadian Literature* asserts that 'the small literary publishers' provided 'the real impetus' in the publishing of short stories. He cites in particular the activities of Oberon Press, founded in 1966, as central to the vigour of the short story in Canada. It is not quite clear whether he means to suggest that 'the small literary publishers' discovered and elicited new work or whether existing work suddenly found outlets previously denied it by commercial houses. Whichever, the evidence would seem to suggest that the relationship between the 'explosion' and 'the small literary publishers' needs to be reconsidered.

Of the seventeen story collections cited so far only five were published with 'small literary publishers' and only one of those five with Oberon – and that single title was not a talent discovered by Oberon but was the veteran writer Hugh Hood whose work had already been published internationally. Oberon's importance to the story – apart from the anthology series founded by David Helwig and Tom Marshall which evolved from *Fourteen Stories High* to *New Canadian Stories* to *Best Canadian Stories* – dates from about 1974 or 1975, some years after the 'explosion'. The House of Anansi published very few collections of stories; I can only call to mind three or four titles. And Coach House – apart from a series of anthologies entitled *The Story So Far* – foundered in pretentiousness and raving obscurity.

If the 'explosion' in the genre cannot be linked to the founding of the literary presses – and the proposition does seem more than dubious – what else might account for it? I have often heard the explanation offered that the work was called forth by the *Zeitgeist*, by the intensity of nationalist yearning gripping the country at that time. This explanation explains much less than it might seem to. A little thought soon shows that the origins of the work pre-date the rise of fervent nationalism.

Alice Munro had been publishing in magazines since the early fifties; she once described *Dance of the Happy Shades* as having had a fourteen-year apprenticeship. Blaise's dazzling and innovative work had been appearing in magazines in the States long before his first publication here with Clarke, Irwin. Smith's *Cape Breton* collection in 1969 had been preceded by two novels, one unpublished and one abandoned, which reflected no nationalistic interests whatsoever. My own first stories, all with British settings, were written in 1962 and 1963 and appeared in *Prism International* in 1964. Nor should we forget that not all the writers were of the same generation. In 1961 Ethel Wilson had published *Mrs. Golightly and Other Stories* and Norman Levine had published *One Way Ticket*. Hugh Hood had published *Flying a Red Kite* in 1962. Margaret Laurence had published *The Tomorrow-Tamer* in 1963.

But if the writing itself was in gestation long before its birth at this period, it is true that the intensifying nationalism provided a receptive climate and the illusion of an audience. Our involvement in the dream of a national literature was less in harnessing our writing to some grand National Vision and more in proselytizing. We thought it proper – and I still think it proper – for Canadians to read Canadian writing and to that end we taught, performed, and anthologized. It is also true that most of us then felt that we were writing at a unique moment in Canada's history, that we were engaged in the building of a national literature.

This euphoria lasted almost until 1975.

No explanation for the 'explosion' seems to accommodate all the facts; no single explanation seems to accommodate the gestation periods of the writing, the ages of the authors, the differing countries of origin or residence, the differing influences, styles. Literary historians have come along in our wake inventing bizarre 'traditions' to which they assert we belong and generally trying to cram too much string into too small a bag but the reality seems to me, looking back, to be that much of the 'explosion' in the story genre was, at the beginning, coincidental and accidental, that we all invented ourselves largely independently as I suspect all writers do, taking what was needed or delightful from whatever sources presented themselves.

But if I'm at a loss to explain *why* this group appeared when it did, I'm not at all at a loss to explain what we were all doing. That we all found ourselves publishing within the same period was most probably coincidental, but after initial publications many of us became acquaintances and friends and discovered a common agenda. The interactions among many of the writers represented in this book resulted in something close to a very informal and undefined movement.

Though 'movement' isn't quite the word I want.

Might 'network' be more precise?

Certainly there was a sense of separate but shared endeavour. Here are some of the ways we discovered it and each other.

I remember sitting in my apartment one night in Montreal listening to Alice Munro's story 'Images' on CBC *Anthology*. This was before she had published *Dance of the Happy Shades*. I was delighted, amazed, and envious. The story had succeeded brilliantly at exactly the same problems of construction that I myself was messing about with and trying to solve. As I listened to the story, I instantly *recognized* what Alice was doing. Of course, I wrote to her immediately and entered into a discussion of technical problems that went on intermittently for the next seven or eight years.

Some of us got to know each other better not only through Robert Weaver's *Anthology* programme but also through his *Tamarack Review*.

Kent Thompson was known to most of us through his fiction and through his editorship of *The Fiddlehead* in the years 1966-70. During that period he raised the magazine to a level it has not attained since. His sustaining enthusiasm for new writing and his love of contentious debate about technique helped many of us to define further what we were driving towards.

In Montreal, Hugh Hood, Ray Fraser, Ray Smith, Clark Blaise, and I came together to form Montreal Story Teller though Ray Smith and I had been close friends for some time before this. We all shared a passionate interest in craft and probably influenced each other in all kinds of subtle ways. I would certainly acknowledge the influence of Hood, Blaise, and Smith.

In 1970 Kent Thompson staged a conference at the University of New Brunswick in Fredericton on the state of Canadian fiction, inviting writers and academics. This three-day event intensified debate amongst the writers and confirmed for some of us that academic grasp of what we were doing lagged years behind us and that we'd be well advised to take care of our own analysis and criticism.

Out of that conference came my second Canadian story text, *The Narrative Voice* (1972).

And with each passing year the network expanded.

What *was* the common agenda?

What we were so passionately talking about was, in essence, how to go beyond – even escape from – the 'epiphany' story into new forms which could express new worlds, new sensibilities. Kent Thompson was speaking for many of us when he described our inheritance as having become Academy Stuff. Our education had been the great modernist story writers of the earlier part of the century, *The Garden Party*, *Dubliners*, monumentally and inescapably *In Our Time*, *A Curtain of Green*... Our problem was that the forms these masters had created had hardened into a classicism. We could no longer write in *their* forms.

(*Our education had been...* The idea currently being promoted by scholars like W.H. New and literary journalists like Wayne Grady that Canadian story writers are all the literary descendants of Duncan Campbell Scott is simply nationalist looney tunes and should be firmly scotched whenever it appears.)

There was no point in our writing yet another Hemingway or Eudora Welty story yet the shadow they cast was long. It should be remembered also that thirty years ago the dominance of these writers was even greater than it is now; these Ogres were then much closer to the poor Pygmies we were. In the fifties, I had actually *met* Hemingway in – of all places – Pamplona. Much of our early work was derivative – what else *could* it be? – but gradually we achieved new shapes, independence, new life. The record of all this struggle is quite plain to see.

(An aside.

It is ironic that most criticism of my work describes me as 'traditional' while *I* would consider myself an experimental writer having spent most of my writing life so far struggling with problems of form and technique. Ray Smith credits me with having invented a new form in the story 'The Teeth of My Father' and I would suggest to those critics who consider me 'traditional' that they read the paragraphs from 'Polly Ongle' discussed in 'That Damn Clock Again' and the paragraphs from *Going Down Slow* discussed in 'Punctuation as Score').

Over the last few years I've seen for the first time since our efforts in the sixties and seventies to forge new shapes a new generation of writers engaged in exactly the same task. It is heartening to know that the story is alive and doing what it must to stay alive. These new shapes and new principles of construction can be seen, for example, in the work of Keath Fraser, Linda Svendsen, Dayv James-French, Terry Griggs, Douglas Glover, and Diane Schoemperlen.

These emerging writers – and many others younger than they – are luckier than we were when we started writing. They're luckier in that they have *us* as audience to understand them, to help, to encourage. Our job was to break away from out-moded forms. This we succeeded in doing quite brilliantly. But the problem then facing us was audience. For whatever reasons – literary conservatism, xenophobia, The Great Canadian Time-Warp, simple dullness – our audience wasn't sufficiently sophisticated to have come to grips with even the Academy Stuff we were trying to displace.

I can recall with nightmare vividness my first year in Canada in 1962 and the first Canadian high school in which I taught. The head of the English department was a faded lady of ghastly, dentured gentility who wrote poems and had a volume of them published at her own expense. I can see that little book in my mind's eye even now; it was bound in nasty blue fabrikoid. Once a term she would correct a set of essays from each of my classes to discipline me and to show me how a seasoned professional did the job. All her corrections were neatly written in the margins in red ink.

She once ringed in red in a student's essay the sentence 'My father just grunted' and wrote in the margin: 'Only *piggies* grunt!!'

Even now, some thirty years later, I still remember fragments of one of her poems. Some things do not leave one. The poem made the case for abstaining from alcoholic beverages. It was entitled 'Modern Menace' and began:

No longer drunkards lie about,
  Nor often now the wine-drenched shout...

Some stanzas later it continued:

For ways we have against this Brute:
  If offered sherry, say '*Make mine fruit!*'

I can also recall the mind-numbing meetings of the department. One of the compulsory textbooks in literature contained Hemingway's story 'After the Storm' and it baffled them. How could one teach it? What, Miss Perkins wanted to know, constituted a correct answer about it on the exam? Why couldn't he *say* what he wanted to say? *Exactly!* Quite right. *Get his point across.* Whatever the point might *be.* What in God's name, demanded Mr Lumley, was it *about?*

It was like watching frowning chimps trying to extract a peanut from a medicine bottle.

It is probably difficult for young writers now (thank God!) to imagine the *dimness* of the Canadian literary world in the early sixties. Only the poets were showing vital signs. The appearance of Hugh Hood's *Flying a Red Kite* in 1962 caused hardly a ripple. Few people in Canada would have been aware that Margaret Laurence published *The Tomorrow-Tamer* in 1963. Richler and Levine had fled.

In 1952 The Ryerson Press had halted the printing of Earle Birney's *The Damnation of Vancouver*. The title was changed to *Trial of a City*. Birney commented in 1977: 'Ryersons..., for reasons explicable only to United Churchmen, refused at the last moment to accept "damnation". The word was O.K. in the text, but too shocking on the cover.' And I can guess that in their deliberations and in their conversations with Birney they used the word 'strong' because 'strong' was the word they were using with me in 1964.

This scene, this relationship, that line ... 'is, perhaps, rather *strong*.'

As late as 1968 an innocuous little story I'd written about two small boys playing in the woods and happening upon a used sanitary napkin caused Bill Clarke of Clarke, Irwin to declare that such a story would never be published by any decent and respectable house and most certainly never by his.

It was rumoured that Signing the Pledge was one of the conditions of employment at Clarke, Irwin. That may have been rumour but it was certainly true that Clarke, Irwin and Ryerson were teetotal; no wine-drenched shouts at *their* launching parties.

Tea and biccies.

Alice Munro's *Dance of the Happy Shades* seemed so revolutionary in 1968 that The Ryerson Press thought it prudent to have it introduced by Hugh Garner who then bestrode our narrow stage. As I've written elsewhere, this was rather like having an exhibition catalogue of Edward Hopper introduced by Norman Rockwell. Of Alice's stories, Garner wrote: 'These are women's stories that will appeal to women and men alike, unless somebody's been kidding me all this time.'

A sophisticate he wasn't.

At my high school I was teaching a bowdlerized edition of *Two Solitudes*, bowdlerized, disgracefully enough, by none other than Claude T. Bissell M.A., PH.D., President of the University of Toronto from 1958 to 1971.

It was felt, apparently, that to allow students of sixteen and seventeen to learn that Marius felt sexual desire for his stepmother would...

But who now can even guess what mastodons felt?

These anecdotes suggest something of the resolutely unliterary society we were working in and for. Our task was to forge new shapes and at the same time teach an audience how to read them, a task made doubly difficult because the audience had never understood or accepted the material we were writing in reaction to and attempting to replace. Our audience, if it was puzzling at all, was puzzling how to shake Hemingway, as it were, out of the medicine bottle. The essays and pieces gathered in this book, plus the ten essays especially written for it, are a record of our educational endeavour over a quarter of a century. But the book is far more than archival. It offers endless insights into how writers write which in turn suggest how stories mean and how we should read and experience them.

The idea of compiling this book was reinforced for us by the shining example of Louis Dudek's and Michael Gnarowski's *The Making of Modern Poetry in Canada*. The title of the book is a bow to John Ciardi's sterling text *How Does a Poem Mean?*.

Kent Thompson

THE CANADIAN SHORT STORY IN ENGLISH
AND THE LITTLE MAGAZINES: 1971

IT MUST BE ADMITTED that the title of this article is somewhat confusing. That is appropriate, if nothing else. The fact is that the state of the short story in Canada is tied closely to the operations of the little magazines in Canada, and the entire matter is somewhat confusing. In short, it's a jumble. And if certain generalizations can be drawn from this jumble (like threads from a tangle of yarn), it will not be a straightforward matter, nor will it be accomplished easily. Knots and tangles remain.

To begin with the first difficulty, and, at the same time, with a disclaimer. This discussion is necessarily limited to the short story and the little magazine *in English*. As nearly as I can tell, there is virtually no communication between English and French writers. They write for different magazines; they read different magazines. They do not, as a rule, read one another. When I was the editor of one of the English magazines, *The Fiddlehead*, from 1966 through 1970, I attempted to find and publish French prose. I had no success whatever. One of the leading French writers eventually told me that it would be awkward, perhaps even unwise, for a French writer to publish in such an English magazine. I hope that I do not imply any value judgements in that statement. It is merely a description of the way things are. If there is no communication, there is no antipathy, either, as far as I can see. To borrow the French phrase, it is a matter of being *maîtres chez nous*. If the two writers do come together, it is only in the anthology in the classroom.

Therefore what I propose to discuss is the matter of the short story in English and the little magazine. And this, of course, has a certain traditional

First published in *World Literature Written in English* 11.1 (1972).

ring to it. It is one of the academic truisms that the growth, development, and health of the short story as a form is dependent upon the health and influence of the periodical. That is where the short story began; that is where it generally remains. Yet the truism is misleading. It is also a fact that there is *no* mass circulation magazine in Canada which publishes short stories. The only magazine which even approaches such a description and continues to publish short stories is the regionally-oriented *Atlantic Advocate*. It remains one of the three best-paying 'markets' in Canada. Because, to put it bluntly, there is no 'market' whatever for the short story in Canada. There is no way that a writer in Canada can make anything more than beer-money (or, all right, buy a pair of skates for his children) from the sale of his short stories. Indeed, the only place he can publish them is in the little magazines.

And the little magazines, few of them as there are, fall into at least three separate categories. First of all, and most important to the writer, are those magazines which are exclusively interested in creative literature. There are five of them: *Prism International, West Coast Review, Quarry, The Tamarack Review*, and *The Fiddlehead*. Only *The Tamarack Review* and *The Fiddlehead* pay anything more than a token honorarium (that is to say, anything more than $25). By and large these are the Establishment literary periodicals. They are (with the exception of *The Tamarack Review*) edited and published by people associated with the universities (not, necessarily, by the universities). They do tend to publish more established writers – those who have clearly achieved some mastery of their craft. Because they are largely edited by academics it might seem that they would favour the short story in its traditional forms, and this would be only natural – scholars tend to look to the past for their standards. That they do not do this any more than they do is perhaps a surprise – and may indicate one of the reasons for the surprising health of the short story in Canada. And there is one other important fact about the relatively high-paying magazines – *The Tamarack Review* and *The Fiddlehead*. Both are supported by The Canada Council in order to pay their contributors. Thus, they are indirectly supported by the Government of Canada. The significance of this will, I hope, be seen by the end of this article.

A second category of little magazine in Canada is the scholarly magazine which prints some creative work alongside its scholarly articles. Magazines in this category include *Queen's Quarterly, The Malahat Review, Wascana*

Review, *The University of Windsor Review*, and *Dalhousie Review*. With their emphasis on scholarship, it is not surprising that these magazines – with the notable exception of *The University of Windsor Review* (where writers Alistair MacLeod, Joyce Carol Oates, and Eugene McNamara have been the fiction editors) – tend to publish the strictly traditional short stories. This is not to denigrate the stories which appear in these magazines – they are often very fine – but one does know what to expect from them. The *form* of the short story is rarely challenged.

The third category of little magazine is the lively little mimeographed magazine which leaps up in surprising places, usually around a group of young, un-established writers. The health and life-span of these magazines obviously varies. *Intercourse*, in Montreal, has been surprisingly vital, and despite (or because of) its slap-happy attitude toward respectability and the world of academe, its standards have often been quite high. Others, like *Tide* and *Salt* – and on a slightly more exalted level, *Copperfield* – get out when they can, as they can. They publish the young writers, the experimental writers (of successful and failed experiments), and, in a very real way, the continuing health of the literary culture is dependent upon them. It seems to me, in fact, that any country which does not have magazines analogous to these is fated to repeat itself with consistently diminishing returns. As long as they exist to instigate a continuing dialectic, the literature will develop.

All of these statements are, of course, truisms. But they need to be laid against that often overwhelming one, that as the periodical goes, so goes the short story. The short story in English in Canada is very healthy, and it is surprising that it is: there is no obvious market for the writer's work.

But this in turn breeds one of the anomalies. Because the short-story writer in Canada cannot write for a market, he doesn't. Because there is no money to be made anyway, the writer feels quite free to write as he pleases. He may feel that he is read only by other writers – but that does not need to be stultifying. His audience is a demanding one in terms of art; it sets very high standards. Consequently, there is very little 'slick' fiction being written in Canada. Much of it aims at that elusive ideal – art. And this, in turn, may explain the *kind* of vitality which exists.

II: Now, to continue further into the jumble.

Although the short story in English in Canada is alive and well, its vitality has gone largely unnoticed. The writer works with only a very small readership; he works largely without criticism. The fact is that there is very little criticism of contemporary Canadian prose being written, and none whatever about the short story. (This article is no adequate substitute, nor even a beginning; I am not a critic; I'm an ex-editor and a reader.)

Perhaps part of the blame for the lack of criticism might be laid on the university Departments of English, which provide most of what little contemporary criticism exists. Fashion has made its point even in the universities, however, and the short story is no longer a fashionable genre. When short stories are studied, they are usually studied as the minor work of a major novelist. Seldom are figures studied who are primarily short-story writers, or who have done their best work in the short-story genre: writers like Frank O'Connor, Flannery O'Connor, Seán O'Faoláin, Irwin Shaw, H.E. Bates, or J.F. Powers, for example.

It might be wondered if this is necessarily a bad thing. The criticism which exists in universities relies upon certain natural premises, but I am not at all sure that they are the best ones. For example, university courses tend to be organized around concepts of historical development – a procedure which is both convenient and traditional. As a result, emphasis has come to be placed on those writers who develop the form. Thus a hypothetical course on the 'Development of the Short Story from Poe to Borges (3 credits)' would naturally value very highly the Joycean epiphany.

But the resulting ironies make me dubious of this sort of premise. (We have seen it happen with novelists.) First of all, because the critics are also scholars, and therefore involved in preserving the traditions of the past, they tend to praise only *past* innovations. Their standards being locked in the past, therefore, they are quite scathing about contemporary ones, and thus tend to praise that work which most clearly emulates the past masters. (Herein lies the danger of magazines edited by scholar-critics at universities. Thus the 'scholarly' magazines have one set of premises, and the literary periodicals – often edited by writers who happen to teach for a living – have quite other ones.) But in the current situation, there is always an impulse toward an academy technique. This, in turn, is fought by the writer – but not always wisely.

Because there is yet another danger. The writer, naturally desiring immortality, and perceiving that it is to be obtained by achieving his inclusion in *future* courses in the development of the genre, tends to over-value innovation. Indeed, the very fellow who is often most vehement in his anti-academic expressions is also often the one most enslaved by the academy. To get into the academy of the future anthology, he warps his syntax obviously, he plays typographical games. Thus he, as well as the critic, can easily be conditioned by what is nothing more than a convenient habit of the universities in their organization of literature courses.

Consequently, it is possible that the writer in Canada, existing without a market, a large readership, or criticism, is better off. No criticism at all is better than the possible stultification of what might emerge. (In the u.s. a popular groundswell of interest might force a writer onto the reading list – a Brautigan, or a Vonnegut. But inasmuch as there is no public readership in Canada, this is an impossible dream for a Canadian writer.)

III: Deeper still into the jumble.

Who are the Canadian writers of the short story, and how are they to be categorized? Naming them is fairly easy. Those actively at work and publishing in the little magazines are: Margaret Laurence, Alice Munro, Hugh Hood, John Metcalf, Alden Nowlan, Mordecai Richler, David Helwig, Rudy Wiebe, Dave Godfrey, Shirley Faessler, Jack Ludwig, Mavis Gallant (although she publishes chiefly in the u.s.), Ray Smith, Raymond Fraser, George Bowering, Alistair MacLeod, Beth Harvor, W.D. Valgardson, Michael Yates, Andreas Schroeder, Hugh Garner, Don Bailey, David Lewis Stein, Doug Spettigue, C.J. Newman, and Clark Blaise. That is today's list. Tomorrow's would be different, as would yesterday's.

Categorizing them is another matter.

The first problem is that many of the writers are known chiefly for their work in other genres, as Alden Nowlan is known chiefly as a poet, and Margaret Laurence as a novelist. (Or, to take similar cases, George Bowering and Mordecai Richler – who is also an essayist, of course.) David Helwig, in fact, is a poet and a playwright as well.

But even greater complexities are presented by the particular conditions of the Canadian literary situation. It is impossible to categorize writers according to subject matter, or style, or even place of birth. And this, indeed, makes nonsense of any attempt to assert the presence of a tradition.

For example, the most eminent Canadian prose writers are Margaret

Laurence and Mordecai Richler. Both live in London, England. Richler writes about his Jewish Montreal background and Britain; Laurence now writes chiefly about Canada, although she has written extensively about Africa. But both, in a general sense, are quite influential on the Canadian scene. We talk about them a lot.

In turn, the chief Canadian nationalist might be considered. He is Dave Godfrey, who will not permit his work to be published by a Canadian subsidiary of an American publishing firm. He is a great admirer of Laurence, and went to Africa in something like emulation of her. The result was his novel, *The New Ancestors*, which won the Governor General's Award for Fiction in 1970 – and is set in Africa. Stylistically, too, Godfrey is quite different from Laurence. But Godfrey also studied at the University of Iowa Writers Workshop – as did Rudy Wiebe, W.D. Valgardson, Robert Kroetsch (the novelist, who teaches in the U.S.), and Clark Blaise. But Blaise, although American-born, is the bilingual son of English- and French-Canadian parents and continues to write often about the U.S., where he was raised. The immigrant factor must be considered. Another Canadian writer is British-born John Metcalf who, like Margaret Laurence, is a great admirer of the work of the late British novelist Joyce Cary.

Confusing?

Yes, and that's not the half of it. As in most ex-colonies, Canada's literary tradition is not yet fully formed – which ought not to be confused with accomplishment. That is, there is no *strong* national tradition. Canadian writers are not influenced only, or even chiefly, by other Canadian writers. This presents a problem for university professors when organizing a course – or the writer of an article like this one. Indeed, eminent writers of Canada's past often looked to London or New York for their publishers, their standards, and their public. Morley Callaghan, the friend of Fitzgerald and Hemingway, is a case in point.

And contemporary Canadian writers, besides reading their own contemporaries in the little magazines, as well as the writers published in London and New York, also read Commonwealth writers. At a conference in Fredericton in 1970, both Hugh Hood and Dave Godfrey cited their admiration for the work of the Nigerian writer Chinua Achebe. Yet Hood and Godfrey, although both committed strongly to certain *Canadian* attitudes, are quite different *kinds* of writers. Furthermore, given the rapidity of communications and the rapidity of development, it is no longer even reasonable to assume that a developing literature is somehow inferior to a more established one. (The twentieth century frees the writer from national traditions, I suppose, as well as condemns him to a certain rootlessness.) Thus, while some Canadian writers – I haven't named them, as it happens – might imitate James Joyce or Henry Miller and think themselves 'modern', this kind of activity is generally considered to be provincial aping at its worst, and is justly ignored.

But the matter is complicated further still by the fact of regional differences. Canada is so vast, and its historical progression westward was so rapid, that quite different cultures exist. The result is not merely different subjects and different settings, but different styles as well. (Remember the great Canadian motto: the medium is the message.) What is perfectly natural for the East Coast is alien for the West Coast – which is looked upon (perhaps unjustly) as the California of Canada. (My East Coast perspectives and prejudices are showing; to me, California represents the dictatorship of Kresge's.) But it is on the West Coast that there exists the only discernible 'school' of writers in Canada – the neo-surrealists around Michael Yates, who was, until recently, in the Department of Creative Writing at the University of British Columbia. (The University of British Columbia has the only Department of Creative Writing in Canada and is the only university to offer graduate courses and degrees in creative writing. Other universities generally offer an undergraduate course. The University of New Brunswick offers the option of a creative thesis for the M.A. in English.) The neo-surrealists, with their concentration on the realities akin to dream, are, in fact, a minority group among Canadian writers. If there were a mainstream – which there is not – the neo-surrealists would be set against it. Not at all surprisingly, the neo-surrealists have recently begun their own little magazine, *Canadian Fiction Magazine*. Even less surprisingly, a new little magazine of a different orientation is being organized by a group of graduate students at the University of New Brunswick. But, it ought to be noted, the neo-surrealists are perhaps the most active writers in Canada – perhaps because of the graduate programme.

At the same time that there are regional differences, there is a paradox. The writers might live vast distances from one another, but they tend to publish in and read the same magazines. Furthermore, thanks to the encouragement of The Canada Council (in travel grants, conference grants, and the like), the writers tend to know one another. Thus, if one wishes to imagine the Canadian short-story scene (a difficult image, I grant you), one would have to imagine a great circle of writers, most of whom know one another and read one another, but each of whom brings into the circle his own, often extra-national, reading. Again, it seems to me that this contributes to the vitality of the art form as much as it detracts from any kind of homogeneity.

Because, as I mentioned above, there is no 'mainstream' of Canadian short fiction, he who asserts that there is leaves himself open to brickbats – perhaps from the neo-surrealists, perhaps from the writers of understated, often wacky prose (represented, perhaps, by Raymond Fraser, who worked for a time for the Montreal scandal-tabloid *Midnight*), perhaps from the writers who work in the more traditional forms.

But if there is no mainstream, the ferment remains. For example, there are the experimentalists. The most avowed experimenter in the form of the short story would be, I suppose, Ray Smith, whose work at its best is represented by the title story in his first collection, *Cape Breton is the Thought-Control Centre of Canada* (House of Anansi). His style might best be described briefly as Swiftian satire in something of a short-story context. His other stories have not proven to be as successful, but he does challenge the form. Again, one would have to mention Dave Godfrey, whose story 'The Hard-headed Collector' is a very impressive piece of work which also challenges the traditional concepts of the genre.

Interestingly, both of those stories are anti-American ones, and perhaps it might – *might*, mind you – be safe to say that the chief innovations now under way in Canada are part of the attempt of Canadian writers to deal with the complexities of *Canadian* experience in a 'new' way. (American readers might be surprised to learn that Canada is, historically, the 'Yes, but' to the U.S. Right now the emphasis is on the 'but' – and anti-Americanism is part of the Canadian tradition.) I am led to this statement, however, as much by a recent story of Rudy Wiebe's as I am by Smith's and Godfrey's work. In Wiebe's 'Where Is the Voice Coming From?', there is the attempt to deal with an aspect of Canadian history in terms of uncluttered immediacy; the traditional sense of *story* is replaced with other techniques of direct communication.

And perhaps something of the same kind of impulse is present in the work of Hugh Hood. To make my position clear: in my opinion, Hugh Hood is probably the master of the short story in Canada. He, too, is immensely concerned with Canada as a nation, although not in an anti-American sense. (For example, he accepts the challenge of the older Canadian writer Hugh MacLennan to write of the specifically Canadian problems – as he has done in his first and third novels – and he accepts also the challenge of Morley Callaghan to deal with moral problems.) Hood, too, has challenged the form – but so subtly that few readers are entirely aware of it. The dimensions of his work are vast: he can deal with the problems of human identity, time and space, moral assertion, and has done so, all in a *specifically* Canadian context, in 'Three Halves of a House'. (Hood, too, is deliberately Canadian. Born and educated in Toronto, he taught in the U.S. before returning to Canada, to Montreal, where he has become, as he says, 'imperfectly bilingual'.) But it is Hood, also, who can cite his reading of Turgenev and Proust as well as Achebe, MacLennan, and Callaghan. Most important of all, I suppose, he has developed his own styles; there is no hint of imitation in his work; he is a practising artist. But it is Hood also who, despite his own challenging of the short-story form, can say (as he has) that the tradition of Canadian literature is not that of developing technique, but that of developing moral concern.

Perhaps he is quite right. And it ought to be mentioned that only Hood and Laurence have attempted to use the short-story form as a tool toward the writing of a complete, whole book. Laurence's coherent collection is *A Bird in the House*; and in it, the narrator – the same person throughout – grows as the result of telling each story about herself. Thus, the narrator at the end of the book is a different person than she was at the beginning. The emphasis, interestingly, is on the difficulty of moral decisions. Hood's coherent collection is *Around the Mountain: Scenes from Montreal Life*, in which Hood uses himself as a character to begin what seem to be essays but which slip quietly into experiential stories which contain the different perspectives of life to be found around Mount Royal, in Montreal. The implications of the stories are not merely cultural, but moral – and even religious – as well.

Hood and Laurence, then, might serve as exemplars of the mainstream, if there were one. But a mainstream exists only if it can dominate the tradition, and as yet not even the tradition exists. Perhaps it might be said that at the moment there seems to be a preponderance of writing which, represented by the work of Alice Munro, concentrates on story, on epiphany, on character, and on the invocation of experience by the careful use of detail. She, for example, is greatly admired for her quality of craft – particularly by John Metcalf, whose work, thus far, has been set entirely in his native Britain.

One can only conclude that the jumble is fertile.

IV: But if the short-story writers and the little magazines are vigorous, the same cannot be said of the usual associates of the art form. The magazines do not have a publishing industry to 'feed into', for instance. Nor is there – as I indicated earlier – any critical activity taking place. If the short story is alive and well in the little magazines, it nonetheless dies outside of them.

Part of this is due, again, to fashion. Clearly the short story is out of fashion as a genre read and enjoyed by the general public. Publishers in both the U.S. and Britain seem to recognize this, and thus are loath to publish collections of short stories. And the Canadian publishing industry, which is sick almost unto death – as the result of American competition, high overheads, and dwindling markets – finds it virtually impossible to publish collections of short stories. The major writers I have mentioned have published collections, but never easily, and the sales have been poor. (It might be argued, and not unreasonably, that they might have done better with more extensive promotion; the Canadian publishing industry is not famous for its hustle.) Two collections of Hugh Hood's stories have appeared and been acclaimed, but not purchased in encouraging numbers. Even Margaret Laurence, Canada's big 'name' writer, had difficulty persuading her U.S. publishers to bring out her coherent collection, *A Bird in the House*. They asked wistfully if perhaps she 'couldn't turn it into a novel'. And rumour has it that Alice Munro's widely praised *Dance of the Happy Shades* did not sell at all well – even after it was given the Governor General's Award.

This is discouraging for the writer, of course, and he can take scant sympathy from the fact that no creative book in Canada – novel or otherwise – seems to be selling well.

However, two reactions have taken place. First, small publishing houses, with more ideals than capital, have sprung up. Dave Godfrey helped found one, the House of Anansi, which published his first collection, *Death Goes*

Better with Coca-Cola. His novel was published by the next firm he helped to establish, New Press. In Ottawa the small Oberon Press has published David Helwig and is scheduled to bring out Hood's next collection. Prism International Press at the University of British Columbia and Michael Yates's Sono Nis Press have both been active.

Yet these publishers work on limited budgets; and if they are able to get their books into university libraries, they do not have the distribution apparatus (which is largely, in effect, in the hands of American publishers) to get their books into the hands of the general public.

However, a second new direction is being explored. The present wave of interest in Canadian nationalism has resulted in a clamour for courses in Canadian literature in Canadian universities. These courses naturally require texts. Anthologies, therefore, have begun to appear in order to meet the demand. In the end they may create a new audience. It is interesting, furthermore, that the anthologies are often edited by writers, and writers, furthermore, whose work is associated with the little magazines. Thus, the first anthology which put the Canadian short story into an international and historical context was Rudy Wiebe's *The Story-Makers*. Then John Metcalf's *Sixteen by Twelve* appeared. This year, two more are to appear: an anthology of contemporary fiction and theory edited by Metcalf and an anthology of previously unpublished stories edited by David Helwig and Tom Marshall, who were previously associated with the little magazine *Quarry*. Other 'international' anthologies – including stories from Canada and from the other nations of the Commonwealth – include W.H. New's *Four Hemispheres* and Anna Rutherford's *Commonwealth Short Stories*.

Consequently, it would appear that The Canada Council, in its endeavours to stimulate Canadian art, has been at least partly successful. By its grants to the writers and some of the little magazines, The Canada Council has assured the continuing life of the short-story genre, at least in a small way. In effect, the indirect government support of the art has resulted in a certain kind of life. The anthologies, in turn, have depended upon the magazines. Now, perhaps, if we're very, very lucky, the anthologies will breed a new audience and then – faint, faint hope – a revitalized publishing industry. Indirect government support can have an effect. But the fact remains that if the art is lively, there is no audience to know of it. In that, thus far, we may have failed.

Finally, I suppose, there is the matter of quality. I have contended that the short story in Canada is 'lively', that it is 'healthy'. I have argued that the competition among writers has produced excellent results. But is it really any good? (I am obviously less than disinterested.) I think that the reader of this article might do well to pick up any copy of the current 'Best' anthologies – *Best American* (sic) *Short Stories, Best Little Magazine Fiction*, etc., etc. – and read the stories and take a look at the editor's 'distinguished' list. Certain names will be prominent: Laurence, Hood, Nowlan, Metcalf, MacLeod, Harvor. For a country with a relatively small population in a vast amount of space, Canada is not doing badly at all – even if it is, like the famous lost tribe, calling out: 'Where in the hell *are* we?'

Hugh Hood

GET YOURSELF A REPUTATION, BABY!

I'M AMUSED and a little rueful to find myself making my first contribution to *The Kenyon Review* in this symposium, because I've been trying to place a story here, on and off, for more than a decade, and I see that one of the preoccupations of contributors to the discussion is the supposedly dwindling market for the short story. If this condition did exist, my recommendation would be: let *The Kenyon Review* and the other reviews run plenty of stories, mine among them.

On a first look at the situation it does seem as if demand for the story has about dried up. Thirty years ago, the argument runs, even the mass-circulation magazines would run good stories. *Esquire, Collier's*, the *Saturday Evening Post, Atlantic, Harper's, Scribner's* and several others would pay large fees for stories and present them to enormous audiences. Where are they now? If they still exist, they run fact-fiction or straight documentary. Publishers won't consider collections of stories, which are notorious money-losers. The story writer should switch to documentary, where his command of language and his traditional attachment to social fact will place him in the first rank.

One of the few competent newspaper reviewers in North America, Robert Fulford of the *Toronto Daily Star*, recently wrote an article on my fiction in which he advised me to do exactly that. He said that writers like Mailer and Baldwin were wasting their time on fiction when their talents so plainly fitted them for superior journalism. He did me the honour of bracketing me with them, as the outstanding example of a Canadian writer who is wasting his time writing fiction when he is really a reporter. A writer like

First published in *The Kenyon Review* 30 (1968). Republished in Hugh Hood, *The Governor's Bridge is Closed* (Ottawa: Oberon, 1973).

me, devoid of psychological penetration, who sees and records very accurately from the outside, shouldn't 'recklessly expend his energy in writing novels'.

Pace Robert Fulford, I don't believe that the new documentary has supplanted fiction, any more than I think that a writer who isn't endowed from birth with every gift of the great novelist is wasting his time trying to write good novels and stories. This question has two obvious aspects, the economic and the artistic, and they are most profitably discussed separately. As far as markets and payments go, I'll admit that the best-paying buyers of fiction are buying much less of it than they used to. Where *Esquire* ran three or four stories in every issue in the 1930s, they now run one, rarely two. The *Post* uses fiction very sparingly and in any case is shaky financially. The biggest magazine in Canada, *Maclean's*, used to run fiction regularly, but hasn't done so for ten years. *Harper's* runs no fiction, so far as I'm aware, and *Atlantic* relatively little.

Nevertheless I can report that I have several times earned fees totalling well over a thousand dollars for individual stories. In one case, I sold a story to *Esquire* for $500, then saw it reprinted several times in Europe and in anthologies; that story earned me close to $1500. Another example: I placed a piece first with *Prism* for $25; but the National Film Board bought it and made a short film of it, the CBC put it on the radio several times, each time paying me a substantial fee, and it was reprinted here and there. A third example: last fall the CBC paid me a flat thousand dollars to write a story for them, for broadcast on a series they were running to help celebrate Canada's centennial. No editorial restrictions; I could write whatever I liked.

I see of course that these are not payments on the most grandiose scale, that of Michener, Uris, Robbins, Wallace. But they are substantial fees. I consider a thousand dollars a very reasonable fee for a short story, whether a single payment or the sum of a series of permissions sales. What's more, I'll bet that writers everywhere in the world except perhaps around New York will agree with me. I don't have to please anybody but myself when I write a story. I needn't observe any editorial restrictions whatsoever, and in fact I never have. If the magazine doesn't want the piece, jolly good luck to them, it's their decision after all. Acting on these principles I've managed to write without censorship of any kind (except that of my own unconscious motives) and I've sold stories – fifty of them – for a perfectly satisfactory return to every imaginable kind of market except the very richest, here and in Europe. I have no complaint whatsoever about payments or markets.

The biggest single reason for this is the CBC, whose producers have for many years bought and broadcast fiction as a service to their audience and to the literature of the country. The CBC is far and away the most receptive and the fairest – though not the highest-paying – market for stories that I know of, almost the only paying market in Canada.

The commercial media apart, there's another market for stories, of indefinite but very large proportions. I mean the literary magazines, and here again there are complexities, and qualifications to be made. *Any good story can be published somewhere, in* The Carleton Miscellany *or* The Kenyon Review *or* The Canadian Forum *or* Northwest Review. In many cases a small fee will be paid, often a page rate, or one based on a word count; but nobody is going to get rich writing for the reviews. If you think over the people who write stories for the reviews, you recognize that most of them like Jack Ludwig or Stephen Minot or Jesse Bier have a teaching job, or do some editorial work, or write ad copy. Maybe they make a living by taking every writing job that's going: reviewing, jacket copy, continuity articles. Did anybody ever make a living writing nothing but serious fiction? Chekhov, Turgenev, Tolstoy, Henry James, Joyce, Hemingway, all supported themselves in a variety of ways, partly by writing stories no doubt, but mainly on inherited income, or by patronage, or by the practice of a profession, or by doing a little quiet starving until their reputation was established. If poetry is a mug's game, as Eliot said, so is serious fiction. And yet, as every good poet or story-writer discovers as soon as he becomes known, even regionally, there are lots of people who will press money on you to write other things, once you've got the reputation of a serious artist. It's a case of 'Get yourself a reputation, baby!'

Why is that? *The Star Weekly*, which wouldn't run a story of mine for fear of the heavens falling, will pay me $800 for a short article on the expansion teams in the National Hockey League. If one is to live by writing, the normal order of things is the slow acquisition of a name, by publishing stories in the literary magazines, followed by highly paid journalism or lecturing or broadcasting. There's something funny going on here. A story-writer I know, a very good one, who also does factual sports pieces for one of the larger Canadian magazines, told me that the magazine once took a poll of its readership to find out how many of its readers had read from start to finish the prize-winning story in their annual contest – a contest with a large prize that attracted many excellent writers. Four per cent of the sample read the story from start to finish. Eighty-five per cent of the readership customarily finished my friend's sports stories and he, and I, found this extremely puzzling. The magazine in question has mainly an upper-middle-class circulation. Its readers apparently don't read fiction, but do read sports copy (by a writer of fiction) that's a hundred times easier to write.

Even if this were a general condition (and it may be, I don't know) there would still be a demand for serious writing, because poetry and fiction are the heavyweight division of literature. In boxing, as is well known, the whole sport lapses into desuetude when the heavyweight title is vacant or not frequently contested by worthy challengers. Even the greatest featherweight or middleweight champion can't maintain interest in the sport the way even a fairly good heavy can. You have to have plenty of good poets and story-writers using the language at peak intensity – straining it to its limits – if the other forms of writing are to stay sweet.

A critic like Robert Fulford is wrong to maintain that Mailer has the gifts of a journalist. Watching Mailer at work at reportage is like watching somebody sharpen a pencil with a laser. He wouldn't be nearly so interesting to read if he didn't have gifts and disciplines superior in kind to those of the most talented journalist. A good writer of fiction is disciplined to observe carefully and to arrange patterns of social behaviour in artistic form with a degree of finesse beyond that of any journalist I can think of. It's because Mailer and Baldwin have written fiction well that they, and Turgenev and Hemingway too, have become good journalists.

All the other kinds of writing, technical writing, copy writing, political journalism, biography, live off poetry and fiction, though not always parasitically. They learn what can be done with language from the artists the same way that industrial designers and textile designers have learned from, say, Mondrian. I've seen ad copy that was very close to Joyce, derived a generation later from his practice.

In default of the mass audience, therefore, the story-writer will probably persist in placing his work where he can, for moderate but satisfactory returns. I've managed to get two collections of stories into print, an extraordinary feat, as any writer will tell you. The first of these, *Flying a Red Kite*, was published in an edition of 1,100 copies, and went out of print in about eighteen months. After that there was a small but steady demand for it, and the publishers reissued it last fall in an edition of 4,000 copies in a quality paperback format. I suppose it will sell a couple of hundred copies a year almost indefinitely. My second collection, *Around the Mountain: Scenes from Montreal Life*, appeared last year in a first printing of 3,000 copies, of which two-thirds were sold in the first year.

What are we to make of this? 5,000 copies manufactured of a first book, a collection of stories by an unknown writer, in a country with a reading audience a twelfth that of the United States. 2,000 copies of a second gone in twelve months. I say that this is a credit to the Canadian reading public, and I think that these are highly satisfactory sales, and immensely pleasing to me. *Dubliners* sold 379 copies in its first six months, in a country with a large reading public, without competition from television or films. Of course it's doing pretty well now.

The fact is that human beings *need* stories just as they need food or sex or religion. The need to hear stories is as deeply rooted as these others, and won't disappear before they do. It doesn't much matter to people whether the story is told by this or that means, so long as they get to hear it, but there seem to be two kinds of stories, what we may call (to keep the nomenclature simple) the long and the short.

The long story comprises epic, romance, the myth cycle, the novel, certain kinds of chronicle drama and most feature-length films. The feature still hasn't emancipated itself from the tyranny of the story.

The short story likewise comprises a multiplicity of forms: anecdote, reminiscence, tale, folktale, memoir, *conte* or *fabliau*, the novella and mainly and centrally the story of 5,000 words, what editors of literary magazines think of as the normal story, what Henry James was always planning to write before the thing got out of control. To these purely literary categories might be added certain one-act plays that are thinly disguised stories, likewise many half-hour television plays that are mainly narrative in form, having no specially visual form beyond what's necessary to get them on the screen. Finally there are stories written for radio broadcast, as were many of my own.

Anything *written to be read aloud* is apt to be paradoxical in structure, and the paradox points to a second root distinction in the theory of fictional genres. Stories may be divided into two kinds: those spoken aloud and those meant to be read silently. The construction of the two kinds is radically dissimilar because of the brute fact that an orally delivered tale is not physically present in packaged form. It can't be re-read. The audience can't turn back several pages to re-establish in their minds some crucial aspect of artistic pattern. The reaction times and the apperceptive rates of hearers and readers differ significantly. When I write a story for broadcast, I pace it differently from one designed mainly to be read in print. The diction must be less polysyllabic, and there will be a lot of direct address. I'm more likely to use a first-person narrator, who ought to be of the same sex as the person who will read the piece on the air. I won't use any of the language of ethical meditation, such as one finds in Proust, because it's very hard to speak. The differences between oral and written form are endless, and can lead writers into traps. A deliberate written imitation of a tale in oral form can give the reader an uncomfortable impression of fakery. If this story-teller is so close to the heart of the folk, such an unsophisticated simple fellow, why is he appearing on news-stands in a 75¢ paperback, and why does he have a literary agent? Self-conscious imitation of folk form, unless supremely successful, is apt to seem bogus. The one really brilliant success in this line is 'The Rime of the Ancient Mariner' and I know of nothing in fiction to equal it, nothing by Malamud, nothing by Singer. I've tried to do a literary treatment of folktale now and then and I've had trouble with it because I keep saying to myself: 'Come off it; basically you're not a simple sage who wanders the streets and lives off the generosity of the folk.' Yeats got into difficulties with this kind of self-projection, and there are writers practising at this moment who aren't avoiding the traps.

I use the oral forms with my children at bedtime, not as a rule elsewhere. The written, deliberately literary form is after all one's *métier* and no matter what the mass-media people may assert, books are far from dead. Written literature has predictably a very long life ahead of it, as any professional librarian will attest. A book is a machine of the most elegant kind (if we are to consider the matter in the terms of contemporary technology) for storing and releasing information. It needs no fuel or electrical connection. You don't have to plug it in or oil it or repair it. It is easily transported and stored, and an example of excellent industrial design because it fits your hands and your lap very neatly. All you have to do to operate it is open it and turn the pages. The threatened disappearance of print-culture seems to me a bogey to frighten young readers with, not at all imminent. Certainly there have been cultures without books printed from movable type, even cultures without written records. There may be similar societies in the distant future. But nothing that I can observe in North American society at the present time convinces me that written records and written literature are about to disappear, not this millennium, maybe later.

Memory is the mother of the Muses, written record of history. I wouldn't assign the sole central source of literary creation to the historical instinct, the need to preserve, interpret and make present the past. Much poetry seems to me to lie to one side of this strictly social function of literature: the lyric, the poem of linguistic experiment, the poem treated as physical object (found poetry, concrete poetry), determinedly symbolic poetry. But the historical motive, the creation of the conscience of the race, seems to me to lie at the sources of the great prose forms: legal codes, liturgies, religious histories, sacred scriptures, records of myth, some epic narratives and finally the novel and the story. I think that the chief *telos* of fiction in all its forms, whether in verse or prose, the long story or the short, epic, romance, myth, novel, tale, story, is located in the story-teller's function, which is that of giving assurance to his readers or hearers of the persistence of the inner values of their culture. Story is by nature 'realist', and the great story forms are realistic and historical, and have to do with the behaviour of men and women (as they are capable of being represented within literary conventions) in real observable human societies. I think of myself as a realist in the tradition of Homer and Dante and Tolstoy and Joyce. I recognize that there are other aspects to literary art. Fiction may exhibit a high degree of formal organization in its language, its *montage*, in those parts of the craft which lie close to poetry. But I will never concede that language is about language, that a linguistic system is purely self-reflexive, that the universe of language closes on itself. That seems to me nonsense, whatever Lucien Goldmann and Roland Barthes may teach to the contrary. Language and its structures help to condition the act of the writer of fiction, but don't control it or determine its shape.

Story is very close to liturgy, which is why one's children like to have a story repeated exactly as they heard it the night before. The scribe ought not to deviate from the prescribed form. That is because the myths at the core of story are always going on. Cuchulain is always and everywhere fighting the waves, Oedipus blinding himself, Christ dying and rising again. Myth exists to reassure us of the persistence of some of the fundamental forms of human action. It has always seemed to me a profoundly interesting bit of literary psychology that Chaucer would invent an authority for his story if one didn't exist. He didn't think of himself as writing originals but as following 'myn auctoritee' and this for the reasons I've been adducing. Spenser had no copyright on the story of Britain, nor Ariosto on that of the *douzepers*. Cash-nexus economics are the accident of history, stories the permanent possession of mankind.

John Metcalf

EDITING THE BEST

DESPITE THE PLENTIFUL GREY HAIRS I see every morning in the mirror, it still came as a shock to me to realize that I am about to write something which can only be described as history.

I came to Canada in 1962 on a ship called the *Carinthia*. It was a miserable voyage; I started vomiting when the ship was still attached to the dock in Liverpool and continued well past Trois-Rivières. As the *Carinthia* drew into the mouth of the St. Lawrence I was blind to the opening wonders of the New World. My world had contracted. Again.

Although I was entirely unaware of it then, 1962 was the year that Hugh Hood published with The Ryerson Press his first book, the story collection *Flying a Red Kite*. The *Carinthia* has long gone to the breaker's yard, The Ryerson Press survives only as a hyphenated appendage of McGraw-Hill, and Hugh Hood, now working on his eighteenth or nineteenth book, is no longer quite so fresh of face as the young man who is looking out of the window on that first dust-jacket.

I came to Canada more or less by accident. I could as easily have gone to Hong Kong or Australia or Burma. I applied for a job with the British Council in Lima, for a job as a manager of a plantation in Burma. I nearly secured a job in a private school in the West Indies but proved 'unsuitable' after questioning the pittances to be paid to my various servants.

The great attraction of all these places, and of Canada, was that they were not England.

After leaving university, I had drifted into a job in a secondary modern boys' school in Bristol. It was a school over-stocked with the sons of the

First published in John Metcalf, *Kicking Against the Pricks* (Downsview, ON: ECW, 1982; 2nd ed. Guelph, ON: Red Kite, 1986).

proletariat and run by a man who was clinically insane. My flat was in the once-fashionable Georgian and Regency area of the city where I had lived as a student, huge limestone houses in rows and crescents divided now and subdivided into flats, flatlets, and bedsitters but still beautiful in their decline. The bus journey from my flat to the Bluebell Secondary Modern School was an expedition to another world.

The bus lumbered down towards the city centre, through all the commerce, on through the drab streets of terraced houses and small shops – newsagents, fish and chips, turf accountants – towards the decaying prefabs and the rawness of the housing estate served by Bluebell School. The invisible dividing line between the city I lived in and the city I worked in was marked for me each morning by a butcher's shop whose windows announced in whitewash capitals: UDDER 9D PER POUND.

This daily journey soon presented itself to me as a metaphor. My life was split between a decaying past which exercised a great power over me and a present which was unbearable and stretched ahead like a life sentence. Even then, I realized that it was futile and deadening to live for the past and I knew that I had to get out of England and escape from its dream.

Had my job been interesting and comfortable, I'd doubtless have succumbed to the dream and lived out the rest of my life clad in tweed with vacations spent taking brass rubbings in medieval churches. But life at Bluebell Secondary Modern was neither interesting nor comfortable. The school was a compelling argument against the desirability of compulsory education. The staff were caricatures. The headmaster was downright alarming. The pupils ranged from the merely drooling to the psychopathically loutish.

It was the sort of school where homework was rarely assigned because the pupils returned with notes written on torn brown bags which said:

Dear Teacher,
    He have not done his sums because its
    bad for his nerves
    Thanking You I Remain
    Signed Mary Brown (Mrs)

The remedial mornings were divided by School Dinner from the remedial afternoons.

In a container of medieval proportions, greasy stew studded with emerald processed peas followed by steamed pudding and aluminum jugs of custard topped by a thickening skin.

When emissaries of the Protestant School Board of Greater Montreal set themselves up in a suite in one of the city's posher hotels to drum up custom, I was one of the first in line.

The formalities were simple. I merely had to furnish evidence of sobriety and moral probity attested to by a Minister of Religion and the results of a Wasserman Test proving that I was not riddled with the pox or clap. I promptly wrote a sickening letter and signed it as the Vicar of St. Michael and All Hallows and some days later took my place in a long line of subdued Jamaicans at the Bristol Royal Infirmary's V.D. Clinic. Two men in white lab coats were indulging themselves in unseemly badinage with the clientele.

When my turn came, one of the men said, 'Well then, where have *you* been sticking it?'

'I haven't recently', I said with some asperity, 'been "sticking it" anywhere. I'm not here for medical reasons. I only need a test because I'm emigrating.'

He stared at me.

Then he shouted, 'Hey, George! Come over here! You're not going to believe this but I've actually heard a new one!'

The high school to which I was posted had a reputation, I was warned, for toughness. Rosemount High was in the eastern part of the city – the area that in those carefree days of Anglo power was referred to as 'the French part'. Compared with any British secondary modern school, this reputedly tough establishment was like a luxury rest-home.

After an initial period of gawking at the strangeness of everything and after figuring out, theoretically, the shape and extent of Canada, for, typically and criminally, I had been ordered to teach Canadian history, I began to look about me to find the literature.

WHAT FOLLOWS, THEN, is an impressionistic sketch of how Canadian literature appeared to an immigrant teacher of literature in the early sixties.

The first observation I made was that there was precious little literature in evidence. Nor did there seem to be much of a literary world. The literary landscape was dominated by Hugh MacLennan, Morley Callaghan, Hugh Garner, Sinclair Ross, and W.O. Mitchell.

(Margaret Laurence had at this time written little and Richler's first books were published by Deutsch. Both were living in England.)

As far as the schools were concerned, awareness of Canadian writing was restricted to MacLennan's *Two Solitudes* in a bowdlerized version, the odd story by Callaghan, a handful of poems by Bliss Carman, Archibald Lampman, and Sir Charles G.D. Roberts, and one or two pieces by that Monarch of Mirth, Stephen Leacock. Everything else was British and American with the scales heavily weighted on the British side. And horrid stuff it was. Bad poems of the W.H. Davies variety and arch, personal essays of the 'On Preparing To Garden' school. It was as if students and teachers had been caught in a time-warp which preserved the faded diction and gentilities of what had been a peculiarly barren and bankrupt period in the literature of the 'Mother Country'.

The literature was a perfect complement to the *social* environment which the school board was attempting to maintain – or imagine. This also was British – school uniform, division into 'Houses', discipline backed by violence, decorum. Teachers were imported every year from England to stiffen the system's backbone. It was a colonial situation analogous with, say, modern Nigeria.

In brief, it would not be unfair to say that in the early sixties in Canada the literature being taught and celebrated was some of the worst that had been produced in England in the first thirty years of this century.

Even the literary revolution of the seventies has not broken that strange loyalty to outmoded forms. The awful tradition of consciously 'comic' writing which expired in *Punch* so many years ago has been institutionalized here with the Stephen Leacock Award for Humour which honours staggeringly unfunny books which are positively archaic in sensibility. It's interesting to compare a contemporary collection of Canadian humorous pieces with the work of contemporary practitioners in England such as Patrick Campbell and Paul Jennings. Or with much earlier practitioners in the States such as Thurber and Joseph Mitchell.

Or even Ring Lardner.

This 'dead hand' of bankrupt tradition which seems to me so typical of Canadian literary history is exemplified by the Canadian branch of P.E.N. A world organization of writers dedicated to protesting against electrodes on genitals is, in Canada, an organization which is confined to Westmount. Everyone in Canada *not* in Westmount is defined as an *out-of-town member* – a marvellously myopic phrase. The Canadian branch of the organization does not vehemently concern itself with human rights; it saves its energies for tea and buns with favourite sons like Sir Edwin Leather.

In the early sixties, Montreal was far more sophisticated than any other city in Canada. Let us not speak of the other cities. Those students who were bright and desirous of being hip were plugged into a certain extra-curricular awareness of poetry by the precious buffooneries of Layton and Cohen who were showing the flag for literature in the city's bistros, taverns, and universities. The female population was peculiarly open to instruction.

It's a sad comment that such flag waving was necessary.

Cohen's poetry was exactly right for the twelve-to-sixteen-year-old 'naughty' set. Romantic stuff, rebellious, not too difficult to grasp, touches of surrealism which were whimsical rather than arresting, and all produced by a handsome young man who 'suffered' prominently. Why his poetry ever engaged adults always baffled me. His later dirges such as the world-famous 'Suzanne' are, of course, pseudomystically incomprehensible which doubt-less explains their popularity.

Layton was, and is, a considerable poet.

Prose, however, lacked any such charismatic practitioners.

Callaghan struck me as an extremely *clumsy* writer. I was not charmed by the obtrusive didacticism of the novels or by their cardboard characters. The stories, which were accounted better than the novels, seemed to me even worse. They were badly written and mawkish. The language was plod-ding. I was offended all the time by Callaghan's telling me what every damn thing meant; he was unable to leave the reader alone.

Quite recently, one of these early stories, 'The Little Business Man', was reprinted in the *Reader's Digest* and it's hard to think of a more fitting home.

Sinclair Ross is a much better writer but it's *As For Me and My House* which commands respect rather than the stories. John Moss has recently called the stories in *The Lamp at Noon* 'some of the finest in the language'. Most of the stories are basically plot stories; when we've found out 'what happens', we've gone a long way towards exhausting them. The language and imagery are, however, much more involving than is usual in plot stories. They're *good* plot stories but finally they're only that. To say of them that they're 'some of the finest in the language' is to invite comparison with Hemingway, Katherine Mansfield, James Joyce, Eudora Welty, Caroline Gordon, Flannery O'Connor, Thurber, Lardner, Anderson, Faulkner, etc. Which is to be foolish.

There is a considerable element of poetry in Ross's stories – particularly in the best stories such as 'Cornet at Night'. The weakness of the stories is that the insistence on 'meaning' often clashes with the *experience* of the story. The stories are far too much *tales*; they are deformed by plot. Ross is unable to let meaning grow from our experience of the story's world; he editorializes. 'Cornet at Night' is brutalized by Ross's final paragraph which summarizes and explains the story. In 'One's a Heifer', as another example, there is some good and involving writing, particularly the rather complicated identification of the physically damaged owl with the mentally damaged farmer, but our experience of place and person is diluted by the demands of the form Ross chose to write in – the 'whodunnit' or 'whodunwhat'; story writers would not now choose a form which crippled their real interests. Ross is a writer who, in his stories, was poised for flight but remained earthbound, weighted down by traditional baggage he was unable to jettison.

(*The Lamp at Noon* in the New Canadian Library edition is introduced by Margaret Laurence who was influenced by Ross at quite a young age. She is a vastly more sophisticated story writer than Ross but it's interesting to note that she, too, in the stories in *A Bird in the House* often intrudes to summarize or add obtrusive comment. This is particularly noticeable in 'The Loons' where the story is progressively weakened by the final two paragraphs. It is almost as if her trust in the reader falters. It is puzzling to compare this story with the very much earlier work in *The Tomorrow-Tamer* which contains such glowing stories as 'The Perfume Sea'.)

Hugh Garner's writing is primitive and uncouth.

(I remember Garner writing a piece for me to accompany a story in an anthology for students. I wrote back questioning a few points of grammar. He replied: 'Change whatever you want. Hell! It isn't Holy Writ.'

Any writer who *doesn't* regard his work as Holy Writ is not worth much time or consideration.)

The only writers of stories who might have become interesting figures were Ethel Wilson and Raymond Knister.

In 1962, Hugh Hood published *Flying a Red Kite*. This was the first book of modern stories published in this country. Or perhaps it might be more accurate to say 'traditionally modern'. These stories were in the line of descent of all modern stories. Relatively few people have grasped how centrally important this book is to Canadian literature. The stories have withstood the passage of the years magnificently. The only bad story in the book – significantly enough a story first published in *Esquire* and quite uncharacteristic of Hood's genius – is 'After the Sirens'. For the rest, they are as fresh as the day they were first written.

So it had taken some forty years for a world movement to impinge on Canada. The interesting question is how Canada had managed to remain almost untouched for so long. The monuments of the modern movement were as available to Canadians as they were to anyone else; they were no further away than the nearest bookshop. It seems that Canada was isolated from the rest of the world by some inexplicable time-lag. Raymond Souster as late as the fifties and sixties, for example, was still working in what was basically an Imagist manner. A partial explanation may be a ponderous conservatism and the total lack of an informed audience. I haven't read enough to *know* but I have a suspicion that literature in Canada up until, say, 1950 was so largely crappy because it was a narrow class preserve. Audience *and* writers, I suspect, were part of an Establishment which was characterized by ghastly good taste, gentility, and doctorates – an Anglican world of pianoforte and good posture with attachments to Empire and 'Beauty'.

The year before *Flying a Red Kite* was published, W.O. Mitchell published *Jake and the Kid*; these two books beautifully represent voices from two different worlds. It would not be unfair to say that the sensibility behind *Jake and the Kid* remains to this day the more popular and dominant.

(A *potpourri* of that dominant sensibility: W.P. Kinsella, Indian 'art', Inuit 'art', William Kurelek, landscape with old barn.)

The reputations of MacLennan, Callaghan, Garner, Ross, and Mitchell seem, if anything, to have grown even larger in the intervening years. Reputations in Canada take years to build and then, once built, stand copper-clad for ever like vast CN Hotels.

I'm not criticizing writers older than myself to be unpleasant or

controversial. I would hope that by now I'm not really *being* controversial.
We are mired at the moment in hopeless dishonesty about our literature. It's
necessary to put these writers who have grossly inflated reputations in Canada into some sort of critical perspective, to compare them with their contemporaries in the rest of the English-speaking world. If this task is not
undertaken by responsible critics, the lies will continue to be propagated
and we will all sink beneath the burden of absurdity. We must not forget
that one of the critical fraternity has already produced an explication of
Garner's mindless *oeuvre*.

My interest in this is not totally disinterested. If we cannot honestly
evaluate the past, we cannot make intelligent judgements about the present.
As a working writer, I'm terrified of having what tiny audience there is put
to sleep by the charismatic fans of Frederick Philip Grove. If I were a bright
young student instructed by the owner of a Ph.D. that the works of Callaghan, Garner, and Grove were of great interest and literary importance,
I'd be happy to reject CanLit forever in favour of a Frisbee.

There have been attempts over the last few years to assert a native Canadian tradition in short story writing. David Arnason claims in his *Nineteenth
Century Canadian Stories* that the Canadian story can be considered as 'the
development of the Letter to the Editor as a specialized literary form'.
Wayne Grady in his preface to *The Penguin Book of Canadian Short Stories*,
following Arnason, suggests that the characteristic feature of Canadian
stories – realism – is inherited from pioneer journalism.

Grady's preface seems to suggest – vaguely, tenuously – that Richler,
Hood, Margaret Laurence, and Alice Munro somehow stand in some sort of
obscure relationship to letter writers to *The Daily Stump and Stone Picker*.
Common sense alone would suggest that this is nonsense.

It's interesting to read what Raymond Knister wrote of this alleged tradition in his introduction to the anthology *Canadian Short Stories* published in
1928:

The short story has shared in the disadvantages of other types of literature
and of culture as a whole in Canada. It is vain to say that it might have
sprung from the soil as a new variant of the traditional form. There has
been no national Burbank to create a Canadian subspecies of the short story
as there was to breed Marquis wheat. It emerged, as the short story in the

United States did, in a spirited emulation at best, or a shallow imitativeness at worst, of foreign models.

I would assert that the interesting story writers in Canada are writing in the world tradition of the 'modern'; others would assert that the *interesting* writers are working in the tradition of the 'post-modern'. The revisionist attempt to create an indigenous literary tradition is damaging in two ways; it's damaging to the obvious truth and it's damaging to CanLit's future because the monuments of this spurious tradition are so ineffably boring that only the dullest of students will endure them. And it is these sons of dullness who will go on in future generations to cast the blight of their scholarship over other appalling hacks who will in turn join the pantheon of the Canadian literary great.

The federal government has recently granted a million dollars to pay for the preparation of standard texts of some of this early Canadian fascination; it's obvious before the project has even got under way that they'll only get shot of these volumes by donating sets of them to remote Indian bands and to non-English-speaking visiting dignitaries. What's depressing, though, is that a million dollars equals entrenchment.

Grady's claim in his preface to *The Penguin Book of Canadian Short Stories* that 'realism' is the characteristic feature of Canadian stories may be historically accurate but to cite specifically the writing of Alice Munro, Hugh Hood, and Margaret Laurence as examples of realism seems to me to reveal an inability to read. Or it may be that the determination to hold an untenable thesis is causing him to read what he wishes to read.

Alice Munro, for example, is not a 'realist'; she is a marvellously *poetic* writer. She is no mere recorder of surfaces. Her 'realism' is like that of one of her favourite painters – Edward Hopper. The experience of *reading aloud* the first few paragraphs of, say, 'Walker Brothers Cowboy' or 'Images' should be enough to persuade even dim readers that Alice Munro is, to borrow a term, a very *painterly* writer.

Similarly, it is a profound mistake to think of Hood as a 'realist'. He is obsessively concerned with names, distances, weights, colours, and procedures – but he is not a 'realist'. Hood had, in his first book, mastered the 'modern' short story and indeed had started to go beyond the confines of the 'classical' epiphany story. A careful reading of 'Silver Bugles, Cymbals,

Golden Silks' reveals his early brilliance. Since then, Hood's work in the short story has been continually innovative and experimental. The deceptive surface 'realism' of *Around the Mountain* conceals work of incredible complexity; the only critics who have begun to grapple with Hood's short fiction are Kent Thompson and Robert Lecker. Those stories which have been described as 'journalistic' or 'documentary' are not at all what they might appear to be; the stories are deeply revolutionary, radically different from anything ever written in Canada or indeed anywhere else in the world. In all of Hood's work the mundane and the eternal intersect and coexist; in Hood's world, God manifests Himself unto us in a variety of surprising and unlikely things. Hood has largely abandoned the flash and filigree of his earliest rhetoric because, I should imagine, his mastery of it bored him and because he is working a new kind of rhetoric whose austerity seems to him better suited to the largeness of his themes.

This whole question of an indigenous literary tradition is merely nationalism in a literary guise. The reinvention of the past is bad enough but critics are also inventing the shape of the present.

It's unfortunate that our literature is so precarious that were it not for the universities and, to a lesser extent, the schools, the whole house of cards might very well collapse. It is unfortunate that contemporary work is so quickly seized on by universities and turned into 'courses'. The strong, and understandable, desire for Canadian masterworks *creates* masterworks; the critical judgements are almost bound to be unbalanced. Writers quickly become entrenched; they become the 'property' of those academics who dared champion them. Responsible criticism is soon seen almost as blasphemy. Such a situation applies to Mordecai Richler, Margaret Laurence, Margaret Atwood, and Robertson Davies. The old pattern is being repeated. In my own case, the inadequacies of my novels are not as widely criticized as they should be while the felicities of my stories seem largely ignored.

It would be preferable that contemporary writing were not taught at all, but if the universities and colleges withdrew their interest writing probably would not survive. Critical buffoonery can flourish only because the literary base is so narrow. It is a vaguely remembered dream to suggest that time and the Common Reader will winnow out the wheat.

But I am getting wildly ahead of myself.

As the sixties progressed, things were happening beneath the obvious surface. Story writers were scribbling away and publishing in the largely unknown little magazines, writers whose names were unknown then and are not much better known now: Hugh Hood, Clark Blaise, Alice Munro, Dave Godfrey, Ray Smith, David Helwig, Kent Thompson, Shirley Faessler, Audrey Thomas, etc. Weaver's *Tamarack Review* and *The Fiddlehead* under the editorship of Kent Thompson were alive with exciting work. I can remember listening to CBC *Anthology* one night and hearing Alice Munro's 'Images'; I was envious, excited, and amazed.

Blaise's first publication in book form was in 1968, Godfrey's in 1967 and 1968, mine in 1969 and 1970, Ray Smith's in 1969, Alice Munro's in 1968. Hugh Hood's second book of short fiction appeared in 1967.

(It's worth noting that the powers that be, or were, at The Ryerson Press thought it prudent to have *Dance of the Happy Shades* introduced to the public in a foreword by Hugh Garner – rather like having an exhibition catalogue of Edward Hopper introduced by Norman Rockwell.)

In 1972 Margaret Atwood published *Survival* which did a lot for nationalism and the idea of a Canadian literature but which probably set *literary* appreciation back by a decade.

The literary flowering of the seventies was under way. Quite simply, this 'revolution' was the writing of people who had absorbed the far earlier revolution of the 'modern' and were writing within *its* tradition. This simple fact was sometimes obscured by the nationalist sentiments of the leaders of the movement. Dave Godfrey, for example, might have *liked* to have been writing in some indigenous tradition but his work is derived from obvious foreign models and his training as a writer was at the hands of the running dogs at Iowa.

It's interesting to consider the influx of 'foreigners' at this period and their impact not only on Canadian writing but on the Canadian literary world. The list is impressive: Kent Thompson, Audrey Thomas, Jane Rule, Austin Clarke, Leon Rooke, Clark Blaise, Chris Scott, John Mills, Sonny Ladoo, Leo Simpson, etc. Our expatriates, too, funnelled in the winds of change: Mavis Gallant, Norman Levine, Dave Godfrey, Margaret Laurence, and Mordecai Richler.

There has been for years a resentment against the 'foreignness' of some of these people – even if they are, in fact, Canadian citizens. The literary renaissance was international in style but narrowly nationalist in sentiment. I will very soon have lived more than half my life in Canada but I still arouse hostilities in certain quarters less for my behaviour than for the fact that I am not native-born. In 1977 Clark Blaise and I edited an anthology of Canadian stories called *Here & Now*. We wished to put together a book which illustrated the strengths of the Canadian story and the gains made in the seventies. Our introduction concluded: 'We have not defined a literature because the literature is still defining itself.' Not, I would have thought, a wildly provocative statement. Canadian writer Peter Such, who was born in England, reviewed the book, snottily, and described Blaise as an American and me as an Englishman. We are, in fact, Canadian. I wrote to the *Toronto Star* in an attempt to get them to print an apology on the grounds that 'Englishman', in the context, and under the provisions of the Ontario Human Rights Code, was a racially abusive epithet. They were not persuaded by the brilliance of my argument.

I agonized a great deal over becoming a Canadian citizen. While I had no wish to return to England, I had been born and formed there and had a deep love of the country and its history. But as the years passed and I found myself with a Canadian wife and a Canadian daughter, I found growing within me a genuine and deep attachment to Canada and its future. I finally became a citizen in 1970.

It was a quintessentially Canadian transaction.

I knew nothing of the procedures for becoming a citizen other than that I thought that one was supposed to know the words to 'O Canada' and was supposed to be able to answer questions about the political system. And it may well have been that I was confusing all this with movies about the U.S.A. and Ellis Island. But I was *emotionally* prepared. I was willing, if such a radical step were demanded, to forswear allegiance to the Queen and the heirs of her body for ever. I gathered together all my bits of paper and found the correct federal institution on Dorchester Street in Montreal – a building only slightly less brutal than the British Labour Exchange.

I was directed into a cubicle and stood facing an official who was writing on some forms. While I waited, I ran a mental check over the names of the provinces, provincial capitals, the sequence of the Great Lakes, etc. I rehearsed the names and portfolios of the current cabinet. An old Greek in the next bullpen was attempting to deal in broken English with a very

French Canadian and was in danger of having his name entered as that of the boat on which he'd arrived.

My official took out a clean form and said, 'Do you 'ave a passport?'

'Yes.'

'Nationality?'

'British.'

'What is de number?'

He wrote it on the form.

'Sign here.'

I signed.

'That', he said, 'will cost you twelve dollar.'

In my editing of *Best Canadian Stories* I've paid little attention to the exact legal status of the writers I've published. It's enough for me that they are here. For example, I have no idea whether Elizabeth Spencer is a Canadian citizen. She has lived in Montreal for many years and occasionally writes stories with a Canadian setting. If faced with two stories by Elizabeth Spencer, one set in the Southern States and one set in Montreal, I wouldn't automatically favour the one set in Montreal. I'd select the better of the two.

While I would describe myself as an ardent Canadian nationalist, I have little time for narrow nationalist concerns *in literature*; history has dictated that writing in English transcends national boundaries. It was to England's credit, and *great* advantage, that the British literary world did not say, 'Yanks Go Home!' to Henry James and T.S. Eliot. Or complain that Kipling wrote about *India*. Or spurn Conrad's Polack origins. Or reject the woggishness of V.S. Naipaul.

Canada finds it more difficult to be tolerant and welcoming.

The modern story in English was shaped by the work of writers from the U.S.A., Ireland, and New Zealand. The sensibility of the English-speaking world may next be shaken and transformed by someone from Hong Kong or Belize. Or even Moose Jaw. Who knows? Closed-shop cultural policies in literature – and in any of the arts – can only lead us back into the mediocrity from which we've recently struggled. It is not totally unlikely that fine Canadian writing in the future will link us with India and Vietnam, Germany, Poland, Italy and Portugal. This is a prospect that I can only consider reasonable and pleasing.

Canadian literature is a young and tender plant in need of nurture but over the last ten years I've come to believe that any form of protectionism does more harm than good. I've come to believe that the remorselessly logical and crisp economic arguments of quota, subsidy, distribution, and tariff are a dangerous delusion. Literature is not oil or auto parts. Our response to our literature is *our* problem. We will win by winning hearts and minds. I have seen the enemy and the enemy is not the economic might of the U.S.A. or the cultural power of England.

The Enemy is Us.

IN 1971, David Helwig and Tom Marshall edited a story anthology for Oberon entitled *Fourteen Stories High*. This was followed in 1972 by an anthology called *New Canadian Stories* which became the title of the series which was to follow. David Helwig resigned from editing the series in 1975 because he had accepted a job with the CBC Drama Department which precluded outside work and I was offered the job as co-editor with Joan Harcourt.

The policy of the series when I took over was to publish previously unpublished work. Helwig had started the series with the intention of providing another outlet for new work and new writers. Joan Harcourt and I were receiving manuscripts by the hundred. Nearly all of them were atrocious. I was soon driven to begging friends for unpublished stories – and at that, I wasn't getting the cream because Oberon could not afford to match the payments offered by some of the magazines, nominal though they were. It dawned on me slowly that we were in direct competition with the literary magazines for a very small crop of good work. There was not much point in this and I began to get restless with the whole policy and purpose of the series.

Although Joan and I got on well together, I began to hanker after the idea of a fresh co-editor, someone not quite so *nice* as Joan, someone harsher in judgement. I decided on Clark Blaise. Joan resigned by mutual agreement in 1977 and I persuaded Michael Macklem, Oberon's publisher, to change both the title and the policy of the anthology.

The title was now to be *Best Canadian Stories* and the policy was to concentrate on republishing the best stories from the literary magazines. I *had* wanted an outright policy of republication but Macklem persuaded me that such a policy would be bad PR and would result in reviewers berating

Oberon for closing off yet another publishing outlet. Under pressure, I agreed that we would continue to read and consider unsolicited manuscripts. When the first *Best* appeared, reviewers lamented and berated anyway even though five of the ten writers in the volume were new and young.

I'm still uncomfortable about the policy because I think there are sufficient literary magazines to provide a home for good work. These magazines do not represent an Establishment or an Orthodoxy; there are magazines which cater to every literary taste from dodo to Dada. Most of the magazines, however, are eclectic and their editors are dedicated and avid for new talent of whatever stripe. If a story writer can't get published in a Canadian literary magazine, I'm prepared to believe there's probably something wrong with his writing.

I also believe that the period the young writer spends battering at the literary gates is strengthening; during this period when the gatekeepers seem to be deaf he will possibly come to see for himself some of the flaws and shortcomings in his work. If he goes away from the gates sore of heart and fist never to return, then that, too, is to his advantage.

I would *like* to be able to watch young writers establishing their credentials in the literary magazines over a period of a couple of years before accepting them for *Best Canadian Stories* but such a policy would be unrealistic at the moment; we have problems enough finding ten first-rate stories in any year without setting up additional hurdles.

Joan Harcourt, in her farewell introduction to the 1978 book, said:

I learned some things during my stint as co-editor of *New* (now *Best*) *Canadian Stories*, many of them small, some that I didn't want to know, but learn I did. Mostly I learned that this country is full of people shrouded in arctic light, trapped in their Canadian loneliness, sometimes writing badly about it, sometimes well, occasionally brilliantly. Probably I've read as many stories typed on kitchen tables in efficiency apartments and in echoing old houses in small towns as has anyone in the country. Some of the writers whose stories I read cut slightly ridiculous figures, but they were fighting the battle the best way they knew. Courage is where you find it, and I do dignify them with the title 'writer' even when the stories were less than good: they had a faith and that's more important than the product.

I think I learned that there is little real fiction in Canada. What we have instead are personal histories with the names changed and the facts slightly bent. ... [T]he large run of the stories we received presented carefully crafted reliquaries, little boxes in which were enshrined little memories. Some of these reliquaries were elaborately enamelled, but mostly they were simple, sturdy constructions.

This extract from her introduction illustrates what I meant when I said that Joan was *nice*. I have no disagreement with her second paragraph except that I found the 'constructions' less 'carefully crafted' than she did.

(Mavis Gallant, in a letter, described them disdainfully as 'pallid little "I" stories' though she was talking about the ones we'd *selected*.)

It is with Joan's first paragraph that I am in violent disagreement.

'... they had a faith and that's more important than the product.'

No!

Although Joan is saying this of *inadequate* writers, it's an attitude which has condoned and fostered the mediocrity of *all* Canadian writing from its beginnings to the present.

When I was small and aunts for my birthday gave me socks, my mother used to say to my disgruntled little self, 'It's the thought that counts.' I considered this argument but it seemed to me that what I was left with was, inescapably, *socks*.

My desire to change the title and direction of *New Canadian Stories* was prompted by a belief that 'product' was more important than 'faith'.

I was tired of socks.

It was not until 1977-78 that I felt our story writing was generally strong enough to dare, in emulation of Martha Foley's book, the new title. The manuscripts flooding in were a constant reminder that the fight for excellence was by no means won and that only the thin red rejection-slip was holding off the positive hordes of ink-stained savages. At any given moment, there are hundreds of writers in Canada writing short stories that begin: *Pig-Eye Pete and the boys were shooting the breeze out back with a six-pack of Bud and....*

Best has only been going a few years and it has not yet taught the lessons of technique and sophistication that I hope will eventually be learned. The anthology must be seen in context. It is still a young venture and it mustn't be forgotten that it is only a *very* few years ago that Garner's crudities were highly valued. It mustn't be forgotten that the anthology sells only 2,000 copies in a good year. I would regard the anthology and what it stands for as being still in an embattled position. Squat, unblinking, ready to engulf and absorb it leaving not a trace, sits the vast warty toad of Canadian taste. The most popular writers of stories in Canada are not Mavis Gallant, Alice Munro, Margaret Laurence, and Hugh Hood. The most popular writers of stories are W.P. Kinsella and W.D. Valgardson. It is salutary to remember this.

Kinsella's stories about Indians sell in their thousands. The stories are, for the most part, bad. His Indians are basically a racist creation in the sense that they speak fractured English but are graced with poetic perceptions denied to the insensitive white men – that is, they're relatively noble savages with shining teeth and a natural sense of rhythm. Kinsella writes these stories somewhat cynically, I am sure, because he is talented and has written much better stories on non-Indian themes. The second most popular writer of stories in Canada is W.D. Valgardson. Many academic critics – and even the usually lucid George Woodcock – consider him as one of the three or four best story writers in the country. I profoundly disagree. I find his writing crudely drawn and *thin*. I recently reread all his work when I was compiling an anthology for school children: I was appalled to discover that there was not a single story that was not suitable.

Were these two writers merely popular, the fact would not be worth mentioning; what is worth stressing is that they are accepted as important literary writers by a surprising number of academic critics and literary anthologists. There is no critical consensus in Canada about Canadian writing and very little critical writing worth the paper it's printed on. I harbour the suspicion that many academic critics in English know as much about fiction as I do about nuclear fission. The situation of *Best Canadian Stories* is, at best, precarious.

Under the headline 'Required: Boldness', Anthony Dawson reviewed *80: Best Canadian Stories* in *Canadian Literature*.

Anthologies do not simply respond to what's going on, they aren't merely repositories. They help to shape a national culture, to formulate a sense of what can or should be done by collecting the best of what has been done.

But this brings up the issue of *choice*, and the responsibility for their choices that the editors must assume. And related to this is the problem of context and purpose. Bringing together diverse pieces needs to be done with an eye on the context so created, which in turn raises the question of why such a context should be created. If anthologies are to be culturally as well as commercially successful, their editors have to face this problem boldly, and not, as seems the case with the books under review, just gather material that they happen to like; rather, they have to use the material to reflect, if not a vision, at least more than a glimpse of cultural reality.

I feel that I've *had* 'more than a glimpse' of cultural reality in the last seven years of editing *New* and *Best Canadian Stories* and it's not a vision one would wish to dwell on. An attentive reading of Dawson's review left me with a pain between the eyes; I simply didn't understand what he was getting at though I was tantalized by feeling that it might be something important.

I don't really know what he means by 'cultural reality'. If he means, 'our culture as it really is', I could put together a book that reflected *that* from one week's rejected manuscripts. But I suspect that isn't what he means. I'm made uncomfortable by his assertion that editors should 'use the material to reflect ... cultural reality'. I wouldn't want to 'use' stories for anything. I don't think of stories as 'material'.

Could it be that by 'reflect ... a vision' he means selecting stories that together promote something? National unity, perhaps? Canadian identity? The importance of the North? The Westward shift of power? Or can he possibly mean that editors should promote a particular *kind* of writing?

I can understand editing an anthology to promote a particular *school* of writers and writing – such as the 'Movement' anthologies in England or the 'Fugitive' anthologies in the southern States – but surely it would be immoral to edit an *annual* anthology with the title *Best* from some narrowly partisan point of view? I have always insisted on working with a co-editor precisely because I'm aware of blind spots and prejudices and feel that another sensibility is a safeguard against imposing my purely personal taste – and lack of it.

I had always thought Blaise, Rooke, and I *had* a vision. That vision is simply one of excellence. We're arrogant enough to believe that we can recognize excellence but we're not arrogant enough to assert that there's only one kind. I'd contend that an annual gathering of excellence *does* shape a national culture and does formulate 'a sense of what can or should be done'. It stands, annually, as a beacon against the general dark.

We do not, of course, operate with the conscious burden of formulating a national culture. How unbelievably pompous and deluded we would be if we imagined any such thing possible. That Seal of Approval approach to Culture has always struck me as comically Gallic. We're simply concerned with finding ten good stories which stand up to rereadings. It's impossible to 'formulate' a national culture whatever the Liberal Government may think to the contrary. That's the sort of loopy bureaucratic idea that emerges from slow Fridays at Secretary of State. Our national culture will eventually be found to be, quite simply, the sum of individual excellences.

Dawson goes on to say:

80: Best Canadian Stories has at least the unity provided by its exhibition of a single genre, and the influence the series has had on the development of that genre over the past 10 years has undoubtedly been significant, although it may not have been entirely beneficial. Judging by the present, anniversary volume, the boundaries of the genre do not seem to have been extensively tested or expanded. Excepting 'Speck's Idea', the selection is rather drab, predictable, cautious, though there is some deft work by newcomers Martin Avery, Linda Svendsen, and Guy Vanderhaeghe. As a whole, the volume has not been sufficiently *built* around its impressive centrepiece.

My general reaction to this kind of flatulence is to wish that I could rub the reviewer's nose in the mountains of manuscript and mounds of magazines I trudge through every year. Dawson – and others with similar complaints – surely *must* be aware that editors of annual anthologies *can't* 'build' what they might *like* to 'build'. They are obviously restricted to the stories published in any given year. I do agree that it would be lovely if we had ten writers as good as Mavis Gallant each of whom published new work every year and each of whom agreed to its republication for the nominal sum that Oberon can afford to offer. But such is not the case.

Dawson is not alone in thinking our selections 'drab, predictable, cautious'. Some reviewer or another has described every single volume as 'conservative'. Perhaps all these reviewers are aware of wild and innovative stories which have escaped our attention entirely for years. In the book Dawson is discussing there appears the story by drab, cautious, old Leon Rooke entitled 'Sixteen-Year-Old Susan March Confesses to the Innocent Murder of All the Devious Strangers Who Would Drag Her Down' – as weird a piece of scrivening as one would find in a day's march. But perhaps, as the grumpy millennial leader in the *Beyond the Fringe* skit says, perhaps I'm *very* old-fashioned.

Something I've noticed over the last few years is the way that new writers are seized on and then quickly discarded. Fashion meets CanLit. Boring old Alice Munro, positively antiquated old Hood. Of course, few people have managed to read either very carefully. Soon, I have no doubt, Rooke will be consigned to the rear shelves as a toothless mumbler and Hodgins will be issued his walking-stick. Such blasé attitudes in so short a span of years – as though all these critics and reviewers are operating ahistorically, entirely unaware or forgetful of the fact that it was *only fourteen years ago* that it was felt necessary to use Hugh Garner to introduce the revolutionary new Alice Munro.

It could be argued, I suppose, that this desire for the new, non-drab, and unpredictable illustrates the distance we've travelled in fourteen years and is welcome evidence of a new literary sophistication sweeping the land. The only problem with such a claim is that, in my experience at least, readers simply do not fully understand even the earliest of Alice Munro's stories. Her work has suffered at the hands of dim feminists who have quarried it for ammunition and who have, inevitably, diminished it as literature. When Alice Munro turned out not to be a prophet of escalating sexual violence or indeed a propagandist of any sort, the more volatile in her following drifted away. All this, of course, had little to do with Alice; she simply continued writing stories which was all she'd been interested in doing in the first place. The quest for the fashionably new continues; it is not a literary quest.

Some jaded reviewer can always be relied upon to drag in the avant-garde. Why, they cry, doesn't *Best Canadian Stories* feature the work of x or y? Some reviewers see *Best* as an Establishment anthology but how they manage to do so when it has an open-arms policy to talent and regularly prints the work of young newcomers writing in any style baffles me. I wish I had the leather chair and decanter of port to go with the reputation.

(Cockburn '92 is always mentioned respectfully if anyone's in a donating mood.)

Why doesn't *Best* publish the avant-garde? The best answer I can give is to quote a review I wrote in 1975 of the avant-garde anti-Establishment anthology *The Story So Far 3* published by the Coach House Press. It must be understood that this review does not necessarily reflect the views of my co-editor, Leon Rooke, some of whose own work is capable of causing the eyebrow to rise.

This anthology of twenty-five short stories is the third in what threatens to become an annual event. The contents of the book might be described as antiquarian avant-garde. The titles of some of the offerings indicate the nauseating pretensions of the whole – 'The Nazz: ...scenario for a comic-book', 'three untitled pieces', 'Counting Combinations: A legend of partial distance'. No doubt we are dealing here with Art.

Many of the pieces are free from such conformist conventions as ortho-dox spelling and punctuation. Those which are not entirely liberated indulge mainly in ellipsis.

'And now I begin. I rub ... I push. I rub you with my body. So hard ... so humid. No, don't touch me ... wait, not now.'

Oh, God ...

George Bowering who describes himself as 'living & writhing in Van-couver' is still addicted to the ampersand.

It saddened me to see Terry Heath in such company; he published a good book in 1972 entitled *the truth & other stories.* Daphne Marlatt is cap-able of better things. Matt Cohen is vastly more gifted than the present sample would indicate.

I was intrigued to encounter A.S.A. Harrison again if only because she edited an unintentionally comic masterpiece (also for the Coach House coterie) entitled *Twenty-two Women Talk Frankly About Their Orgasms.* I was immensely taken with the acknowledgements in that book. They read, in part, 'I am grateful to the women who granted me interviews, including Pascal, Granada, Rosy, Angela, whose orgasms are not included here.'

The piece that appealed to me most was 'The Mole' by Martin Howard Vaughn-James, inventor of the 'visual novel', because it contained only sixty words. I was grateful, too, for George Bowering's maunderings

because the funny spelling reminded me of Ring Lardner and I went back
to 'The Young Immigrunts' which contains the lines:

> Are you lost daddy I arsked tenderly.
> Shut up he explained.

The book is illustrated with photographs of the authors who present
brief autobiographical and bibliographical credentials:

Noddy McCoy 'did have a nervous breakdown at the top of the Torre del
Mangia, Siena.... She does not cook or sew.'

Gerry Gilbert says 'I write in the dark' and 'I squat to crap'.

Steve McCaffery 'aetat 4: imagained a colour to be black. practised "a
secret thing". aetat 8: attempted to see a spot. trebled it. read gertrude stein
aetat 24.'

It's all very sad isn't it?

The book was funded by The Canada Council.

There are hundreds of aspiring writers in Canada and I have read the
work of most of them; it has had permanent effects on my disposition. Since
New Canadian Stories became *Best Canadian Stories*, the flood of manuscripts has slowed, thank God, to a trickle. This is pleasing for two reasons.
First, I don't have to wade through five stories a week that begin: *Brrrr! The
alarm-clock....* Second, it suggests that *Best*'s growing reputation has per-
colated right down even to the hardcore literasts who had previously submitted, repeatedly, stories and even articles they had originally published in
their parish magazines in 1924.

My years of experience led me to formulate four general rules about
unsolicited manuscripts which I am willing to pass on for the edification of
those who might in the future become involved in editorial work.

1) *Any unsolicited manuscript sent by Registered Mail or Special Delivery will
   turn out to be peculiarly awful.*
2) Many manuscripts arrive in folders, glassine binders, or pastel dockets, or
   are secured with intricate clips and clamps, or are bound by gay ribbons.
   Many of these are introduced by several pages of front matter – title page,
   half-title, epigraph, etc. – often on paper of contrasting colours.
   The fancier the package, the worse the contents.

3) *Manuscripts tend to be ghastly in proportion to the order and number of the following notations found on the title page:*

  a) *The number of the words to the nearest thousand.*

  b) *The number of words to the nearest hundred.*

  c) *The exact number of words.*

  d) *North American Serial Rights Only.*

  e) *A circle containing the letter c in indication of copyright.*

      If a title page bears c), the manuscript is bad. If a title page bears c), d), and e), the manuscript should be returned unread.

4) There is a surprising number of aspirants who seem convinced that their work is likely to be plagiarized by the mailman.

      Those authors who are most obviously paranoid about copyright are those with the least cause for anxiety.

I'm not an excessively formal person but it irritates me to receive letters on square bits of paper headed: Memo From The Desk Of. Some correspondents favour Holiday Inn stationery. Others write on elaborate letterhead which incorporates their photograph and advertises their other artistic ventures such as Pastel Portraiture and Scissor Silhouettes. Some authors, invariably female, decorate their letters with magic marker flowers and Happy Faces.

Salutations, too, often depart from convention:

'Dear Oberon,'
'Dear Eds'
'Hello there!'
'Hi!'

It may be of sociological interest that letters which begin 'Hi!' are always from women, are usually decorated with Happy Faces or flowers, *and are invariably from British Columbia.*

Many authors include a curriculum vitae which details volunteer work in hospitals and lists their prior publications in *Container and Contents* – the house organ of the Canadian Reinforced Cardboard Box Company.

More than one covering letter has resorted to emotional blackmail describing recent open-heart surgery and suggesting that acceptance of the enclosed would speed recovery ...

It is sometimes hard to keep alive the necessary faith and enthusiasm for this task, hard to keep in mind that it is a project that by its nature must take years to bear fruit abundantly.

In one manuscript, *adhering to*, almost *fused with*, was an uncooked hamburger.

THE TWENTY YEARS that have passed since my arrival in Canada have seen vast changes in our literature. At first glance, the difference between 1962 and 1982 is like the difference between desert and oasis. There are more writers and better writers. Some six or seven bookstores specialize in Canadian books and most bookstores, with the exception of the large chains, carry a passable selection of Canadian fiction. The Canada Council buys its own products and donates them generously. Going to or returning from a public reading of one's work, it is impossible not to bump into fellow-writers in airports.

If forced to generalities, I'd say that the strongest genre in Canada is the short story and the weakest the novel. It would not be realistic to hope for more than one major poet in any fifty-year period. In any country. Our two most important poets are Irving Layton and John Newlove but it's far too early to assess their achievement. I suspect that the idea of a 'major poet' – one who changes our emotional landscape and recharges our language – is now a historical concept; impact requires audience and poetry has become dangerously marginal. The sensibility and manner of our best story writers is basically poetic and it may well be that there is something about our times that prompts people who might once have written poetry to write prose instead.

There has been a blurring of the lines between poetry and prose for some sixty years now; Hemingway's brief 'vignettes' which separate the stories in *In Our Time* are more concentratedly poetic than most verse since. The opening paragraphs of Katherine Mansfield's 'Miss Brill' rise above the normal rhythms of conventional prose into something more highly charged. The verse, on the other hand, of both Hemingway and Katherine Mansfield is unbelievably inept and embarrassing.

Odd.

Where twenty years ago Canadian stories stressed content – what a story was *about* – the main emphasis now is on the story as verbal and rhetorical *performance*. Our best writers are concerned with the story as *thing to be experienced* rather than as *thing to be understood*. This more than anything else is what seems to baffle some readers – and not a few critics; it is difficult for those of us writing stories to understand why this is so since these concerns have been dominant since about 1920.

In an essay that Alice Munro wrote for me this year for a book I was editing, she said:

> I will start by explaining how I read stories written by other people. For one thing, I can start reading them anywhere; from beginning to end, from end to beginning, from any point in between in either direction. So obviously I don't take up a story and follow it as if it were a road, taking me somewhere, with views and neat diversions along the way. I go into it, and move back and forth and settle here and there, and stay in it for a while. It's more like a house. Everybody knows what a house does, how it encloses space and makes connections between one enclosed space and another and presents what is outside in a new way. This is the nearest I can come to explaining what a story does for me, and what I want my stories to do for other people.

The implications of this paragraph alone should be enough to give pause to those who consider Alice Munro a simple 'realist'. What she says here is very like some notes for school children I wrote in 1980 for a junior high-school text called *New Worlds*:

> The 'What does it mean?' approach to the story could be compared with the package-tour traveller who 'does' Europe or Africa in fourteen days. I suggest settling down in a place, learning the language, observing the ways of the inhabitants until you begin to understand their world.

It's probably a very dangerous analogy to make because painting and writing really cannot be compared, but the changes in the short story in Canada over the last twenty years are not wildly unlike the changes in painting at a slightly earlier period. I'd suggest that the story pre-1962 could be compared with traditional representative painting and that the changes since have moved the story closer to an equivalent of abstraction. Though it's precisely there that the analogy collapses – for words have meanings. I don't mean to suggest by 'abstraction' that the modern story lacks immediate reference to the external world. Obviously not. I mean rather that formal concerns are becoming increasingly important.

It possibly makes little sense and sheds no light but the Canadian painter with whom I, for example, tend to identify immediately is David Milne. His concerns in the watercolours and drypoints seem to me exactly the sort of things that I'm trying to do with words.

Our major story writers are Mavis Gallant, Norman Levine, Hugh Hood, Alice Munro, Leon Rooke, and Clark Blaise. Of these writers, Levine and Rooke are the ones most obviously concerned with rhetoric and form. Rooke is writing in a relatively contemporary American tradition, Levine in an older American, now international, tradition. In 1972 when I seemed to know more than I do now, I wrote the following review of *I Don't Want To Know Anyone Too Well* for *The Canadian Forum*.

The fifteen stories in Norman Levine's new collection explore loss of youth, loneliness, varieties of failure, and death, and express a stoicism in the face of these adversities. Nearly all the stories are constructed in much the same way – an incident or a memory is recounted, usually in the first person, and the events are put down one after the other in almost reportorial fashion. The end of the story is usually off-hand, seemingly casual, determinedly flat.

The end of 'A True Story' illustrates the manner. The story recounts the beginnings of a hoped-for affair and ends with the girl's sudden death. On his way back from the funeral, the narrator meets a colleague.

'Isn't it a glorious day', he said.
'It is', I said.
The sun was shining. The snow on the ground and on the trees glistened. We could see our breath in the cold still air.

In other words, Levine is writing text-book examples of 'the modern short story'.

A typical Hemingway story, 'The End of Something', finishes:

'Have a scene?'

'No, there wasn't any scene.'

'How do you feel?'

'Oh, go away, Bill! Go away for a while.'

Bill selected a sandwich from the lunch basket and walked over to have a look at the rods.

But that was in 1923.

The determinedly flat is, of course, as much a piece of rhetoric as is the final speech of a corpse-strewn Elizabethan play; the fact that we can recognize and discuss it as a device shows us that it, too, is a *historical* rhetoric.

When the device succeeds, it can still produce moving work. Levine more than succeeds with such stories as 'A Small Piece of Blue', 'By the Richelieu', 'My Wife Has Left Me', 'A Canadian Upbringing', and 'South of Montreal'. These stories are haunting. In each of them certain details are so fictionally *right* that they are unforgettable – the alcoholic doctor at the northern mine who ritually shoots at a candle-flame with an air rifle in his office; Marsden, the exile and ex-writer, who makes toy roundabouts. Yet even in these most successful stories, an invisible worm eats away at one's pleasure.

One is always aware of Hemingway's looming bulk and sadly aware that such stories in 1971 are a cliché; the pattern of their rhetoric is predictable. I know; I've written them myself.

Just as some good people are trapped and made rigid by some concept of 'good breeding', so Levine is trapped in a delicate but out-moded form. That form no longer delivers the poetry. There is no point now in writing Joyce novels or rhyming couplets. Levine is writing superbly within what is now a formula. Gulley Jimson said Lady Beeder's water-colours were 'like farting Annie Laurie through a keyhole. It may be clever but is it worth the trouble.'

Because Levine has not challenged himself in terms of form and style, his very mastery becomes boring – like watching Minnesota Fats playing billiards. His chasteness and perfection made me long for struggle and vulgarity.

The succeeding ten years of reading and rereading have taught me that I was wrong, that Levine's rhetoric does still deliver the poetry. I've reprinted this review not only so that I could apologize for it but also because it interests me, looking back ten years, to realize how firmly I was locked into rhetorical interests.

Sophistication in style and rhetoric is now more widespread than it was even five years ago. During the last few years the general quality of story writing in the country has improved dramatically. I'm not really sure why this should be. I would like to flatter myself that *Best Canadian Stories* has played a part but this probably isn't true in the sense of its offering literary models to younger writers; it must be remembered that the best writers in the world are only as far away as a bookstore or library. Canadian writing at the moment is only a small and minor current in a very big river. *Best Canadian Stories* may have had some indirect effect, however, simply by existing and offering evidence, perhaps imperfect, that it is possible to be Canadian *in Canada* and still be in touch with a larger sense of excellence. When our best writers publish in international magazines and are republished in *Best Canadian Stories*, it should be an encouragement to all younger writers to know that it is indeed possible to become something more than a spine with a maple leaf stuck on it.

One of the pleasures of editing *Best Canadian Stories* is in the recognition and launching of new talent. Writing, oddly enough, is not a particularly competitive business. Most writers are wise enough to know that all writing is unique and that all writers are part of a tradition which is larger and more important than personal vanities. It has given me great pleasure to be of use to writers at the beginnings of their careers. It's probably invidious to refer to particular people but I've been deeply impressed and excited by the work of Linda Svendsen and Keath Fraser; I have few doubts that they will forge important literary careers.

My hopes for the anthology are that it will come to have such a reputation that writers will consider themselves honoured to be selected. I don't intend this in any arrogant way or mean to imply that our imprimatur is the source of the honour; rather, that the book should become, if this makes any sense, a *communal* expression of excellence in writing. Our stance is not Olympian; we are genuinely grateful if readers and other writers draw work to our attention.

As our writing matures and we develop *more* writers of quality, it is not perhaps silly to imagine beginners here reading *Best Canadian Stories* as attentively as they should be reading *Best American Stories* and *Winter's Tales* from England. I am idealistic enough to hope that one day readers and young writers in England and the U.S.A. will look forward to the annual appearance of *Best Canadian Stories* as a normal and unremarked feature of the literary life.

Although our literature has improved beyond recognition in the last twenty years, the literary situation remains precarious. Although there are books and visible authors and although there are new young writers dedicating themselves to a life of extremely hard work with meagre rewards, there is still one huge fly in the Canadian ointment; nearly all the gains made since 1962 are reflections of the various activities of The Canada Council. The literary base is so narrow that the superstructure is ludicrously unstable. As I've said over and over again, the one thing we still lack – and it's the most important thing – is an audience. Money can subsidize the writers, the magazines, the printers, and the publishers, but an audience can't be bought.

I have no solution to the problem.

I do have vague Sunday School memories of a hymn which involved the general idea of the prevailing darkness of sin illuminated here and there by the individual candles of *good* girls and boys. The words 'You in your small corner and I in mine' somehow linger. Or possibly, 'me in mine'. Or perhaps that was another hymn altogether. But what I'm getting at is the power of individual points of light to dispel dark. It's an answer of sorts and Despair is a sin.

WHEN I MOVED from Delta to live in Ottawa, I spent my first few weeks pottering about finding out where life's essentials were. One of my first stops was the main branch of the Ottawa Public Library. Naturally, I wanted to see how many of my books they had. Curiosity satisfied on that score, I decided to check out the situation with *Best Canadian Stories*.

'I think we'll find them', said the library lady, 'under "B" in "Fiction in English". Or possibly ...'

I followed her Wallabies.

'... under "W". A very good series.'

I nodded and smiled.

'I do so enjoy his historical novels.'

'Pardon?'

'Here you are', she said, gesturing at a rank of familiar spines.

'Ah! Thank you', I said. 'Why might they have been under "w"?'

Spectacles decorated with rhinestone butterflies.

'They're edited', she said, 'by Rudy Wiebe.'

Kent Thompson

ACADEMY STUFF

LIKE MOST 'LITERARY THEORIES', my ideas on the short story form are less 'theories' than they are simple 'reactions' – on the one hand – and 'working principles' – on the other. And although they may have some relationship to that great grey Thing known as Literature, they are first and foremost (as far as I am concerned) the tools of my own individual trade. If I am called upon to justify them in the Grand Arena of Criticism (as I am here doing) I think that I can do so, but I must issue the warning that I am doing something 'after the fact'. That is, having committed the crime of passion (as it were), I am now trying to explain how rational I was all the time.

But most theories, I believe, are developed in reaction to something or other – perhaps something even so vague as 'the way things are'. And the fact is that in the past ten years, as writer, teacher, and editor (of *The Fiddlehead*, for four years), I have found myself growing more and more dissatisfied with the stories I have been reading.

This does not mean that I have much sympathy with what passes for 'avant-garde'. What is usually meant by that term is the use of typographical techniques which were developed fifty years ago (half a century!) and are now used in an attempt to finesse the writer into the future courses of the 'Development of Literature', or whatever. Most 'avant-garde' is all flash and no substance. Worse, it is ridiculously easy to imitate and fake. Worse yet, it is imitative of the fresh fashion of the 1920s. Nothing could be more provincial than the aping of a fashion of fifty years ago, nothing is more futile, and nothing is done more often. (It might be worth reminding oneself that the real avant-garde writer rarely thinks of himself as such, and that we have

First published in John Metcalf, ed., *The Narrative Voice: Short Stories and Reflections by Canadian Authors* (Toronto: McGraw-Hill Ryerson, 1972).

blithely forgotten most of the so-called 'avant-garde'. Who has read Wyndham Lewis lately? Tried him myself once. Got bored; quit.)

In another way, however, I have reacted against some of the writing which was submitted to me when I was the editor of *The Fiddlehead*. This was quite often the symbol-sodden maundering parable of the beginning writer, and when I worked my way through it I thought to myself, 'Oho, somebody's been reading Coleridge and Kafka on the same afternoon.' Mind you, I was less dissatisfied with this kind of attempt than I might have been. I began writing symbol-sodden parables when I was young and reading Coleridge and Kafka on the same afternoon. My friends said it was 'pretty impressive stuff', although somehow it was never accepted for publication. Yes, and it was pretty pretentious stuff, too – a papering-over of an insufficient conception with a flowered wall-paper of prose. One thinks one can disguise one's weakness – or one's youth – with great gobs of obscure prose. Its chief characteristic is that it is only obscure, and not worth the effort of disentangling it.

But I think that the writing which I have reacted most strongly against is what I call the 'Academy' work – that is, the successful story of fifty years ago which I now teach three or four days a week, and the contemporary imitation of it. When this work is done by one of the masters, I am full of admiration for it. When it is a lesser imitation, it seems like pretty weak stuff.

This is the kind of story developed to an incredible degree by the skills of Chekhov, Hemingway, Fitzgerald, or James Joyce. It was a grand era for the short story, and the results were so astonishing that their conventions have hardened into something very like rules. We study the masters in literature classes; we study them in creative writing courses. It is not difficult to see what has happened.

But I can hear myself standing in front of my English 2010 class and intoning: 'The chief characteristic of the short story in the twentieth century is the use of *implication*.' Then, while my minions are writing that down in their dubious spellings, I go on to explain how James Joyce, et al, worked by *patterns of implication*. They get that down; underline it, too. I continue: 'The writer implies; you infer.' I follow this with a brief two minutes on the different meanings of the two words.) And in a moment I am launched into an explanation of the *epiphany*. The writer is God showing the truth to Saul on the Road to Damascus. We the readers, or the characters in the short story, or all of us, infer a certain *truth* about a character's entire life from the circumstances of the story. We discover that Mr Duffy of 'A Painful Case' was a moral coward because he was afraid of sin. The boy in 'Araby' deluded himself about the nature of Romance. In other words, we 'work it out', we 'solve the problem', we 'see the point'.

It is neat and intellectually satisfying. We academics have been making a living out of it for years. But I think we have been less than kind toward that great grey Animal of Literature.

First of all, is anyone's entire life revealed in one moment or one set of circumstances? This is the basic tenet of the short story as we commonly know it. It throws a man's life into focus, as it were. But I am uneasy about this. I know too well that human life is more complex than that, and that one moment, however dramatic, does not sum up a person's life nor does it even throw it into focus. It seems to me to be too arbitrary: a rough handling of humanity for a quick effect which is not fair to the multiplicity of mankind. I realize that it is a useful convention, but I am not too sure that it has not outlived its usefulness.

Then there is the more fundamental matter of the Joycean *epiphany*. The writer *makes his point* by throwing the character's life into focus. But I would argue that by making us 'see the point' the author has turned his story into an intellectual exercise. And worse, the moment we 'see the point' the characters themselves are erased from our consciousness. We put the point down in our copious notebooks and forget the humans at the core of the story. Mr Duffy disappears in our comment about his moral cowardice. Mrs Sinico is only the means of revealing his moral cowardice; she has ceased entirely to be a person.

And indeed, this may not have been what Joyce intended at all, but this is what we have done by our methods of criticism. We tend to read all stories as parables – and this is not surprising because the parable is one of the basic forms of the short story in our culture – but I think that such a reading is unfair to the art of writing, which I see as the business of invoking humanity. (One of my favourite poets is Browning; one of my favourite poems is 'Fra Lippo Lippi'.)

But because we read stories in this way, it is inevitable that we should write them in the same way. And consequently writers – some very *good* writers – are still using the convention of the epiphany. The lesser writers are being used by it, and their characters have become algebraic symbols by which the reader is driven toward a 'solution to the problem'.

The result of the pervasive use of the epiphany, then, is an 'Academy' technique: what were once techniques have become conventions, and the conventions show every indication of hardening into rules. The result of writing by the rules is usually academically respectable, but the work produced is imitative, conventional writing. It is 'Academy Stuff'.

And perhaps because of this discovery, I have come to see the bones of dead structures everywhere. I find the syllogistic form of the Shakespearean sonnet concealed among free verse forms: Point A (image) is contrasted with Point B (image) and results in Synthesis C (image). A small image serves as the concluding couplet. Worse, I have found the same thing in the work of some short-story writers. Dramatic conflict is constructed from Points A and B through C, and zippered up by the final imagistic paragraphs of the short story. The intellectual point is not only *made* – it is made *neatly*.

So I have come to the conclusion that the fine old techniques have become conventions, and have become worn-out.

II: These 'reactions', of course, are not and have never been quite as rational as perhaps I have made them sound. There have been vague feelings of uneasiness which I have here attempted to codify into something resembling coherence. And it is quite possible that in what follows I shall simply drag in under new names techniques which I think I have thrown out under old ones. But my reactions against the current forms of the short story have been sufficient, at any rate, to set me off on what I hope is my own direction, and as a result I have been forced to develop what I call, grandly, my 'working principles'.

But the starting point is essentially negative. I know only what I do *not* want. I do not want the reader of my stories to clap his hands and say, 'I see the point.' I do not want the intellectual progress toward an epiphany.

What do I want then? I think I want to control an emotional experience. That is, I want to send the reader through a set of circumstances which will alter his emotional awareness. I do not want to 'change the reader's mind'. I want to 'change his emotions'. (I am well aware that this might be a Romantic – and false – dichotomy.) In other words, I want to induce an emotional attitude, and to do this I try to take the reader through a number of attitudes and circumstances. The total accumulation of these experiences is to be the effect of the short story. Inevitably, I think, my way of writing a short story throws the emphasis of the short story away from the dramatic point or the intellectual insight and onto the immediate *experiencing* of the character.

For example, I find that I am particularly drawn to the first-person point of view. It gets me out of myself, for one thing, and of course it invokes the immediately human dimension of the human voice. The reader is told something directly in the words of the central character. The relationship between the reader and the character is therefore one-to-one; there is no mediating author to judge or analyse for the reader. The reader has to judge or know the character as he might a close friend – with all the restrictions of 'knowing' that that entails, but with all the humanity of it, too. The reader knows the narrator in a human dimension – not in the god-like omniscience of the third-person point of view. And of course, with this approach, the teller of the story is at least as important as the story itself. Quite often he *is* the story. In 'Because I Am Drunk', for example, I wanted Seeg to speak directly and also to see himself as a character, and consequently I moved back and forth from the first-person to the third-person. It is not an uncharacteristic feature of a drunk: he sees himself doing strange things and wonders at himself for doing them, but does them anyway because something within him makes it impossible for him to stop. (Think about F. Scott Fitzgerald, for example, drunk and dancing on a table with Zelda, and taking mental notes about himself, his behaviour, and the party.) The narrator of 'The Problems of a Truancy', on the other hand, is very much aware of his physical and historical surroundings, but he is not aware of the despair he feels at his failure to 'connect' with them – the despair of the alienation of his knowledge. If the torn-up Seeg is a man of violent love who is trying to be civilized, then the narrator of 'The Problems of a Truancy' is more suicidal than he recognizes. (Incidentally, 'The Problems of a Truancy' is much less autobiographical than it might appear; most importantly – I am *not* the narrator.)

But if I want to *induce* a particular emotional effect, the trick is to *control* it. I have tried to do this by inducing attitudes, and one of the qualifications of the inducement is that it must go unnoticed – and yet it must be *felt*. To this end I have tried to utilize certain literary techniques to perhaps an uncommon degree.

For example, I think of my stories as consisting of a series of 'weights'. I even use the term as a verb. I think to myself: 'I'll weight this section "heavy", and that next one "light", "quick", or "sharp", and that last one "very heavy".' This is the structure of 'Because I Am Drunk'. In other words, I am attempting to structure the story by means of emotional 'weights'. I want the story to 'weigh on one'.

But I very seldom plan the 'weighting' in any formal sense. I try to catch the tone I want, the voice of my narrator, and then hope that the story will generate its own energy.

And in fact it occurs to me that my so-called 'working principles' are really little more than metaphoric descriptions of things which I feel while I am working. The terms are drawn chiefly from the art of painting (about which I know almost nothing – but a number of my friends are painters), and in fact the term 'weight' might best be thought of as something analogous to the painter's or sculptor's use of *mass*.

But the 'weight' of a section can be controlled by several means. For example, an incident told from a long perspective (the view from across the Square in 'The Problems of a Truancy') is, to my feeling at any rate, much lighter than the 'heavy' density of details in the close perspective. The reader (and narrator) are simply farther away. But *very* close perspective (as in the last paragraph of 'Because I Am Drunk') is very heavy. If you are close to a person, you are weighed down by him. The narrator of 'The Problems of a Truancy' is weighed down by the consciousness which notices the infinity of details in the restaurant. The mass of them oppresses him, although he tries to control them by his carefully ordered thought.

Pace and syntax, therefore, also contribute to 'weight'. The reader of 'The Problems of a Truancy' may not realize it intellectually (and perhaps I prefer him not to), but he feels the narrator trying to order his consciousness; the reader feels this because of the pace and the sentence structure. Then in the last paragraph of 'Because I Am Drunk' the release of the emotion is indicated by the turned-loose sentence structure. Or again, in the same story, the sharp moral debate which takes place in Section II is indicated less by what is said than it is (I hope) by the quickness of the dialogue, the brevity of the sentences. It is a moral battle, and the moral knives are quick and sharp.

Diction contributes as well. Abstract words are heavy, I think. (See what

Faulkner does with a carefully placed Latinate word.) And metaphors are heavy because they slow the pace; a mass of metaphors bundled into a paragraph is very heavy indeed.

The rhythm of the story (which is probably my substitute for the intellectual or confrontational dramatic structure) is achieved by playing the weight of one section against another. The design of the story is the relationship of the parts to one another.

But in addition to all of these 'principles of composition', there are other factors which do not fit into anything so coherent as a theory, yet which may be more important in the production of the story. For example, I write myself little notes which gradually accumulate across my desk until they are either filed away or composed into a short story. Whatever it is that is behind the notes is probably responsible for the short story, although it might not appear in the story itself. But why do I write the notes?

Usually the notes are simply phrases (that is how 'Because I Am Drunk' began) or a scrap of dialogue or an image. I know I do not begin with an idea or a character, much less a 'theory of fiction'. And it is also true that a story which one has read, or which has been told by a friend, can have much more influence on the story at hand than any literary theory, however sincerely or strongly held.

In other words, it seems to me that there are other factors contributing to a story which are perhaps more important than the 'theory', but which are too incoherent to fit into any kind of rationally explicable pattern. These are the individual, personal offerings of the individual writer, and these are the things which indicate his style – perhaps more accurately than his literary philosophy.

At any rate, I know that I think a short story is finished when all of these facts seem somehow contained; when I can no longer separate the thinking about the short story from the doing of it.

Ray Smith

DINOSAUR

1. WHAT I DO NOT WRITE

Walter wanted to stay with her, he did not want to go outside again. Outside you were jostled by people, the eyes of strangers stared at you and hated you for being different from them. Down into the subway, bustle and push, sweat and rush, and up again into the street to those bloody big doors of Jaspers, VanDamme & Co. 'Have you finished the Commissions Post-Due Statement?' And you'd hardly finished your coffee....

'Penny for them', said Carol.

He squeezed her small body to him and looked desperately about him.

'The light on the ceiling', he replied. 'I was wondering what you call that shape. A trapezium?'

'Funny man', and nibbled his ear.

My God, if only she knew, and he squeezed her to him again, squeezing shut his eyes to keep out the terror and failing.

Who wrote that? When? Where? Obviously part of a novel. Twentieth-century. English or North American. 'Subway' is American or Toronto. 'Penny for them' sounds rather English. Let's leave it for a while.

Call it the bone of a dinosaur and try to reconstruct the rest of the book. It began the previous Friday afternoon, inside Walter's head. He should have been working on Commissions Post-Due but was instead making bad metaphors on the slow passage of time. For a page or two he reflects on past injuries inflicted by the fat pig of a supervisor, daydreams of revenge. Miles, another clerk about Walter's age but better looking, a hotshot, owner of

---

First published in John Metcalf, ed., *The Narrative Voice: Short Stories and Reflections by Canadian Authors* (Toronto: McGraw-Hill Ryerson, 1972).

sports car, with connections, slips a needle or two into him. Closing time, home for a weekend with Carol. He likes her, thinks he might marry her, but she's a bit dumb and he finds he's coming to hate that one stray strand of hair.... Rest of novel: Miles gets Carol, Walter makes fool of himself at office party, has several smoothly plotted perceptions about life and people (including another woman), Carol sees too late she was wrong, and the novel ends with Walter coming to a largish symbolic, metaphoric, and/or psychological perception about life. He acts upon this at about 3:06 a.m. on the dark night of his soul by attacking those bloody big doors at Jaspers, Van-Damme & Co. with a blow torch. We are left to guess if he goes insane, gets arrested, dies as the doors fall on him, or writes a novel about the spiritual agonies of a Commissions Post-Due clerk.

Does your reconstruction look much different from mine? You included a couple of awful parents? A bit different, but not much. Right: the point is, we both have dinosaurs on our hands. If we can reconstruct a novel from a fragment it is a dinosaur, extinct, and no damn use to a writer today. It was useful thirty, forty years ago: alive, flexible, adventurous, still growing, still discovering. In a word: healthy.

2. AND WHY

The author? Me, of course. I wrote it an hour ago. It is part of a novel, a large pastiche novel floating about in my head, a novel I hope I never bother to write. Apart from a slight archness in tone which I think is understandable under the circumstances, it seems to me a reasonably convincing bit. It satisfies all the conventions of a standard twentieth-century novel. The damnation of it is that I could whip it off in ten minutes. If a writer can do that with a style, with a form, it is dead.

The problem of the artist is to make a representation of the world. That seems general enough to be taken as acceptable by anyone. The question immediately following is how to make it.

I deliberately began the last paragraph with 'the problem of the *artist*'. Depending on his talents the artist can make his representation in words, music, painting, dance, whatever. Seen in this light, the hows of the artist extend through a very broad range and my little pastiche fragment is but one of an immense number of hows.

The style of my fragment has been widely used for at least a hundred years. Dickens didn't much use it, Tolstoy used it to a degree, so does Norman Mailer. I use aspects of it. But in the twentieth century almost all novels have used it exclusively. Like any other style it has its advantages and its limitations.

The most important characteristic of the style is that it allows a representation of human thought in words. Not symbols (like the big doors), not just figures of speech (having eyes hate), but a sober, prose account of a character's thought. The whole of the book will be contained inside Walter's head, the reader will see the world through his eyes. We find Walter lying in bed, presumably having just made love with Carol. He thinks of going to work tomorrow morning and we follow his mental journey. Certain aspects of the trip are selected so that the reader can fill in the feeling of the trip from his own experience. We are told what Carol says, Walter's reaction and words, we see him squeeze her, but we are not told what she is thinking or what is going on somewhere across town, although some novels allow this shift. In addition we can be sure that no character of importance will appear suddenly more than halfway through the book; that Carol's appearances will be carefully spaced through the story; so also Miles, the supervisor, the landlady. The novel will have a calm rhythm of event, conversation, reflection, action. Walter's problems will gradually mount; they won't fall on him like a load of bricks in the first or the second last chapter. But the defining point is that the book, or the world the book shows us, is filtered through Walter's mind.

The advantage of this approach is that it gives the writer a tool to represent the minds of any number of different people in any number of different situations. (One mind, twenty situations per novel.) The tool can be used in poetry but must be subordinated to the poet's other more important concerns. It can be used in movies, but awkwardly as voice-over narration. It can even be used in painting by lettering the words onto the ground. But it is most at home in prose fiction.

The limitations of the style are several. A lot of thought seems to be in words of a language. But a lot apparently is not. Over a normal day people will have a lot of repetitive thought: 'Christ, what a hangover.... Where did I leave my wallet?... I wonder if she loves me.... Hope it's roast beef for supper....' A lot of thought is specific to a profession. Novelists, being novelists, are not accountants or used-car salesmen or farmers in Uzbekistan. They do specialize in imaginatively constructing how other people think and, since young novelists rarely make living expenses from their writing, their biographies often include a sentence like this: 'MacSnurf has been a lumberjack, dishwasher, skip tracer, cabby ...'. Unfortunately these lists rarely include 'Uzbekistani goatherd, astronaut, banker, senator, ship's captain ...'. Sometimes one of these more recherché types will take up writing as a second profession. If he is good at it, like Joseph Conrad, readers will have something truly unique on their hands. Doctors, lawyers, the odd soldier does this. But very few bankers or Uzbekistani (or Manitoban) farmers. Several generations of writers have tried their hands at creating the thoughts of these people. We have had bankers, bankers with dull wives, interesting wives, mistresses; bankers who hated their jobs, loved their jobs, who didn't care one way or the other; bankers who drank, took drugs, or fondled little girls in parks. A notable feature of such books, though, is that one rarely sees the banker banking. Although I don't know of any books about Uzbekistani farmers, I expect the hero spends a lot of time philosophizing about sky and hills and grasslands; and damn little worrying about diseases of goats or wheat.

This attempt to construct the mentality of various types became a major object of the novel. Books were touted with blurbs like this: 'Here is MacSnurf's brilliant and incisive probe of the corrupt world of high finance. Through the eyes of Payon Dumand, the dynamic and ruthless director of ...'. This from MacSnurf who, without the aid of the Encyclopaedia, would have thought a kited cheque was a native of Prague aloft at the end of a string.

Not only is the imagination limited factually, but it runs out of new people. In his next book, MacSnurf will have to try harder. We have met a thousand Payon Dumands, we want someone with a few extra elements to his character. The end of the process is a hero who is the son of a Bombay brothel keeper and an Arizona cowgirl eight feet tall. Hero was brought up in the north woods of Finland and has had a career as a notary and white slaver in Beirut. Married to a gorgeous but insane Eskimo ballerina, he has retired to Melanesia to catalogue butterflies. The novel relates his train of thought through the ten seconds it takes him to lace up his battered running shoes.

But perhaps the crux of the question lies in the phrase 'Through the eyes of ...'. Point of view: once a useful tool, it has become an end in itself, and so a tyranny.

In a sense, of course, there is always point of view. But writers and readers have come to think that a single point of view is right, is the norm, the proper form. It is acceptable to get into Walter's mind for a chapter, then into Carol's in the next. But there will be an overall narrative point of view. Anything more extreme and the writer is being deliberately arty, is using artificial contrivance because he can't master the real thing.

But the only criterion for judging a how is: does it work? A normal beginning for an artist is: 'I wonder what would happen if ...'. Right. I wonder what would happen if we said the hell with point of view. Let's try a ten-page story with a hundred and twelve points of view. Explode it all over everywhere. Will it work? Yes. I have tried it and so have lots of other artists and it does work. The reader has to be willing to suspend his expectations, but any reader worth a damn should be ready for this from time to time.

Any style, then, has its limitations. Until those limits have been reached the style is alive. The writer says: 'I wonder what would happen if, in this style, I tried to represent children ... love-making ... Marco Polo ... green men from Mars ... housewives with itchy crotches ... turtles ...'. And he struggles and finds that he can. To reread the book in which some previously untested limit has been tested is continually refreshing. We can go back to Henry James and watch as he explores the limits of point of view. We can read Hemingway or Cary or D.H. Lawrence for their original representations of the world as seen through the eyes of a man with no testicles, a wacky-wonderful painter, or a horny English lady. But MacSnurf's novel using point of view as found in *The Ambassadors* and creating a horny English lady with the hots for her gamekeeper will be three hundred pages of cliché, stereotype, and unintentional parody.

As I said, I'm quite willing to use the style of Walter and Carol, but in limited bits, probably for intentional irony, and, I hope, in some new context. But to write entire works that way is to cheat the reader and oneself. The most obvious cheat involves the extensions of the world in the work. The implication of any work is: here is a way of seeing the world. Hemingway says: life can be seen as a struggle to face death with honour. Lawrence says screwing is good. Any book written from a single point of view says the world can be seen this way. But to say that all good novels (or valid novels) show the world from one or a limited few points of view is tyranny and a cheat.

Another extension and another cheat in the Walter and Carol book is the extension of plot. The statement of any sort of plot is: this is a way of seeing the relations between events; or, this kind of relation between events is a significant kind. Men have used all sorts of plots. The Greeks accepted *deus ex machina*; we call it a cheat. Dickens and Shakespeare both used lots of coincidence. Their imitators used coincidence as a crutch and a reaction took place. The twentieth-century plot is, in this sense, a massive reaction against the plots of shameless junk like the Horatio Alger books. This sort of shift happens when a fresh writer says, 'Hold it a moment, it may look fine to you and your readers, but my world is not full of long lost brothers, millionaires in disguise, and runaway horses bearing terrified virgins. In fact, my world hasn't included a coincidence since last Christmas when two of my gift books contained the word "Zeugma". And furthermore, I think it is far more interesting to look at a series of rather subtle, low key events to see if they will lead a character to some significant perception of the world.'

Right: and this attitude gave the world fifty to a hundred years of fine prose fiction. But again, this tool has been used to work just about every sort of material. Its use has become obsessive. Writers who use it without conviction can be seen hiding chance meetings inside pages of elaborate disguise: 'How long had it been since Walter had taken a stroll along the river?...'. So we wade through half a chapter of desultory description of coal barges and used condoms before we come to: 'Dolores, what a surprise to run into you!' 'Oh, I often walk along the river....' and a few bad metaphors about time passing.

The extension, then, is that there are no coincidences in life. But obviously there are and some of them are damn important and a whole literature which excludes them denies their existence and so misrepresents the world.

3. WHAT I WRITE

'A Cynical Tale' and 'Peril' for your pleasure, gentle reader. In the hope that you see in them, in their extensions, something of the world around you, perhaps even that you see the world in a new and fresh way. A pair of (I hope new) 'I-wonder-what-would-happen-ifs'. Isn't that what it's all about?

I don't really consider them very odd or very new. You should be able to place them, but if you can't, here's a very brief and incomplete context.

They are part of a body of work called 'speculative fiction'. Generally ironic in tone. Aesthetic in approach; which means, I suppose, an indirect approach to the many social and political problems of the world around us. This is in clear contrast to the other rising body of writing which includes things like revolutionary writings, the new journalism, documentary novels, and the like, all of which try to grapple directly with the aforementioned social and political problems. I should emphasize, or repeat, that speculative fiction doesn't ignore the world, but approaches it somewhat indirectly. The telling point is that both types have pretty much rejected the whole creaking apparatus of the Walter-Carol psychological-realism (or whatever it's called) form of writing.

Some big dogs in speculative fiction: Jorge Luis Borges, Vladimir Nabokov. Coming big dog: Kurt Vonnegut, Jr. Prominent younger dogs: Thomas Pynchon, John Barth, Donald Barthelme, Richard Brautigan. Incidentally, from considering these writers, their views, careers, antecedents, and whatnot, you can see speculative fiction as a continuing historical alternative, trace its ups and downs, off-shoots, roots, and other such aspects as critical enquiry can profitably illuminate.

Some specific notes on:

'A Cynical Tale'. A modern fantasy re-write of the English ballad 'Barbara Allan' by the prolific and versatile lyricist, Anon. It is about italics, capital letters, parentheses, the semi-colon, a floating point of view, *non sequiturs*, over-plotting, flat characters, spy thrillers, high rise apartments, lingerie, short stories, overstatement, understatement, dropped endings, and plum cordial. It is not, I swear, about homosexuality.

and:

'Peril'. Three incidents which each contain a hidden peril. Three young-ish men, rather similar, rather different, take a walk. They meet a stranger or strangers and converse about one thing and another, then go on. In the graveyard walk, the peril is in the necromancer's sanity. (His description of his introduction to the art is, incidentally, a loving parody of Gulley Jimson explaining his conversion to painting.) The peril in the park is in the question: Is either of them sane? The peril of the beach is that, if everything is as it is presented, then Purlieu has lunched with a god and a goddess.

I often use 'Peril' to illustrate how I write. I began with a cluster of images, moods, words, people that took the shape of a line starting out in front of my eyes toward the right, but curving gracefully to the left, and disappearing in the hazy distance. A very relaxing vision. Obviously the curve took shape as the beach in Part 3, but I hadn't thought of the beach when I began to write. It did come out, but the way I consciously tried to produce it in the reader's mind was by arranging and manipulating his expectations. When we read things, it seems to me, we are continually trying to guess what comes next. A long series of correct guesses, as in our reconstruction of the Carol-Walter Dinosaur, would be a straight line. An ingenious and convincing thriller like *The Spy Who Came In from the Cold* would produce a jagged line with a jag for every time Le Carré caught you going in the wrong direction. I figured I could make the curve by fooling you just a little every paragraph or so. So if your expectation of outcome had been a straight line running out at thirty degrees on the starboard bow, and if each jolt brought the line a degree or so to port, then the completed line would be a long gentle curve.

But whether you saw the curve or not (and I don't suppose you did) the story should have left you in a gentle curving mood. It should have given you some pictures you can't quite explain but which will stay with you for many years, pictures which will return when that sort of mood is upon you or which, returning, bring that mood on. If it did that, then the story worked, and I am happy. If it didn't work for you, then you can use the pages to make paper airplanes to fly in gentle curves and perhaps that will make you happy.

4. AND WHY

Because they were there.

Carol Shields

IS THERE A FEMININE VOICE IN LITERATURE?

LET ME SAY at once that I would be happy to embrace the altogether attractive myth of the feminine voice. It is a temptation to believe that delicacy, fluidity, subtlety, and elegance are more pronounced in the writing of women – though one must bear in mind that these qualities in their over-ripe stages produce preciousness, whimsy, and flatulence.

Many of you here will be familiar with Frances Brooke's Quebec novel, *The History of Emily Montague*. Published in 1769, it is regarded by some as North America's first novel. In the story one of the characters, a vivacious young coquette, writes to a friend in England promising that with her very next letter she will enclose a frost piece, a frost piece being a silvery little bit of wintery description, an exercise in pure style, the kind of genteel piece-work which ladies of the time turned out much as they produced water colours or embroidered cushions. The important thing is, I think, that even then, in 1769, Frances Brooke was gently mocking this tradition.

Female chauvinism would be gladly served by a belief that women are masters of rich language patterns, intricate clustered metaphors, or a syntax which is artful, supple, and suggestive – but all these things are difficult to prove. What is somewhat more apparent, in Canadian writing at least, is a difference in tone. And what is very different is the sort of topics women have chosen to write about.

First, to talk briefly about tone, the women who are writing fiction in Canada at the moment – and there are many – seem to speak in a voice which is both present and personal. The first person is often used, and there has been an increased use of the present rather than the past tense. The settings tend to be simple enclosures, patiently explored. I think I see, too, a

First published in *Atlantis* 4.1 (1978).

shift away from the tone of irony which has marked much of Canadian women's writing.

It is really the question of content which marks the difference between men and women writers. Think of Canadian men novelists – Richardson, Kirby, Grove, Callaghan, Davies, and Cohen; what they have written about is man and landscape, man and history, man and moral issues. Think of our women writers – Moodie, Duncan, Laurence, and Munro. Almost from the start in this country women have chosen to write about the relationships between people and particularly between men and women.

You may say this is not really surprising. Women have also been mothers and therefore witness the growth and development of human personality. Then there is the question of confinement and expectation: cut off from the world of affairs and from a history of their own, women may have turned instinctively to the present moment and to the immediate concern of what it means to be a woman.

Susanna Moodie was a nineteenth-century writer of prose and poetry whose stated desire was simply to entertain and divert with tales about her family and neighbours. Her views on the role of women were not advanced. The serious matters of the world, she said, should be left to men. Consciously she may have believed all of this. But in her writing one sees again and again the tableau of the failed man and the heroic woman. Men died, lost money, drank, and acted foolishly; women survived, held together families, guarded the public morality, and gave to society its art and its meaning.

Sara Jeannette Duncan wrote novels about women at the turn of the last century, a time when the question of women's rights was at issue. In her novels *The Imperialist* and *Cousin Cinderella*, there is a consistent pattern which in many ways echoes Moodie. Women are adaptive, pragmatic, and realistic while men give way to ill-defined idealism and bouts of romanticism which are as damaging as disease.

And in the present day we find that the stories by the Canadian writer Alice Munro are about what it means to be a woman. She deals not with problems of civil rights but with the more central issue which is the struggle of the feminine spirit to survive. In her story 'Boys and Girls', for example, she looks at the kind of compromise women have had to make, surrendering power in order to remain human.

Briefly then the isolating of the feminine voice in terms of language is a difficult, perhaps impossible, task. But listening to what the voice is saying is immediately revealing.

Carol Shields

THE SAME TICKING CLOCK

MY FRIEND SARAH was worried about her five-year-old son, Simon. 'I hear voices in my head,' he told her, 'and they're talking all the time.'

It took her a few days to figure out that the buzzings in his brain were nothing more than his own thoughts, the beginning of that lifelong monologue that occupies and imprisons the self.

It's here in the private, talky cave of our minds that we spend the greater part of our lives – whether we like it or not. And mostly, it seems, we do like it – 'The Soul selects her own Society' – but there are times when the interior tissues thin and when the endless conversation grows unbearably monotonous, when it seems to be going back and forth across the same grooves of experience, the same channels of persuasion, and we long for release. Long, in fact, to become someone else. Even the most fortunate of us lead lives that are sadly limited; we can inhabit only so many places, follow so many lines of work, and can love a finite number of people. We're enclosed not just by the margins of time and by the accident of geography, but by gender and perspective, and by the stubborn resistance of language to certain modes of meditation.

Our own stories, moreover, are not quite enough; why else are our newspapers filled with Dear Abby and Ann Landers, with problem columns for golden-agers, for adolescents, mid-lifers, parents, consumers, patients, and professionals? It's not for the solutions that we devour this often execrable journalese, but for a glimpse of human dilemma, the inaccessible stories of others. Even the smallest narrative fragments have the power to seduce.

First published in Libby Schier, Sarah Sheard, and Eleanor Wachtel, eds., *Language in Her Eye: Views on Writing and Gender by Canadian Women Writing in English* (Toronto: Coach House, 1990).

School children read in their arithmetic books about Mary Brown who buys three pounds of turnips at twenty cents a pound and a kilo and a half of cheese at five dollars a kilo. How much change will she get back from a twenty-dollar bill? The answer arrives easily, or not so easily, but leaves us hungering after the narrative thread – who is this Mary Brown, what will she do with all that cheese, and what of her wider life, her passions and disappointments? A phrase overheard on a bus or perhaps a single name scratched on a wall has the power to call up the world. We want, need, the stories of others. We need, too, to place our own stories beside theirs, to compare, weigh, judge, forgive, and to find, by becoming something other than ourselves, an angle of vision that renews our image of the world.

Writers draw on their own experiences, though only a few draw directly. We want to imbue our fictions with emotional truth; does this require that we stay imprisoned in the tight little outline of our official résumés, that we must write about the Prairies because that's where we live, that we cannot make forays into the swamps of Florida or Mars or Baloneyland, that we must concentrate our steady eyes on the socio-economic class we come from and know best, that we must play it safe – because this is what it amounts to – and write about people of our own generation? A lot of energy has been lost in the name of authenticity; we fear far too much that critical charge – 'it doesn't ring true' – and worry too little that it may not ring at all.

'When I write, I am free', Cynthia Ozick argues in one of her essays, collected in her book *Art and Ardor* – and she means utterly free, free to be 'a stone, or a raindrop, or a block of wood, or a Tibetan, or the spine of a cactus.' Our circumscription is largely of our own making, and at least a portion of it flows from a peculiar reluctance – whether caused by a stance of political purity or a fear of trespassing or 'getting it wrong' – to experiment with different points of view, and, in particular, with shifts of gender.

We all know that a fully-furnished universe is made up of men and women, and that women writers are often called upon to write about men, and male writers about women. Writers go even further at times, not just writing about the other sex, but speaking through its consciousness, using its voice. The question can be asked, and often is, how successful is this gender-hopping? Does any truth at all seep through? Maybe more than we think. Oscar Wilde had the notion that we can hear more of the author's true voice in her or his fictional impersonations than we can hear in any autobiography. (Not that he bothered with the niceties of gender pronouns.) 'Man is least himself', he said, 'when he talks in his own person. Give him a mask, and he will tell you the truth.' A mask, he said, but he might also have said, a skirt. Or a small pointy beard.

This is not to say that crossing gender lines consists of trickery or sleight of hand; nor is it a masquerade as Anne Robinson Taylor, in her book *Male Novelists and Their Female Voices*, would like us to think; and certainly not an impersonation as Oscar Wilde suggests. To believe this is to deny the writer the powers of observation and imagination and also to resist the true composition of the universe, real or created, in which men and women exist in more or less equal numbers.

Nevertheless it is still considered a rare achievement for a man to have created a believable and significant woman, and a woman a believable and significant man. We point to these gender trips as exceptions, as marvels. Isn't it amazing, we say, that Brian Moore could get inside the head of Judith Hearne and make us believe in her? And Flaubert – how remarkable that he was able to comprehend the temperament of a French housewife, her yearnings and passion! And there must be a couple of others out there – aren't there? Jane Austen gave us a few men who were worth waiting three or four hundred pages for, although there's a chilliness about even the best of them. Charlotte Brontë uses the male voice in her novel *The Professor*, but the tone is painfully awkward. In writing the male character, Brontë says, she was working under a disadvantage; when writing about women she was surer of her ground. Joyce Carol Oates once remarked that she did badly with male narrators because for her the angle of vision was restricted, and too much feeling and self-awareness had to be sacrificed.

A few years ago women could point to their own lack of experience in the world of men, but this situation has been extraordinarily altered by legislation and by a revolution in thinking. What has also been altered is the kind of experience that can legitimately be brought to art – birth, motherhood, the rhythms of the female body, a yearning for love and the domestic component of our lives – which serious literature had previously suppressed. But the news is out: we all, male and female alike, possess a domestic life. The texture of the quotidian is rich with meaning, and the old problem-solution trick is beginning to look like a set-up, a photo opportunity for artificial crisis and faked confrontation. Acknowledgement of that fact leads us to the hypothesis that we are all born with a full range of sympathy toward both men and women – yet something, somewhere, gets in our way and makes us strangers. This is puzzling since, despite the inequities of the power structure, men have always had mothers, sisters, wives, daughters, just as women have had access, albeit limited, to the lives of fathers and brothers, husbands and sons. We have been living under the same roofs all these years and listening to the same ticking clock.

It seems baffling, then, that in this day there should be so few men and women writing well about the other sex and even sadder that they are not writing *for* the other sex. The world we are being offered as readers is only half-realized, a world divided down its middle. As readers we are being misled; as writers we are cheated. I wonder sometimes if the loneliness writers complain about isn't a result of scraping a single personality, our own, down to its last nuance.

What is needed is permission to leave our own skins, worrying less about verisimilitude and trusting the human core we all share. Of course our experiences are necessarily limited – this is part of the human conundrum – but observation and imagination may lead us to what we intuitively know, and have known all along.

Carol Shields

NEWS FROM ANOTHER COUNTRY

EVERYWHERE it seems there is an impatience with the conventions of literary realism, and with good reason, for the 'real world' is too often shown as fragmentary, a sort of secondary lesion of the senses, trailing off in *diminuendo*, interrogated on every side by technology, unwilling to stand still long enough to be captured by definition. Language itself, our prized system of signs and references, frequently appears emptied out or else suspiciously charged.

Post-modernism – it's sometimes forgotten that post-modernism is a theory, not a mode of writing or a methodology – seemed for a time to offer a new perspective. Writers were relieved of the responsibility to create a believable world and to invest that world with meaning, to tell a story that derived its tensions from the springs of cause and effect, from psychological motivation or moral consequence. Writers could lean in their inarticulateness on the absurdity of the endeavour, and their *texts*, that curious but useful word, could be crisped and refreshed by the knowledge that this was, after all, a game.

But how anxious theory is, and how arbitrary. This 'beautiful nonsense', as it has been called, proved all too tendentious, too labyrinthine, too much a hypothesis deduced from materials that were themselves unproven. How disappointing it was to find that even a theory that illuminated and delighted the intellect could fail to convince. There was also, and from the beginning, a disparity between theory and practice that signalled a certain effort of accommodation and an easy forgiveness of imprecise expression or ironic aloofness – some would say élitism. Language, which might have

First published in John Metcalf and Leon Rooke, eds., *The Second Macmillan Anthology* (Toronto: Macmillan, 1989).

been liberated, instead shrivelled; we have seen how writers, overdosed on theory, became incomprehensible. (The poet Don Coles has written about a tragic Portuguese child who was kept by her parents in a chicken coop and who, when finally rescued by neighbours, was found to 'talk' like a chicken.)

But if post-modernism has proven a synthetic discourse, unanimated by personal concerns, it has at least given writers a breath of that precious oxygen of permission and, more important, time to see in what way the old realism failed us.

It was, perhaps, not real enough. It focused too compulsively on those phantom inventions, comedy and tragedy. It trafficked too freely in moments of crisis, imposed artificial structures, searched too diligently for large themes and too preciously for graceful epiphanies (*mea culpa*). It banished certain parts of our language to certain emotional parts of the house. The people who appeared in 'realistic' fiction were almost never allowed the full exercise of their reality, their daydreams, their sneezes, their offended appetites, their birthday parties, their tooth-aches, their alternating fits of grotesque wickedness and godly virtue. Their meditative life was neglected. Realistic fiction passed too quickly through the territory of the quotidian, and it dismissed, as though they didn't exist, those currents of sensation that leak around the boundaries of vocabulary. The realistic tradition stressed – why? because it was more 'dramatic'? – the divisiveness of human society and shrugged at that rich, potent, endlessly mysterious cement that binds us together.

These are interesting times for a writer. The crisis of meaning, and we nearly died of it, has brought us a new set of options. The strands of reality that enter the newest of our fictions are looser, more random and discursive. More altogether seems possible. The visual media, television and the cinema, have appropriated the old linear set-ups, leaving fiction, by default, the more interesting territory of the reflective consciousness, the inside of the head where nine-tenths of our lives are lived. And writers seem more happily aware of their intimate connection with readers and with other writing. (I love the work of Audrey Thomas because she understands that the books we read form part of the tissue of experience.)

In the books I read – and I find it hard to separate my life as a reader from that as a writer – I look first for language that possesses an accuracy that cannot really exist without leaving its trace of deliberation. I want, too, the risky articulation of what I recognize but haven't yet articulated myself. And, finally, I hope for some fresh news from another country which satisfies, by its modesty, a microscopic enlargement of my vision of the world. I wouldn't dream of asking for more.

George Bowering

UNDONE TRADITION

SINCE THE TWENTIES, approved North American fiction has been conservative, falling behind the other arts in adaptation to changing ways of looking at the world. In France the innovators have been the major figures, while in the U.S. and Canada they have been underground cult figures or almost totally ignored. But in the past couple decades there has been a great undoing of the tradition. American critic Jerome Klinkowitz takes the publishing season of 1967–68 as a watershed. It was then that John Barth described the fiction of Exhaustion in a major literary slick, while some critics were confidently albeit crankily proclaiming the death of the novel (and who would not, reading only Bellow and Updike?). More important, that was the year that a large number of odd crackpot books appeared: Barthelme's *Snow White*, William H. Gass's *In the Heart of the Heart of the Country* and Vonnegut's *Welcome to the Monkey House*, to name a few books of stories.

How are the new writers different from those who were busy ravelling the end of the tired tradition? We are still struggling with the terminology needed for a departure. Readers who really have for some time disbelieved the ruses of 'leading characters, plots, themes, morals, beginnings, middles and ends' have to have some vocabulary to half-settle in. A lot of people are looking for a way to distinguish the new, and to find a means of discrediting the old. Many readers, especially those who could read before television came into the reading-room, are not so much bewildered as resentful because of the 'chaotic' page offered by the new fiction. They have spent time learning the rules and they want to protect their investment.

The new fiction's act reminds one often of what has happened in non-

First published in *Open Letter* 3rd ser. 4 (1976). Republished in George Bowering, *Craft Slices* (Ottawa: Oberon, 1985).

academic poetry. For instance the abandoning of an attempt to describe the world in favour of transforming it by way of the shaping imagination. The writers beginning the new can take content, that flimsiest of things, and, transmuting it through the imagination, making metaphor, allow the language to tell its own story. This will not be a description of life, but ultimately as real as life (without making life be like it any more than *vice versa*, as was supposed to happen in the contract of realist writing). This means that the novel becomes opaque, perhaps as opaque as the world we spin on.

Some of the new fiction writers speak their versions of that idea. Barthelme: 'art is not about something but *is* something.' Kosinski: 'you are actually creating this situation when you are reading about it; in a way you are staging it as an event in your own life.' Sukenick: 'it would be hard to overestimate the importance of the imagination in confronting and even creating the world in which we live.' Sorrentino: 'no art can succeed when it is willingly mistaken for reality.'

Often in realist fiction, imagination meant sympathy, usually with the central character. Now it means the aroused ability to put together a world, a place to live, for writer as well as reader. Klinkowitz says that Kurt Vonnegut has had the world 'overpopulated, technologically revolutionized, firebombed, invaded by zombies from Mars and formally destroyed'. Barthelme does not try to found new structures, exactly. He takes the ones he finds around him, enlivening street and apartment languages by picking them like cherries and dropping them into novel and oddly recognized places. Snow White, remember, is trapped in her world of dwarfs because she cannot *imagine* anything better.

Ray Smith

WERNER WHO?

SHOULD LITERATURE ever come to be understood and defined by someone with proper philosophical training, it will be seen to be fuzzy.

Critical labels for movements – realism, post-modernism, metafiction – name bulges, tendencies; they serve fashion, not truth; they are crutches for those who need help reading, judging; crutches for editors, agents, journalists, and other such literary middlemen.

A successful critical theory must be analogue and multidimensional; it must be able to deal in unknowns and indeterminates. But most critical theories are digital and two- or three-dimensional, puny constructs one can walk around in an hour or two.

Any paradigm of the social role of the artist and his work must allow for Jane Austen as well as Solzhenitsyn; for Rembrandt's self-portraits and Vermeer's interiors as well as *Guernica* and *Los Desastres de la Guerra*; for *Der Rosenkavalier* as well as *Fidelio*. The arts and politics are arts of the possible; but the possibles are different. The great political artist finds his soul in the great world, the great private artist finds the great world in his soul; the little political practitioner is a hack, the little private practitioner pares the nails on his effetes. (Clearly I mean that the artists and works that begin this paragraph are great; anyone who thinks I mean they are equally great cannot read.)

Art is a just rendering of the world. The better the work, the more just the rendering. By 'just', 'rendering', and 'world' I mean things beyond the complexity I can get at in this paper (or anywhere). I mean this not in the (properly) limited sense of the endeavours of the statistician, the lawyer, or

First published in John Metcalf and Leon Rooke, eds. *The Second Macmillan Anthology* (Toronto: Macmillan, 1989).

the historian: *Tristram Shandy, Wuthering Heights,* and *Finnegans Wake* render the world with a justice of a quality with *Emma, War and Peace,* or *Madame Bovary*; all sing in their different fullnesses. Let some critic take it from here; let us have some useful and generous delineations, distinctions, definitions; let us have a vocabulary of fiction. My own attempt at such a vocabulary is described in a letter to John Metcalf and published in his *Carry On Bumping*; the same letter includes my readings of modern critical theory.

While I was writer-in-residence at the University of Alberta, I wrote a piece for aspiring writers entitled 'Three Propositions on the Art of Writing'. They are:

1) Writing is an activity. (It is the doing of it that matters to a writer.)
2) A writer is someone engaged in the activity of writing. (Not in research, thinking, planning, drinking, talk-showing, award-receiving.)
3) All writer's questions about a piece of writing can only be resolved through the act of writing. (A writer needs practical answers to such questions as 'Will it work?', 'Does it fit?', or 'Can I manage it?'. Theoretical answers here are meaningless.)

The most important aesthetic perception a writer has is that the dichotomy between style and content is false, does not exist for a working artist. It should also be false for a reader reading or a critic cricketing; but you can't undo two millennia of western thought based upon the dichotomy.

I have read lots of interesting critical theory (along with lots of trashy theory), but the only stuff of any use to me in my writing was done by other writers or painters or musicians.

I am constantly amazed at the certainty of critics: the only large certainties in the arts must embrace uncertainties. Critics are never uncertain; writers always are; I am a writer.

Who Heisenberg?

Hugh Hood

SOBER COLOURING:
THE ONTOLOGY OF SUPER-REALISM

SUPER-REALISM, yes, because that is how I think of my fiction, quite deliberately and consciously, very likely unconsciously too. When I started to write novels and stories about the year 1956, I had no clear idea of what I was doing. I had had a literary education, and knew something about critical theory and method as applied to the work of other writers, the classics especially, and some moderns. I got a Ph.D. in English in late 1955. After that I did more or less what I wanted. I began to write independently, feeling liberated from the need to defer to what other people might think. I was glad to get out of the graduate school.

I had no theory of my own writing, and belonged to no school, so I wrote most of a novel which was never published, and a dozen stories, in 1956 and 1957, instinctively, making all the important artistic decisions as I went along, with no theoretical bias for one kind of writing as against all the others. Instinctively, then, I turned out to be a moral realist, not a naturalist or a surrealist or a magic realist or in any way an experimental or advance guard writer. That was in effect where I began.

All my early writing dealt with the affairs of credible characters in more or less credible situations. As I look back, I see that this instinctive moral realism was tempered by an inclination to show these credible characters, in perfectly ordinary situations, nevertheless doing violent and unpredictable, and even melodramatic, things. A brother and sister go to visit their

---

First published in *Canadian Literature* 49 (1971). Republished in John Metcalf, ed., *The Narrative Voice: Short Stories and Reflections by Canadian Authors* (Toronto: McGraw–Hill Ryerson, 1972) and in Hugh Hood, *The Governor's Bridge is Closed* (Ottawa: Oberon, 1973).

mother's grave and are unable to find it in a cemetery of nightmarish proportions; a man kills his newly-baptized girlfriend thinking that she will go
straight to Heaven; a young priest molests a child sexually; a young boy goes
mad under great strain. A yachtsman runs his boat on a rock and sinks it,
drowning his wife and her lover, who are trapped below deck. I would never
choose actions like these nowadays, not because of their violence but
because of their improbability. I still write about intense feelings which lead
to impulsive and sometimes violent acts, but I am better able to locate these
feelings in credible occasions.

In those days, and for several years afterwards, I tried to control these
melodramatic tendencies – murder, suicide, hanging about in cemeteries,
drowning in burst boats – by a strong sense of the physical form of stories. I
arranged my pieces according to complex numerologies. A novel might have
seven main sections, one for each day of a specific week in a given year, so
that the reader could tell exactly what time it was when something happened. Or the book might be divided in three main parts, each with a
specific number of subdivisions. I once wrote the rough draft of a book in
two main sections and when I had finished each half of the manuscript was
precisely a hundred and forty-four pages long: twelve twelves doubled.
This play with numbers is a recurrent feature of my work. *Around the Mountain* follows the calendar very precisely, with one story for each month from
one Christmas to the next. I have always had a fondness for the cycle of the
Christian liturgical year. My first, unpublished, novel was called *God Rest
You Merry*, and covered the seven days from Christmas Night to New Year's
Eve, in a most elaborate arrangement.

I still do this. My new novel, which will appear in the fall of 1972, *You
Cant Get There From Here*, is in three parts. The first and third sections have
ten chapters each; the middle part has twenty, which gives us: 10/20/10.
The Christian numerological symbolism implied is very extensive. It makes
a kind of scaffolding for the imagination.

I had then, and still have, an acute sense of the possibilities of close formal organization of the sentence, syntactically and grammatically, and in its
phonemic sequences. I paid much attention to the difficulties of writing
long sentences because I knew that simple-minded naturalists wrote short
sentences, using lots of 'ands'. I did not want to be a simple-minded naturalist. I hoped to write syntactically various and graceful prose. I took care to

vary the number of sentences in succeeding paragraphs. I rarely used the one-sentence paragraph; when I did so I felt mighty daring. I kept a careful eye upon the clause-structure of each sentence. I wouldn't use the ellipsis mark (...) because Arthur Mizener wrote to me that he considered it a weak, cop-out sort of punctuation.

I sometimes use the ellipsis now ... and feel guilty.

My interest in the sound of sentences, in the use of colour words and of the names of places, in practical stylistics, showed me that prose fiction might have an abstract element, a purely formal element, even though it continued to be strictly, morally, realistic. It might be possible to think of prose fiction the way one thinks of abstract elements in representational painting, or of highly formal music. I now began to see affinities between the art I was willy-nilly practising and the other arts, first poetry, then painting and music. I have always been passionately attached to music and painting – I have gone so far as to marry a painter on mixed grounds – and have written many stories about the arts: film-making, painting, music less often because it is on the surface such a non-narrative art. I find that it is hard to speak about music.

I have also written some stories about a kind of experience close to that of the artist: metaphysical thought. My stories 'A Season of Calm Weather' (with its consciously Wordsworthian title) and 'The Hole' are about metaphysicians. The second of the two tries to show a philosopher's intelligence actually at work, a hard thing to do. Like musical thought, metaphysical thought seems to take place in a non-verbal region of consciousness, if there is such a thing, and it is therefore hard to write about, but to me an irresistible challenge.

My novels, *White Figure, White Ground* and *The Camera Always Lies*, dealt respectively with the problems of a painter and a group of film-makers. It is the seeing-into-things, the capacity for meditative abstraction, that interests me about philosophy, the arts and religious practice. I love most in painting an art which exhibits the transcendental element dwelling in living things. I think of this as true *super-realism*. And I think of Vermeer, or among American artists, of Edward Hopper, whose paintings of ordinary places, seaside cottages, a roadside snack bar and gasoline station, have touched some level of my own imagination which I can only express in fictional images. In my story 'Getting to Williamstown' there is a description of a roadside refreshment stand beside an abandoned gas pump, which is pretty directly imitated from a painting of Hopper's. I see this now, though I didn't when I wrote the story. That is what I mean by the unconscious elements in my work which co-operate with my deliberate intentions.

I have to admit at this point that my PH.D. thesis discussed the theory of the imagination of the Romantic poets and its background. The argument of the thesis was that Romantic imagination-theory was fundamentally a revision of the theory of abstraction as it was taught by Aristotle and the mediaeval philosophers. The kind of knowing which Wordsworth called 'reason in its most exalted mood', and which Coleridge exalted as creative artistic imagination, *does the same thing* as that power which Saint Thomas Aquinas thought of as the active intellect. I do not think of the imagination and the active intellect as separate and opposed to one another. No more are emotion and thought *lived* distinct and apart. The power of abstraction, in the terms of traditional psychology, is not a murderous dissection of living beings; on the contrary it is an intimate penetration into their physical reality. 'No ideas but in things' said William Carlos Williams. I believe that Aquinas would concur in that – the idea lives in the singular real being. The intellect is not set over against emotion, feelings, instincts, memory and the imagination, but intimately united to them. The artist and the metaphysician are equally contemplatives; so are the saints.

Like Vermeer or Hopper or that great creator of musical form, Joseph Haydn, I am trying to concentrate on knowable form as it lives in the physical world. These forms are abstract, not in the sense of being inhumanly non-physical, but in the sense of communicating the perfection of the essences of things – the formal realities which create things as they are in themselves. A transcendentalist must first study the things of this world, and get as far inside them as possible. My story 'The Hole' tries to show a philosopher working out this idea in his own experience. Here, as everywhere in my writing, I have studied as closely and intensely as I can the *insides* of things which are not me. The great metaphor in human experience for truly apprehending another being is sexual practice. Here, perhaps only here, do we get inside another being. Alas, the entrance is only metaphorical. In plain fact no true penetration happens in love-making. It is not possible for one physical being to merge into another, as D.H. Lawrence finally realized. Bodies occupy different places; there is nothing to be done about this. Sex is a metaphor for union, not itself achieved union.

What we are united to in this world is not the physical insides of persons or things, but the knowable principle in them. Inside everything that exists is essence, not in physical space and time, but as forming space and time and the perceptions possible within them. What I know, love and desire in another person isn't inside him like a nut in its shell, but it is everywhere that he is, forming him. My identity isn't inside me – it is *how I am*. It is hard to express the way we know the forms of things, but this is the knowing that art exercises.

Art after all, like every other human act, implies a philosophical stance: either you think that there is nothing to things that is not delivered in their appearances, or you think that immaterial forms exist in these things, conferring identity on them. These are not the only ontological alternatives, but they are extreme ones, and they state a classical ontological opposition. The bias of most contemporary thought has been towards the first alternative, until the very recent past. But perhaps we are again beginning to be able to think about the noumenal element in things, their essential and intelligible principles, what Newman called the 'illative' aspect of being. The danger of this sort of noumenalism is that you may dissolve the hard, substantial shapes of things, as they can be seen to be, into an idealistic mish-mash – something I'm not inclined to do. I'm not a Platonist or a dualist of any kind. I think with Aristotle that the body and the soul are one; the form of a thing is totally united to its matter. The soul is the body. No ideas but in things.

That is where I come out: the spirit is totally *in* the flesh. If you pay close enough attention to things, stare at them, concentrate on them as hard as you can, not just with your intelligence, but with your feelings and instincts – with your prick too – you will begin to apprehend the forms in them. Knowing is not a matter of sitting in an armchair while engaged in some abstruse conceptual calculus of weights and measures and geometrical spaces. Knowing includes making love, and making pieces of art, and wanting and worshipping *and* calculating (because calculation is also part of knowing) and in fact knowing is what Wordsworth called it, a 'spousal union' of the knower and the known, a marriage full of flesh.

I want to propose the Wordsworthian account of the marriage of the mind and the thing as a model of artistic activity. I don't think that the Romantic movement failed. I think we are still in the middle of it. Of the Romantic masters, Wordsworth seems to me to have understood best how things move in themselves, how they exist as they are when they are possessing themselves, having their identities, living. Wordsworth has an extraordinary grasp of the movement, the running motion, of the physical, the roll of water or sweep of wind, changing textures of fog or mist, all that is impalpable and yet material. In this fleeting, running movement of physical existence, for Wordsworth there is always the threat of an illumination, splendour in the grass, glory in the flower. Things are full of the visionary gleam.

The illuminations in things are there, really and truly *there*, in those things. They are not run over them by projective intelligence, and yet there is a sense in which the mind, in uniting itself to things, creates illumination in them.

> The Clouds that gather round the setting sun
> Do take a sober colouring from an eye
> That hath kept watch o'er man's mortality.

This is a triple eye, that of the setting sun which colours the clouds, and that of the sober human moral imagination, and finally that of God as brooding, creative Father of all. The colouring of the clouds is given to them by the Deity in the original act of creation. Every evening the sun re-enacts the illumination. The moral imagination operates in the same way, though it is not originally creative; it projects colouring into things, true, but the colouring has already been put there by the divine creation. The act of the human knower is an act of reciprocity. It half creates and half perceives the mighty world of eye and ear.

'I have at all times endeavoured to look steadily at my subject', said Wordsworth, very justly. His regard to things is concentrated and accurate; he insists everywhere on the utter necessity of the sensory process, of seeing and hearing, of taking in the sensible world and transforming it. He proposed 'to throw a certain colouring of the imagination over incidents and situations taken from common life'. This is the same metaphor as that of the final stanza of the 'Intimations Ode'. The eye in seeing gives colour to things; but the colour is there.

The poetry of Wordsworth supplies us again and again with examples of this colouring of imagination spread over incidents and situations from common life. The figure of the old Leech-Gatherer in 'Resolution and Independence' is perhaps the most overwhelming example of this capacity of very ordinary persons and scenes to yield, on close inspection, an almost intolerable significance.

> In my mind's eye I seemed to see him pace
> About the weary moors continually,
> Wandering about alone and silently.

The concentrating eye, interior/exterior, giving to things their sober hues, is constant in Wordsworth. I have imitated it from him in my work. In the deliberately paired stories 'Socks' and 'Boots' I have chosen incidents from ordinary life and characters such as may be met with everywhere, and I have attempted to look steadily at these persons in the hope that something of the noumenal will emerge.

These stories are, to begin with, political; they are about the ways in which living in society modifies our personal desires, a very Wordsworthian theme. Domenico Lercaro in 'Socks' does not want to work so hard. Nobody wants to work that hard. He doesn't want to work on a garbage truck or do snow removal, but he is driven to it by the need to survive. The fictional 'my wife' in the story 'Boots' wants to buy a certain specific kind of winter foot-wear, but the stores simply don't stock the boots she wants. We can buy only what we are offered, and our range of choice is surprisingly limited.

I have tried to move beyond the fiction of social circumstance by taking a very attentive look at my two main characters. In 'Socks' poor Domenico sees the enormous, noisy snow-removal machine turn before his eyes into a divine beast or Leviathan. Everyone who has seen these machines at work recognizes their intimations of violence, in their noise and in the sharpness of their rotary blades. They have actually killed and eaten people. Modern life is full of these mechanical beasts.

'My wife' in 'Boots' feels trivialized by fashion; most women in middle-class circumstances do, I think. To wear high heels and a girdle is to enslave yourself – to adopt the badges of a humiliating subservience. This story tries to make its readers sense of the galling limits on their activities felt by intelligent women in the face of the clothes which fashion and *chic* propose for them: the necessary sexual exhibitionism, the silly posturing, the faked little-girlishness.

The two stories insinuate larger issues than their subjects would suggest; they are following Wordsworth's prescription. I have at all times endeavoured to look steadily at my subjects. I hope that my gaze has helped to light them up.

Audrey Thomas

BASMATI RICE: AN ESSAY ABOUT WORDS

MY STUDY is on the second floor of our house and faces East. I like that and I get up early to write, perhaps not simply because I enjoy the sunrise (especially in winter, when all has been so black, and then gradually light, like hope, returns) but out of some atavistic hope that my thoughts, too, will rise with the sun and illumine the blank pages in front of me.

We live in a corner house and my study is right above a busy street. People whom I cannot see often pass beneath my window and throw up snatches of conversation before moving out of earshot. And I hear footsteps, light, heavy, singly or in groups, and the sound of buggy wheels or grocery carts. Now, I can see the sidewalk on the other side of the street, see people hurrying along or dawdling, the young woman from the St. James Daycare a block away, out for a walk with her little charges who all seem to march (or skip or run) to a different drummer, a father with his baby tucked inside his ski jacket, a blind man, a woman with her arms full of grocery bags. I cannot hear their footsteps or anything they might be saying and sometimes a wonderful thing happens where someone will pass beneath my window, and say something while someone is walking by on the other side of the street, and so I get the wonderful absurdity of seeing the old lady in the red coat who lives at the Senior Citizen Lodge at 16th and Macdonald (I know because she asked me to take her picture, waving her hand-made Union Jack, the day the Queen came down 16th Avenue) going by on one side and hearing a gruff teenage male voice saying, 'so I said to him nobody talks like that to me and....' The movie I watch has the wrong soundtrack!

I am interested in such absurdities, in the word *absurd* itself, from the Latin for inharmonious, foolish. L. *ab*, from, *surdus*, deaf, inaudible, harsh

First published in *Canadian Literature* 100 (1984).

(used metaphorically here, deaf to reason, hence irrational). I am interested in the fact that I spend a lot of my days at a desk, or table, and that the desk or table needs always to face a window. This is not just so I will have something to look at when 'illumination' comes slowly (or not at all) but because, in what is essentially an inside occupation (and a very lonely one at that, I can't even stand to have a radio on when I'm working), I am able to feel even a little bit connected with the outside. I often see myself like a diver in one of those old-fashioned diving bells, both in and apart from everything in the universe around me. There is a little piece of brown paper taped to the window frame. I got it from a bread wrapper several years ago when I was spending a winter in Montreal. It says

PAIN

FRAIS DU JOUR

in blue letters and underneath

BREAD

BAKED FRESH DAILY

Some days, if I'm wrestling with a piece or a passage that seems especially difficult, I fold the paper so that it reads:

PAIN

BAKED FRESH DAILY

and for some perverse reason this cheers me up. That the French word for bread and the English word for misery of one kind or another *look* alike is another of those absurdities that interest me. There is no real connection, as there is, say, with the English *blessed* and the French *blesser*, to wound – it's just chance. But my mind, when in a certain state of heightened awareness (which, I might point out, can just as easily be brought on by laughter as by tears), makes that kind of connection easily.

Here's another. It was early November when I began thinking about this essay, and the tree outside my window was almost bare of leaves. The weather was turning cold and a cold rain was falling. 'Autumn leaves' I wrote on my pad, 'Autumn leaves'. Over and over. And then suddenly

'Winter enters'. Again, no real linguistic connection, but writing the phrase over and over gave me a new way of looking at the leaves.

I love words. I love the way they suddenly surprise you; I love the way *everyone*, high or low, uses them to paint pictures – that is to say metaphorically. In the past week a phrase, not new, but surely not much in vogue of recent years, has been said in my hearing, or I've read it in the paper, no less than five times: so and so is 'between a rock and a hard place'. Once in a line-up at the main post office downtown, once spoken by a friend and in three different newspaper articles. Where does this phrase come from? I can't find it in Bartlett's, at least not under 'rock', or 'place', or 'hard'. Why is it suddenly being said? It is certainly a most poetic (and uncomfortable) image. I wouldn't want to be there, nor would you. Somebody says, of somebody else, 'I've got him eating out of my hand', probably unaware of the root of the word 'manipulate'. When I was a child I heard constant warnings about kids who were 'too big for their britches' or 'too big for their boots' and we were all, without exception, potential 'big-eared little pitchers'. And yet it seemed to me that all the adults I knew – parents, relatives, teachers – corrected me if I played around with words or grammar or sentence structure myself. It was as though all the metaphorical language in the world had already been invented and I wasn't there on the day that it happened. Once I started reading poetry I realized that poets seemed to have a certain freedom that ordinary, hard-working decent folks didn't (or didn't allow themselves) to have. They invented and re-invented language all the time. (Prose that got too metaphorical was considered suspect unless it were in the Sunday Sermon or spoken by Roosevelt or Churchill.) That was when I decided I would become a poet, and probably why. My poems were terrible – a lot of them were very 'Christian' in a romantic way, full of Crusaders, lepers, infidels and angels – and some of them, I regret to say, won prizes. But I do remember the day we were asked to write limericks (Grade 4? Grade 5?) and I came up with this in about five minutes:

There was once a fellow named Farrell
Whose life was in terrible peril
He fell in with some rogues
Who stole all but his brogues
And had to slink home in a barrel.

(I don't know where I got 'brogues' from or how I knew what it meant; it certainly wasn't a word used in our family.)

I wrote dozens of limericks after that first one. I knew it wasn't Real Poetry but I also suspected the other stuff, the stuff my teachers and my mother and various judges liked, wasn't Real Poetry either. Nevertheless, for all my desire to write poetry, what I was always better at was prose. Who knows why one writer works better in one genre than another? What I'd really like to be is 'ambidextrous', like Michael Ondaatje or Margaret Atwood, but I'm not. It's always prose for me. (Why do most of us see poetry as 'higher'? Because it seems more of a distillate of the creative unconscious than prose? Perfume as opposed to cologne? I once had a poet in a graduate prose class in Montreal. He needed one more course to get his degree and had chosen mine. We were all working on stories and one night he said to me, in much despair, 'I've never written "he said" and "she said" before.' Of course he wasn't a *narrative* poet: not for him *Beowulf* or *Idylls of the King*, or, closer to home, *The Titanic*, or *Brébeuf and His Brethren*.) I still sometimes have the awful feeling that I failed because I failed to write poetry, even while I know that prose can be just as exciting or dense, 'packed', innovative as any poem. It probably has something to do with the fact that we write our notes, our memos, our letters, in prose, we speak in prose to one another, even when we speak metaphorically: 'Lay off me, will you?', 'I'm really blue today', 'What's for dinner, honey?', 'You're driving me up the wall'.

Sometimes a sentence or a phrase gives me the idea for an entire story (once, even, for the very last line of a novel I didn't write for another three years, when I overheard a man in a pay phone say to whoever was on the other end: 'Get rid of it.' That's all I heard him say and then he hung up). This summer my daughter and I were in Greece. We witnessed a very bizarre incident involving a young English boy, an octopus and a man in a panama hat. I knew that that in itself could provide the central image for a new story but then, a few days later, I heard a French woman on another beach say '*La méduse; il faut prendre garde*', and suddenly, because of this incident with the octopus, I saw not the jellyfish to which she had been referring but the great snaky tentacles of an octopus and *then* I saw that what I really wanted to write about was all that sexuality that was there on the beach, in that heat, under the intense blue sky: the bare-breasted European women, the young Greek men showing off to their girlfriends and whoever else would watch. All the bodies. The story is seen through the eyes of a twelve-year-old English boy, very properly brought up, for whom the octopus becomes the symbol of everything most feared and most desired, 'the nightmare spread out upon the rock'. Later on, on quite a different island, a Greek man said two things that have become incorporated into the octopus story. He said, when we were listening to some very sad Greek music, 'There are no happy men in Greece, only happy childrens.' He also asked 'You like this ice-land?' and since the temperature was over 80°F. we stared at him. He meant 'island' but it took us a while to figure that out. Now, in my story, the young boy hears words and phrases he doesn't completely understand (*'La méduse; il faut prendre garde'*, 'You like this ice-land?') and this just adds to his general sense of unease.

Another recent story was inspired by a newspaper clipping about a man who had been charged with common assault for massaging the feet of strange women. I began to do some foot research and discovered something I must have learned in my university zoology course, that the number of bones in the human foot is the same as the number of letters in the alphabet. And so the story begins: 'There are twenty-six bones in the foot; that is the alphabet of the foot' and goes on to tell a story which is a complete fabrication except for the fact that both men (the 'real' man and the man in my story) get arrested, charged and fined.

Another story, which is the title story of the collection I'm presently working on, came as a message written on a mirror in the George Dawson Inn in Dawson Creek. The message was not intended for me but showed up on the mirror in the bathroom after my daughter had taken a very hot shower. It said 'Good-bye Harold, Good Luck' and whoever had written it must have counted on the fact that Harold would take a shower. (And the maid had obviously not gone over the mirror with Windex.) We had a lot of fun trying to figure out who Harold was and whether the message was written in anger or love. In the story, 'they' (a mother who is contemplating a divorce and her child) do meet up with Harold, but of course he doesn't know that they have seen the message (and they're not absolutely sure he has).

I cut things out of newspapers, often really horrible things, and I'm never sure why.

MURDERER SET WIFE ADRIFT ON RAFT

AUDREY THOMAS

TIGER BITES TRAINER TO DEATH
(Horrified Wife Looks On)

DOLPHINS NUDGE BOY'S BODY TO SHORE

That last one really haunts me, not just the image, but that word 'nudge'. The dolphins with their blunt 'noses', gently nudging the dead boy towards the shore. That one will probably end up in a story.

PLAN YOUR PLOT

(this one was in the gardening column of the *Province*) and one from the *Vancouver Courier* recently prompted a note to a friend:

POUND WARNS PETS

I cut this one out, and wrote underneath, 'You're an old bitch gone in the teeth.'

And so it goes. And so it goes. And so it goes on and on. I read Rev. Skeat, I read Bartlett's, I read Fowler's *Modern English Usage*, given to me by an ex-boyfriend who wrote, as a greeting, the definition of *oxymoron*, which just about summed up our relationship! I have *The Shorter Oxford English Dictionary* but long to have the real one, all those volumes as full of goodies as good Christmas puddings. I have the Bible, the Book of Common Prayer, Shakespeare and *Partridge's Origins*. I have Collins' phrase books in several languages ('that man is following me everywhere'). I have maps and rocks and shells and bits of coral from various places to which I have travelled. I scan the personal columns, the names of the ships in port. And I have my eyes and ears.

I am a dilettante (related to the Italian for 'delight'). I never learn any language properly but love to dabble in them. I have studied, at one time or another, Latin, Anglo-Saxon, Middle English, Old Norse, French, Italian and, most recently, Greek. I spent a winter in Athens a few years ago and saw, every day, little green vans scurrying around the city with ΜΕΤΑΦΟΡΗ posted on a card in the front windshield. 'Metaphors.' When I enquired I discovered that these vans are for hire and they *transfer* goods from one section of the city to another. Now I long to write an essay called 'A Meta-phor is not a Truck'.

Last year I took two terms of sign language at night school. I was amused by the fact that in ASL (American Sign Language) the sign for 'woman' has to do with the tying of bonnet strings and the sign for 'man' with the tipping of a hat. These are charming archaisms, like 'horsepower' in English. (I am also interested in mirrors, mirror images, going into and through mirrors, so signing, which one does to someone facing you, is fascinating – and very difficult. I often came home with an aching hand.) I would like to take more sign language; I would like to become, as an African man once said to me, about English, 'absolutely fluid in that language'.

Words words words. Sometimes it all gets on top of me and I feel like the monster made out of words in *The Faerie Queene*. I can't leave them alone; I am obsessed. I move through the city watching for signs with letters miss-ing ('Beef live with onions' advertises a cheap café near Granville and Broadway, ' ELF SERVE' says a gas station out on Hastings) and I am always on the lookout for messages within words: can you see the harm in phar-macy, the dent in accident, the over in lover? In short, I play.

There is a phenomenon, most commonly observed in photography but also talked about by people who make stained glass. It is called 'halation' and it refers to the spreading of light beyond its proper boundary. (With stained glass it happens when two colours are next to one another.) I think words can do that too, or perhaps I should say that I would like to think that there is no 'proper boundary' for words. Let them spill over from one language to another, let them leap out at us like kittens at play. 'Wit', said Mark Van Doren, 'is the only wall between us and the dark.' If a writer, if an artist of *any* sort, stops approaching his materials with wit, with laughter, then he is lost. The other day I was making a curry and listening to some old Beatles songs on the radio. John or Paul was yelling 'Can't Buy Me Love' and I was thinking about Basmati rice. Suddenly I realized 'Basmati rice' had the same number of syllables as 'Can't Buy Me Love', so every time John or Paul or whoever got to the chorus I yelled out 'Basmati rice!' and did a little soft-shoe shuffle while I stirred the curry sauce. (Everybody had a good time.)

Audrey Thomas

BASMATI RICE: PART TWO

I WROTE THAT PIECE a long time ago – five years, six years? The house where I wrote it has been sold; the story about the writing on the mirror has been published, ditto the story about the boy and the octopus. The first turned out very differently from its original conception; the second almost 'wrote itself' exactly as I had first imagined it. Both stories have to do with parents and children (mother and daughter, father and son) – a point I shall come back to later on. Another collection of stories is out this month; a novel is nearly finished. Whatever it is that compels me to write has not diminished in intensity, in fact the reverse. As I grow older it more and more strikes me how lucky writers are – unlike singers, dancers or baseball players they can just go on and on (even, perhaps, when they shouldn't). All we really have to worry about is the little grey cells, not the little grey hairs or the bad shoulder, the aching feet. I realize that so long as I can hold a pen or a phrase I shall continue to write.

As I pen this – and I must be one of the few writers in Canada who can say that and mean it literally – I am sitting in a pleasant apartment in Montreal, September 1990, not facing a window but facing a wall and a door. The window, which looks out onto the street, is to my left. My apartment is on the second floor and the green leaves of a maple tree almost completely shut out the view of the houses across the street, including the wonderful house on the corner, which has something resembling a gold samovar on its front gable. The window is open and the sounds of footsteps and voices float up to me, just as they did in Vancouver, only here the voices are speaking French, a rapid, nasal, slangy French that I have trouble understanding, equipped as I am with high-school and university French, every word carefully

_____

First published in *How Stories Mean*.

enunciated, every sentence spoken *adagio* or *moderato*. A girl on Mont Royal asks me if I have the air and I wonder what in hell she is talking about. 'Air, air' she says impatiently, pointing to where a watch would be on her wrist. Oh, say I, 'l'er'. I tell her the time and we both laugh. (And this place is paradise for someone as word-besotted as myself. I notice the night deposit at the Immaculate Conception Bank nearby and think of Mary and the Holy Ghost. I hear someone, speaking in English, mention the Minister of Transports.) Church bells ring at noon and at the angelus; *les pompiers* from the fire station on rue Rachel flash by, sirens howling, on their way to yet another Montreal fire; stickers in windows warn of guard dogs (on rue Boyer a smug calico cat sits in the window behind just such a sticker); placards with the Quebec flag say '*Fier d'être québécois*'. The news on the radio – I listen in both languages – is of Oka and Iraq. The shops advertise ethnic clothes and 'earth colours'. Considering what we're doing to the earth this last gives me pause for thought. (How about scum green, pollution pink, stuff like that?)

One thing that is different with me since I wrote 'Basmati Rice' is the fact that I have become interested in the past, my family's past. I am lucky enough to have a mother (whom I sometimes refer to as my 'Agèd P.') who is over ninety and possesses an amazing memory. I began to ask her to write down whatever she could remember, partly as a make-work project for her – she suffers from loneliness and depression – but mostly out of genuine curiosity. Small children ask 'Where did *I* come from?' Older ones, much older, say 'Where did *we* come from?', wanting now some sort of connection back into the long winding river of history. 'Out of Mummy's tummy' is no longer enough.

And one day my mother told me something so extraordinary that the novelist in me sat up straight, all lights flashing (like the fire station on rue Rachel, I know a signal when I hear one). She saw something, she said, when she was quite small, and it changed her relationship with her parents forever.

'What did you see?'

'I don't want to talk about it', she said. 'I mustn't get upset.'

(But of course she did, later on. She wouldn't have brought it up if she hadn't wanted – eventually – to talk about it.)

I'm quite near what I hope is the final draft now. It has all my usual quirks and eccentricities: definitions, word play, references to children's books and childhood. A friend of mine told me that I always write about 'the lost child', even when I start out in an entirely different vein. I now accept that he is right, although I argued the point vigorously a few years ago.

That – in one guise or another – is my 'theme'. It's not a bad theme to be stuck with; it's not *trivial*. (Look up that word sometime – you might be surprised.)

A woman I was introduced to on Galiano said, 'Oh yes, I know who you are. Mind you, I haven't read all your books.'

For once, I thought of the appropriate remark right then, not that evening or weeks later:

'I haven't written them all yet', I said.

Mavis Gallant

WHAT IS STYLE?

I DO NOT reread my own work unless I have to; I fancy no writer does. The reason why, probably, is that during the making of the story every line has been read and rewritten and read again to the point of glut. I am unable to 'see' the style of the stories 'Baum, Gabriel' and 'His Mother' and would not recognize its characteristics if they were pointed out to me. Once too close, the stories are already too distant. If I read a passage aloud, I am conscious of a prose rhythm easy for me to follow, that must be near to the way I think and speak. It seems to be my only link with a finished work.

The manner of writing, the thread spun out of the story itself, may with time have grown instinctive. I know that the thread must hold from beginning to end, and that I would like it to be invisible. Rereading 'Baum, Gabriel' and 'His Mother', all I can relate is that they are about loss and bewilderment, that I cannot imagine the people described living with any degree of willingness anywhere but in a city – in spite of Gabriel's imaginings about country life – and that a café as a home more congenial than home appears in both. The atmosphere, particularized, is of a fading world, though such a thing was far from my mind when the stories were written. It may be that the Europe of the nineteen-seventies already secreted the first dangerous sign of nostalgia, like a pervasive mist: I cannot say. And it is not what I have been asked to discuss.

Leaving aside the one analysis closed to me, of my own writing, let me say what style is *not*: it is not a last-minute addition to prose, a charming and universal slipcover, a coat of paint used to mask the failings of a structure.

First published in John Metcalf, ed., *Making It New: Contemporary Canadian Stories* (Toronto: Methuen, 1982). Republished in Mavis Gallant, *Paris Notebooks: Essays & Reviews* (Toronto: Macmillan, 1986).

Style is inseparable from structure, part of the conformation of whatever the author has to say. What he says – this is what fiction is about – is that something is taking place and that nothing lasts. Against the sustained tick of a watch, fiction takes the measure of a life, a season, a look exchanged, the turning point, desire as brief as a dream, the grief and terror that after childhood we cease to express. The life, the look, the grief are without permanence. The watch continues to tick where the story stops.

A loose, a wavering, a slipshod, an affected, a false way of transmitting even a fragment of this leaves the reader suspicious: What is this too elaborate or too simple language hiding? What is the author trying to disguise? Probably he doesn't know. He has shown the works of the watch instead of its message. He may be untalented, just as he may be a gifted author who for some deeply private reason (doubt, panic, the pressures of a life unsuited to writing) has taken to rearranging the works in increasingly meaningless patterns. All this is to say that content, meaning, intention, and form must make up a whole, and must above all have a reason to be.

There are rules of style. By applying them doggedly any literate, ambitious, and determined person should be able to write like Somerset Maugham. Maugham was conscious of his limitations and deserves appreciation on that account: 'I knew that I had no lyrical quality, I had a small vocabulary.... I had little gift for metaphors; the original or striking simile seldom occurred to me. Poetic flights and the great imaginative sweep were beyond my powers.' He decided, sensibly, to write 'as well as my natural defects allowed' and to aim at 'lucidity, simplicity, and euphony'. The chance that some other indispensable quality had been overlooked must have been blanketed by a lifetime of celebrity. Now, of course, first principles are there to be heeded or, at the least, considered with care; but no guided tour of literature, no commitment to the right formula or to good taste (which is changeable anyway) can provide, let alone supplant, the inborn vitality and tension of living prose.

Like every other form of art, literature is no more and nothing less than a matter of life and death. The only question worth asking about a story – or a poem, or a piece of sculpture, or a new concert hall – is, 'Is it dead or alive?' If a work of the imagination needs to be coaxed into life, it is better scrapped and forgotten. Working to rule, trying to make a barely breathing work of fiction simpler and more lucid and more euphonious merely injects into the desperate author's voice a tone of suppressed hysteria, the result of what E.M. Forster called 'confusing order with orders'. And then, how reliable are the rules? Listen to Pablo Picasso's rejection of a fellow-artist: 'He looks up at the sky and says, "Ah, the sky is blue", and he paints a blue sky. Then he takes another look and says, "The sky is mauve, too", and he adds some mauve. The next time he looks he notices a trace of pink, and he adds a little pink.' It sounds a proper mess, but Picasso was talking about Pierre Bonnard. As soon as we learn the name, the blues, mauves, and pinks acquire a meaning, a reason to be. Picasso was right, but only in theory. In the end, everything depends on the artist himself.

Style in writing, as in painting, is the author's thumbprint, his mark. I do not mean that it establishes him as finer or greater than other writers, though that can happen too. I am thinking now of prose style as a writer's armorial bearings, his name and address. In a privately printed and libellous pamphlet, Colette's first husband, Willy, who had fraudulently signed her early novels, tried to prove she had gone on to plagiarize and plunder different things he had written. As evidence he offered random sentences from work he was supposed to have influenced or inspired. Nothing, from his point of view, could have been more self-defeating. Colette's manner, robust and personal, seems to leap from the page. Willy believed he had taught Colette 'everything', and it may have been true – 'everything', that is, except her instinct for language, her talent for perceiving the movement of life, and a faculty for describing it. He was bound to have influenced her writing; it couldn't be helped. But by the time he chose to print a broadside on the subject, his influence had been absorbed, transmuted, and – most humbling for the teacher – had left no visible trace.

There is no such a thing as a writer who has escaped being influenced. I have never heard a professional writer of any quality or standing talk about 'pure' style, or say he would not read this or that for fear of corrupting or affecting his own; but I have heard it from would-be writers and amateurs. Corruption – if that is the word – sets in from the moment a child learns to speak and to hear language used and misused. A young person who does not read, and read widely, will never write anything – at least, nothing of interest. From time to time, in France, a novel is published purporting to come from a shepherd whose only influence has been the baaing of lambs on some God-forsaken slope of the Pyrenees. His artless and untampered-with mode of expression arouses the hope that there will be many more like him, but as a rule he is never heard from again. For 'influences' I would be inclined to substitute 'acquisitions'. What they consist of, and amount to, are affected by taste and environment, preferences and upbringing (even, and sometimes particularly, when the latter has been rejected), instinctive selection. The beginning writer has to choose, tear to pieces, spit out, chew up, and assimilate as naturally as a young animal – as naturally and as ruthlessly. Style cannot be copied, except by the untalented. It is, finally, the distillation of a lifetime of reading and listening, of selection and rejection. But if it is not a true voice, it is nothing.

John Metcalf

INTERVIEW: CLARK BLAISE

METCALF: What are your working methods? How much rewriting do you do?

BLAISE: I'm a reluctant first-draftsman, a wretched second-draftsman, and it's only when the shape and tone of the story is really ascendent that I start to become warm to the story. Then I can go through draft after draft, growing more and more neurotic as I go, and I begin to see every little typographical and grammatical nicety as part of the voice, every comma as essential as every paragraph.

I write a first draft longhand, then I type a working draft from the longhand that is so haphazard I don't even capitalize. Then I go through with pen and type again. I might cut 40% and add about 15%. Then I'll cut a little and add a little less. When a draft seems not to require cutting or addition, I type out a neurotically clean fair copy – polishing the keys with a rag before embarking.

METCALF: You studied at The Iowa Writers Workshop. What did you learn there?

BLAISE: Well, none of what I've just been saying comes from having attended the Writers Workshop, or Malamud's class at Harvard before that – I'm predisposed to short stories and to kinds of stories that borrow a lot from poetry and I have the work habits of someone with that predisposition. Iowa I don't think teaches anything but a sense of obligation to craft and community and standards and articulateness about aims.

METCALF: Are creative writing courses a good idea?

BLAISE: I don't want to get involved too much in the 'Can you really teach writing?' trap except to say that it's the most valuable thing a literature

First published in *Journal of Canadian Fiction* 2.4 (1973).

student can do. And if you're the kind of writer I've been describing, it's not a harmful or wasteful way to earn a living.

METCALF: How do you accommodate to the life as writer and as academic? Does the teaching of technique make you too conscious as a writer? Or is that romanticism?

BLAISE: I learn a lot from teaching and there are numerous instances in my own writing of direct inspiration. I enjoy teaching writing and I especially enjoy teaching literature (*my* favourite authors) from the point of view of the writer's concern. I'm less fond of lecture sections of standard authors for indifferent arts and science students who are frankly baffled or bored or contemptuous of a digressive lecturer and of the slow approach to a book through its associations, its 'world', and its minute details.

METCALF: Can you give me the chronology of the stories in *A North American Education*?

BLAISE: Yes, the stories were written more or less as follows: 'Continent of Strangers' 1963-65. 'A Class of New Canadians' 1967. 'Eyes' in 1968. 'Words for the Winter' 1971. 'Extractions and Contractions' 1968. 'Going to India' 1970. And the Thibidault stories 1968-71, with 'Snow People' completed in the winter of 1971.

METCALF: I remember your telling me that the Thibidault stories were reworked from what was to have been a novel. Why did it abort and what was involved in the reworking?

BLAISE: Those stories were part of a novel which was not taken on by three different agents and not well received by Jerry Newman (an impeccable guide) and politely refused by a friendly independent editor who was really anxious to publish me – all of this I take to be pretty conclusive.

The parts of the novel that I worked into the stories – they were published, except for 'Snow People', in 1970 and '71 in *Florida Quarterly, Tamarack*, and *Shenandoah* – were the 'remembered' parts of the novel; the 'present action' of the book never really built on its 'textured' foundation. I botched it and I'm on my way now for a year in India to write a book that will show me I can do it now – or never.

In rewriting the fragments of the novel into stories, I concentrated on the handling of *time*, trying to make for each of them a self-contained temporality that was lacking in the larger context of the novel. That accounts for the playing with time in three of those stories – the historical/episodic in the title story, the woven back-to-front quality in 'The Salesman's Son Grows Older', and the rather more elliptical nature of 'Snow People'.

METCALF: Why do you describe 'Snow People' as a novella? Length and form don't seem to me to differ substantially from some of the stories.

BLAISE: Well, first of all because it was cut by twenty pages – the transition was written on the galleys, taking about eight lines, which shows how a good editor can benefit a still-developing writer. So the notion of 'Snow People' as a denser and longer piece stuck in my mind, the thing that must be read in the book if you're to get as many of the tones of 'North America' and 'Education' as I could put in.

METCALF: Landscape and cityscape appear in your work as a *moral* landscape. Any comment?

BLAISE: I think I've been raised in two places where there is a continuity between the moral and the physical – the Deep South and Montreal. I think all writers I've read in Montreal (French and English) and all writers from the Deep South have essentially been writing the 'moral history' of their place and have found the incongruities and contradictions too great and too absorbing to go beyond. If I had lived all my life in Pittsburgh – where I spent my high school years – or in some comparable Canadian city or suburbs, I would never have seen the moral dimension in the physical, or the very real passion in even the passively perceived. Flannery O'Connor has written on that – 'the roots of the eye are in the heart' – and it's true.

My subject matter is – and has been for five years – Montreal, and one of the books I'm taking with me to Calcutta for the year is Spark's *Mandelbaum Gate* because I want a sharp rendering of a tripartite city, and Spark's Jerusalem is at least perfectly done. All works written in Montreal are finally laments or celebrations. (Montreal was the Dublin of North America for the majority of its citizens.) And the number of cities in the world of which this can be said are few – Paris, New York, London, and certainly Calcutta.

Of *regions*, the South was one, and so, if I understand the critics, is the Canadian Prairie. These are places where setting is not merely an excuse, but where setting is in fact the mystery and the manner.

METCALF: How do short stories arrive for you? As much of your work is 'autobiographical', how do the elements coalesce? How do you transpose and juxtapose events to make a piece of fiction?

BLAISE: It's true that I rely on 'autobiography' – whatever that is. I mean, when I am living my own life and dreaming someone else's? Most of my life is lived in dreams and in my vivid dreams I am obviously not myself. What I return with from my dreams and finally incorporate into my own reality is a story – or, at worst, a lecture-topic.

METCALF: Apart from 'Continent of Strangers', which I considered the most conventional and the weakest story in *A North American Education,* you've moved a long way from any conventional ideas of 'plot'. Much of your writing is more a 'collage' held together by theme but more particularly by *tone.* Can you comment on the voice that speaks in your stories?

BLAISE: I think the real reason I'm fond of 'personal' fiction is that two things move me in fiction – texture and voice.

Texture is detail arranged and selected and enhanced. It is the inclusion of detail from several planes of reference: dialogue, fantasy, direct passive observation ('I am a camera'), allusion, psychic wound, symbol, straight fact, etc. etc. – the sum of all that is *voice.*

So small wonder I'm drawn to writers who are themselves obvious texture-workers. John Hawkes, Malamud – lesser-known story writers like Richard Yates, Tillie Olsen, and Cynthia Ozick. Among the dead masters – Flaubert, Céline, Faulkner. They all have the power to arrest me, really strike me in such a way as to block my approach through similar material.

Texture implies both vitality and unevenness – it probably rules out most satire. I think the job of fiction is to view life through a microscope so that every grain gets its due and no one can confuse salt with sugar. You hear a lot about cinema being the visual medium – this is false. It *degrades* the visual by its inability to focus. It takes the visual for granted. Only the word – for me – is truly visual. I'm reminded of something from Nabokov's *Speak, Memory* where he speaks of the words learned in his childhood always possessing a *colour,* and in later life he sought the proper word with precisely the sensual involvement of a painter seeking a tone. That's what I mean by language as (for me) a visual experience and only secondarily a musical (poetic) one. It seems that the expressive gift, when it occurs in language, is frequently visual or aural. Otherwise, presumably, it is legalistic or journalistic, an expediency to communicate data.

By *voice* I am referring to the control, what is commonly referred to when we mention the 'world' of a certain author; the limits of probability and chance in his construction, the sanctions he leaves us for our own variations, what we sense of his own final concerns and bafflements. Again, my interest in voice is not one of 'character'. I see the construction of 'character' as an honourable but not necessarily compelling occupation.

When I 'see' a story it is always in terms of its images and situation, the tone and texture and discovery that seems immanent in that situation – and very rarely do these intimations demand a thirty-eight-year-old spinster or a college drop-out on an acid trip. I try to work out a voice that will allow for a simultaneity of image and action. Sometimes it is 'second-person', frequently first-person, commonly present tense. Sometimes it will have no time-referent beyond the present moment. In my book *A North American Education*, most of the Montreal stories – 'Eyes', 'Words for the Winter', 'Extractions and Contractions', and 'Going to India' – follow, at least in part, this pattern. Those are stories of texture and voice – details selected with an eye to their aptness but also to their 'vapour trails', their slow dissolve into something more diffuse and nameless.

One learns the traffic congestion in unfamiliar cities from helicopter reports, one notes that dogs outnumber children and that garbage gets deposited in pizza boxes ... it is a matter of texture to select those details and a matter of voice that allows for wider interpretation. Voice allows the reader a confidence that he is in a shaping vision with a tone coloration that is different from the actual 'character's'. That's one reason why 'autobiographical' is accurate but insufficient; there is no such thing as an 'autobiographical voice'.

In a story like 'Extractions and Contractions' I had very little to do with the actual events – heightened in scale with what I felt to be the voice of the experience, they were all based on – or suggested by – a shade of event. But I worked a year with the basic situation: teeth, pregnancy, roaches, buildings going up and down, protest (it was 1968), before seeing that the best I could do would be to openly insist on the disruptive, non-sequential nature of teasingly similar events. The actual story was written in Amsterdam in the early summer of 1968 and typed up when I got back to Montreal in July. It was revised a few more times that summer and sent out in the fall and immediately accepted by *Tri-Quarterly*. It was the second story I'd written in and about Montreal and the first that had an immediately favourable response from my friends George Bowering and Jerry Newman. I read it at The University of Western Ontario when I received the President's Medal for a story I'd published in *Tamarack* the year before and there, too, Michael Ondaatje received it enthusiastically. I read it in the States a week later when I was writer-in-residence at Denison University (where I thought I'd have to explain nearly everything in it) and a professor in the audience immediately contracted it for an anthology. I read it so many times in the space of the year and came to think of it as so obviously the best thing I'd done that I haven't been able to read a single line of it in the last four years.

I thought the form was original when I hit upon it but William Gass had published *In the Heart of the Heart of the Country* a few months earlier and I've seen similar 'collages' altogether too many times – it's become a trite format.

METCALF: You handle dialogue well but you seem to avoid it as much as possible. Is this related to your ideas about voice?

BLAISE: Dialogue, for me, has only one purpose and that's to reveal a compulsion that has been hidden to the 'eye' of the story until its utterance. Dialogue is a terribly inefficient way to set up anything or to impart information. It only works for me as an instance of inadvertence, or pressure released. My aborted novel was crammed with dialogue, it filled the pages effortlessly, but after fifteen pages of dialogue very little had gotten out that wasn't already obvious or – if revealed in speech – suddenly too obvious. So I'm overly sensitive to dialogue. I like it for its obvious *authenticating* quality – but I don't have the ear to sustain a story through dialogue. Though I *do* have more dialogue in a book for Doubleday in 1974 – it's called *Tribal Justice*. Obviously, I'm going to have to find a way of working dialogue back into the kinds of stories I want to write. Otherwise, they'll become nothing more than meditations or neurotic internal monologues.

Dialogue's nice also to vary the reader's sense of the author's omniscience – whenever a character speaks, there's an illusion of freedom in the world of the book.

METCALF: The 'plots' of your stories are carried also by an unobtrusive chain of images much in the manner of poems – I read your work *as* poems – and the Montreal stories seem to be moving into a bleak and mysterious world similar to the worlds of Margaret Atwood or John Newlove.

BLAISE: This might be a kind of poetry, especially of the kind associated with Atwood. I used to call it my 'aged eagle' stance and Jerry Newman still calls me on it nine times out of ten. But I don't read poetry with any kind of enthusiasm. I attend poetry readings for the old Iowa sense of community and also in the hopes of hearing a 'voice' that will stimulate my own thinking.

Poems have a voice, as do paintings, music, and especially film. But only Satyajit Ray and Truffaut among world directors today (fleetingly Rohmer) have a voice that I find inherently appealing, or even embarrassing, to my own concerns. I can admire Bergman of course, but he's rather like Joyce or Borges or Nabokov in being outside my greedy cannibalistic needs.

METCALF: I think that *A North American Education* is one of the best collections of stories published in Canada. Can you tell me anything of its publishing history? Why an American company, for example?

BLAISE: I submitted a combined manuscript of *A North American Education* and *Tribal Justice* − with some changes − to academic presses in the States. They each took eight months to turn the book down. Then I sent the full manuscript to Clarke, Irwin who had published four stories in *New Canadian Writing, 1968*. They thought they couldn't afford a book that simply wouldn't earn a profit. A friend advised me to submit the book to McClelland and Stewart. I sent them the book in its present form and I was told that it didn't have 'enough meat' and while the stories were good and generally successful, they were rather academic and the reader just didn't come away with a feeling of having had 'a literary experience'.

So I sent the book to Doubleday on the advice of Malcolm Foster and I was called by my editor-to-be three weeks later with an acceptance. They've been all-supportive and concerned with the *ensemble* of the book from editing to binding to promotion and even though they are very large and I'm very small − Park Avenue conglomerate to débutant Canadian short story writer, to draw out an obvious point − I've been dealt with as a private sort of citizen with dignified 'aged eagle' ways and keen sense of self-promotion.

METCALF: That's a sad history.

BLAISE: There's something I'd like to come back to − the autobiographical thing. I'm content for now − and have been for years − to write from a reasonably settled psychic point of view ... i.e. roughly my own, as I understand it ... and to seek variety not in certain 'character-frames' − you know, like the lenses that an eye doctor keeps dropping in those heavy frames during an eye test − but in rendering the texture of a situation in a voice appropriate to it. I have no defence against those critics who've commented on the 'ego-involvement' and the 'obviously autobiographical' nature of this 'first work'. I'd say that most of *A North American Education* is a 'twenty-fifth' work and that the interchangeableness of the various characters is not meant as a particularly well-disguised secret.

In that, I would agree a bit with John Hawkes who said once in an interview that he began writing fiction with the assumption that the true enemies of the novel were theme, plot, and character. I only wish I'd begun writing with as clear a sense.

John Metcalf

SOAPING A MEDITATIVE FOOT: NOTES FOR A YOUNG WRITER

1) If you write as balm for a broken heart, if you find writing therapeutic, read no further.

2) If you find offensive the assertion that writing has little or nothing to do with 'sincerity' and spontaneity, read no further.

3) Do not confuse politics with writing. Party political positions are necessary in the larger world; the literary world is necessarily aristocratic.

Do not hope to write for the masses – it is a fate worse than death.

Don't write propaganda – be warned by the example of those who did. (Read the poetry which came out of the Spanish Civil War. Or worse, the bad poetry by some excellent poets which is coming out of the Viet Nam War.)

Do not feel ashamed that you are not carrying a gun or digging a ditch. Let the cobbler stick to his last.

Remember that all writing is political, all great writing subversive.

4) Stories, novels, and poems are neither idea nor opinion. They are the distillation of experience.

> Particular life is still the best map to truth. When we search our hearts and strip our pretences, we all know this. Particular life – we know only what we *know*. (Herbert Gold.)

If you have an idea, don't start writing until you feel better.

First published in John Metcalf, ed., *The Narrative Voice: Short Stories and Reflections by Canadian Authors* (Toronto: McGraw-Hill Ryerson, 1972).

5) To sustain, nourish and enrich the climate for creative growth and progress, Titanic is embarked on the most comprehensive quest for new ideas
in the company's history.

    The formal vehicle for this quest is an imaginative and long-range
planning programme that was launched last year and is being executed
with skill and vigour. The programme is a continuing, in-depth effort
that is adding and will add new directions and novel dimensions to the
on-going and imaginative activities of the company's strategic planning
department.

    (Extract from *Annual Report* of Titanic Oil Company.)

This is not *merely* effluent; it is your *active* enemy, the tide against which
you must swim.

6) Take joy in the Placing of words.

How had he made his bad impression? The most likely thing, he always
thought, was his having inflicted a superficial wound on the Professor of
English in his first week. This man, a youngish ex-Fellow of a Cambridge
college, had been standing on the front steps when Dixon, coming round
the corner from the library, had kicked violently at a small round stone
lying on the macadam. Before reaching the top of its trajectory it had
struck the other just below the left kneecap at a distance of fifteen yards
or more. Averting his head, Dixon had watched in terrified amazement; it
had been useless to run, as the nearest cover was far beyond reach. At the
moment of impact he'd turned and begun to walk down the drive, but
knew well enough that he was the only visible entity capable of stone-
propulsion. He looked back once and saw the Professor of English
huddled up on one leg and looking at him.

    (From *Lucky Jim*. Kingsley Amis. Gollancz, London, 1957.)

Consider the word 'looking' and its setting.

7) It is understandable but futile to take the twentieth century as a personal affront.

8) Know the weight, colour, and texture of *things*.

> For what seemed an immensely long time, I gazed without knowing, even without wishing to know, what it was that confronted me. At any other time I would have seen a chair barred with alternate light and shade. Today the percept had swallowed up the concept. I was so completely absorbed in looking, so thunderstruck by what I actually saw, that I could not be aware of anything else. Where the shadows fell on the canvas upholstery, stripes of a deep but glowing indigo alternated with stripes of an incandescence so intensely bright that it was hard to believe that they could be made of anything but blue fire. Garden furniture, laths, sunlight, shadow – these were no more than names and notions, mere verbalizations, for utilitarian purposes, after the event. The event was this succession of azure furnace doors separated by gulfs of unfathomable gentian. It was inexpressibly wonderful, wonderful to the point, almost, of being terrifying. And suddenly I had an inkling of what it must feel like to be mad.
>
> (From *The Doors of Perception*. Aldous Huxley. Harper and Brothers, New York, 1954.)

9) The real poetry – the names of materials and tools in the trades. Visit hardware stores.

10) Avoid, so far as possible, articles made of plastic.

11) Certain foods should be avoided on aesthetic and spiritual grounds. (E.g. all forms of styrofoam 'bread'.)

12) Do not watch television. It is debilitating and leads to the belief that one or two programmes are not really all that bad.

13) The consumption of vast amounts of alcohol or dope or both is not necessarily the outward and visible sign of genius.

14) Fill your mind with useless information. *Brewer's Dictionary of Phrase and Fable* is invaluable.

15) Buy the SOED and *Webster's*.

16) Consult Fowler's *Modern English Usage*.

17) Read Jane Austen.

18) Avoid literary criticism which moves away from the word on the printed page and ascends to theories of God, Archetypes, Myth, Psyche, The Garden of Eden, The New Jerusalem, and Orgone Boxes. Stick to the study of the placement of commas.

19) If your main interest is prose, study poets.

20) Good films are cross-fertilizing.

21) ... a good talker can talk away the substance of twenty books in as many evenings. He will describe the central idea of the book he means to write until it revolts him.
   (From *Enemies of Promise*. Cyril Connolly. Routledge and Kegan Paul, London, Revised Edition, 1949.)

22) Read *Enemies of Promise*.

23) Study Arthur Waley's translations of Chinese poetry – the modern short story in capsule form.

24) Don't be pious about Literature. Take what you need and don't feel too guilty about what you leave. (With the exception of Jane Austen.)

25) Approach Dylan Thomas with extreme caution; he is insidious and, on prose writers, a Bad Influence.
   Avoid *richness*. A love of Keats and a love of sweet sherry are not unrelated.
   Tio Pepe for preference.

26) Study the Grand Masters. For years. After you've decided who they are.

Shakespeare has been widely praised for the audacity of his quintuple 'Never' and for the poignant simplicity of 'I pray you undo this button' but who has praised P.G. Wodehouse for daring to write:

> Tum tiddle umpty-pum
> Tum tiddle umpty-pum
> Tum tiddle umpty-pum?

These masterly lines are enshrined in the following context.

I don't know if you happen to be familiar with a poem called 'The Charge of the Light Brigade' by the bird Tennyson whom Jeeves had mentioned when speaking of the fellow whose strength was as the strength of ten. It is, I believe, fairly well known, and I used to have to recite it at the age of seven or thereabouts when summoned to the drawing-room to give visitors a glimpse of the young Wooster. 'Bertie recites so nicely', my mother used to say – getting her facts twisted, I may mention, because I practically always fluffed my lines – and after trying to duck for safety and being hauled back I would snap into it. And very unpleasant the whole thing was, so people have told me.

Well, what I was about to say, when I rambled off a bit on the subject of the dear old days, was that though in the course of the years most of the poem of which I speak has slid from memory, I still recall its punch line. The thing goes, as you probably know,

> Tum tiddle umpty-pum
> Tum tiddle umpty-pum
> Tum tiddle umpty-pum

and this brought you to the snapperoo or pay-off, which was

> Someone had blundered.

I always remember that bit, and the reason I bring it up now is that, as I stood blinking at this pink-boudoir-capped girl, I was feeling just as those Light Brigade fellows must have felt. Obviously someone had blundered here, and that someone was Aunt Dahlia.

(From *Jeeves and the Feudal Spirit*. P.G. Wodehouse. Herbert Jenkins, London, 1954.)

'Grand Master?'

'Well, in one way, yes.'

The tragedy of Wodehouse is that he is not a comic writer but, rather, a comedian. If only C.P. Snow, Doris Lessing, or Joseph Heller had shared his grace.

(Examine a few paragraphs of Heller's lumbering humour in *Catch-22*; soggy as old bread pudding.)

'But Grand Master!'

'Don't be pious!'

Here is Wodehouse doing Nature. It is a performance, a comedian's routine, but it can teach you more of the art of writing than all the Writers' Conferences and Schools advertised in the summer issues of *Saturday Review*.

A thing I never know when I'm telling a story is how much scenery to bung in. I've asked one or two scriveners of my acquaintance, and their views differ. A fellow I met at a cocktail party in Bloomsbury said that he was all for describing kitchen sinks and frowsty bedrooms and squalor generally, but the beauties of Nature no. Whereas, Freddie Oaker, of the Drones, who does tales of pure love for the weeklies under the pen-name of Alicia Seymour, once told me that he reckoned that flowery meadows in springtime alone were worth at least a hundred quid a year to him.

Personally, I've always rather barred long descriptions of the terrain, so I will be on the brief side. As I stood there that morning, what the eye rested on was the following. There was a nice little splash of garden, containing a bush, a tree, a couple of flower beds, a lily pond with a statue of a nude child with a bit of tummy on him, and to the right a hedge. Across this hedge, Brinkley, my new man, was chatting with our neighbour, Police Sergeant Voules, who seemed to have looked in with a view to selling eggs.

There was another hedge straight ahead, with the garden gate in it, and over this one espied the placid waters of the harbour, which was much about the same as any other harbour, except that sometime during the night a whacking great yacht had rolled up and cast anchor in it. And of all the objects under my immediate advisement I noted this yacht with the most pleasure and approval. White in colour, in size resembling a young liner, it lent a decided tone to the Chuffnell Regis foreshore.

Well, such was the spreading prospect. Add a cat sniffing at a snail on the path and me at the door smoking a gasper, and you have the complete picture.

(From *Thank You Jeeves*. P.G. Wodehouse. Herbert Jenkins, London, 1934.)

27) Do not expect much recognition financial or critical for the years of hard work ahead of you.

In 1968, Alice Munro gave us *Dance of the Happy Shades* – the finest collection of short stories yet published in Canada. You can *still* buy (and should) copies of the first printing. Allen Ginsberg once said that most critics couldn't recognize good poetry if it came up and buggered them in broad daylight. Canadian critics seem equally insensitive to quality in the short story.

28) A reply to those who ask you what your stories *mean*.

There is easy reading. And there is literature. There are easy writers, and there are writers. There are people whose ears have never grown, or have fallen off, or have merely lost the power to listen. And there are people with ears....

'I write. Let the reader learn to read.' I must be as skilful as I can. I am obliged to be the best craftsman I can be. I must be free to choose my subject and my language, and I am at liberty to experiment, to grow, to express, if need be, the complexity of my experience with whatever resources are at hand. I will talk baby talk to babies and dog talk to dogs, but I cannot tell you in baby talk or dog talk of the excitement of being an adult human being in a world so wondrous with hope and sorrow and loyalty and defeat and anguish and delight.

All of us who *write* once made the decision to write out the best that is in us. It had nothing to do with Integrity, only with taste and preference. Loath to tape our ears to our skulls, we said, instead, We shall let our ears grow up and away and see what happens.

We want to tell the jokes we want to tell, and we can tell them only to people with ears to listen, people who will bring to the evening talents to challenge our own, who will work as goddam hard to read as we work who write.

(From 'Easy Does It Not'. Mark Harris. In *The Living Novel: A Symposium*. Ed. Granville Hicks. Macmillan, New York, 1957.)

29) Rewrite.

30) Rewrite.

Norman Levine

THE GIRL IN THE DRUGSTORE

I MUST HAVE BEEN about ten or eleven when my parents arranged for my sister and me to spend the summer holidays at Markovitch's farm on the outskirts of Ottawa. I was a city kid – but that summer I was taught how to pitch horseshoes, drink water out of a tin ladle, gather corn, ride a horse, throw a lasso, listen to cowboy songs on the wooden verandah from the gramophone inside. There were five other Ottawa kids on the farm for the summer. One of them was a girl called Mona. I liked her. And I decided to write a play for her. We put it on in one of the barns and charged the adults a button by way of admission.

Then later in high school (I went to the High School of Commerce) they had a magazine called *The Argosy*. It carried short stories. I wrote a short story for it, about a hangman who has to hang his own son. I called it 'A piece of string'. When I showed the story to Mr Benoit, our English teacher who was also my basketball coach, he said:

'You can't use that title. Maupassant has a story called that.'

I didn't know who Maupassant was. For we had no books in the house. My main home reading was the funnies. My uncle, who lived on the Drive-way, used to get American newspapers and he would save me the funnies. Once, a second-hand book did get in the house. It was a novel. All about Vienna. I read the first chapter – about the hero wandering through the streets of Vienna with his coat-collar turned up. And that was enough to make me do imitation after imitation in exercise books.

As soon as I could leave high school legally I did and went to work for the government in the Department of National Defence. One of my jobs was to operate the duplicating machine, running off specifications. Some evenings

First published in *Canadian Literature* 41 (1969).

I would come back and do stencils of something I had written – short sketches, mostly descriptions – like going out fishing very early in the morning near Ottawa in a boat on a river with the mist close to the ground. I would then give these mimeographed pieces to my friends.

In 1942, when I was eighteen, I joined the air force and eventually ended up on Lancasters with 429 Squadron in Yorkshire. When the war in Europe was over, and while waiting to go back to Canada, I went to Trinity College, Cambridge on a special leave course. There a lecturer gave me a thin wartime production of Pound's *Selected Poems*. It was the first modern verse I had read.

Four months after returning to Canada I went to McGill. And it was at McGill that I started to catch up, and how, for my lack of good reading. Perhaps it was because I read too many classics too quickly. Or perhaps I read these books knowing I had to pass exams on them. Whatever the reason – I have only the haziest notion of these books today, unless I have reread them since leaving McGill. The only book, from all the reading lists, that has left a definite memory is *The Sound and the Fury*. And the reason is not entirely because of the book.

I began to read it one evening in the basement room, on the corner of Guy and Sherbrooke, that I rented from the Dean of Christ Church Cathedral; he lived with his family above. I read it right through at one sitting. And when I finished, it was early in the morning and I was far too excited to go to sleep. So I put on my black winter coat and went out. It was very cold. Hard-packed snow on the ground, icicles from the roofs. The only place open at this time was the drugstore on St. Catherine near Guy. I walked down the few blocks. And went in. The place was empty except for a woman sitting on a stool by the counter having a cup of coffee and smoking a cigarette. She was in her twenties. She had on a fur coat that was undone. She had her legs crossed. She wore galoshes. We both looked at each other. Then she crossed herself. I turned and walked out.

After twenty-two years *The Sound and the Fury* has become vague and hazy. But that girl in the drugstore crossing herself has remained vivid and there are times when she haunts me still. Later, I was to find out in writing that this is the way things emerge.

At McGill I had some flying war-poems, full of bad alliteration, published in the *McGill Daily*. And for a year I edited *Forge*, the university's literary magazine. I also took Professor Files' course in writing. This meant going to see Professor Files once a fortnight with something new I had written. In this way I started to write what I called a novel, which turned out to be *The Angled Road*. Every second Saturday morning I would go into his office and show him a chapter or part of a chapter. Often I wrote it the night before. And he would go over it, sometimes correcting the grammar of a sentence. Sometimes suggesting parts to leave out.

I am unable to read *The Angled Road* today. But at that time Files' encouragement was vital. He helped to build up confidence on the shakiest of foundations.

My wartime stay in England was very unliterary. But when I returned there in 1949 with the manuscript of *The Angled Road* in my Gladstone bag and a chapbook of juvenile poems that Ryerson had brought out and a promise from McClelland to look after my books in Canada if I could get them published in England – I thought of myself as a writer and headed for literary London.

I had no letters of introduction nor did I know anyone. But it wasn't the kind of time when you needed these things. A lot of people had come to London from different parts of Britain and the Commonwealth. Writers and painters congregated in certain pubs. And there was still a hangover of the war in the loosened class barriers, the romanticism, the idealism. Wanting to be a painter or a writer was equated with wanting the good life. The rationing, the bomb-damage, the general seediness, also helped. And because of the wartime boom in reading it was still, comparatively speaking, easy to find a publisher for one's work. Literary standards were, on the whole, not high. What I didn't know, at the time, was that I had come in on the end of something that was in the process of breaking up.

I spent the summers down in Cornwall. And while St. Ives, then, was an outpost of what was going on in London, especially in the painting – the physical impact of Cornwall was another thing.

I had come straight from city life. And to be exposed, unexpectedly, to so much varied nature gave me an exhilarating sense of personal freedom. I spent most of the time outside just walking and looking. For much of what I was seeing was totally unknown to me. The names of the birds (apart from plain gull and sparrow) I didn't know. I didn't know the names of the flowers or what was gorse or bracken or heather or blackberries or these stunted

English trees. The fish I saw up for auction every morning at the slipway with their fat human lips and small eyes were anonymous. A hard and new physical world seemed to have suddenly opened before me, and in such splendid colour. I'd get up before six in the morning and go out. And late at night I'd be sitting by the window, just so I wouldn't miss anything.

Then it was seeing the painters go among the beached boats with a sketch pad and do sketches that probably made me go out with a pencil and notebook and try to describe what I saw. I would spend a whole morning on a beach trying to describe the way a wave broke, how the far-shore fields changed colour with the passing clouds. Then in the harbour: there were the boats, the gulls on the sand bar facing the wind, the sand eels swimming by the harbour wall, the way the sunlight fractured like fishing nets on the sandy bottom.

The physical presence of Cornwall and these exercises stopped me from writing self-indulgent prose-poetry in the prose. And cut out all those inflated rhetorical bits in the verse. The writing became much more simple and direct.

But I still had to come to terms with something else.

At McGill I was running away from being a Jew. It sounds silly now. But at the time it was mixed up with coming from Murray Street, Ottawa, with the peddlers' horses and sleighs, and going around with boys and girls from rich parents. I made up so many identities. It all depended on who I was with. This helped to give my life there a certain dangerous edge. But it was to prove near fatal to the writing. For at that time I was writing *The Angled Road*. And in it I cut out the fact that my characters were Jewish. And by doing this, a whole dimension is missing; I made them smaller than they should have been.

Then, when I came over to England I was running away from Canada. All my early stories, which were to do with Canadian life, I set in England. The result was the same sense of paleness and unreality. And I find that none of that early writing means anything now to me.

A couple more years had to go by before I was able to recognize my material and use it without trying to make it more acceptable. And the first book to come out after that was *Canada Made Me*. My writing begins with that book.

It seems a complicated and long way to have to go in order to come to terms with one's material. But then some people take longer than others to grow up. And perhaps it also took longer because I had to recognize that one of the conditions of my being a writer is of living in exile. I felt it in Canada, as the son of orthodox Jewish parents in Ottawa; then as the poor boy among the rich at McGill. And now I feel it as a Canadian living in England. It's not the way I would have planned it. And I still have fantasies of some day living in a community where I will take an active part in its everyday affairs.

George Bowering

HOW TO WRITE

A BUNCH of local fellers are sitting around, and a politician or preacher or some such comes around and tries to sell them a verbal bill of goods; they might listen to what he says (content) – but they pay more attention, in terms of offering their belief or trust, to HOW he says it, his vocabulary and accent or dialect, and the amount of familiarity he adopts. If he sounds like a city-slicker or uppity, or condescending, or too abstract, etcetera, etcetera, they arent likely to believe him.

I think the same applies to poetry.

First published in IS 8 (1970). Republished in George Bowering, *Craft Slices* (Ottawa: Oberon, 1985).

Jack Hodgins

SOME THOUGHTS ON WRITING FICTION:
BRIEF NOTES TO MYSELF

The following thoughts do not suggest rules, or even a consistent philosophical position. For myself, they are capsule reminders of matters to be thought about while writing. For my students, they are merely statements to be considered for discussion.

BEFORE THE FIRST DRAFT. Resist starting on a 'first draft' of a story so long as you have only 'an idea' or 'a character'. Instead, write 'pieces' – bits of description, snatches of dialogue, notes on ideas, etc. Do this until one of the pieces catches fire and you can't bear not to keep going, or else until staring at all these pieces causes an explosion of insight, some new understanding that comes from the connection amongst them, giving you a richer sense of what you're up to.

CHARACTER. Eventually, amongst those bits and pieces, there will be some half-imagined people beginning to take on life. They may be totally invented, they may be imitations of real people you've observed, they may be artificially manufactured out of bits and pieces collected in your notebook. One of them, or some of them, will start to haunt you. Puzzle you. Intrigue you. 'What makes *him* tick?' 'Why do I keep thinking about *her*? Where did she come from anyway?' Since writing will include both *discovering* these people for yourself and *revealing* them to your reader, it may be a good idea to hold off writing anything except more bits and pieces until you stumble upon something that jolts you – frightens you, alarms you, startles you, delights you, makes you laugh. 'Okay, now *you're* someone I'm going to

First published in *How Stories Mean*.

pursue!' (What was it the boy said to the elephant in *The Jungle Book*? 'There's something about you I don't understand and I'm going to sit on your head until morning.')

WRITING THE FIRST DRAFT.   Write the first draft for no one but yourself. Write to find out what you're writing about. Think of this as just a way of nailing the story down so that it can't get away. No eyes but yours will see it. Writing the first draft should be fun (you're telling yourself a story, after all) and surprising (you're making a journey, where people will reveal things you hadn't anticipated) and free (you can change your mind or change direction as often as you want so long as you feel you're getting somewhere that might pay off). When you look back at what you've done, however, it will be as though you have just completed ploughing a field. What will be interesting (and important) now is to discover what – besides predictable soil – you've unearthed along the way.

STARING AT THE FIRST DRAFT.   Walk over the field and have a good look at the surprises. What rocks and broken bottles and mammoth bones came to the surface without your permission? Don't be too quick to throw them away. (Don't be too quick to make them welcome either.) This is your chance to discover that your material has more to offer than you'd suspected. If you're a writer who doesn't want a story to do anything more or less than you'd decided ahead of time, you'll throw them all out and brush the dirt from your hands and gaze with pride at your perfectly ploughed field. If you're a writer who suspects that a million unfathomable reasons lie behind your choice of a particular piece of material to write about, you may also suspect the material contains more than first appears. Stare. Stare. Flannery O'Connor said it takes a certain kind of stupidity to be a good fiction writer – the kind of stupidity that requires you to stare at something before you begin to understand it. This means staring not only at the world out there but at the lumps and bumps and glittery things that surface during the writing of your own work. Assume there is a secret story hidden within the story you thought you were writing, then search for its clues, think what the clues might mean; have enough respect for both the material and the process to believe there's more going on here than you have consciously done. A good story, honestly written, will have a life of its own, like

the natural terrain, and before the writer goes through and tosses out everything that wasn't consciously intended he or she ought to take a good close
look at everything. That donkey jawbone or that broken bottle may come in
handy yet. They may even be clues to help you understand what you're up
to. Potential is what you're looking for here – what *does* this story want to
become?

CHARACTERS AGAIN. Those 'people' who began as scraps of paper, or as
bits and pieces of memory, or as voices heard, and who talked and strutted
and fought their way through your first draft, may or may not have taken on
full-blown life. Sooner or later you want them to sit up and start to breathe
on their own. Staring at the first draft can help bring this about. In the
fiction I admire, it seems to me the most vivid characters leap to life not
from an accumulation of information – although description and background and explanation might have been necessary too, to get us started –
but from some unique and peculiar detail of manner, or some unique and
peculiar turn of phrase in dialogue. Something, in other words, that causes
my imagination to make the leap from that collection of impressions which
is the fictional character to a sharp flash of recognition: 'I know this person.'
(New Zealand novelist Maurice Shadbolt refers to that 'precious particle'
which must be sought out to define a character. Milan Kundera insists that
nothing is necessary except to capture the 'essence' of the character.) It may
be that there is someone in real life I'm reminded of; more likely it is that the
telling detail or revealing speech pattern is so sharp and fresh and unique
that it automatically contains within it all the rest I need to know about the
character. The narrator of William Goyen's story 'Bridge of Music, River of
Sand' leaps almost instantly to life with his opening words: 'Do you remember the bridge that we crossed over the river to get to Riverside? And if you
looked over yonder you saw the railroad trestle? High and narrow? Well
that's what he jumped off of. Into a nothing river. "River!" I could laugh. I
can spit more than runs in that dry bed.' In Elizabeth Bowen's *Eva Trout*,
the narrator tells us: 'Anyway here was Eva, right back on top of one. Eva as
ever, extra heavily breathing, about to twitch the ignition key.' In both cases,
the rhythm of the sentences conveys as much as the words. (Seeing Eva
throw her ocelot coat over her shoulders and heave herself into her Jaguar
helps too!) I imagine I would recognize either of these 'characters' on the

street or in a theatre foyer in a way I would never recognize someone I'd read about in the newspaper. If this is my experience as a reader, it makes sense as a writer that I try to cause this sort of thing to happen to *my* readers. To look for the unique spark – whether mannerism or habit of speech or personality quirk – and let it ride at the very centre of all the accumulating experiences and reactions that make up the story.

It doesn't hurt to remind yourself of what the how-to books have to say – that you can get information about your characters across to a reader by telling it yourself, by letting the character tell it, by letting some other character express it, or by letting the character's actions suggest it to the reader. The first is easiest, but the last is the one the readers will believe. They saw it with their own eyes, so to speak. They decided for themselves. Eva Trout is a formidable woman, and inescapable, blundering her way through the world.

Student writers struggling with characters who resist all attempts to force life upon them have sometimes found it useful to do some serious thinking about the people who most affected them as young children, those people who became the archetypes that haunt their lives. (Your first bus driver, your first nun, your first bully, your first scandalous adult, your first drunk, your first spineless adult, your first terrifying old person.) Find out what those people have to offer. Frankly, I sometimes suspect that much of writing is an attempt to get these figures off our backs, or at least to understand them, or to bring them down to human level so we can look them squarely in the eye.

PLOT. 'A series of causally related events, involving some sort of conflict (or tension), leading (probably) to a climax and (possibly) to a resolution.' Something to be aware of but not to be governed by. Australian novelist Kate Grenville: 'The great danger of the conventional plot is that it becomes so contrived and unlifelike that it becomes dead: a pale, shallow imitation of the richness of real life. The great danger of the plotless narrative is that there isn't enough forward movement for the reader to stay interested' (*The Writing Book*). Plot (which is not nearly as interesting or important as design or structure in a story) is an artificial device to ensure that the 'story' does not become so shapeless and purposeless as to lose its reader's interest. (Someone once suggested that a writer should ask himself or herself at the bottom of each manuscript page, 'Would a reader pay a dollar to turn this page?' Impossible to know. Why is the reader reading at all? The way you wrote the first page told the reader what to expect. If you *caused* your readers to read with their hearts in their throat, wanting to find out what happened next, then you'll have to live with that and try to satisfy that expectation right to the end. If your opening page invited your reader along on another sort of journey and the reader accepts the invitation, that is another matter. Stories without traditional or obvious plots often have substituted something else that satisfies the same need in the reader – to have a reason to keep reading. A forward-moving impulse. If it isn't to be 'What happens next?' or 'Will he/she get out of this mess or not?' (the traditional plot) then it may be 'What am I going to learn about this person next?' or at least 'Is there no end to the surprises (or insights, or fresh observations) this writer can come up with?' If the character is sufficiently vivid and interesting, and if I have a 'story' I want to tell, it is probably enough to ask 'What does he/she want?' and 'What obstacles stand in the way?' in order to ensure enough tension and interest to get things going. If a story seems limp and indifferent, often the most important question to ask is 'What's at stake?' Student writers find this a cruel question. If 'Nothing' is the answer, then 'Why are we reading this story?' is the next question. If the reader even thinks to ask 'Why am I reading this story?' you've probably lost the whole thing. The important thing in both plotted and unplotted stories is to be so intensely interested yourself in this journey you're taking (for whatever reasons – action or character or revelation or the joy of using language) that others may want to take the journey too. It's probably a good idea to reckon that the reader will be only about 1/100th as interested in your story as you are yourself. If this is a discouraging thought, then why are you writing this story anyway? To learn how to write it better.

SETTING. Perhaps the first job of the fiction writer is to make the reader believe in the world of the story – at least temporarily. One way to begin accomplishing this is through the creation of a convincing geographical world, whether imagined or faithful to some original. This is an extension of character development; the people you write about take on clearer and more forceful reality if they have a geographical and cultural and historical context. Setting can be nothing more than minimal backdrop but it can contribute much more than that. Most locations, if stared at long enough, offer up more than geography. A front porch of a family home is only the front porch of a family home in the geographical world; but a front porch of a family home in a story about a family struggling with a horrible secret offers much more. Porches have under-the-porches. Families talking on their front porches are sitting above the dark secretive world only children and dogs and chickens know, a world of old bones and lost toys and hurt feelings and frightening monsters. What kind of fiction writer would sit on a porch and not think about the gold mine beneath it? The world is offering us gifts every minute if we pay attention. Eudora Welty writes: 'The truth is, fiction depends for its life on place. Location is the crossroads of circumstance, the proving ground of "What happened? Who's here? Who's coming?" – and that is the heart's field' (*The Eye of the Story*). If fiction depends for its life on place, so does the fiction writer. David Malouf: 'What I will be after is ... a description of how the elements of a place and our inner lives cross and illuminate one another, how we interpret space, and in so doing make our first maps of reality, how we mythologize spaces and through that mythology (a good deal of it inherited) find our way into a culture' ('A First Place: The Mapping of a World', *Southerly*, 45, 1985). The tourist may look at a place and think 'What does it do? What is it like? How much does it please me?' but the fiction writer must look at a place and think 'What does it suggest? What does it mean to me? What does it mean to my characters?' An extreme example occurs in Shirley Hazzard's *The Transit of Venus* where she locates a meeting between two people (one of them about to give information which will destroy the life of the other) in Harrod's rug department, 'which had the space and solemnity of a cathedral', and where 'thick rolled strips of carpet stood or lay like the fallen drums of columns in a temple'. One character's inner world of sacred hope is then devastated before our eyes. To follow this model too seriously is to risk disaster of another kind, but the hint is worth consideration: since you're in the business of weaving a spell, of creating a world and its effects, you may as well enrol the help of every element, including setting, in the task.

SETTING AND STYLE.   If landscape can be seen as contributing to the characters, the actions, and even the meaning in a fiction, the writer might want to consider the extent to which a particular landscape, or landscapes, may have affected him or her. Was Larry McMurtry's spare lean horizontal style influenced by a childhood in Texas? (He says it was.) Would the novels of Patrick White have been less sprawling, his sentences shorter, his casts smaller, his plots less complex, if he were writing about tiny, cramped, and crowded Poland, say, instead of vast Australia? (In a 1977 speech, he said 'I believe that geography ... is what makes us.') I once complained to a writer friend that every time I start a new story my goal is to write it in fast, tight, clean, clear prose – *The Old Man and the Sea*; *The Bridge of San Luis Rey* – but that once I get into the job, prose springs up all around me like a jungle; new people get into the act, the story becomes more complex and mysterious than I'd anticipated, all of the world seems to want to be part of the action. Less puzzled than I was by this, my friend laughed. He suggested things could not be otherwise. 'You were born and raised in a rainforest. You have a rainforest brain. Your imagination – and so your prose – has the fecundity and the complexity of a jungle. Don't fight it. So long as you're writing *about* the Vancouver Island world, this is not only inevitable, it is appropriate.' What does this mean? I don't know what it means. I don't even know if he's right. But it's something to think about, occasionally.

WHERE TO BEGIN THE READER'S STORY. Just because you wrote your first draft from A to Z (probably from what you thought was the beginning to what you thought was the end) does not mean the reader must experience it that way. I once heard a fiction writer say that a story is like a house; it doesn't matter which door or window you enter by so long as you visit all the rooms before you leave. I agree. But I also think that choosing this door instead of that door, visiting this room before that room, results in quite a different story experience than other choices would have made. The house itself may look approximately the same by the time you step out of it at the end of your visit and stand back far enough to get some perspective, whatever order you chose, but this will not change the fact that the order in which you chose to visit the rooms will have had as much effect upon *you* as the content of the rooms themselves. (Imagine visiting Manhattan immediately after visiting Elsa, the tiny mining village north of Whitehorse; imagine visiting the two places in the reverse order.) People who design the interiors of department stores know the importance of this. Remember when you could walk into a department store and make a bee-line straight to the back wall where you knew you could quickly buy that record you'd been saving for? Not any more. People have been paid big money to find ways of making that impossible. They have decided to take you by the hand and make sure you're forced to take a circuitous route so that you are forced to visit as many departments as possible before you get to where you thought you wanted to go (which won't be there any more anyway). They will determine your journey through the store. Around a semi-circle you go, tilting like a motorbike on a sharp corner and looking for an opportunity to take a short cut – no short cuts are possible any more, without extreme awkwardness – exposed at every step to a rapid succession of merchandise set out to compete for your lust. The journey from the door to the record department has become a series of emotional encounters, hardly escapable. Like it or not, if the reader's experience of your story is to be an emotional journey, you are the floor-designer who gets to decide what kind of journey it will be. If you push him through the smells of the fishmarket on his way to cosmetics he'll come out with quite a different impression than if you'd taken him to cosmetics by way of the toy department. This is not to suggest a story's structure should be determined with the T-squares and compasses of a cold-blooded retailer plotting to separate people from their money. But it is a reminder that you have choices. If you are told who the murderer is right at the beginning of the story, you read about the detective's search with quite a different feeling than if you are stumbling along from clue to clue as confused and ignorant as he.

POINT OF VIEW. This is the killer. Sitting around trying to make the best choice can paralyse you. Whose story is it? Who will tell it? How much time has gone by between the events and the telling? Should the story be told by the main character himself? If so, what has happened to him since the story happened and how does he feel about the experience now? Should it be told by a witness? Why? Should it be told in the third person? If so, who is this third person, and how much is he capable of knowing? Omniscient, objective, or limited in his 'omniscience' to the thoughts and motives of only the main character? It's one thing to know what the choices are; it's important to know the limitations and possibilities of each; it's also important to know the responsibilities that go along with each choice. Any story could be written in any point of view. The thing is to try them all, or at least to imagine how different the effect would be in each case before trying the ones you think will be the most satisfying. Chances are you will choose the point of view you 'feel like' writing, but who knows what mysterious factors lie behind that urge? Why do pre-school girls (according to educational studies) tell stories in the first person, boys in the third? Does it matter? What matters is the difference in effect, the difference in the reader's (listener's) experience of the story. What matters is that you give some thought to the effect you want to have, the effect the material needs to have. Perhaps by the time all other aspects of the story have been thought about, and experimented with, there is no real need to make a choice of point of view. There may, if you're fortunate, be only one choice which can help you carry out all the other things you want to do. Often, even when I'm content that I've chosen the best point of view, I find it useful to convert the entire story to another, quite different point of view. Fresh discoveries can sometimes be taken with you back to the original.

VOICE. If the story is written in the first person, this is a matter of getting the idiom and the rhythms of the narrator not only 'right' but also 'right' in some unique way that brings him to life. If the story is written in the third person, then comes the question of what persona you've adopted to tell it. Voice is what you hear when you pick up Wright Morris's *In Orbit* and read, 'This boy comes riding with his arms high and wide, his head dipped low, his ass light in the saddle, as if about to be shot into orbit from a forked sling.' *This* boy, not *that* boy. *Comes riding*, not *rides*. Word choice. Angle of vision. Cadence. Morris has adopted the voice of someone wound up and ready to let fly, someone who taps you on the shoulder and points out what you're to look at and even makes you feel a little tense about it. *This* boy seems a little threatening to me. Quite another sort of voice is what you hear when you pick up Saul Bellow's *Mr. Sammler's Planet* and read, 'Shortly after dawn, or what would have been dawn in a normal sky, Mr. Artur Sammler with his bushy eye took in the books and papers of his West Side bedroom and suspected strongly that they were the wrong books, the wrong papers.' A different cadence, a different attitude, a different sort of vocabulary. No wound-up spring here. We're hearing the voice of someone calm and sympathetic who knows the power you can give the words you save for the end of a sentence. Who will *you* be, for this story you're writing? Will you assume the stance of a wise old grandfather, perhaps, placid and unsurprised? A wise-cracking youth? Will you be emotional about your material, involved – or will you be distanced? Much of this will depend upon your attitude to the character or characters you are obsessed with. Are you an intimate of the characters, or an ironic observer? The voice you adopt, the narrative persona, informs every line you write, establishes and maintains whatever relationship there is between story and reader. What can be more important? Voice assigns the reader a role to play in the drama: if you've chosen to adopt the voice of a historian (whether or not you are *identified* as a historian) you are asking the reader to be a student of history, if you've chosen to adopt the voice of a rural gossip you've made the reader a rural gossip too, or party to it at least, if you've chosen to adopt the voice of a flashy smartmouth sneering at your characters you're asking the reader to be the impressed audience and to sneer along with you. Not something to be taken lightly. Neither is it something to be added afterwards. It is a part of every word you write.

SYMBOL. Not to be added afterwards either. (And yet not to be *thought* much about until most of the other work is done.) Back to that ploughed field, the first draft. Where did these rocks come from? What does this jaw-bone mean? How did this shattered nineteenth-century bottle get here? Now who would ever expect to turn up a toy sailboat in a place like this? Much of this will be hauled away, thrown out – the result of taking a false turn in your writing, of daydreaming, of suffering from heartburn from lunch, of brooding about that last remark someone made in this morning's phonecall. Some, however, can be seen to be connected to others: the old bottle has the picture of a sailboat on it? The jawbone, held at a certain angle, has something of the shape of the toy sailboat? Or connected to the characters: Old George is preparing for an ocean voyage but is frightened of going? Stop! Leave it alone! It is enough merely to suspect the connections for now. It is enough simply to decide not to throw something out – to let it hang around and grow with the various drafts. Maybe, eventually, it will earn its keep. Maybe it will even become indispensable. Maybe you will even want to give it a place of honour – in the title, say, or in the final sentence of the story. The literary scholars will talk about symbol. Don't be coy – so will you. But you will know that it was something that had to stay there because it gave the story something it would be hollow without – some insight into motives, some glimpse into character, some hint at a connection between your story and the outside world.

REVISIONS. Editing and 'fixing up' are important, but don't pretend they're revisions. They can make a story better but they aren't likely to cause a story to leap into a newer, fresher, richer form of life. Revising requires re-visioning. The work has only just begun. All 'breakthroughs' which I've experienced or observed, causing good-enough stories to become very good or even superb stories, have come about after the writer has done everything he knows how to do – the editor in him has had his say – and then steps back, abandons the 'almost wonderful' story, and begins afresh. That is, after staring at the existing story until he knows it intimately, he sits down at the desk and begins a brand new 'first draft' from scratch. If the story is alive, new insights are more likely to occur while writing this way than while tinkering with a manuscript. In this new draft you will be writing from the position of having done all the work, of having no fear of losing the story-so-far, of relaxing in a way you may not have relaxed since doing the 'first draft', and this relaxed and joyful retelling of the story is more likely than anything else I can think of to throw up fresh insights and new angles and fresh ways of saying things. If you are lazy about the physical work of writing or typing, and if you are impatient to get to the end to see what sort of new story you've got on your hands, this approach will encourage you to leave out everything that isn't necessary to the story – all those beautiful but irrelevant passages and all those sentences that take too long to say what they need to say. The story may be better off without them. If not, if their absence is felt and you really think they earn their keep, they can still be imported from the earlier story and given a second chance. In my many years of teaching, most of the best students have been able to take their stories through draft after draft to a point where they're very good and could be abandoned with satisfaction and pride, but those students who have taken their stories all the way to 'superb' and seen them accepted for publication and praise have most often gone through a process similar to this. It requires a decision to treat all the hard work of draft after draft right up to the 'very good' draft as mere background research and practice exercise for the experience of writing the 'final, fresh, real' version of the story. Then if you put it away for a good long time and then take it out and read and find yourself thinking 'Hey, this story is better than anything *I* could have written, I wish it were mine!' then maybe it's just about ready for people.

CAUTION. Having reminded yourself of all this stuff, forget it. Well, don't forget it, just push it aside. Who could lift a finger if he thought about everything necessary to make that finger move in a natural way? Assumed 'knowledge' too consciously adhered to can paralyse. The trick is to know all this stuff and then somehow, despite it, find a way of writing with all the abandonment and energy and joy that was once the product of a happy innocence. Perhaps this is why I like the idea of doing more than one 'first draft'. In the 'first draft' you can quite happily be the half-blind explorer stumbling joyfully through a landscape full of surprises. (Or, if I must be consistent and return to my original metaphor, ploughing up an unfamiliar field in a dim light.) In that last 'first draft' you are sitting down with the experience of having explored the territory thoroughly before withdrawing from it, and can now take your ideal reader (yourself) on a joyful journey through a landscape where everything is already in place, suitably lighted, and where the most important landmarks can be visited with a confidence that all that *isn't* specifically visited is nevertheless *there* and lending the recorded story its reflected light. Even the thoroughly prepared guide, if he still cares, will find new breathing things to surprise and puzzle him. In fact, it's the well-prepared guide who is most likely to be aware of the newly-uncovered mysteries. Beware the story that doesn't leave you just a little puzzled. If *you* can thoroughly understand your story, Hodgins, the story can't be doing very much.

Leon Rooke

AUTHOR'S COMMENTARY ON
'IF LOST RETURN TO THE SWISS ARMS'

'If Lost Return to the Swiss Arms' is about an old man, lonely and poor, on his way to a slow death, but it is a story that makes *me* happy. I will explain. The story is twenty years old but I recall everything about it with total illumination. It is one of about ten stories (I was primarily writing plays then) I wrote while a student at the University of North Carolina. I too was poor, and *felt* old, so had no difficulty identifying with my character. (I was also lonely, like him I had a habit of waiting for mail, and I often dreamed that one day a nice girl would bring me soup and let me hold her hand. The old man was *lucky*; I was the person deprived.) My instructor at the time, Max Steele, a fine American story writer, sent 'Swiss Arms' to his editors at *The Atlantic, Harper's, Esquire, The New Yorker*, etc. They replied that they wanted *his* stories, not mine, not those of a yokel who could not spell *besieged* and who apparently thought the semi-colon was something one wore on the head. Steele ran out of editors, so I took over the story's submission. I submitted the manuscript monthly, tri-monthly, as regularly as it was returned. *Tree, Cloud, Goose, Grit*, and *Gumball*, among others, were each given their chance to snap it up. 'Sorry,' the reports came back, 'your story does not fit into our publishing programme.'

This reaction didn't faze me. What else were editors for? Such shoddy treatment, I perceived, could only toughen me up. I would go on as long as necessary drinking thin lemonade rather than Fitzgerald's champagne or Faulkner's bourbon. I had learned to delight in my rejections, and spent a

---

First published in John Metcalf, ed., *Stories Plus: Canadian Stories with Authors' Commentaries* (Toronto: McGraw-Hill Ryerson, 1979).

lot of evenings keeping them alphabetized. Why should I worry? I still believed 'Swiss Arms' to be a fair story.

Dish, Protoplasm, Melting Pot, and *The Yale Review* didn't think so.

I then acquired my first agent. Here was a man in New York City, a real go-getter in the largest agency in the world, what editor in his right mind would refuse good work sent to them from MCA? His favourite editors at *The Atlantic, Harper's, Esquire, The New Yorker* (*Vogue, Harper's Bazaar,* on and on) refused to give in. They didn't want a Rooke, they declared, they wanted a Flannery O'Connor, a Cheever, a Malamud, or more Letters to Peter from Catherine Marshall. 'You send us their work and you can bet your martini our response will be up-beat.'

Once again the story's fate was left to me.

Mush, Ilk, Groom, Bridebone, Dog, Punk, Gristle, Swampstump, The Antioch Review, and numerous other celebrated magazines subsequently turned down the story, a few 'after careful consideration'.

Four years passed. *Toad, Lug, Highwire, Flag, Truce, Kenyon,* and *The Virginia Quarterly Review* responded with thumbs down. The same at *Mother, Seed,* and *Air.*

Periodically during these years I toyed with and rewrote the opening sentence. Eventually I owned 447 drafts of that sentence, each beautiful. Sometimes, depressed, I would include these drafts with my submission, and invite an editor with wit to take his choice. No deal. 'Sorry, your story does not fit into our publishing programme.' Thinking more sentimentality might win the day, I added a weepy alternate title, 'Lay Me Down Like the Sun'. *Bash, Oink, Dingaling, Sewanee,* and *The Quarterly Review of Literature,* after lengthy waits, shot it back. Some claimed the story lacked beginning, middle, *or* end, others said it was too short or too long, or that it was insufficiently pithy.

Here was true criticism! My spirit soared, I was, I thought, well on the road. Smart men and women all over North America were beginning to take me seriously, and a most intelligent fellow in the Yukon Territories had even told me to 'Try again.'

Mug, Ointment, Blue Movie, Metcalf's Revenge, discovery, Frigate, A Stovepipe Hat, Oilcan, and *The Paris Review* were less enthusiastic.

I had of course during this long interval not been putting all my eggs under one chicken. Seven *other* stories had appeared, and it was rumoured that a much-talked-about national magazine was soon to publish a short novel of mine. As I saw it I had a firm reputation and it was with less and less frequency that I was stopping strangers on the street to complain that an editor wouldn't know a good story if he saw it. At about this time too the editor of *The Carolina Quarterly* went to a party and there overheard a woman complaining to other assembled females that I was 'the one to watch'.

So after 39 rejections 'Swiss Arms' finally saw print.

The following year, at that time to my surprise and later to my chagrin (not altogether: *worse* stories have been included), the story was selected for one of Doubleday's *O. Henry Prize Story of the Year* awards.

That made me happy.

The experience with 'Swiss Arms' taught me much that I consider of value in my survival as a writer: keep on paddling; the writer is his own best editor; write all your stories as if inside a church; don't begrudge the postage and never curse a postman; avoid *The Atlantic, Harper's, Esquire*, etc. (unless asked); develop satisfying hobbies; marry young to a rich and loyal person (who can and will type); keep out of bars until sunset; complain only to strangers; don't fall asleep in deep trenches; rewrite, if you must, your opening line (what is the biggest lie this man ever told?); make your characters nice people if you want your story to be loved; view every incident, however trivial, as a matter of life and death; never sit down in a restaurant unless you have money; learn how to spell *besieged*; accept that any blank page is your best friend and the deadliest of enemies; sleep in the nude except perhaps in winter; run off to Mexico or Greece or at least go out the back door once in a while; buy yourself a neck brace and a good back harness; mind your form; never write the same story twice; admit to no limitations; map the traditional, advance into the unknown; *all* subjects are taboo until tried; engage in no sleazy act as they deplete the soul; be a moralist; be God; be scores of different individuals and be faithful to each of them; have a notebook but never put anything of value in it; deliver finished manuscripts by night for fear of the Evil Eye; examine your face daily in the mirror as eyes have a habit of closing; should people ask what you do be quick to let them know you are a union electrician; to clean copper, brass, or bronze take one teaspoon salt, the juice of one lemon, and apply with steel wool; be versed in home remedies; always expect, demand, and work for miracles; always end with something a reader can sink his teeth into; be prepared to live with all your mistakes (such as this one); recognize clichés and know when to stop (them); never employ a title that can't tolerate an explanation.

TITLE EXPLANATION: It is my impression that readers customarily respond more warmly to my titles than they do to my texts. Friends, for instance, will avoid at all cost asking where I got a story – 'Swiss Arms' has as its model my grandfather – or what it means (too trapped, they would have me believe, by the glue of what happens), but they may ask where I got the title. (They are more interested in their own lives than they are in mine; from my point of view this is unfortunate.) ITEM: A hotel I once stayed in was known as The Swiss Arms. Naturally, in return for one's money one received a room key. Mine came, as often they do, with a plastic handle. On one side were the words THE SWISS ARMS. On the other it said IF LOST RETURN. A verity: behind every mystery resides simplicity. (Subterfuge breeds chaos is the corollary.) Of course I could have made use of the other words imprinted on the handle: POSTAGE PREPAID PLEASE DROP IN MAIL BOX THANK YOU THE MANAGEMENT. While I believe most good short stories are every bit as *complete* as good novels, I have to acknowledge that the story writer must be discreet about what he puts in. Also the rhythm seemed wrong.

Clark Blaise

TO BEGIN, TO BEGIN

Endings are elusive, middles are nowhere to be found, but worst of all is to begin, to begin, to begin.   (Donald Barthelme)

THE MOST INTERESTING THING about a story is not its climax or dénouement – both dated terms – nor even its style and characterization. It is its beginning, its first paragraph, often its first sentence. More decisions are made on the basis of the first few sentences of a story than on any other part, and it would seem to me after having read thousands of stories, and beginning hundreds of my own (completing, I should add, only about fifty), that something more than luck accounts for the occasional success of the operation. What I propose is theoretical, yet rooted in the practice of writing and of reading-as-a-writer; good stories *can* start unpromisingly, and well-begun stories can obviously degenerate, but the observation generally holds: the story seeks its beginning, the story many times *is* its beginning, amplified.

The first sentence of a story is an act of faith – or astonishing bravado. A story screams for attention, as it must, for it breaks a silence. It removes the reader from the everyday (no such imperative attaches to the novel, for which the reader makes his own preparations). It is an act of perfect rhythmic balance, the single crisp gesture, the drop of the baton that gathers a hundred disparate forces into a single note. The first paragraph is a microcosm of the whole, but in a way that only the whole can reveal. If the story begins one sentence too soon, or a sentence too late, the balance is lost, the energy diffused.

First published in John Metcalf, ed., *The Narrative Voice: Short Stories and Reflections by Canadian Authors* (Toronto: McGraw-Hill Ryerson, 1972).

It is in the first line that the story reveals its kinship to poetry. Not that the first line is necessarily 'beautiful', merely that it can exist utterly alone, and that its force draws a series of sentences behind it. The line doesn't have to 'grab' or 'hook' but it should be striking. Good examples I'll offer further on, but consider first some bad ones:

> Catelli plunged the dagger deeper into her breast, the dark blood oozed like cherry syrup....
> The President's procession would pass under the window at 12:03, and Slattery would be ready....

Such sentences can be wearying; they strike a note too heavily, too prematurely. They 'start' where they should be ending. The advantages wrested will quickly dissipate. On the other hand, the 'casual' opening can be just as damaging:

> When I saw Bob in the cafeteria he asked me to a party at his house that evening and since I wasn't doing much anyway I said sure, I wouldn't mind. Bob's kind of an ass, but his old man's loaded and there's always a lot of grass around....

Or, *in medias res*:

> 'Linda, toast is ready! Linda, are you awake?'

Now what's wrong with these sentences? The tone is right. The action is promising. They're real, they communicate. Yet no experienced reader would go past them. The last two start too early (what the critics might call an imitative fallacy) and the real story is still imprisoned somewhere in the body.

Lesson One: as in poetry, a good first sentence of prose implies its opposite. If I describe a sunny morning in May (the buds, the wet-winged flies, the warm sun and cool breeze), I am also implying the perishing quality of a morning in May, and a good sensuous description of May sets up the possibility of a May disaster. It is the singular quality of that experience that counts. May follows from the sludge of April and leads to the drone of summer, and in a careful story the action will be mindful of May; it must be. May is unstable, treacherous, beguiling, seductive, and whatever experience follows from a first sentence will be, in essence, a story about the May-ness of human affairs.

What is it, for example, in this sentence from Hugh Hood's story 'Fallings from Us, Vanishings' that hints so strongly at disappointment:

> Brandishing a cornucopia of daffodils, flowers for Gloria, in his right hand, Arthur Merlin crossed the dusky oak-panelled foyer of his apartment building and came into the welcoming sunlit avenue.

The name Merlin? The flourish of the opening clause, associations of the name Gloria? Here is a lover doomed to loneliness, yet a lover who seeks it, despite appearances. Nowhere, however, is it stated. Yet no one, I trust, would miss it.

Such openings are everywhere, at least in authors I admire:

> The girl stood with her back to the bar, slightly in everyone's way. (Frank Tuohy)
>
> The thick ticking of the tin clock stopped. Mendel, dozing, awoke in fright. (Bernard Malamud)
>
> I owe the discovery of Uqbar to the conjunction of a mirror and an encyclopedia. (Jorge Luis Borges)
>
> For a little while when Walter Henderson was nine years old, he thought falling dead was the very zenith of romance, and so did a number of his friends. (Richard Yates)
>
> Our group is against the war. But the war goes on. (Donald Barthelme)
>
> The principal dish at dinner had been croquettes made of turnip greens. (Thomas Mann)
>
> The sky had been overcast since early morning; it was a still day, not hot, but tedious, as it usually is when the weather is gray and dull, when clouds have been hanging over the fields for a long time, and you wait for the rain that does not come. (Anton Chekhov)
>
> I wanted terribly to own a dovecot when I was a child. (Isaac Babel – *and I didn't even know what a dovecot was when I started reading.*)

At least two or three times a day a story strikes me in the same way, and I read it through. By then I don't care if the climax and dénouement are elegantly turned – chances are they will be – I'm reading it because the first paragraph gave me confidence in the power and vision of the author.

Lesson Two: art wishes to begin, even more than end. Fashionable criticism – much of it very intelligent – has emphasized the so-called 'apocalyptic impulse', the desire of fiction to bring the house down. I can understand the interest in endings – it's easier to explain why things end than how they begin, for one thing. For another, the ending is a contrivance – artistic and believable, yet in many ways predictable; the beginning, however, is always a mystery. Criticism likes contrivances, and has little to say of mysteries. My own experience, as a writer and especially as a 'working' reader, is closer to genesis than apocalypse, and I cherish openings more than endings. My memory of any given story is likely to be its first few lines.

Lesson Three: art wishes to begin *again*. The impulse is not only to finish, it is to capture. In the stories I admire, there is a sense of a continuum disrupted, then re-established, and both the disruption and re-ordering are part of the *beginning* of a story. The first paragraph tells us, in effect, that 'this is how things have always been', or, at least, how they have been until the arrival of the story. It may summarize, as Faulkner does in 'That Evening Sun':

> Monday is no different from any other weekday in Jefferson now. The streets are paved now, and the telephone and electric companies are cutting down more and more of the shade trees....

Or it may envelop a life in a single sentence, as Bernard Malamud's often do:

> Manischevitz, a tailor, in his fifty-first year suffered many reverses and indignities.

Whereupon Malamud embellishes the history, a few sentences more of indignities, aches, curses, until the fateful word that occurs in almost all stories, the simple terrifying adverb:

Then.

Then, which means to the reader: 'I am ready.' The moment of change is at hand, the story shifts gears, and, for the first time, *plot* intrudes on poetry. In Malamud's story, a Negro angel suddenly ('then') appears in the tailor's living room, reading a newspaper.

> Suddenly there appeared ...
> Then one morning ...
> Then one evening she wasn't home to greet him ...

Or, in the chilling construction of Flannery O'Connor:

> ... there appeared at her door three young men ... they walked single file, the middle one bent to the side carrying a black pig-shaped valise....

A pig-shaped valise! This is the apocalypse, if the reader needs one; whatever the plot may reveal a few pages later is really redundant. The mysterious part of the story – that which *is* poetic yet sets it (why not?) above poetry – is over. The rest of the story will be an attempt to draw out the inferences of that earlier upheaval. What is often meant by 'climax' in the conventional short story is merely the moment that the *character* realizes the true, the devastating, meaning of 'then'. He will try to ignore it, he will try to start again (in my story 'Eyes' the character thinks he can escape the voyeurs – himself, essentially – by moving to a rougher part of town); he can't of course.

Young readers, especially young readers who want to write, should forget what they're taught of 'themes' and all the rest. Stories aren't written that way. Stories are delicate interplays of action and description; 'character' is that force which tries to maintain balance between the two. 'Action' I equate with danger, fear, apocalypse, life itself; 'description' with quiescence, peace, death itself. And the purest part of a story, I think, is from its beginning to its 'then'. 'Then' is the moment of the slightest tremor, the moment when the author is satisfied that all the forces are deployed, the unruffled surface perfectly cast, and the insertion, gross or delicate, can now take place. It is the cracking of the perfect, smug egg of possibility.

Clark Blaise

THE CAST AND THE MOULD

WHEN WE TRULY *apprehend* something from a story, when, years after we've read it, we are suddenly struck by the *appropriateness* of a word or an image or a character, it's often because we've gone beyond simple comprehension (comprehension is what they teach in schools), well beyond anything deliberately in the story or consciously provided by the author. It is because we have finally grasped the *world* of the story and have found ourselves suddenly viewing the surface of the story from precisely the same angle as the author. And instead of a shimmering reflection – beautiful, undeniably – we've suddenly seen far below the surface. We see structure and purpose and meaning and metaphor and we see the hidden nine-tenths of everything superficial in the story. We see, in fact, that the story was only a single example of something much larger, more diffuse, and practically unnameable. We may even return to that story ('I must go back and read that Cheever story ...') – and be disappointed by it. Was it really there? Or did we over-endow it? It's only when our own experience in some way unites us with the same meaning that the story (or the poem-painting-movie-or-music) will take on dimension, become permanent and living in our own imagination. Until that happens, art is cold and attractive and perhaps even admirable, but it remains basically an intellectual exercise. It's not yet *true*, and it's not haunting enough to be beautiful.

That cold, attractive entity we call a story is often a casting, something plastic poured into a mould, allowed to set, and then extracted, polished, and exhibited. The plastic is event; the mould is something akin to impulse, a trigger, an urgency to set it all down. A hall of castings is a book, like this

First published in John Metcalf, ed., *Stories Plus: Canadian Stories with Authors' Commentaries* (Toronto: McGraw-Hill Ryerson, 1979).

one. And what of that shaggy, disreputable, rusting, unlovely thing called a mould? That larger, encompassing, all-embracing *world* that contained all the delicate flutings within its heavy, iron-or-clay shell? Usually it's lost to us, smashed open by the artist as he extracts his finished product. And yet, I would argue, it very often *is* the story; it contained the story and gave it form and guided that molten flow in a thousand invisible ways. But once the flow had hardened, its purpose was served. It disappeared.

The reader's job, like the archaeologist's, is to reconstruct that mould, re-imagine it, to admire both the hand (the story) and the glove, that crumpled world that once contained it. No writer is comfortable confronting his theme head-on; it's practically impossible to say precisely what you want to say *and* to gain the effects you want to gain. That's a job for salesmen. But because the artist's message is mindful of so many things (including its own futility), the message is necessarily coded, textured, qualified. The writer trusts instead to the diligence of the reader and to time itself being on his side; time which will resurrect his work because part of his work – the mould of his work – always resided in timelessness, slightly beyond and above the story.

My stories 'Broward Dowdy' and 'The Fabulous Eddie Brewster' are 'war stories' or stories of a separate peace. 'Broward Dowdy' contrasts the squalor, intolerance, poverty, and brutishness of central Florida with a certain nobility of character, humility, and fundamental human decency. Two boys confront each other over the gulf of literacy and the all-important determinant of class. The narrator's family has temporarily fallen (due to the War), and that fall enables the narrator to glimpse at a life he would otherwise have dismissed. The War – an event that Broward knows nothing about, can know nothing about – has brought them together. Squalor and dignity can co-exist; the war is not confined to unnamed islands in the Pacific – the last image in the story conveys strongly the possibility that Broward Dowdy will also be a casualty.

'The Fabulous Eddie Brewster' is, of course, more comic; more of a 'tall tale'. It assumes a certain similarity between central Florida of the '40s and Vichy (Nazi-occupied) France during World War II. A man of many disguises who could prosper during one régime should do well under the other. And Etienne-Eddie manages very well. But I was also, consciously, talking about Canada and the French-English conflict, about losers and survivors, those who hang back (from moral scruples), those who dream but can't really act, and, finally, those who can take The Big Plunge, no matter what the consequences. I rather like the character of Eddie Brewster – sure he's a hustler and a cheat and a collaborator – he's not terribly admirable, but he's also around to establish a dynasty in his second, perhaps even his third, country. The *story* is about an immigrant hustler with a blot on his record; the *mould* (to me at least) is about extending oneself, from never leaving Regina, to never leaving the French-speaking ghettos of New England, to not taking the final plunge (in backing the brother with a little money), to ploughing ahead like some force of nature, starting over rather than yielding to bitterness, envy, or self-pity. Resistance, semi-transformation, and utter collaboration are all under scrutiny in this story (and they are the terms of our national dilemma); they were all attractive notions in my parents' generation, and that's what this story is about.

Clark Blaise

ON ENDING STORIES

STORIES BEGIN MYSTERIOUSLY but end deliberately. A writer can't really *will* a story to open, but, in the act of writing, the appropriate ending (event, tone, revelation, effect) will probably suggest itself. Most endings arise in the act of writing (a few stories 'arrive' so fully formed that the ending is as mysterious as the opening; the writer is rarely so fortunate), and they all share a single purpose: to give a final emphasis to a particular aspect of the story. Literally, it's the writer's last word on the subject: he'd better choose those words carefully. The opening anticipates the conflict. The ending immortalizes the resolution.

There are only two kinds of endings: those that lead you back into the story, and those that lead you – gently, or violently – away. I associate the first kind of ending with de Maupassant and Chekhov, and with modernists who adapted those stories for their own purposes – Hemingway, Joyce, James. Of authors who lead away from the story, who wish to emphasize the artifice of the story, or wish to address the reader directly, I associate dozens of our contemporaries. Impatience with art is as old as faith in art; the choice of ending is the battlefield for those particular feelings.

You are aware of stories that end with a let-down. 'That's it? It's over?' you ask yourself. There's a Hemingway story there are many Hemingway stories like it) that ends, 'Bill selected a sandwich from the lunch basket and walked over to have a look at the rods.' That's an ending? Norman Levine can fade out in the same way. It's subversive, of course, a subversion of the expected neatness of closure, the gathering up of narrative and thematic threads, the welling-up of music, the frozen gesture that summarizes *the*

First published in John Metcalf, ed., *Making It New: Contemporary Canadian Stories* (Toronto: Methuen, 1982).

whole meaning of the story.... We realize that the short story initially paid its debts to theatre, or to fable; audiences expected a big pay-off at the end. When it didn't happen, it was revolution, it was art. Chekhov subverted the expectation dramatically: his vision of a static, purposeless society required the destruction of climax and resolution; the lack of an expected ending makes us feel the lack of resolution, vitality, movement. It preserves tension. You can read that last paragraph, then go back in a circular fashion to the first sentence, and *it almost makes sense.* Joyce adapted the Russian vision to the Irish reality, seeing in that paralysis and indecision an opening to unconscious inhibitions. The so-called 'epiphanies' that end his stories are merely the revelation of the subconscious exerting mastery over the blighted, conscious lives. Joyce's stories end when the buried life is suddenly manifest. In their separate ways, James and Hemingway and a number of other modernists and their followers have done the same: sunk the ending deep in the story's texture, forced the reader to dig up the whole story in order to resolve its tensions. The author is not overtly helping the reader: the story *is* its ending.

I think of these endings as the most disturbing. They hit a glancing blow at the reader, but generally ignore him. By approximating the most casual of voices, they manage (in the hands of masters) to sound most urgent. By ignoring us, they speak to us directly. What remains unresolved and undisclosed becomes inviting and forbidding. They offer us no way out of their bland circularity; thus, they linger with us. For me, they are the saddest stories. (Certainly a mastery of that kind of openness, and that kind of 'dropped' ending, accounts for the remarkable power of the American author Ray Carver – a very contemporary Hemingway-like voice.)

Endings that lead us away from the story can do so gently or abruptly. The most traditional kind of ending is the one that serves as a prose equivalent to the theatrical last scene, the rising of music and receding of the camera, as lights go out, one-by-one, and characters fade off together in a figurative sunset. Such endings announce a faith in continuity, order, harmony – no matter what particular horrors may have been investigated in the story. They are sophisticated and traditional ways of updating the old 'happily ever after' ending so familiar from the fables. Even if the endings are thematically 'sad', they are formally (or cosmically) 'happy'; they lead us away from the specific exemplum (the story) to a generalized harmony.

They are religious in form, if not in content.

How can you detect such an ending? Well, they *sound* like endings. From Eudora Welty we get, 'Outside the redbirds were flying and criss-crossing, the sun was in all the bottles on the prisoned trees, and the young peach was shining in the middle of them with the bursting light of spring.' From Margaret Laurence's first collection, 'The sea spray was bitter and salt, but to them it was warm, too. They watched on the sand their exaggerated shadows, one squat and bulbous, the other bone-slight and clumsily elongated, pigeon and crane. The shadows walked with hands entwined like children who walk through the dark.' Again, from Laurence's second volume of stories, 'It seemed to me now that in some unconscious and totally unrecognized way, Piquette might have been the only one, after all, who had heard the crying of the loons.'

Such endings strike me as reassuring, reconciling. A writer with a disturbing, alienated vision probably would not employ such an ending (and, indeed, individual authors hold a number of endings in their repertory; as I said earlier, it all depends on the effect desired from any particular story). These endings, however, are 'safe', and they grow out of essentially recollective experiences; they are mellow, and they are the kinds of endings that self-conscious writers have instinctively subverted.

There are other endings to be discussed: they are violent or playful; metafictional or accusatory. In some stories, I think of the image of a trapdoor – Cheever does this well – in which the last paragraph is so *utterly* at odds with the material that has come before that an entirely new, last-minute interpretation is forced onto the whole story. (Why not? Anything that works is legitimate.) Cheever himself seems particularly fond of the ending to 'The Country Husband' (he even mentions it in the foreword to his *Collected Stories*). It goes like this:

'Here, pussy, here, poor pussy!' But the cat gives her a skeptical look and stumbles away in its skirts. The last to come is Jupiter. He prances through the tomato vines, holding in his generous mouth the remains of an evening slipper. Then it is dark; it is a night where kings in golden suits ride elephants over the mountains.

A rhetorical flourish, then – the opposite of the stoical close of Hemingway and friends. An impulsive reaching out; the tension between the dreamer and the fouled dreamland is always present in Cheever (it has its terse side, too; the ending of 'O Youth and Beauty!' reads, 'The pistol went off and Louise got him in midair. She shot him dead.'); Cheever's endings never slide off the page, and if they close with the music welling up, it's a full symphonic number.

I must confess to my own fondness for this kind of close – as though the full possibility of the story did not occur to the author (or to me, since I often use it) until the last minute. In both stories selected for this anthology, I used variants of this ending, choosing to close the nightmare of a Cincinnati school-day with questions about the promised land, and rounding off the tale of generational conflict, sexual discovery, disillusionment (all that stuff that won't let go of me) with a deliberately skewed vision taken from a different time and place, emphasizing the titanic force of connectedness, on the one occasion it had indisputably happened. (As Hemingway said in a different close, 'It was a good thing to have in reserve.' And as he said in another one, one that also won't let me go, 'Seems like when they get started they don't leave a guy nothing.')

There are other endings: the interrogative, ending with an accusing question that throws the whole story up in the air, but aiming it for the reader's heart. There are Judgemental endings, such as Flannery O'Connor's: 'The tide of darkness seemed to sweep him back to her, postponing from moment to moment his entry into the world of guilt and sorrow.'

All I would leave a good reader with is the injunction to look at endings as urgent, final communications. They are the cords we have bitten (sometimes only raggedly chewed) in the act of giving birth.

Margaret Atwood

HAPPY ENDINGS

John and Mary meet.
What happens next?
If you want a happy ending, try A.

A.   John and Mary fall in love and get married. They both have worthwhile and remunerative jobs which they find stimulating and challenging. They buy a charming house. Real estate values go up. Eventually, when they can afford live-in help, they have two children, to whom they are devoted. The children turn out well. John and Mary have a stimulating and challenging sex life and worthwhile friends. They go on fun vacations together. They retire. They both have hobbies which they find stimulating and challenging. Eventually they die. This is the end of the story.

B.   Mary falls in love with John but John doesn't fall in love with Mary. He merely uses her body for selfish pleasure and ego gratification of a tepid kind. He comes to her apartment twice a week and she cooks him dinner, you'll notice that he doesn't even consider her worth the price of a dinner out, and after he's eaten the dinner he fucks her and after that he falls asleep, while she does the dishes so he won't think she's untidy, having all those dirty dishes lying around, and puts on fresh lipstick so she'll look good when he wakes up, but when he wakes up he doesn't even notice, he puts on his socks and his shorts and his pants and his shirt and his tie and his shoes, the reverse order from the one in which he took them off. He doesn't take off Mary's clothes, she takes them off herself, she acts as if she's

First published in Margaret Atwood, *Murder in the Dark: Short Fictions and Prose Poems* (Toronto: Coach House, 1983).

dying for it every time, not because she likes sex exactly, she doesn't, but she wants John to think she does because if they do it often enough surely he'll get used to her, he'll come to depend on her and they will get married, but John goes out the door with hardly so much as a goodnight and three days later he turns up at six o'clock and they do the whole thing over again.

Mary gets run down. Crying is bad for your face, everyone knows that and so does Mary but she can't stop. People at work notice. Her friends tell her John is a rat, a pig, a dog, he isn't good enough for her, but she can't believe it. Inside John, she thinks, is another John, who is much nicer. This other John will emerge like a butterfly from a cocoon, a Jack from a box, a pit from a prune, if the first John is only squeezed enough.

One evening John complains about the food. He has never complained about the food before. Mary is hurt.

Her friends tell her they've seen him in a restaurant with another woman, whose name is Madge. It's not even Madge that finally gets to Mary: it's the restaurant. John has never taken Mary to a restaurant. Mary collects all the sleeping pills and aspirins she can find, and takes them and half a bottle of sherry. You can see what kind of a woman she is by the fact that it's not even whiskey. She leaves a note for John. She hopes he'll discover her and get her to the hospital in time and repent and then they can get married, but this fails to happen and she dies.

John marries Madge and everything continues as in A.

c. John, who is an older man, falls in love with Mary, and Mary, who is only twenty-two, feels sorry for him because he's worried about his hair falling out. She sleeps with him even though she's not in love with him. She met him at work. She's in love with someone called James, who is twenty-two also and not yet ready to settle down.

John on the contrary settled down long ago: this is what is bothering him. John has a steady respectable job and is getting ahead in his field, but Mary isn't impressed by him, she's impressed by James, who has a motorcycle and a fabulous record collection. But James is often away on his motorcycle, being free. Freedom isn't the same for girls, so in the meantime Mary spends Thursday evenings with John. Thursdays are the only days John can get away.

John is married to a woman called Madge and they have two children, a charming house which they bought just before the real estate values went up, and hobbies which they find stimulating and challenging, when they have the time. John tells Mary how important she is to him, but of course he can't leave his wife because a commitment is a commitment. He goes on about this more than is necessary and Mary finds it boring, but older men can keep it up longer so on the whole she has a fairly good time.

One day James breezes in on his motorcycle with some top grade California hybrid and James and Mary get higher than you'd believe possible and they climb into bed. Everything becomes very underwater, but along comes John, who has a key to Mary's apartment. He finds them stoned and entwined. He's hardly in any position to be jealous, considering Madge, but nevertheless he's overcome with despair. Finally he's middle-aged, in two years he'll be bald as an egg and he can't stand it. He purchases a handgun, saying he needs it for target practice – this is the thin part of the plot, but it can be dealt with later – and shoots the two of them and himself.

Madge, after a suitable period of mourning, marries an understanding man called Fred and everything continues as in A, but under different names.

D.   Fred and Madge have no problems. They get along exceptionally well and are good at working out any little difficulties that may arise. But their charming house is by the seashore and one day a giant tidal wave approaches. Real estate values go down. The rest of the story is about what caused the tidal wave and how they escape from it. They do, though thousands drown. Some of the story is about how the thousands drown, but Fred and Madge are virtuous and lucky. Finally on high ground they clasp each other, wet and dripping and grateful, and continue as in A.

E.   Yes, but Fred has a bad heart. The rest of the story is about how kind and understanding they both are until Fred dies. Then Madge devotes herself to charity work until the end of A. If you like, it can be 'Madge', cancer', 'guilty and confused', and 'bird watching'.

F.   If you think this is all too bourgeois, make John a revolutionary and Mary a counterespionage agent and see how far that gets you. Remember, this is Canada. You'll still end up with A, though in between you may get a lustful brawling saga of passionate involvement, a chronicle of our times, sort of.

*

You'll have to face it, the endings are the same however you slice it. Don't be deluded by any other endings, they're all fake, either deliberately fake, with malicious intent to deceive, or just motivated by excessive optimism if not by downright sentimentality.

The only authentic ending is the one provided here:

John and Mary die. John and Mary die. John and Mary die.

*

So much for endings. Beginnings are always more fun. True connoisseurs, however, are known to favour the stretch in between, since it's the hardest to do anything with.

That's about all that can be said for plots, which anyway are just one thing after another, a what and a what and a what.

Now try How and Why.

Norman Levine

I WROTE 'A Small Piece of Blue' towards the end of 1955 in St. Ives, Cornwall. I was waiting to go to Canada in order to do a trip across the country (the trip was to form the backbone of the book *Canada Made Me*) and had made a list of the places I would be going to visit. One of the places was Helen Mine, an iron mine in northern Ontario, where I had worked during the summer of 1948 after graduating from McGill University. In the autumn I would return to McGill for my M.A., then go off to England. Meanwhile I had to earn some money. A summer job, in the past, usually meant working in Ottawa, for the government, in an office. But there had been a war. I had been in the RCAF. And I didn't want to go back to what I was used to. So going to work in the mine was also an act of bravado.

I didn't have a clear notion of the story when I started. Only a definite intention – of wanting to show something of what living and working in this iron mine was really like. Yet, some of the ingredients in this story came not from the mine but from people and incidents that I had met elsewhere.

The woman with no nose – she came from Barnstaple, in North Devon. She was a music teacher and let out a room. I took it for a few months in 1954.

The shooting with the gun, indoors, at a lit candle was told to me about what went on aboard the French crabbers, anchored in the bay off St. Ives, at night.

First published in John Metcalf, ed., *Making It New: Contemporary Canadian Stories* (Toronto: Methuen, 1982).

The poem that begins:

All your experiences:
Those bits.
Those pieces you carried away with you.
How long will they last?

I wrote that separately, as a poem, in 1952. I had not long been married and we were staying, very briefly, with my wife's parents in London. I remember I was in a pub reading a newspaper. An American professor had come over to England to exhume a tomb to try and prove that Bacon had written Shakespeare's plays. There was another customer in the pub as well. We got talking. He said he worked at an undertaker's. And he told me some technical things about his job: what was the best wood to have and how even that didn't last very long ...

I did not think of these separate pieces as parts of a jigsaw that I had to get to fit in order to make this story. As I remember it, all I wanted was to write a story about the experience of living and working in the mine. And it was the pressure of writing the story that made me remember these disconnected memories. The pressure of writing the story was like a magnet that pulled these pieces from my past. And by the time I came to the part of the doctor I found I had to invent him in order to make the story work.

A few months after finishing 'A Small Piece of Blue' I was in northern Ontario again, at Helen Mine. And one of the first things I did was to go to the lake to see if it was shaped like a heart. It wasn't. And I don't know why I expected it to be.

'We All Begin in a Little Magazine' was written in the autumn of 1971. And I remember the circumstances clearly.

I had spent four years (1965-69) writing and revising the novel *From a Seaside Town*. It was published in 1970. Then I made a selection of some of the early stories and most of the recent ones for *I Don't Want To Know Anyone Too Well*. And that was published in 1971. All I had left were a few odd stories I had not included. I tried to earn some money by sending these to Robert Weaver at the CBC. He kept returning them. After returning the same story twice he asked me if I would write a new story for him, as a commission, for his radio series *Anthology*. (Ten years later, in Toronto, he told me it was the first time the CBC had commissioned anyone to write a short story.) I received Weaver's letter in Mordecai Richler's house on Kingston Hill, in Surrey. We had come up from St. Ives to stay in his house and have a London holiday, while he and his family went off for a holiday in Ireland. (It was not the first time that Mordecai let us have his house in this way.)

Two years earlier, in the summer of 1969, when I finished the novel, we had come to London for a three-week holiday, and found that the person whose house we had rented ran a little magazine. Somehow being in Mordecai's house surrounded by books and the magazines that I knew from my past ... and having been in a previous house in London where the person edited a little magazine ... then the commission by Robert Weaver who edited *Tamarack Review* – all these combined to get me thinking about my early years in post-war England. The ambitions to be a writer. The life we led. And the difference, now that I was one. It was this confrontation, of the past with the present, that set off the story.

As with 'A Small Piece of Blue', I can pick out bits and pieces taken from a variety of places and times. And George Smith, and his visit, is an invention. But the feeling of the life we lived (and a feeling of that time) before we became writers and painters – it was this that I tried to trap.

And I remember during that holiday in 1971 deciding, on an impulse, to go and see a painter who had been a good friend in those early years. And who I had not seen since. He was considered, then, one of the most promising young painters in England. A well-known London gallery had promised him a show when he had enough paintings. But that exhibition never did take place ... I finally traced him to his present address. He wasn't in. I'm sure that if we had met I'd have seen the changes in his face as he would in mine. But in the way of life (the bare rooms with the windows wide open, the paint peeling from the walls, the different bell-buttons by the front door that were not working) – in that he hadn't changed. And, it seemed, I had.

I sent the manuscript off to Weaver. He (promptly arranging for a new commission) said he liked it. And thought it was 'a sad story'.

Kent Thompson

I FIND ESSAY-WRITING DIFFICULT. I much prefer fiction. That's because, in essay-writing, you have to do one thing at a time; you must present facts, information, ideas, in a logical sequence. In fiction you can do everything at once, and there are so many tools available: dialogue, metaphor, tone, rhythm, punctuation, etc. You can do almost anything in fiction, particularly in the short story form, because you can suggest an infinite number of things.

One of the easiest parts of fiction writing is – at least for me – the 'significant' part: the underpinning of the story, the philosophical premise, the thoughtful aspect. That's because I've been teaching literature for some years now, and, besides that, I studied philosophy – and religion – as an undergraduate. The intellectual concern is virtually automatic.

When I was writing 'Perhaps the Church Building Itself' I began playing almost immediately with the ambiguity in that word *church*. We use the same word to refer to the building, the congregation, the dogma and creed, and the tradition. So the word opened up all sorts of opportunities. And one of the major emphases of the story is, I guess, that to me the Christian church as an institution has become middle-class and wishy-washy, and is therefore unable to reply to Benjamin Wilson's hard questions about life and death. He and his elderly friends – who make up the Church of the Old – want reassurance that their faith will be rewarded. They have given their faith to the church and have been promised Everlasting Life in return. Now they are worried about their investment.

First published in John Metcalf, ed., *Stories Plus: Canadian Stories with Authors' Commentaries* (Toronto: McGraw-Hill Ryerson, 1979).

But Reverend Williams does not understand that. He sees his duties as a clergyman as akin to those of a psychological counsellor and teacher, and he looks upon the Old People as if they were recalcitrant children. Therefore he tries to re-direct their attention. It's an old trick, well known to every Grade One teacher. He sends Benjamin Wilson off to prepare a report on *current events*.

And Wilson goes because he's a polite man. But of course, because he is old and very much concerned with his death, he spends most of his time evaluating his life. That's how we value life: we measure it against our inevitable death. So he tries to do his assignment as quickly and as easily as he can – like a lazy schoolboy – by looking for the black-bordered box in *Time* magazine.

It has been pointed out to me that this search is very symbolic – death and *Time* – and I won't deny that for a moment. However, I must admit that I did not realize the symbolism when I was writing the passage. Like Wilson, I was trying to do the assignment. The symbolism was a happy accident of the narrative.

Anyhow, Wilson looks back over his mortal, sensual existence for values, and finds them: the smell of the farm, the vistas of landscape, the white flash of a woman's thigh. And then he realizes it is too late. All that life is past him. He therefore – typically, perhaps – runs to the church. He wants reassurance, he wants an answer. And in crying out that he wants to die he is trying to get rid of his shame, atone for his lifelong ineptitude and guilt, and get safely to the other side to the promised salvation. His motives are in fact contradictory. Of course. But consider the verse which his mother chose by chance for his father's stained-glass window: 'Whosoever shall seek to save his life shall lose it; and whosoever shall lose his life shall preserve it' (Luke 17:33). That paradox is what I wanted: the dramatic paradox of life and death in the person of Benjamin Wilson.

Of course, Reverend Williams does not understand that dimension at all. He is ignorant of all theology. Perhaps I am here a little hard on the middle-class Protestant church.

But when I was writing the scene where Benjamin Wilson falls down on the steps of the altar, I was not much aware of the Christian paradoxes or the failings of the middle-class church. I was chiefly concerned with language. I was childishly pleased with the phrase I found to describe Wilson's slowly rolling hat: 'its openness upward'.

It is because fiction does so many things at once – particularly short fiction – that much of the composition is in fact unconscious. One works with intuition and the verbal imagination and the act of story-making creates the story in the same way that dreaming creates the dream. The activity takes over and fulfils itself.

And odd things do happen. For example, when I was writing the passage in which Wilson's mother flips through the Bible to find a suitable verse for his father's stained-glass window, I did not take the time to look up a verse right then. In fact, I simply left a blank space in the manuscript. It's still there. It wasn't until I was doing the first typed version that I took the time to look for something suitable. And when I did so, I used Wilson's mother's method. I flipped through the Bible and let my finger fall on a verse. It was Luke 17:33. It was the perfect verse. Not the *good* one. Not the *suitable* one. The *perfect* one. A shiver ran up my spine. That sort of thing is unsettling to those of us who live usually in what we think is a world governed by natural laws and principles. It's as if a prayer had been actually answered, immediately.

But that part of the writing – all the religious and philosophical concern – was at the back of my mind. I was more immediately interested in punctuating Benjamin Wilson's voice and getting the rhythm right. Northrop Frye tells an anecdote in *The Educated Imagination* which I think is instructive. He remembers that one of his teachers told him that if he got the rhythm right the sense would take care of itself. Frye says that although he himself would hesitate to give that advice to a student these days, there's a great deal of truth in it. I agree.

It is the rhythm, I think, which gives us our thoughts – our ideas, our characters, our voices. When all of them cohere they can sometimes astound us with awkward – maybe profound – revelations. And hard questions get asked of this too-easy world. Benjamin Wilson challenges his church. If the church cannot answer our questions of life and death, where shall we go for knowledge?

Where, indeed?

Hugh Hood

FLOATING SOUTHWARDS

AS OF DATE OF WRITING, December 1981, I've written ninety-three short stories, all of them published or about to be published, and I've written eight published novels, two early unpublished novels and a bit of a third, and I'm preparing another to be published sometime in 1984. I'm the only Canadian fiction-writer who has done so much in both forms. Richler? Goodish novelist but not much of a story-writer and wouldn't claim to be one. Laurence? Close, but the stories are clearly of secondary importance. Gallant? Primarily a story writer. Munro? Same thing. When I try to think of Canadian fiction writers who have excelled in both forms, my memory throws out the Morley Callaghan card and that's all. Davies? No stories. Aha, what about John Metcalf and Audrey Thomas? There are two writers who have written well in both longer and shorter forms. I can't think of any more.

My work has divided itself naturally and easily – with a smoothness that always surprises me – into two intimately related, co-operating parts. I have made it a habit for many years to work on a novel in the months from January to May. I'll do a first draft, take the ensuing summer and fall for other matters, then return to the novel the following winter and finish a final draft in May of the second year. For example, I wrote the first draft of *Black and White Keys* from January to May of 1980, and the final draft in the corresponding period of 1981.

In the summers I sail my boat, swim, insulate another bedroom at the cottage, mind my own business – my very favourite pastime. In the fall I'll write three or four stories. Novels: winter and spring. Stories: summer and

First published in John Metcalf, ed., *Making It New: Contemporary Canadian Stories* (Toronto: Methuen, 1982).

fall. Sometime or other I ought to sit down with a really competent literary theorist − not a deconstructionist − to see if any constant and specific relation can be found between the two interacting bodies of material, bundles of modalities. What do they have in common and what divides them, *for me?* I suppose that some writers can work easily on a novel and a short story at the same time − there have been times in my life when I did this − but now I instinctively prefer to keep the two enterprises rigorously separate as to time. I did write the opening of *The Swing in the Garden* in October and November one year, and that's the last time I undertook such a thing. I don't see any reason why stories come quicker and better in the fall than in the spring − and of course they don't. I think about my stories all the time I'm writing one or another draft of a novel. I keep a list pinned up beside my table of the next six to eight stories I intend to write, and I see it every morning. Right now, for instance, I'm thinking about three stories I plan to write in the fall of 1982, called 'The Blackmailer's Wasted Afternoon', 'We Outnumber the Dead' and 'Moskowitz's Moustache'. My experience has been that when a story gets far enough forward in my head for me to give it a title, I'll proceed at some time or other to write it. I expect to die with six or eight stories quite clear in my head, unwritten simply because I never got around to them. I'd better write the titles down somewhere before I go. Maybe one of my kids will want to carry on the business.

I could easily switch things around and write stories from January to May, and novels from September to December; it isn't the inner demands of form that dictate the arrangement, it's a matter of convenience more than anything else. Mind you, what seems mere convenience may be dictated by deep inner necessity. I like very much (suspiciously much?) to have a very long work to concentrate on through the depths of winter. January through to my birthday (April 30th), those are the times for novels. After Christmas, right at New Year's, you grit your teeth, type out your scenario and plunge into those heavenly opening pages with all the world of the possible before you; 'we were the first that ever burst into that silent sea.' There is no feeling quite like that in my experience. Those first sixteen to twenty pages, where you close off so many thought-over likelihoods and begin to see which avenues you will choose to follow, which reject. You refuse all invitations − and what bliss that is − and descend into the depths of the narrative. Writing a novel is a lot like dying, and very much like undergoing deep analysis. Then comes that extraordinary day when you pass the halfway mark in your outline and you perceive that everything from here on will be downhill racing, hazardous and speedy. The last hundred pages of a novel are like being reborn. I suppose novel writing is inwardly a wintertime process. Novels take time.

Stories intensify moments: there's the trace of the difference. I write stories in September, October, November, and I begin to flag in early December when I can sense the next novel-writing exercise looming big in my imaginings and feelings. When I'm writing stories, the year is beginning for me. As I've spent a large part of my life teaching, September is of all the months the one in which my life starts all over again.

What it is to write a story in September or October! You only have to look through the sunny warm fully lighted lemon-coloured atmosphere of 'The Small Birds' to see what my feelings can give me in mid-September. The story was composed in September of 1980.

Having said this much, I have now to confess that 'Breaking Off' was written in January of 1979, as one of a series of six stories that I wrote from October 1978 to May 1979 to complete the collection *None Genuine Without This Signature*. The story written immediately before 'Breaking Off' was 'New Country', in December 1978, and the following story, written in February 1979, was, appropriately enough, 'February Mama'. That brief period was the first for years, and will probably be the last for many more years, in which I was free to work on stories in mid-winter, and the reason is clear. I had taken a year off from novel-writing, something I will likely only be able to do once more in my life, for reasons which will be perfectly clear to readers of *The New Age/ Le nouveau siècle*.

If I'm to have my novel-sequence work out according to design, the final volume will have to appear in 1999, if possible on New Year's Eve, when the odometer turns over and we'll have the three zeros showing, two-zero-zero-zero, for only the second time since the beginning of the Christian Era. This is called taking the long view. If I'm to have my novels in the nineties coming out in the odd-numbered years, such that they end with 1999, I'll have to take one more year off sometime around the end of the present decade. At that time I'll probably write a few more stories around the beginning of a year. I hope they turn out like 'Breaking Off' and 'February Mama'.

From these notes you can readily draw three conclusions: 1. I'm obsessed with minute and specific arrangements of form, behaviour very familiar to psychoanalysis; 2. my stories and novels are fitted in and around each other in very close symbiosis like the yolk and white in one shell. Which is yolk, which egg? You tell me. Every reader has his own opinion. 3. a September story and a January story should show striking differences of form. In fact 'The Small Birds' and 'Breaking Off' do display very distinct qualities. When I wrote 'Breaking Off' I was doing it at a time when I felt like I should be working on long fiction. The story feels novelistic to me. It is the closest I have come to the novella or long story, and is based on a subject I had been mulling over since about 1948, more than thirty years. It is a very heavily charged *donnée*, too large really for the short story form. As I was writing it, I knew that I must condense, squeeze, truncate, compress, elide. As my novels do, this story signals the significance of extremely complex patterns of group behaviour – and linguistic usage – using individual lives as enactments of social forms; the story has embedded in it an ongoing criticism of various types of communication, such as, for example, the strange speech of parrots. I'm not talking about mere social history – any idiot can write social history – and I'm not primarily concerned with the multiplication of observed detail, although many of my critics have said that I am. I mean the way that membership in an army, a church, a big business, a social class, a language group, circulates like arterial blood (ha, a metaphor, no, a simile, anyway an explicit comparison for a change) into personal conduct in such a way as to make of occasional selected individuals immensely expressive representatives of what is happening in their world. Emmy and Basil are representative people in this specific sense, doing representative things. Not trendy things or symbolic things. Here I'm placing myself in a relation with Emerson, in his essay on 'Representative Men', and with Scott Fitzgerald, who considered himself all his life to be a man peculiarly endowed with a power to express in his life/work the immense social forces that were swirling around him.

Emerson was somewhat more ready than Fitzgerald to see the source of these forces in the will of the Almighty. To that will I would add the Divine Intelligence which is one with that will, and am happy to trace these currents to such a spring. In 'Breaking Off' my central imaginative preoccupation – the powerfully apprehended sensory schema which was lodged in my consciousness as I wrote – is that of an enormous chunk of ice, a part of the glacier, separating itself from the Arctic icecap and floating southwards on the current, gradually diminishing somewhat in size until it becomes an iceberg, smaller than at birth but still immense and capable of destroying the greatest human enterprise. This image is not found in the overt text of the story, except in the implications of the title. The social groups, the language systems, the courtship patterns, which Basil and Emmy share, form a mass like that of the southwards-moving iceberg with nine-tenths of its significance below the surface, but deadly. This isolated chunk of human culture – ourselves in the last third of this century – cannot speak to the times which went before us, cannot hear their voices. 'Breaking Off'.

The September story 'The Small Birds' is much less novelistic, much more characteristically what the textbook twentieth-century story is supposed to be: a compressed single image of a moment of experience so intense as to eternize itself and stand for the significance of many lives, perhaps all lives. It is for such moments that we live. The most important sentence in 'The Small Birds' comes close to the end. 'Invisible influences crossed in the upper air.' I originally wrote 'Invisible voices crossed in the upper air', but realized at once that some captious critic would insist that voices are definitively invisible, and so changed the word to 'influences', which gives a pleasing suggestion of the in-flowing (*Einfluss*) of spirits, water or grace. 'Crossed' fits in nicely too. The story builds up from our apprehension of the presence of spirits, and I don't think that I'll say any more about it. It might be my best story. It might be my only one.

Alice Munro

AUTHOR'S COMMENTARY ON
'AN OUNCE OF CURE' AND 'BOYS AND GIRLS'

'An Ounce of Cure' is a story I found ready-made, the only story I ever found like that. A friend told me an anecdote; there it was. Of course I used a lot of my own memories, my own teenage self, my own home-town. One thing in it I think is interesting, now that I look back on it: when the girl's circumstances become hopelessly messy, when nothing is going to go right for her, she gets out of it by looking at the way things happen – by changing from a participant into an observer. This is what I used to do myself, it is what a writer does; I think it may be one of the things that make a writer in the first place. When I started to write the dreadful things I did write when I was about fifteen, I made the glorious leap from being a victim of my own ineptness and self-conscious miseries to being a godlike arranger of patterns and destinies, even if they were all in my head; I have never leapt back.

'Boys and Girls' is a very different sort of story. I wrote it rather too purposefully perhaps, to show something, to show what happens to girls and women, then found I had to write about something that happens to boys too. It is one of my favourite stories but not at all one of the most successful; there is some disjointedness about it I have not been able to mend.

This is what I was trying to say: up until the time she is twelve or thirteen years old a girl feels free, able to think of her future in terms of action, to dream of adventure, heroism, power. With the full realization of her sexual nature a change is forced on her, partly from within, mostly from without. (This was true in my generation and, it goes without saying, in previous generations; I have hopes it is much less true today.) She understands that,

First published in John Metcalf, ed., *Sixteen by Twelve: Short Stories by Canadian Writers* (Toronto: Ryerson, 1970).

for her, participation in the world of action is not impossible, but does hold great dangers, the greatest danger being that it will make her not splendid, but grotesque. She must go back inside the house, inside herself, wait, dream of being beautiful rather than courageous. The full human powers she thought she had are seen to be illusory. She cannot make herself; a definition of herself, as a woman, is waiting for her. Unless she has fantastic strength or stubbornness she is going to accept that definition or at least compromise with it. This is painful; something crippling is happening to her.

But this very denial of action, of full responsibility to the girl, gives her a kind of freedom the young male in most societies must give up. To be accepted, to be fully male, he cannot criticize, he must sometimes partici- pate in, whatever bloodstained practices his society believes necessary to itself; that, or become a revolutionary. In this story the family is economi- cally dependent on the systematic killing of animals; if the boy wants into his father's world, he must learn to take part in this. It is the girl, already half shut-out, becoming mutinous, confused, critical, who is permitted the gesture of refusal. She is permitted it because she is 'only a girl'.

That is how the story ends. What it says is something like this: it is per- missible to have fine feelings, impractical sympathies, if you are a girl, because what you say or do does not finally count. On the other hand, if you are a boy, certain feelings are not permissible at all. So taking on these roles, whichever you get, is a hard and damaging thing.

Perhaps that is a big chunk of message for a slight story. Most readers seem to think the story is a nostalgia-piece and there are things in it that come from my own childhood. I did want very much to get the 'feel' of this life, of the economically isolated family, their self-contained world. I wanted to get the sense of childhood horrors, imaginary horrors which are a premonition of the real ones. When I read this story over I have a feeling of failure and despair; I feel that there's so much more that should be there, a whole world really, and I have strained it out into this little story and cannot tell if I got what matters. With 'An Ounce of Cure', on the other hand, I got everything down just as I meant to, there's no shadowy world unrealized behind it, so I'm satisfied, but I don't like it half as well.

It seems to me this is what writing is, when it's real – a straining of some- thing immense and varied, a whole dense vision of the world, into whatever confines the writer has learned to make for it, and this process, unless you are Shakespeare or Tolstoy, must be accompanied by regret; fortunately it is often accompanied by gleeful satisfactions as well.

Alice Munro

THE COLONEL'S HASH RESETTLED

A TORONTO CRITIC, discussing the story 'Images', said that the house in the ground – the roofed-over cellar that the hermit character lives in – symbolized death, of course, and burial, and that it was a heavy gloomy sort of story because there was nothing to symbolize resurrection. Typical of Canadian fiction, he went on to say, but I didn't follow him very far because I was feeling gloomy myself, about what he had said, and angry, and amazingly uneasy. Surely a roofed-over cellar doesn't mean any such thing, I thought, unless I want it to? Surely it's not that simple? I wrote the story, didn't I? If I hadn't sat down and written the story he wouldn't be able to talk about it, and come to all these interesting and perhaps profitable conclusions about Canadian Literature – well, he probably would have come to these conclusions all the same, but he would have had to dig up somebody else's story (I notice the choice of verb and never mind) to do it – so I get to say, don't I, whether a house in the ground is death and burial or whether it is, of all unlikely things, *a house in the ground?*

Well, the answer is no, I do not get to say, and I should have known that already. What you write is an offering; anybody can come and take what they like from it. Nevertheless I went stubbornly back to the real facts, as I saw them, the real house in the real world, and tried to discover what it was doing in the story and how the story was put together in the first place.

I grew up on the untidy, impoverished, wayward edge of a small town,

---

First published in John Metcalf, ed., *The Narrative Voice: Short Stories and Reflections by Canadian Authors* (Toronto: McGraw-Hill Ryerson, 1972). 'Alice Munro's essay was untitled. I entitled it "The Colonel's Hash Resettled" to echo the title of an essay by Mary McCarthy which explores the meaning of "symbol". That essay can be found in *The Humanist in the Bathtub.*' – J.M. (1972).

where houses were casually patched and held together, and there was a man living in a house exactly like that – the roofed-over cellar of a house that had been burned down. Another man and his wife, I remember, lived in the kitchen of a burned-out house, whose blackened front walls still stood, around a roomful of nettles. (What is that going to symbolize, if I use it in a story some day?) Such a choice of living-quarters was thought only mildly eccentric. It was a cheap and practical way of getting shelter, for people with no means to build, or buy, or re-build. And when I think of the slanting, patched roof and the stove-pipe, the house as a marvellous, solid, made, final thing, I feel that I have somehow betrayed it, putting it in a story to be extracted this way, as a bloodless symbol. There is a sort of treachery to innocent objects – to houses, chairs, dresses, dishes, and to roads, fields, landscapes – which a writer removes from their natural, dignified obscurity and sets down in print. There they lie, exposed, often shabbily treated, inadequately, badly, clumsily transformed. Once I've done that to things, I lose them from my private memory. There are primitive people who will not allow themselves to be photographed for fear the camera will steal their souls. That has always seemed to me a not unreasonable belief. And even as I most feverishly, desperately practise it, I am a little afraid that the work with words may turn out to be a questionable trick, an evasion (and never more so than when it is most dazzling, apt, and striking), an unavoidable lie. So I could not go now and look at that house with a perfectly clear conscience, symbol or not.

I do think symbols exist, or rather, that things are symbolic, but I think that their symbolism is infinitely complex and never completely discovered. Are there really writers who sit down and say yes, well, now here I need a symbol, let's see what I have in the files? I don't know; you never know how other writers work. In the case of that house, I gave it to the character without thinking about it, just as I gave him the whisky-drinking cat that actually belonged to the father of a friend of mine. I don't remember deciding to do this. I do remember how the story started. It started with the picture in my mind of the man met in the woods, coming obliquely down the river-bank, carrying the hatchet, and the child watching him, and the father unaware, bending over his traps. For a long time I was carrying this picture in my mind, as I am carrying various pictures now which may or may not turn into stories. Of course the character did not spring from nowhere. His ancestors were a few old men, half hermits, half madmen, often paranoid, occasionally dangerous, living around the country where I grew up, not living in the woods but in old farm-houses, old family homes. I had always heard stories about them; they were established early as semi-legendary figures in my mind.

From this picture the story moved outward, in a dim uncertain way. When this was happening I was not so much making it as remembering it. I remembered the nurse-cousin, though she was not really there to remember; there was no one original for her. I remembered the trip along the river, to look at traps, with my father, although I had never gone. I remembered my mother's bed set up in the dining-room, although it was never there. It has actually become difficult to sort out the real memories – like the house – used in this story from those that are not 'real' at all. I think the others are real because I did not consciously plan, make, or arrange them; I found them. And it is all deeply, perfectly true to me, as a dream might be true, and all I can say, finally, about the making of a story like this is that it must be made in the same way our dreams are made, truth in them being cast, with what seems to us often a rather high-handed frivolity, in any kind of plausible, implausible, giddy, strange, humdrum terms at all. This is the given story (I hate to use that adjective because it calls to mind a writer in some sort of trance, and seems to wrap the whole subject in a lot of trashy notions, but it will have to do) and from that I work, getting no more help, doing the hard repetitive work of putting it in words that are hardly any good at all, then a little better, then quite a bit better, at times satisfactory.

The story 'Dance of the Happy Shades' is done in the form of a memoir more or less as a matter of convenience. I have stories that come from inside and outside. This is a story that came from outside. But now that I write that, I wonder if it is a true distinction. When I get something from outside – in the form of an anecdote told at a family dinner-party, as this was – I have to see it in my own terms, at once, or it isn't going to be a story, however much in superficial points of interest it seems to be crying out to be made fiction. The *I* of the story is a masquerade, she is a little middle-class girl I never was, an attempt to see the story through the eyes of the relative who told it to me. But once I got used to being her I could, as in the other story, remember things – the house, the dresses, Mary Queen of Scots; I was not told any of that.

Writing or talking about writing makes me superstitiously uncomfortable. My explanations have a way of turning treacherous, half-untrue. Now I distrust the way I used the word *remember*, in the last paragraph. I could have said *invent*; the kind of remembering I mean is what fictional invention is; but I wanted to show, too, that it is not quite deliberate. I feel like a juggler trying to describe exactly how he catches the balls, and although he has trained to be a juggler for a long time and has worked hard, he still feels it may be luck, a good deal of the time, and luck is an unhappy thing to talk about, it is not reliable. Some people think it is best when doing any of these things – dancing, say, or making love – to follow very closely what you are about. Some people think differently. I do.

Alice Munro

ON WRITING 'THE OFFICE'

'The Office' is one story whose beginnings I can talk about fairly easily. Most stories don't grow out of a particular incident; they are such elaborations and combinations that it is very hard to figure out what they started from. But 'The Office' is about something that happened to me in 1960 or 1961, in Vancouver. It is the most straightforward autobiographical story I have ever written.

I had started to write a novel but I could not get on with it. I had the usual problems of women trying to work at home. Unexpectedly, I got a bit of money – I think it may have been from the sale of 'Dance of the Happy Shades' to *The Montrealer*, or it may have been from a sale to *Tamarack Review*, either way it would have been a hundred dollars – and I rented an office in the shopping centre near where I was living. I went there four mornings a week when my younger child was at nursery school, and sometimes on Sundays.

From the beginning the experiment was not a success. I had huge ambitions, as most young writers do, and the problem of reconciling those ambitions with my abilities was far greater than the problem of working at home. In the bare room above the drugstore I could not find any more excuses and I could not face the truth, either. I spent hours staring at the walls and the Venetian blinds, drinking cups of instant coffee with canned milk, believing that if I concentrated enough I could pull out of myself a novel that would be a full-blown miracle. The landlord's visits frequently interrupted my concentration. And the fact that they interrupted not my writing, but my painful, sweating, desperate non-writing, made them even more unwelcome

First published in Edward Peck, ed., *Transitions II: Short Fiction. A Source Book of Canadian Literature* (Vancouver: CommCept, 1978).

than if they had halted temporarily a comfortable flow of work.

Perhaps I should have put that into the story. I think I didn't because I couldn't face it at the time.

The landlord kept making suggestions for my comfort, and bringing me things I didn't want, and telling me stories, for instance the one about the chiropractor. My being a woman, young and apparently docile, made me a natural target for his heavy, wheedling, patronizing, never quite offensive attentions; my being, or claiming to be, a writer gave him an opportunity to tell me many of his observations and experiences, in the hope that I might write them down. There was also in his conversation a peculiarly enraging, sanctimonious smuttiness, and the suggestion that maybe a writer wouldn't find these things he related as shocking as he found them, because writers were known to be broad-minded.

At first I loathed this man and myself for putting up with him, for answering his knock, for smiling when I wanted to scream. And then it started to happen, the real small miracle, when something, someone, starts to live and grow in your mind and the story makes itself. I didn't even recognize this as anything to be grateful for. I was annoyed, because my preoccupation with the landlord was cutting into my efforts to bring forth something important and beautiful, some real writing. I didn't want to write another story. For years and years I didn't want to write more stories. I feel that way yet some of the time, but am resigned.

Then I thought I had better write it down and get rid of it so I could get back to my concentration, and I did. It took about three weeks (maybe less). I stayed in the office four months and never wrote another word, but I did get my first ulcer.

It is a little bit rearranged and pointed up to make a story. I think if I were doing it now I'd write it differently. That doesn't mean it might be better, just different. If I were doing it now I'd make the fictionalizing less evident. It is only when you look back over the years you've been writing that you see you have – at least I have – been following certain literary fashions. When I wrote this story, something a bit more definite had to happen in stories than is the case now. Or that's how it seemed to me. And that accounts for the way the story is wrapped up, with the landlord's accusation, the confrontation, the narrator leaving. That isn't quite what I'd do now. I don't know what I would do. I'd like it more open, less pointed, even less contrived; I would like it to seem all artless and accidental, which means that I have adopted another fashion. By fashion I don't mean some currently popular tricks – though there's always a bit of that – but a way of making the story that seems now to get closer to what I want to say.

I hope it will be clear, now, that the incident in a story isn't what seems to me essential. 'What happens' can vary – that is, I could tell this story in another way – but what the story is about, what made me write it in the first place, is always the same. And what is that? It is the landlord's clamorous humanity, his dreadful insistence, which has to get the better of that woman seeking isolation. It is also, but rather incidentally, about a woman's particular difficulties in backing off and doing something lonely and egotistical. And just as the landlord had to break in on the woman in the story, the story had to break in on me and my grand design, but of course I didn't know what was happening, then.

Ray Smith

AUTHOR'S COMMENTARY ON 'COLOURS'

I. INTRODUCTION.   A writer can usually say what his work is, but he cannot so often or so easily or so accurately say what it is about.

'All right, "Colours" is a short story, *so you say*. But what is it *about?*'

'Ohhh ... this and that ... people ... truth and beauty....'

Let me suggest that a story is about what the writer was concerned with
when he wrote it. This seems simple enough. You might say:

'When he wrote "Colours", Smith was concerned with searching. This is
clear from the plot, what there is of it, and especially from the last two paragraphs. We all live in search of something – happiness, contentment, love,
etc. He writes about a man who goes about asking questions. To us these
questions seem idiotic. People like Gerard should be locked away. But Smith
is using extreme exaggeration to show us that we may not always understand
the searches of others, the reasons behind their lives. Just as the business
man may not understand the movie star's search for fame: "Veronica V.
wants publicity", he says, "because it helps her at the box office. The more
famous she is, the more money she gets." He cannot see Veronica except in
terms of his own search; he cannot see that while she enjoys the pleasures
that money can give her, she loves fame more. It is this failure of understanding, failure of sympathy that Smith was concerned with; so this is what
the story is about.'

Well, Smith answers, that's all very true, but it is not the whole truth.
Otherwise I would have written the last two paragraphs and not bothered
with the rest of the story.

First published in John Metcalf, ed., *Sixteen by Twelve: Short Stories by Canadian
Writers* (Toronto: Ryerson, 1970).

2. MAIN TITLE. The writer says what the story is about *in the whole story*. He does this in a variety of sneaky ways and for a variety of sneaky reasons. But he always presents all the evidence. He begins with the title: *War and Peace*; *The Tragedy of King Lear*; *Gone with the Wind*. This last is the sneakiest, being a metaphor and not explaining what exactly is gone.

I have given my story an eight-line title; each part has an additional title. This should seem odd right off: a 1,000-page novel has a three-word title – *War and Peace* – while an eight-to-ten-page story has an immense title. From this you can conclude that I am going out of my way to be sneaky; that I am interested in the technique of titles; that the story is to some extent about titles; that an examination of the titles will help in understanding the story.

'SOED' stands for *Shorter Oxford English Dictionary*. You should be able to read the story without it, but it will help you with certain curious or key words. 'Colour' and its variations are a good example of this. 'A particle of metallic gold' is a metaphor for the breaking of the story into five separate parts, each of which is meant to be pure, glittering, valuable. Some would add precious.

'To misrepresent' is a bit of cuteness: the story is very obviously fictional, fiction also means a lie, while a writer will claim fiction is truer than fact.

'Indirection' refers to the method of the story. An essay, like this one, should proceed in a logical and direct way through an argument or explanation. A story moves by its own rules and reasons which are often not clear, even to the writer, until after the story is done.

'Episodes', as noted, is discussed in Part II. Gerard compares his life to a pearl necklace, and his life is the story. A necklace is valuable because of the value of each pearl. When a woman wears a necklace we do not see the string though we know it must be there. So I have tried to write a story composed of five 'pearls' (like five particles of gold). The reader cannot see the string or plot, but he should be able to deduce it as a line-through from the way the incidents hang together.

3. PILLSBURY. The titles to each part operate in the same way as the main title. 'Q.v.' means 'which see'; that is, look up 'sombre' and 'rich' in the SOED. Neither is quite so applicable as 'colour'. They describe the mood I was trying to catch. 'Rich' is often used to describe the colour of port.

'London (memory of, not locale)' is about atmosphere. The English climate is so cold, damp, and miserable that Englishmen and their writers have a natural interest in cosiness. If you have read some Sherlock Holmes stories you were probably struck by the cosiness of the rooms at 221B Baker Street. Whenever Holmes readers feel cosy while the wind moans outside the window or the fog gathers about the streetlamps, part of that cosiness is due to the memory, however unconscious, of Holmes and Watson in their overstuffed chairs, the fire casting a warm glow, the pipe smoke drifting between them. It was the memory of this London sort of cosiness I was trying to catch.

Pillsbury, an Englishman, has found a London kind of niche, presumably in Canada. He is a bit of an eccentric with his antique bicycle, he is an amateur scholar (not a professional in a university), and he keeps up the old traditions of tea and port.

Cosiness, the peace of finding a niche (his rooms, his research, his small fame), certain English traits – Part I is about these things.

'... a little girl rather like Alice' – in Wonderland.

'EHR' – *English Historical Review.* Scholarly journals are usually referred to by their initials.

'In desperation he alluded ...' – Gerard is rather indirect himself.

'Tibet' – Holmes spent some time there.

4. PATCHOULI: A genre piece is a scene that has been done before and will be done again. Most painters will do a 'Mother and Child' or 'Madonna and Child'. Writers have to do party scenes, waking-up scenes, lovers' goodbye scenes in train stations.

Parts II, IV, and V are genre pieces: the theatre dressing room, the game of chess, the death-bed. You could make a moderate case that the Pillsbury scene is one too. A genre piece gives the writer an extra dimension to work with because the reader can be presumed to have read similar ones. Every dressing room scene you have read (or seen in a movie) will add something to this one.

Dressing rooms are often used by artists to deal with the big question of 'What is real and what is illusion?' Actors have faces but they disguise them with make-up. They can almost become Hamlet or Lady Macbeth. Patchouli's make-up is so extreme that it has no relation to her face. (A friend of mine, a painter, once met a stripper with make-up like this.) She does sexy dances on stage, takes stomach pills in the dressing room. Which is the real Patchouli (surely that's not her legal name?), which the illusory one?

'Patchouli' is a penetrating Indian perfume.

'Kant' – We all ask ourselves the big questions from time to time; philosophers make it their business. Emmanuel Kant (1724-1804) was a German philosopher reputed to be good with big questions.

'Marrakech' – If you don't know where it is, consult an atlas, one of my favourite books.

'... an exotic' – trade term for belly dancer.

5. THE PAINTER.   I suppose this section is about casualness, a sort of indirection. The dialogue is casual, Gerard and the painter are casual with each other, the painter speaks casually of his work. It is also about repetition: the repetition of certain words, especially in the first two paragraphs. This comes up again in the next part. The pork chop game is also repetitive.

There are no extra titles because I am an artist like the painter. Most of what I am is being a writer. I think we all would find it difficult to describe ourselves or our professions in a few words. Besides, the whole story is a commentary on me, on artistry, on the short story. I could have put 'repetition' in the title but did not want to draw attention to it.

'... blue north light' – Light from south or sun windows is yellow. North and south light both affect the tone of paint colour, but painters traditionally consider north light more neutral for some reason.

'... the fanatics' – Would the sculptor in Part IV be one?

'... it's a living.' – An artist is trying to make pictures or stories of truth and beauty. This is his day's work. He doesn't succeed all the time and so needs immense arrogance to keep on. But to make himself bearable to others he will often pretend he is modest or casual about it.

'... thick ankles' – Painters will often become interested in features we do not necessarily consider beautiful.

'... a square' – Friends of mine used to play this game in Dominion Square in Montreal.

6. ASP.   An asp is a poisonous snake found in Egypt and Libya, famous

because Cleopatra committed suicide by embracing one. See the SOED for 'tableau'.

This scene is a formal and elegant one. The style is supposed to be appropriate to the setting and the mood. There is symmetry in the seating of the characters. But by the end certain things have cracked. The symmetry is broken by Gerard's exit; Asp's veneer of poise is cracked when we see her crying; her chess set, room, world appear shattered through her tears; and something in Gerard's so-far polite character is broken for us, we see him a bit differently, a bit selfish or cruel.

The jungle is the world that goes on far below Asp's peaceful penthouse; it is the morbid and violent fate of the sculptor; it is what we glimpse behind Asp's veneer.

Pastel is the colouring of the apartment and the soft colouring of the technique. I was trying to work a number of subtle shifts in tone, mood, character, sentence structure. If I succeeded, you should be able to feel them, but should have difficulty in saying just how it was done.

'Lorraine' – Claude Gellée, known as Le Lorraine because that is where he came from, was an eighteenth-century painter remarkable for his delicate handling of light.

'Tinkle tinkle rasp' – Asp's laugh is part pastel, part jungle.

'9 ... N-K5' – Ask a chess player. Also ask him if the move and its implications are appropriate.

'... and daffodils. God!' – The writer takes an indirect snipe at Wordsworth's poem 'Daffodils'.

'K.550' – Mozart's manuscripts were placed in chronological order by Köchel. His initial precedes the number he gave.

7. MR RUFULUS.   Besides what the SOED tells you about Ultima Thule (see 'Thule') it means the death of Mr Rufulus and the end of the story. It is also the end of whatever suspense the reader has felt over the hidden significance of Gerard's questions: there is none. The reader who believes a story should have a plot must now decide either to throw this one in the garbage or to look for some other point to it. There is no law that a story must have a plot. Most do because a plot holds the reader's attention: 'I want to see how it comes out.' This reader, looking for a satisfactory resolution to the suspense, is liable to be frustrated with 'Colours'. Plot is also seen as a

line-through of actions, causes leading to effects. Clearly, 'Colours' does not have this.

'Crispness' is the hospital atmosphere, the sheets, the nurse's uniform. It is also Gerard's obsession with accuracy and precision which has been evident throughout. Notice his phrasing to Mr Rufulus about the eyelids or the last few lines of Part III.

I am unable to figure out the meaning or reason for the incident with the photograph. It has to do with illusion and reality, with accuracy and evidence, with Gerard's loneliness. Sometimes I feel it works, sometimes I feel I should cut it out. Maybe I will one of these days.

'Thule' is also a town in a most appropriate place.

'Mr Rufulus' orifices' tubes' – This is only the most obvious example of the sort of word play I and some readers find amusing. Others find it annoying, outrageous, disgusting. Depends on your taste.

8. CONCLUSION.   The crispness of Part V is also my own striving for precision and accuracy, for the exact word, phrase, setting. Increased concern for *le mot juste* does not necessarily improve the work. Dostoevsky never used one word when ten would do, Hemingway never one when none would do. In 'Colours' I have tried to write for clear and easy reading: you should always know where the characters are, who is saying what, you should never have to read a sentence over twice to get the sense of it. But if you are willing to linger a bit over the somewhat obtrusive precision work, you may get great pleasure out of Asp's exact chess move or checking to see if the chess books mentioned are real and, if so, how good they are.

You can say that *Hamlet* is about a guy trying to avenge his father; that *Macbeth* is about a guy trying to usurp the throne of Scotland; that 'Colours' is about a guy who goes around asking weird questions. I can't speak for Shakespeare, but I have tried to show that my story is about many other things. I have mentioned most of the important ones: titles, plots, England, a dictionary, make-up, casualness, genre pieces, soft lights, accuracy, etc. I have not mentioned that it is also about the use of the semi-colon (so is this essay); the use of 'he' (first paragraph, Part V); the naming of characters (I figured you'd see that); contrasts (Pillsbury's room and life – Patchouli's); and so on and so on.

A story is many more things to a writer than to any one reader. Even a careful reader would not have seen all the things I have mentioned; but he might have seen things I haven't mentioned, even things I can't see or can't recall putting in. Another might enjoy reading it through quickly, noticing only a few things in passing. You should not have to use the SOED, know where Thule is, or have seen paintings by Lorraine to enjoy the story, though I make it clear they will help. You definitely don't have to play chess.

'I don't know art but I know what I like' is valid to a point. But the more you know about art the more the liking, the more pleasurable the quality of the liking.

Jack Hodgins

BREATHING FROM SOME OTHER WORLD: ON WRITING THE SPIT DELANEY STORIES

ABOUT A YEAR AFTER the 1976 publication of my first book, *Spit Delaney's Island*, an ad appeared in the Classified section of a Victoria newspaper. LOST, a small black spaniel (if I remember correctly), male, answering to the name Spit Delaney. I began to suspect that when you write fiction you may be setting loose much more than you think in the world.

Just *how* much more, I had yet to learn. Recently the two short stories about Spit Delaney were adapted for both radio and the stage. During the intermission of the stage production's preview night, I was approached by a fellow who'd grown up in the same rural community as I had, eager now to talk about the recognitions and memories provoked by the play. He was sure he knew who Spit was, he said, giving me a sideways sort of look that said 'you cheeky bugger'. He recalled several incidents out of his own past as a childhood friend of 'Spit's' – incidents I hadn't known before but which I mentally filed away as material for a future story. 'Old Spit! Old Number One!' He laughed, and shook his head. 'By golly, that's just the way it was!' After the final curtain, however, someone else cornered me to express quite a different reaction. That was certainly not the way *she'd* thought of Spit! She was, in fact, insulted. That the performance had not reinforced precisely her own impression of the character was a personal affront. 'Spit Delaney is us!' she said, indicating members of the departing audience. 'How *dare* they do this thing?'

Driving home down the long dark Island highway that night, I had plenty of time to wonder at what I'd witnessed. What did it mean, that others felt they had taken possession of a character I had released to the world?

First published in *How Stories Mean*.

Were people fooling themselves when they insisted that Spit Delaney spoke, or felt, for them? I didn't know, but I found myself recalling how Spit had come into being – fifteen years before.

Like many of my stories, this one (or rather, these two) began with my parents. Their down-Island visits have always included a round-up of the latest developments in the lives of relatives and friends and acquaintances in the Comox Valley. This time they had news about a certain uncle who worked in the pulp mill north of my parents' farm where he operated the company's steam locomotive, hauling rail-cars of pulp and newsprint on and off the barges. 'I guess you haven't heard what's happened to Fred', my mother suggested, knowing very well that I hadn't.

Her face told me this would be worth pursuing.

'Well,' she said, 'they've sold his locomotive! Just like that. One of the museums in Ottawa bought it. Took it away.'

I knew immediately what a blow this must have been. 'That train was the centre of his life. How's he taking this?'

'Well, *yes!* We always teased him about it. The mill would have to shut down if he wasn't up there every morning exactly at four, getting up his head of steam. Now they're giving him a diesel!'

My father said, 'He's had one of these here painters go into the mill and paint it for him. Old Number One – before they take it away.'

'An oil painting?'

'They've got it hanging over the fireplace', my mother said. She didn't need to say: 'Can't you just *imagine?*'

'And he's got the number off the front hanging on the rec-room wall.'

'And made a tape of the loci before they took it. *Hours* of it! He sits and listens.'

He did more than sit and listen to his tape. He took it with him wherever he went, my parents said. He especially liked to take it into the mountains when he and my aunt went on fishing trips in their truck and camper. 'He waits until all the other people have gone to sleep around the lake – in their tents and campers and RV's – and then he puts the tape on and turns it right up full blast! Watches them come running out, wondering how in hell a train got up where they were!'

'Really,' my mother said, 'it's something that ought to be put in a story.'

It wasn't the first time she'd said these words. In fact she had said them often over the years – still does. This time she was right. And if someone ought to put Uncle Fred in a story, obviously she intended it to be me. I started to work the next day.

It seemed that little needed to be invented. At least at first. I gave my uncle a new name (as I've done again here) and simply recorded what had happened to him in a manner which combined a rapid narrative exposition with brief scenes that included dialogue. But then, when I came to where I was about to set a scene in a lakeside campsite in the Vancouver Island mountains, I found myself thinking *What if he didn't stop there? What if he carried this obsession farther afield? What if he took his tape to some other continent? Europe!* I'd been to Ireland recently, and thought I could imagine the sort of uproar he might create in a foreign country. Part of the fun was watching the exasperation of his poor family.

As I wrote this sequence, though, I began to see that somewhere along the way his wife had lost my aunt's sense of humour about the situation. This wasn't the least bit funny to Stella Delaney. I wasn't at all sure what to do next. Back up and *give* her a sense of humour, let her become his partner in this eccentric performance? Or see how far she could be pushed, see what might happen when she reached the limit of her endurance?

Should I alter a character who seemed to have a mind of her own, in other words, so that she wouldn't spoil a good anecdote? Or should I listen to her (and to him) and follow wherever they might take me? I was stalled. I'd written quite a good anecdote, I thought. It was humorous. It was about an appealing character. It included an entertaining sequence of events. But it was not, I felt, a story. Or at least it was not a story that satisfied me. Something important was missing.

The something important that was missing was something which I'd come to recognize in the fiction I most admired: a richness, a complexity which suggested that the experience, however entertaining, was beginning to catch some small illuminating glimpse of meaning beyond itself.

Excitement died. The original urge to record the anecdote had been satisfied. The part of me which is a lover of good literary fiction had come along and spoiled everything. I put the draft away.

(Of course I might have chosen *not* to put it away. I wonder now what difference that might have made. I was, after all, an avid reader of Erskine Caldwell! If I had believed I had written a satisfying story and had found someone to publish it, would I, by now, be happily and successfully publishing humorous anecdotes about eccentric characters, repeating a happy formula in book after book? Volume Twenty-three of the shenanigans of Spit Delaney and his eccentric relatives! Instead of still trying with only modest success to write fiction which at least *attempts* to track down and secure a glimpse of some small corner of truth, I might be – what? But there is no use thinking about this sort of thing now. However entertaining a well-told anecdote might be, the repetition of any winning formula becomes, I suspect, an accumulating lie. Good fiction, though based on made-up things, endeavours to tell the truth. And the writers I admired most – Faulkner and Chaucer and Steinbeck, amongst others – had managed to do that 'something more' without altogether jettisoning their love of the eccentric tale. Better to risk failure in trying to join the writers I've admired. I thought this then – I still do.)

Spit Delaney lay dormant for a year while life (mine) went on without him. I did some revisions to a collection of stories which had been accepted for publication – my first book, still untitled. I worked on a novel which looked so unlike any novel I'd ever seen that I practically feared for my life. I taught highschool English by day, taught nightschool English by night, directed a television play for students, finished a couple more rooms in the house, fixed broken toys, attended family reunions, read novels and collections of short stories, and dreamed (ludicrously) of one day selling enough fiction to make it possible to quit teaching.

Then, one day, I found the Spit Delaney piece and reread it. It was a good anecdote, just as I'd remembered. But it hadn't, during its time in the drawer, become what I was pretty sure it was capable of becoming.

All at once it was as though an assortment of ideas and images which had been sitting idly by in their various corners (twiddling their thumbs) came rushing in from every direction to collide in a moment, setting off an explosion. It seemed that during that year of Spit Delaney's dormancy I had been preoccupied (on and off) with a number of topics which almost certainly related to Spit and his predicament.

I had, for instance, watched a number of friends go through the anguish of ending a marriage – separation from a companion and from a lifestyle which had been central to their lives for several years. In particular, I was given plenty of opportunity to see what a separation could mean to a man in his forties who had taken his marriage's stability for granted. More than one friend confided his feelings of having been devastated by the experience – nothing remained solid, everything had to be re-evaluated, life had taken on a brand new colour. In more than one case it had happened all at once, a surprise. I imagined how I might react to such a thing myself. If all these people were genuinely surprised by the collapse of their marriages, who would be next?

I had visited the west coast of Vancouver Island during this year, fascinated with its wild spectacular beauty, and more than once had wondered to what extent living on the western edge of a continent affected a people. (Any place which interests me must be stared at until I can glimpse what it must mean to those who live there. Even then, I find myself poking at it until it suggests a metaphor. Where was the metaphor in living at the ragged green edge of the world?) A magazine article drew my attention to the attitude of native Indians to the coastal dividing line between land and sea – stories of Kanikiluk, the monster who came up out of the sea and changed people into fish, fish into people. I read of the fissure that lies beneath the sea not far from here, the crack in the ocean floor which oozes molten stuff from the underworld, pushing the continents apart.

Separation, separation. Land and sea, human and fish, husband and wife, man and family, adult and plaything, man and work ...

During this year I had also, not incidentally, been able to observe how my uncle had recovered from the blow of the lost locomotive. In fact he was doing quite well. While holidaying in California he'd received a call from Ottawa. To his delight, the officials hadn't been able to put Old Number One together again. They needed him. They flew him directly to Ottawa and paid expenses while he lent his expertise to their dilemma. His wife, though almost as exasperated as Stella Delaney by the constantly listened-to tapes, did not show any signs of letting this affect their marriage. She seemed to delight in accepting – as all members of my family seem to accept quite joyfully – that a person's obsession, however eccentric, is what defines him best.

Perhaps this was what I needed. Spit and my uncle had parted company. By reacting so differently from the original, my character had freed himself (in my mind) to take charge of his own life in his own way. I was ready to try a new draft. Remaining as faithful as I knew how to the language and

personality of the Spit of the anecdote (that is, by falling into the remembered idiom of my growing-up place) I allowed those various other related
matters to join the story and help nudge Spit Delaney through his rapidly
collapsing world.

Of course there was more to be done than mere 'nudging'. If Spit and his
experiences were not to be mere entertainments any more, to be observed
with amused smiles, I was faced with the need to build something else. He
and his story – his life – were to be constructed in such a way that a reader
travelling past (or through) the words would be taken on a journey of the
emotions which might approximate Spit's own journey, or might at least
allow the reader to empathize with this imaginary person. And I had nothing at all from which to build this man but words.

He had, of course, a name. A gangly name, with the rise and fall of his
own long step. The first a rude, rustic nickname with some explosion in its
sound. (No passive kindly Trevor, no fancy Roderick, not even an ordinary
solid Pete. His was a name you could put in your hands and *expect things
from*.) An Irish surname, a peasant name, but of the sort that originated
elsewhere in the misty past. French aristocracy well and truly hidden? More
than the eye might see, though the eye be accustomed to stretching things a
little.

Being first a name, he then became an image. 'People driving by don't
notice Spit Delaney.' Why not? If people driving by didn't notice him, was
he worth looking at? Perhaps the reader would like to be someone who
didn't just drive by. (An invitation to read.) If that was the case, then what
was there to see? An old gas station, some second-growth firs, a scalloped
row of half-tires planted instead of a fence, a figure seated on a big rock,
scratching his narrow chest. A man on a rock. Watching the world go by.
Watching the world go by that had no time for watching him sit still. A few
words flung at the page in such a way that they assembled themselves into
something resembling a sketch of a sitting man.

Muttering. He was also a sound. A complaint. An unhappy long-necked
man in an engineer's cap, giving a side-tilted look. Muttering. An attitude:
he despised those who noticed him – hitch-hikers – as much as he was fascinated by them. 'Stupid old fool.' Yet he grinned at the grizzled old man
with the yellowed beard.

And thinking: I am a wifeless man. Spit Delaney was nobody's uncle now, nor was he the full-blown holograph result of some magician's spell. He began to take life, if he took life at all, from the words: a name, a collection of images, a sound, an attitude, a thought, a sentence spoken aloud (though not by him). 'There's enough in the fridge to last you a week.' His wife Stella thus pronounced his doom – which would last, presumably, for quite a bit longer than a week.

Then a hitch-hiker's gaze caught Spit's gaze and something changed. Spit might be made up of words but the words included an assumption. He had assumed that he was a survivor – until now – a man in his forties who thought his marriage was safe. It seemed that it wasn't as safe as he thought. This man-made-of-words was thrown for a loop just before we met him, it seemed, by this shocking discovery. Nothing in life was quite as safe, apparently, as he'd thought.

Thus the process of revising the story was a matter of quite literally re-visioning it – that is, not trying to 'fix up' the earlier draft but seeing it again from a new perspective and starting all over again. This time the impulse was not a tale heard and a desire to retell it – or at least not *only* that – but the explosion that occurred somehow in my imagination when those various elements collided. New life – its own – had begun there. My job was to find it, and keep it breathing, and help it seek out its end. Building it line by line out of words.

Hitch-hikers helped me get started. Because here was something else which had happened during that year. Suddenly you couldn't drive a mile along the highway without feeling you were part of an observed and commented-upon parade. All along the gravel shoulder, hitch-hikers in violently coloured clothing (or in almost no clothing at all) sat or lay or occasionally stood with thumbs upraised, heading for the west coast – nude beaches, make-shift driftwood communities, 'plenty of good grass, man, and friends from all over the planet'. (Earth had ceased being a world about that time and had become a planet instead, making us feel as if we'd just stepped off a space ship and didn't know whether we ought to stay.) If these hitch-hikers had been brought up on Vancouver Island, they would know that the idea was to keep on walking when you weren't thumbing cars – to show you intended to get where you were going with or without the help of someone else's gas. These people took an all-or-nothing approach, not knowing this would offend the native view of things. 'If you don't pick me up, I'll lie here spoiling the view until someone does.' I did not drive over any of them myself. Nor did I especially feel a need to. But I knew many who would, heard many who planned to, saw many come as close as anyone dare. Spit Delaney would hate them, I thought. Going somewhere (while he went nowhere), they thought the next guy ought to take them there. At the same time he would be fascinated by them: if he was forced to look at them, he could also imagine that they might look at him as well. See someone *suffering*, in fact.

Listening. Listening. That's what it took. Not listening to some voice from the clouds, not listening to the characters themselves as though they could stand up and give me orders. But listening to what the story was trying to tell me as it revealed itself. In words. Its secret life. I wasn't changing all that much as far as the sequence of events was concerned. What I had done was allow a cartoon figure to become a human being whose pulse I could take; what I was doing now was keeping that heart beating long enough to let him find out – or not find out – what was happening to him. Words – the sound and shape and meaning of words – supplied the blood. Sentence grew from sentence to complete the job.

When poor Spit, beset like Job, opened his mouth and shouted at me, quite uninvited, from the edge of the sea, I learned very quickly why his story was one I wanted to pursue, why all those related matters had been preoccupying me. They were all shouting the same thing at me that much good writing does, all *living* does: how do you determine where the line is between the real and the unreal, the lasting and the temporal? Spit had simply been unfortunate enough to run headfirst into a question I thought my entire lifetime might be what I'd need in order to answer.

When all this listening and staring and rewriting had finally led me to the moment which I recognized must be the end of the story, right where I'd expected to find a resolution there was not much of a resolution at all. Stripped of his marriage, his family, his job, his home, and his sense of purpose, he had grown only enough to be aware that he *had* a problem. I left him crying out in his anguish: 'Okay, you sonofabitch, where is that dividing line?' However hard I looked I found nothing to suggest any other kind of ending for this story. It was done. A few attempts at closure simply flapped like torn gaudy rags off the end. I threw them away and sent the story to my editor with the suggestion that it be added to the story collection which still awaited publication – and that another be taken out to make room. He agreed. Life – the rest of life, that is – could, I thought, go on.

It did. So, however, did Spit. That story's end may have been good enough for literary purposes – it was definitely over – but somehow it was not good enough for *me*. It took me six months to realize that I was more than a little worried about the welfare of that man I'd left howling out his anguish on the edge of the sea. How was he making out? I found myself thinking: What is Spit Delaney doing at this moment? Have he and Stella got together again? Has he made some sense of his life? Has he fallen apart altogether?

Occasionally I'd felt something similar after reading other people's stories but I'd felt no impulse to do anything about it. This was different. It wasn't someone else who'd left Spit howling like that, it was me. Eventually I determined to find out what had happened to him. And the only way I knew of finding out was to write another story about him. Spit Delaney a year later. No one else need know what I found. I didn't need to publish the results. I'd just do this thing for myself.

I tried several times without success. I planned, mapped out a story. (According to some inherited notion of how a story should take shape, ignoring my own better knowledge.) Tried to employ all the techniques which had gone into the making of the first story. Took up the same narrator's voice, the same language, the same point of view. One paragraph, two paragraphs. It didn't work. Try again. It didn't work. Why? Because I was trying to continue the old story instead of making a new one. Because I was trying to *manufacture* a story. Instead of being the builder who walks onto a piece of land and wonders what it offers that could be used to advantage – how a house could be designed to fit around that beautiful tree, how a garden could make use of that awkward hump of rock, how that creek might run past the living room window instead of being buried in pipes and culverts beneath the ground – I was trying to be that builder who walks onto the lot with a commercial plan designed in some New York office and published in a magazine. 'Cut down those trees. Blast out that rock. We'll put the Cape Cod house right here where it can overlook the Strait of Juan de Fuca.' Maybe there was no real reason to write the second story after all.

But: I could not rid myself of the notion that Spit himself wanted me to do this thing. Apparently I was not to know what his reason was until I'd written it.

The solution, it seemed to me, was to abandon my attempts to tell the story of what happened to him and let him tell it himself. This time instead of being the teller I'd be the listener. Let the bugger surprise me.

He did. I found him in a little seaside motel called the Touch-and-Go, willing to tell me something he would never tell his friend Marsten or his landlady Mrs Bested. Something significant had indeed happened to him since I'd seen him last, or had begun to happen. He'd met this woman –

Naturally the woman who would intrigue Spit enough to start his life back on course (or wreck it altogether) would have to be a member of that class of hippie hitch-hikers he despised. Naturally she would lead this discarded man to a second-hand store; naturally she would challenge this man who'd been too attached to a train with a world of cast-off *things*; naturally she would invite this legless man she'd found floundering at the ocean's edge to come climbing with her in the mountains. The rest was entirely up to him.

This second story, quite unlike the first, presented itself in a single writing, once I'd decided to let it be told in Spit's own voice. Very little revising seemed advisable. I'd received the man's report and read it; there was nothing left to do but send it off to join 'Separating' in that collection of stories which *still* awaited publication, where it would replace another story and give the collection the title it had been waiting for. One story would open the collection, the other end it. Book-ends, reviewers would say. This late-comer would not only give the collection its name and control its structure, he would – it turned out – give the appearance of having got there first and set the agenda. This first collection chosen from stories published over the years in magazines – simply 'my best so far' – had altered its character slightly, taking on a frame that gave the book the feeling almost of a collection of linked stories. Indeed, in the years since then, I have several times seen the book referred to in print as a novel. This is fine with me. I still have the feeling that, in a sense, Spit *deserved* a book of his own.

There is no lesson in any of this. Some stories arrive as gifts to be copied down and passed on, most to be tossed away. Others require planning and sweating and long periods of gestating while waiting for the fortuitous collision of related elements – to be followed by draft after draft of re-visioning, rethinking, reworking.

In subsequent years, stories (and indeed novels) have continued to arrive in one or the other of these two different ways: the collision of separate and apparently disparate elements (some of which were clumsy earlier attempts that failed and some of which were thin and unsatisfying anecdotes and some of which were obsessions and preoccupations I thought were quite outside the world of my writing) or the excited journey spent chasing along after the voice of a character who has something he feels compelled to tell me. Something, I hope, to surprise me.

And that is the one element common to all stories which begin to satisfy me – surprise. The hard long work of rewriting drafts is as much a search for the unexpected and unexplained as it is an attempt to make things better and clearer. I consider any story of little interest if all that it ultimately accomplishes is what I'd intended. I even want to be a little unsure that I fully understand it. The only stories which give me sufficient pleasure that I can bear to send them out into the world for other eyes to see are those which, when I read them, make me wonder where on earth they came from.

I want to discover myself putting down a story and thinking 'I wish I'd written that!' for a split second of wonder and envy before realizing, with joy, 'Hey, I *did* write that!' It doesn't happen often, but it's something I aim for every time.

And all these years later, when I discover the number of people who feel possessive enough about the character of Spit Delaney and his problems to express vehement opinions about the manner in which he is interpreted on the stage, or in the radio adaptation, I realize I do not have the capacity or the tools to explain satisfactorily to myself or to anyone else how it was that this man and his story came into being and got loose in the world. Sometimes I am playing with fire, sometimes with magic, sometimes merely with little black figures on a page. Always, always, though, I am indulging in the marvellous business of constructing a *story*, of building a structure out of words, of spinning out a yarn, of listening to the heavy breathing from that other world.

Norman Levine

SOMETIMES IT WORKS

WHEN I START a story I don't know how it will end. Most of the time I don't know how it will develop. These things happen while I'm working. And how they happen has to do with a method of working that I stumbled on, by chance, and that I have used since.

I began by writing verse. (The first publications were two thin books: *Myssium* and *The Tight-Rope Walker.*) When I started to work on short stories the method I used was the one I used for writing verse. I would write the first sentence then go onto the next. And if I got stuck with the third I worked on that sentence until I had it right. Then I would type out these first three sentences and work on the fourth until I had that right. And so on. By the time I came to the last sentence the story was finished and it was neatly typed.

After a few years of working like this I became bored. And one time, I wrote as far as I could then – instead of working on the next sentence – I made a jump forward. And went on to write a part that may have been suggested by what I had written before. Or it may have been instinctive. Whatever, I felt much freer working this way. And enjoyed it more. And it also opened up the story in ways which I could not foresee.

These jumps ahead – and sometimes the jump went backwards or even sideways – became my normal way of working. And when something like an ending suggested itself I would go back and reread these fragments – for this is what they were – and see what I could do to improve them.

What was, usually, needed was some technical device to hold the fragments together. Later, I found that if I was able to solve this difficulty I often pushed the material onto another level.

First published in *How Stories Mean.*

In 'Because of the War' – the first short story that I wrote when I returned to live in Canada – commissioned by Robert Weaver for *Anthology* – I had these fragments – about Europeans living in Toronto. When I finished it I knew the fragments didn't hold together. No matter what I tried nothing seemed to work. After six or seven months, when I thought I had exhausted the possibilities, I decided to introduce a new character, a Mrs Kronick.

On the way back I saw Mrs Kronick.
    'What have you been doing?' I asked.
    'I was walking down Yonge Street', she said, 'and I thought of the people I knew who are dead. What have I done with my life?'
    I didn't know what to answer.
    'You have a son', I said.
    'Yes', she said gently. 'That's what I have done with my life.'

She appears, in another scene, at the end of the story.

I was walking by the store that showed the time in the capitals of Europe when I saw Mrs Kronick on her way back to the apartment. She had on a smart black and white suit and a large black hat.
    'I'm leaving, Mrs Kronick.'
    She looked at me for a while. Then said,
    'When I leave a person, I don't care if I never see them again.'
    'But what about those you love?'
    'Of course', she said, 'with those you love there's always regret.'

There are only three of these short scenes with Mrs Kronick scattered throughout the story. But they have the effect of stitching the story together. Without Mrs Kronick the story just wouldn't work.[1]

---

[1] *From a letter:* 'I don't know why she draws the fragments together – but she does. As to how – I'm only guessing, but it could be because when she appears she appears in short, *self-contained* scenes. Where all the others are loose, open-ended. Or it could be that when she appears *again* ... it is like a tune in a piece of music. Because it is repeated, it becomes familiar, and holds the thing together.'

This method of working I worked out when I lived in St. Ives, Cornwall. Although coming to St. Ives, in 1949, was an accident, it was no accident that I grew up as a writer by being with painters. It was seeing Ben Nicholson go out with a sketch pad – and draw the beached boats on the sand in the harbour when the tide was out – that made me take out a notebook and try to describe what I could see. Much of what I was seeing was new. As was the way of life. If I noticed anything – I wanted to translate it into words. Watching a crow, or a rook, fly across –

The beat and the still
And the beat, caught, lift,
Of the rook and the gull
Over sea, roof, hill,
Disturb this place from sleep.

The last line was 'comment' which I would drop when I wrote prose. But it was the first line – describing the way the bird flew – that made me realize that the leaner the language the more ambiguous it becomes, and the more suggestive.[2]

Another thing I got from the painters was the need for immediacy. When they finished a painting they wanted me to see it in their studio. And there it was. At a glance. Through the eyes. Onto the nervous system. I remember thinking: how could I get this immediacy in writing? And I remember Peter Lanyon telling me, in his studio, that all that mattered was the work.

'You take something from life. Make something from it. Then you give it back into life.'

Also from the painters was their enthusiasm for writing and for books. They were well-read. They talked well. And, from their conversations, they

---

2 *From a letter:* 'The more you tell – the more you are keeping the reader out from bringing his or her experience in. So if you can reduce a thing to a minimum like 'The beat and the still' – then the reader brings his or her associations to that. So contrary to what people think: the more cryptic you are the more resonance there is. Think what makes a good title. Just a couple of words: *Adult Entertainment* ... *Thin Ice* ... (of course you have to get the right words) ...'

made me want to work more. They also had a good critical sense. And I soon realized that the better the painter the sharper the critical sense.

The one from whom I learned the most, in these conversations, was Francis Bacon. He would talk about the technical difficulties that he encountered in painting. But he would also go off in all kinds of directions, and be very direct. And I remember, after we had talked for hours, that the essence of good conversation was the same as for writing. He talked about so-called ordinary things then, unexpectedly, said something that was memorable. And then went on to talk about ordinary things.

One of the things that he said early on – in November 1959 – was that seeing a painting (we were talking about Rembrandt's late self-portraits) was an emotional experience. 'It unlocks the valves of feeling' was the way he put it. And another painting 'suggested an opening-up into another area of feeling altogether'. I had not thought of painting in that way before. Nor writing – where I felt it even stronger. Until he clarified it.

But these conversations (he was witty about people: 'embroidered hesitancy' was how he described the talk of a painter we both knew) were not entirely one-sided.

I remember once I had gone up from St. Ives to London on the overnight train from Paddington. It would have been 1963 or 1964. And went to see Francis where he lived and painted in a mews in South Kensington. We sat and drank coffee and smoked Gauloises and talked. We got into talking about what was difficult. He said that as soon as you introduce another figure on the canvas the interest divides immediately. And I said that the most difficult thing I found, so far, was trying to describe someone going to the toilet. I ended a bad first novel with just that.

He was silent for about a half-minute.

Then said.

'That would make a good picture.'

Next time I came up to see an exhibition he had at the Marlborough Gallery, with Henry Moore, there was a new triptych. The left-hand panel showed a male nude, his back to you, sitting on the toilet.

I was also lucky to have lived in St. Ives when one way of life (fishing) was dying out and the new one (tourists) hadn't yet arrived. And during this time, I began to get letters from Canada. Some would have a postscript to say that someone I knew had died. And for the next few days I would think about this person. How, for a while, our lives were connected. Then I decided to write a story – as a kind of tribute. The stories 'The English Girl', 'A Father', 'South of Montreal', and 'Hello, Mrs Newman' came about this way. And in writing them I tried to be as close as possible to what I had seen and felt.

That impulse is still there in some of the more recent stories. Except now what sets them off is rarely what the story will be about. I expect it to change in the writing – often in an irrational way – and it will be the better for it.

I started to write 'Django, Karfunkelstein, & Roses' as a tribute to my literary agent. It soon changed into a story about how memory works. 'A Maritime Story' began as a kind of memory of Desmond Pacey who lived in Fredericton and was at the University of New Brunswick. It soon changed into a story about an entirely different character: a German Jewish refugee living in the Maritimes (with his near-senile mother) and missing Europe.

Sometimes a story will come about because of an unexpected confrontation between the past and the present. ('In Lower Town', 'We All Begin in a Little Magazine', 'Class of 1949'.)

Some of the recent stories I have been carrying around for years. ('Gwen John', 'Tricks'.) Then they surface and seem to demand to be written. And I write them quickly. The working out was done while carrying them.

Others come about in a more immediate way.

I was with my wife in France in the summer of 1981. We went to Dieppe for three days before taking the ferry to England to fly back to Toronto.

While in Dieppe we, accidentally, came across the beach where a stone memorial said it was the beach where the Canadians tried to land, on the morning of August 19th, 1942, and most were killed or taken prisoner.

I didn't think I would have any feelings about this. But on the ferry back to England I told my wife that I would like to go to St. Ives (at that time I still rented a place where I could go in order to work) and write a story. Could she fly back to Toronto and I would join her in about a month's time.

I did write the story in St. Ives in a month – but I could not get an ending to it. I would work in the morning then go out at noon for a walk. Up the slope of the steep hill, to the other side, where Porthmeor Beach was with the cemetery above it. And walk towards the small Bronze Age fields, with the stone fences, by the cliffs. Then come back the same way. Still no ending.

This went on for two weeks. Then once, on my way back from the walk, I saw the cemetery above Porthmeor Beach (I must have seen that cemetery, over the years, thousands of times) and noticed that all the gravestones were pointing the other way. What I was seeing were blank gravestones. And I knew I had the ending to the story.

There is often a small part – inside the story, earlier than the ending – which you need to have – which is pivotal – without it – it is usually a sentence or two – the story won't work. And it is only something that comes about while you are writing.

In the Dieppe story, 'Something Happened Here', it is the second sentence of this section.

I sat in a seat on deck, at the stern, facing Dieppe. The ferry turned slowly and I saw Dieppe turn as well. The vertical church with the rounded top, the cathedral, the square, the houses with the tall windows, and wooden shutters, and small iron balconies.[3]

And in the last story, 'Soap Opera', of the new collection it is this:

He said. 'Nothing lasts. Everything changes.'
Was this why we keep making connections? Why do I connect Gino's sculpture to that tall brick chimney to those saplings with Joseph Podobitko

---

3 *From a letter:* 'If I were a teacher, I would think a student bright if they could pounce on the sentence or two where the essence of a story lies – rather than "the main theme" and "the minor theme" that professors seem to reduce things to, as a way of teaching.

'"The ferry turned slowly and I saw Dieppe turn as well."

'(That is another example of the leaner the language the more suggestive.)

'What is visually happening, in the present, connects with the past – what happened in Dieppe in 1942, and earlier. And that is for me the pivotal part of the story.

'Besides this ... I was correcting the galleys for "Django" ... and the key sentence there is: "I had, over the years, changed these things in order to remember them".'

to Mr Thomas Sachs on the door of the hospital room to those little Jewish cemeteries on Roselawn?

But then, whenever I go to a new place and walk around to get to know it, I inevitably end up in a cemetery.

I know that readers often expect an author to comment on what is taking place. And on the significance of the experience that has happened. I usually don't. What I like is for the writer to present things as directly as possible. And let the reader respond to what is on the page. And, especially, what comes off the page.

This leads to a question that I am often asked. How autobiographical is the work? Which is very difficult to explain. (It is not as autobiographical as it reads.) And does it matter?

If readers considered how they live their lives with their wives, their husbands, their children, parents, relatives, close friends, acquaintances, those they work with, strangers they meet. And saw how inventive they are, how evasive, how direct. Even in conversation – while one person is talking – the other listening will interrupt – because of something just said. And by replying will move the conversation away, from what was talked about, onto something else. They would get a glimpse of just how close they are to the way fiction is written.

And of course all this inventiveness, in our everyday life, signifies nothing for the most part. It is just a pleasant way of passing the time. Perhaps it is that for a writer as well. But he does try to connect the personal with something larger. And sometimes it works.

Keath Fraser

NOTES TOWARD A SUPREME FICTION

I WAS BORN in India at the end of World War II. My mother had come to Calcutta in the hope of welcoming my father alive out of Burma where she believed the Japanese had interned him. They had. The Indian army brought him down in a truck to Rangoon from a hospital near Prome. Then, because of a mix-up, instead of his coffin being shipped to Calcutta, it ended up, after a ten-week voyage via Hong Kong (a slow change of holds here), in Vancouver. My mother hadn't realized he was dead until she received a cable at the American Consulate in Calcutta. Her husband, for reasons she later claimed were flimsy, had volunteered for a classified mission against the Japanese in Burma a few months before Truman dropped the Bomb on Hiroshima and Nagasaki. As a pilot in the RCAF he knew how to parachute. He also happened to know some Japanese from working as a teenager on fishboats out of Steveston in the thirties. Perhaps he'd gone into the rain forest to broadcast false messages over the wireless to confound the Japs. But with his accent? My mother later told me he sounded like George Burns speaking Japanese. His being shot for having a comedian's accent isn't something I used to go around telling people in school about my posthumously decorated father. Accounting for him, and I very much wished him to be accounted for, required a degree of limpid fabrication.

Well. Most of this never happened at all.

What has happened, today as I sit down to write, is that the Nobel Prize for Literature has gone to the novelist William Golding. Listening to the Academy's somewhat clotted citation, 'for his novels which with perspicuity of realistic narrative art and the diversity and the universality of myth illuminate the human condition in the world today', I am oddly reassured by

---

First published in *Canadian Literature* 100 (1984).

the rhetoric. Somehow it exonerates the question-begging title I have borrowed. The rhetoric strenuously refuses to accept the demise of great fiction, even today, and attributes to the tattered novelist wandering out of the jungle in shock, carrying with him his book of life, a unique and valuable knowledge. A wry smile of satisfaction comes to the survivor's lips. He feels something of a hero. Wrought as it has been out of the guerrilla warfare characteristic of his own century, his book has not after all been laid to rest on the grander battlefield of the nineteenth-century novel. War and peace, in all of their internecine, cultural, and amorous manifestations, remain poles of 'the human condition in the world today', and the fiction writer today, no matter how uncertain of his audience in a small country like Canada, nevertheless aspires to the same knowledge as his great predecessor. And what is this survivor's unique and valuable knowledge?

Elephant.

At least, coming out of the jungles of Ceylon, this was Lawrence's knowledge in the long poem he wrote by this title. His knowledge through and through is Elephant. We see Elephant, we smell Elephant, we mourn Elephant. The writer says that what we've done to the beast is what we've done to ourselves, crooking the knee to salaam the white man, the Prince, the pale and enervate ideal. A mountain of blood caparisoned at the neck with bells, tong-tong-tong, this is the human condition suggests Lawrence. He ends up wishing *he* were in the pagoda, instead of the visiting wisp of English royalty, for his own supremacy seems to arise from the knowledge that *his* fiction, *his* ideal, is likelier to animate the disappointed people parading past. The assurance is unmistakable. Lesser writers would have said less – and if less sprawlingly, neither with so daring a knowledge. Who of these would not also have toned down the Horse, Ursula's 'lightning of knowledge', at the end of *The Rainbow*, indeed much of the vaulting fiction that precedes it, and ended up with another book? Dickens, Hardy, Melville, Faulkner: these are not perfect novelists, but they are inarguably supreme. What, if it isn't Elephant, is this supremacy founded on?

In Canada we continue to believe we live in a large country, and that this largeness, this landscape, not only defines us but must surely one day account for greatness. Perhaps it will. But not I suspect before an awareness of City begins to refine this accepted definition, and our fiction enables us to see more completely. Man in relation to his environment is only half a vision if there's a failure to understand environment as both Wilderness *and* City: animate as well as inanimate existence, multitudinous as well as reductive. By City I mean a jungle no less various than Wilderness, for the beast it contains is the soul of the culture. Urban and Rural are merely shadows of this fuller, and necessary, vision.

Our literary past, we know, has included the smallness of T.E. Hulme's vision, roused in 1906, when this visiting Englishman and failed philosopher noticed that 'The first time [he] ever felt the necessity or inevitableness of verse, was in the desire to reproduce the peculiar quality of feeling which is induced by the flat spaces and wide horizons of the virgin prairie of Western Canada.' The sort of laconic poems he began to write stimulated Pound who founded Imagism. (I always think of the last three lines of Hulme's little poem 'The Embankment' as Canada's dubious contribution to Modernism.) The odd feeling Hulme got from the Prairies was of a 'chasm' between himself and God, 'the fright of the mind before the unknown'. Interestingly, his response was to return to the City (Brussels) and study more philosophy.

Less familiar is the journey into western Canada three years earlier by another would-be poet, a failed reporter, from New York City. Like Hulme, he was trying to find himself, but instead of stopping on the Prairies he came farther west, for a month of hunting in the B.C. Rockies. The importance of this journey on his next fifty years is evident not only in the frequency with which he spoke of it to his daughter in the weeks before he died, but also, I believe, in his poetry. Like Hulme, Wallace Stevens discerned the tension between Wilderness and City, and an entry in his diary from the summer of 1903 shows this tension becoming part of his imagination.

> There are certain areas of spruce and fir in the forests that take on the appearance of everglades. They are filled with a brownish gloom, still, mysterious. Here the city heart would emit a lyric cry if a bird sang. But we have no music here. The wells of song would freeze overnight.
>
> Lying in one's tent, looking out at the sky, one's thoughts revert to New York: to the trains stopping at the L stations, to the sinuous females, to the male rubbish, to the clerks and stenographers and conductors and Jews, to my friend the footman in front of Wanamakers, to Miss Dunning's steak, to

Siegel and his cigars.

Here come the ants – heads, feet and bellies.

The poles of Stevens' thought became many, and here we can notice the seeds of his interest in North and South, Cold and Tropical, Familiar and Exotic, Wilderness and City. What we also notice is the precise and natural way his mind transmogrifies what it sees into omniscient memory. There's a quality of wonder about such looking, crucial to artists, which I want to return to. Stevens, we know, returned to New York City; indeed living elsewhere he spent the rest of his life returning to New York City, and he evolved slowly into a poet. In the spring of 1904, now away from the Wilderness, he wrote of 'how utterly we have forsaken the Earth, in the sense of excluding it from our thoughts.... The rivers still roar, the mountains still crash, the winds still shatter. Man is an affair of cities.' Stevens seemed to be dedicating himself to revealing what he called the giant's face at the window, to understanding the proper association of Wilderness and City, for even man's 'gardens & orchards & fields are mere scrapings', he concluded, in the face of this Gulliver. Over forty years later in *Transport to Summer* he published his greatest poem whose title I've borrowed for these notes. His poem is the distillation of a lifetime's thought about the nature of poetry. (It Must Be Abstract, he wrote, It Must Change, It Must Give Pleasure.) Unwisely, perhaps, I should like now in my thirties to offer no less didactically than Stevens in his sixties my own, rather dissimilar subtitles in search of the elusive Elephant Stevens glimpsed in this country eighty years ago.

IT MUST BE AUTOBIOGRAPHICAL.   I was born facing west, in Perth. This was the stepping-off city of the world, according to my mother, who along with my father had gone there by freighter from Colombo, where they'd encountered each other after his release from the Japanese in Singapore. He was English, she American. A few months before the war they'd met in London where my mother went in 1939 to find out if she could get an entry into Wimbledon. (In San Francisco she was City Open Champion.) She ended up instead with an invitation from my father to keep in touch. He lived in Chelsea. They exchanged letters. The war intervened and he forgot her. Her later voyage to Colombo on the chance of meeting up with him again was a westward act of love, and a sudden begetting. In Perth they had sun and no winter, regretted this at last, and moved to the world's second stepping-off city, as my mother called it, Vancouver.

Most of this never happened at all.

What then is its use, this failing to understand the conventions of expository writing, this failing to account for parents, this being arch with metaphor?

Suppose you were to write a travel book full of lies; or perhaps a novel that was libellously true. In the first instance, if discovered, you would be called an impostor; in the second, possibly called into court. The travel writer could do well not to count on sales, since no one trusts a liar. Depending on his libel, the novelist might sell out and be reprinted. In his case we have someone pretending to tell lies, and in the traveller's case someone pretending to tell the truth. It's quickly evident who is more admired and read: the one with the smaller imagination, in my example the novelist. But reverse the situation, return it to the conventions of genre, and you end up with the travel writer's reputation restored. His stock is back up. And the novelist? With no libellous *roman à clef* to sell, he should probably forget about money, especially if it's his first or even third novel.

The imagination is distrusted. As readers of fiction we may all be guilty at one time or another of wondering how much of what he writes 'happened' to the author. The question is on the tongue of every talk-show host who has ever interviewed a novelist. Built into this naïve question is the underlying assumption that form and content are separable. This assumption leads to such meaningless, unspoken questions as How much credit should I give this writer for 'making up' what he's written? How interesting is this writer, really? The question of autobiography is a fundamental one because readers, once out of childhood, do not take so easily to made-up worlds. They want their fiction rooted in a reality they recognize and can 'learn' from. (Melville's English publisher had to be convinced that the travels in the South Seas related by Melville in his first novel, *Typee*, had actually happened. At least John Murray published the book. An American firm rejected it because it seemed 'impossible that it could be true'!)

It should be clear that I am attacking the naïve view of autobiography that pervades even our more critical thinking. Fiction of any quality above the level of Harlequin Romance and Potboiler *must be autobiographical by its very nature*. This is to say that writing fiction is an act inseparable from the mind that conceives it. The act of imagining is a real event. It happens. It happens to the author, and it happens to reveal his quality of mind, depth of vision, deftness of touch. (If I record the image of being born in a story, what is the difference between my memory of the image and my memory of the event that took place in Lima?) Fiction when it is true is idiosyncratic, and when it is supreme, profoundly idiosyncratic. It's unique. It particularizes and generalizes concurrently. Its knowledge is Elephant. It is a continuous attempt to account for the author's sense of both man alone in the world and man in society; of what it is to suffer long and to experience oases of joy. (It differs from non-fiction in a way worth returning briefly to later.)

By autobiographical fiction I do not mean fiction written in the first person any more than in the second or third. Neither do I mean a reminiscent style set in the past any less than a dramatic one set in the present. Each of these types can be just as self-regarding, self-indulgent, self-justifying as another, and therefore false, or at least stuck in adolescence. (I wouldn't, as Eliot evidently did, claim there's *necessarily* something suspect about writers who write best about childhood, so long as there is a perceived evolution from rawness to worldliness, from Wilderness to City.) The supremacy of fiction depends first and fundamentally on the thoroughness of its autobiographical voice. Hence the meaninglessness of such remarks as these in one of our national magazines: '... in his second novel, *Lusts*, Blaise begins to push the boundaries of his fiction beyond the autobiographical' – when a few lines later we read, '... if I'd been handed a page of this book without identification I'd have immediately recognized the Clark Blaise voice.' Can you have it both ways? Potboilers and Harlequins are cynical and voiceless works because the author sets himself up (especially if he's only writing for money) as a mind apart from its product, instead of one *engaged in argument with itself*. No fiction worth writing has ever been undertaken, it seems to me, without the writer's doubting his ability to complete it in the way he dares hope. Every completed story or novel should be a miracle, at least to its author, if it has any chance at all of conveying the wonder of its being alive.

IT MUST SUBVERT.   My mother is watching a biography of Bette Davis on '60 Minutes'. When it's over my father switches channels to the middle of a documentary on Bolivian tin miners. Two miners aged thirty-two and twenty-five are dying of TB contracted in the mine. The younger man's in pain in hospital. When he can't afford the bed any longer he goes home, back to the mine. There's a light on his helmet, lights on all the helmets, slipping deeper by tram into the South American mountain. 'This is the price of your tin can', says the narrator. We watch an impoverished family trailing after a casket, round brown faces empty of expression. Before his death the father brought home two dollars a day. 'Now the family has to move out of its company-owned slum', the narrator says. Unionize? Last time the miners tried that the army shot dozens. Increase the price of tin cans? 'Here *we're* the threat', the narrator tells us. 'We'll just turn to more aluminium and plastic.' This poverty's a cycle. The average miner dies at thirty-three. At seventy-two Bette Davis in California is thinking of making a comeback. 'Her spunk really seemed spunky', my mother says to my father, 'till you changed channels.' My father looks moved too. He says we'll do exactly nothing for Bolivian tin miners, Cambodian refugees, starving Somalians. 'What begins at home anyway?' he asks. My mother says, 'What ends?' She picks absently at the hole in her sleeve. Of the three virtues, among those we had any chance of practising when I was young, ours was always Hope.

When we remember our parents they are seldom revolutionaries. It is the same with novels. Thinking of English and American fiction, say, we notice that innovation has never prospered when form was in excess of content, as form often is today in what we sometimes call 'experimental' fiction. True innovation is inseparable from content. And the content of Supreme Fiction is subversive. I am talking about fiction that overturns expectation by juxtaposition, nexus, dislocation. I am talking about fiction that aspires to an understanding of cultural anorexy; fiction that creates the complexity capable of engaging our imaginations; fiction capable of perceiving the many ways that our received culture, for all its splendours of cohesion, for all our diplomacy, is suffering from edema of the soul. It's too easy to accept the belief that the great themes are now in the keeping of dissident writers in totalitarian countries, and thereby to fall into a decadence of technical obsession. For us it may be salutary to remember that the valuable writer in St. Augustine isn't the one of *The City of God*, but of his more earthly City in *Confessions*.

By overthrowing the predictable, which must always be boredom itself, fiction will offer fresh ways of seeing the relationships between people. No less the relationship between man and woman than the one between cultures. Cries for technical subversion, which ignore the figures of life, are merely rhetorical. The lament over technical old-fashionedness in fiction is usually an indulgence of magpie jotters of isms and withinisms. Such jotters, who confuse fashion with innovation, seek a hearing (why so often from within universities?) not a vision. Elephant isn't one of their critical terms. They forget that a truly subversive mind, as the title of one of Stevens' poems has it, is 'A Weak Mind in the Mountains' – in the Wilderness, where 'The wind of Iceland and/The wind of Ceylon' are what 'grapple' for mindfulness. Not, manifestly, hot air.

The fiction I am arguing for aspires to wide appeal and thus to cliché. It wants to be used up by familiarity, swallowed up as idiom, gobbled up and digested as proverb. This is its hope. This is its subversion: the unexpected resulting in the unforgettable, worn-out smile of the *Mona Lisa*, the opening bars of Beethoven's *Fifth*, Hamlet's To Be speech. It's the task of succeeding generations of artists to refurbish traditional ways of seeing, to reinvigorate worn-out idioms, to subvert the familiar. The novelist's hope is to make his own unfamiliarity dangerously familiar to the generation that succeeds him.

It was the best of times, it was the worst of times, it was the age of wisdom, it was the age of foolishness, it was the epoch of belief, it was the epoch of incredulity, it was the season of Light, it was the season of Darkness....

Call me Ishmael.

All happy families are alike but an unhappy family is unhappy after its own fashion.

As Gregor Samsa awoke one morning from uneasy dreams he found himself transformed in his bed into a gigantic insect.

... and yes I said yes I will Yes.

If the skeleton of fiction is narrative, then fiction's flesh is a complex of nerves, brain cells, muscles, features, and senses. The interdependency of all these is taken for granted until the backbone, say, is dislocated, and the mortality of the human condition becomes increasingly apparent, important. The figures of fiction, both fat and starving, stand in awe of the brooding face of death. The resulting juxtaposition is what transfixes us.

IT MUST BE WONDERFUL. By what in fiction are we redeemed if it isn't the writer's love of life, growing out of his awareness of death? No fiction will be supreme unless it is haunted by Death. This is another way of saying it must be haunted by Time. We do not, as Julian Huxley argues, have memory because we are aware of civilization. We have it because we are always facing death.

Death in many forms. The kind of death affecting us least often is the death of people. Even for Charlotte Brontë, whose brother, sisters, and mother all died off like broom blossom, the fact of human death was only one death among many. She, like us, faced deaths of far less dramatic kinds: the death of holidays, the death of years, the death of seasons, the death of meals, the death of days, the death of dreams, the death of visits, the death of books, the death of flowers, the death of altruism, the death of smells, the death of enthusiasms, the death of silences. In fiction as in life an awareness of death is the measure of perspective. Maturity is having learned to appreciate the didactic nature of memory. Growing up in Death's brooding face, our imaginations are educated. This leads to compassion. It offers redemption. The more experiences we have, by which I mean simply the more we *notice* of the world, the more deaths we live through. It was patently wrong of Wittgenstein to say death is the experience we do not live through. Autobiographical (unlike Harlequin) fiction is full of death, death that is lived through, and it's in this way the novelist distinguishes himself from the historian. How to remember what he is looking at is the novelist's obsession. How to look at what he can't remember is the historian's. The perspective we value more, the perspective we *must* value more, is the novelist's. His memories are created in the face of their deaths.

In several of Wallace Stevens' early poems, writes Richard Ellmann in an essay, the poet insists 'that without death, love could not exist.' This is similar to saying that the way we look at something in the present is determined by how we have educated ourselves to see it simultaneously in the future. The subversion of the present is the inevitable consequence of possessing memory. What, for example, do we mean by Here and Now, and what if any are the moral, the cultural, implications of There and Then? (What is Selfishness exactly?) Our interest in fiction accrues in ratio to the wonder we feel it expressing of the Here and Now as an ideal. The supremacy of fiction resides in its capacity to inhabit Time.

The Other Worldness of great fiction makes everything happen, or so it seems, for the writer's mandate isn't to change the world but to show that within the imagination, capable of evoking both the sublime and darkness together, exists a metaphor for God. The fiction we value more is inclusive rather than exclusive. It offers no answers except the order and multiplicity of its vision, the nuances of its humblest details, the miraculousness of its language. It offers a sense of Earth. But it offers more than this, for it is a benevolent and finally human God, interested in understanding the relations of man and nature in the broadest sense of man and man. This God, this imagination, this fiction is Wonderful, for there is no getting through or around the authority of its vision and the intuitive logic of its means.

To be born without a sense of wonder, the supreme novelist tells us, is to die without knowledge. And this knowledge is finally metaphorical. 'All knowledge,' Kafka says in one of his stories, 'the totality of all questions and all answers, is contained in the dog.' Elephant, dog. The supreme writer enters his imagination, as Stevens tells us in 'Notes toward a Supreme Fiction', and 'The elephant/Breaches the darkness of Ceylon with blares'. Stevens conceived of his theory and his fiction as inseparable. His metaphor became him. The hunger of the writer peering into the darkness is always such a becoming.

Dwelling simultaneously in Wilderness and City the writer has visions and revisions to account for his place in the world. Perhaps I was born the day my mother died, the day my father died, the day the war ended. Who can say what matters more than the sheer accident of one's birth? Who can say the wonder of being alive is not the writer's entire theme? Elephant, he speaks, Elephant.

I was born.

Leon Rooke

IS YOU IS OR IS YOU AIN'T MY BABY: CANADIAN FICTION AGAINST THE HEADWINDS

CANADIAN LONGER FICTION – in the darker continents of modern time – has the fixed authority of a nest of recognized classics, both on home and larger soil: Ernest Buckler's *The Mountain and the Valley* was published in 1952, the same year *Waiting for Godot* was published in England and *The Old Man and the Sea* appeared in the U.S. In 1957 Sinclair Ross published *As For Me and My House*, while in England John Osborne's *The Entertainer* appeared and in the U.S. James Agee's *A Death in the Family*. Sheila Watson's *The Double Hook* came out in 1959 ... but whoa! We are, with that date, but six years and a forceps' shine removed from post-modernism.

Our ABCs.

Now the truth is I don't know when it was that Canadian *short* fiction came of age: not, by my stars – but this is old and maudlin stuff – with the 1930s-ish collections of Morley Callaghan – though in truth short stories of a Callaghan gait (I am not speaking here of style but of a prevailing story matrix that consciously (and un) imitated

(early) Hemingway) and

(middle) Everybody Else, and

(late) U.S. President Dwight D. Eisenhower, for the U.S., by sheer number of adherents to the cause, had by the fifties wrestled the short story form away from the British, the Italians, the Germans, the French, and made it indigenously (endemically, inimically, and, pretty soon, 'minimalistically') theirs,

(– this is what prehistory, oral beginnings come to)

First delivered at the Seventh International Conference on Canadian Literature in Catania, Sicily. First published in *Brick: A Journal of Reviews* 33 (1988).

this being the *modus operandi*, fare of the mainstream, by and large (numerous powerful acts of those decades are enshrouded within that phrase), until the end of that cumbersome and encumbered, (re)constructionist

(period.)

(– I do want this sentence to end)

decade.

Some will tell you Hugh Hood (friends of mine in this very audience) recognized the genre's open door policy and brought the Canadian short story whirling into the New World, through fulfilment and command and refinement of contemporary technique, as recently (or as late) as 1962 with the aptly titled collection *Flying a Red Kite*. But this cannot be. And/but this overlooks Friday's child, Ethel Wilson, who surely did not consign all her talent to the making of *Swamp Angel* (1954) and whose *Mrs. Golightly and Other Stories* appeared the year before Hood's estimable *Kite* (as an aside to that, her estimable (& technically accomplished) story 'The Window' (you can see such miscellaneous trivialized footnoting appeals to me) was composed the same year Philip Roth wrote 'The Conversion of the Jews', John Updike wrote 'A Gift from the City', John Cheever wrote 'The Bella Lingua', William H. Gass 'Mrs. Mean', Bernard Malamud 'The Last Mohican'). (Yes, and Julio Cortazar was a UNESCO employee in Paris, Ernesto Cardenal a young Nicaraguan boning up for the priesthood in Cuernavaca, Mexico, and Tommaso Landolfi's famous story 'Gogol's Wife' was seeing its first English print in *Encounter* magazine: how to end this stocking run?) Wilson – Wilson is book-ended (by stories that embrace the full span of her writing life) among annual prize collections from two continents, for instance, with entries in Edward J. O'Brien's *The Best British Short Stories: 1938* and Martha Foley's *Best American Short Stories: 1959*. Nor was she alone on the frontier.

Canada, the invisible nation. Where was Ralph Ellison when we needed him?

We can be thankful that no Canadian author, though Robertson Davies yet might, signed himself 'Papa', as Hemingway did at the age of twenty-eight.

Witness the modest expectations, seen in their eyes and slumping shoulders,

(– Prairie grain is heavy, Nova Scotia fishnets too; in British Columbia it rains a dreadful news)

of plain, simple folk.

(– Another aside: In Canadian universities where I've briefly or longishly taught (if that's the word), beer – and drinking the stuff – has been, among students, fiction's primary subject matter. When instructors favour art's basket with the news 'Write What You Know' – and thus bore yourself – this is what young writers do.)

All the same, despite Margaret Atwood's observation (in *The Journals of Susanna Moodie*) that 'the moving water will not show me/my reflection' – because it *was moving* perhaps – Canada's reflection became over time an ice cap at least tentatively imprinted upon field and (frozen tundra) (if not) stream. Art *was* moving and somehow the reflection (face by itself being nature's paltry compromise) is now in place, and with it redemption and (some degree of) solace too. Canadian literature has come through a lifetime in scarcely thirty years, and now – dollop of Tom Robbins coarseness here – even cowgirls have got the news. (Where *is* Aritha van Herk from?)

'Home ground, foreign territory' reads a phrase in Atwood's *Survival*, now for our critics perhaps no longer the basic (survival) text. (Atwood's phrase is beguilingly discussed by Robert Kroetsch in 'Unhiding the Hidden: Recent Canadian Fiction' in *Essays*, the Kroetsch issue of *Open Letter*, Spring 1983.)

Down here in the ears where my brain resides – where the brain has come to like the drainage of so much effluent from once more noble and higher ground

– *terrain-terrustitus*, a crippling disease;

– I am all that I remember of all I ever heard;

– what the eyes see the ears divide;

– in one eye, we might say, and out the other ear

(– those who have done research on memory functions of the human brain put forward with temerity of indecision the guardedly premature notion that for every five new bits of data, visual image, etc., the brain incorporates, one, mind you, one file, roughly one of what was old and stored becomes erased

– becomes, that is to say, compromised;

– some gender differences, though they strike dread in my heart, do obtain);

– down here, then, at this pit or height from which I speak

– I wander lonely as a cloud and speak to you as a novice parachutist might....

We lean towards Babylon, slouch away from Bethlehem, touch toe to moons – hurtle towards the grave.

Martin Luther hurled his inkpot at the devil. Writers merely with (the posture of) dignity – 'here it is' – may (to the distracted, besieged public) submit a text. We confront the Prince of Darkness with dew that shows his footprints less-than-wistfully there: writers go through awful bogs – oasis *and* bog: groan of flower, whimper of toad, notes of the nightingale

– Virginia Woolf, when mad, is reported to have heard the birds sing in Greek

– Who does not believe this, it may be said, is her-or-him/self mad

ply oasis and bog, we may aver, to bless the washed and unwashed alike with what it is they (in their poems and fictions and dramas) know.

But this innocent question first: Will 'selfconscious fictive constructs' get the reader, never mind the author, into heaven? Will 'fictive forms which process the invention of fiction inventing itself inventing fiction' – forms predating Jesus anyhow, there in our oral-chartered winds – advance us into paradise? Will games? Mirrors revealing the author mirroring ... the fashionable, lethargic self in absorbed, writerly repose?

The mask.

The folly of arrogant (deceitful) prose.

The lion tamer, with cracking whip (cracking air); never the lion.

Fiction's backbone dislocated, the soul's message adrift in surly wind.

Our brightest critics are selling arms to (frequently witty but always and finally insolvent) renegades. Okay, let's reduce that (absurd) overstatement to its more obvious, and deserving, litotes: Paris has never exported philosophy and literary theory in excess of its more strictly (in this context) 'imagined' goods, i.e. poetry, the novel, story, and drama. Existentialism, *l'engagement*, the *Nouveau Roman*, structuralism and its component shelves (if, for instance, semiotics, at this wake, may be said, and it cannot, to occupy a space so small as a shelf. More like, let's say, in the academy, tidal

waves). Yet in France now what enrages most critics is that so many novelists – hordes, it would seem – are reproducing – not works in sojourn from
Robbe-Grillet or Sartre or parroted Flaubert – but Balzacian tomes almost
as old as grapes. In upheaval is the very term 'avant-garde(ism)', a designa-
tion we might have thought adequate for useful flotation through time. All
of which leads me to puzzle whether – not that it is any of my business to –
the French ship all are running to, has not already gone aground, and
whether those who are running, and our 'Balzacs' who *will* follow *them*,
won't in the end find themselves occupying that fabled condition and space
their academic forebears, in North America at any rate, *certainly* held; i.e.
that space where the breaking news is last to go. All right, I grant you, now
that I've said it, with all changes wrought in the academy, there is no possibility of that. So why say it, then?

Because in such a climate too many writers may be influenced to put borrowed theory in front of the material that might otherwise be their salvation? Because all writers who do not aspire to pursue the invention that art
means mask, means hypocrisy, means intellectual play, means commerce in
thin, fraudulent, self-centred goods, will be ignored, and that the author's
inherited obligation to render life-giving evidence in support of genuine
human breath, for both the unshackling of the innocent dead and the
unearthing of the bountiful present whether it be oasis of joy or nightmare
of agony and discontent, will be through our indifference shunted off into
wayward, untrafficable warrens and coves? To my way of thinking, it is
indeed the case that a considerable body of fiction, especially those stories
and novels of pilgrimage and quest, may in one sense be said to be about the
artist's path in and through society, about language and that artistic centre
without which the world would not hold, from J.D. Salinger's *The Catcher
in the Rye* to J.M. Coetzee's *The Life and Times of Michael K.* to John
Gardner's *Grendel* to Michael Ondaatje's *In the Skin of a Lion* to Cormac
McCarthy's *The Orchard Keeper* to Keath Fraser's 'The History of Cambo-
dia', and such a description is serviceable to a point; but confabulations, the
proliferation of mock works, conceits, dirigibles which are determinedly
hatched to reveal the writer posed, the writer as ultimate hero, the writer's
love affair with self, the writer at the desk creating the fiction of him/herself
as constituted, endowable text, are inferior assignments, deflections, texts
which consecrate no ground and which do little for civilization's keeping

because humanity's need, its heart and heartbeat, dwells elsewhere. Dwells off such pages. Such works are prom rehearsals only, gesticulations from the podium, arrogant fillings of (and swillings at) the spurious trough and bear no more likeness to true innovation than does the clinky-clunk of the spinet piano rushed onstage to compete with the concert grand. Fiction is for the unknown, the unadmitted, the strangers ever at humanity's door; it is about the dead who could not speak for themselves, and the living who have not the opportunity (though they have the means, if but to articulate their grievances as an entrapped animal might).

All is fabrication anyhow, say the wizards of conceited prose; the House of Fiction is a mosquito tent collapsible in the first zephyr that blows. Suspend disbelief, enter skins, and be labelled cloistered maniac.

Never the *earned* 'brooding face of death' or its saddle companion, the pristine visage of joy.

Victories have been won, pages turned, for this?

NOW THIS SOUNDS TO ME, as it must to many of you, like tediously reactionary stuff. I note myself in this tissue I proffer the tenebrous glut, and can without serene abstraction ask: 'Without post-modernism where would I be myself?' Theory has liberated text, brought new vigour to corridors of learning where light had scarcely penetrated in fifty years, and in the hawking of new mental tools has rejuvenated the tired language of explication and rightly ravaged the inane meanderings of theme and distillation of jaded plot. But one's full surrender, uncompromising adherence, to *any* single school, I would submit, is the naming that nails the coffin shut.

A line in Tommaso Landolfi's diary *Rien va* (from his *Words in Commotion and Other Stories* [New York: Viking, 1986]) goes this way: 'The truth is that the spirit must lie in chains, regardless of who forged them.' Landolfi is discussing with himself one's inherited fate, determinism, the absence of chance, but out of context, which is mostly how we read, I choose to read this statement as practically a call to arms. The chain is intact, spirit unassailable, the forging ... well, it forges on. To connect, in my devious logic, with Michel Butor's statement (for years we say these things to ourselves and then someone comes along and says them aloud and they are objectively verified. This indicates that a certain forging of chains in a certain shared way is deeply entrenched and has the same explanation as the prevalence on historically untraversable shores of otherwise unexplainable myth) ... with, I was saying, Butor's statement somewhere (in my notes, now limp, but received from the writer's very mouth) that we write – one reason – 'we write to commend and resurrect (pay homage to) the dead'. All right, let's just say that we do so that they may have an easier sleep. One reason only, delivered in a baker's tone, though needing no decoding – nothing to decon-struct.

To paraphrase (and quote) Keath Fraser (in his 'Notes toward a Supreme Fiction' in *Canadian Literature*, number 100, 1984 – republished in *How Stories Mean*), if fiction's backbone is dislocated, 'the morality of the human condition becomes increasingly apparent, important. The figures of fiction, both fat and starving, stand in awe of the brooding face of death. The result-ing juxtaposition is what transfixes us.'

– exhaustive flights
– holding patterns
– allegiance to the human condition
– critical evidence of existing evidence that we live
– and yet survive ...
– assignments from the (sub)(un)conscious. (Literature's face is with us like a ghost town in the Hebrides and (say yes Virginia) there are gold mines in Eldorado, in Brigadoon, in Camelot.)

Men die (people do), says Camus. And they are unhappy.

The universality of human feeling – thought, deed – is not yet in demise.

Dalliance is not the whole show (though it can dishearten us that Russia does not understand North America's and the world's love affair with Che-khov and we can lament their clinging even to a fortress as securely anchored in our own Halls of Grace as Mark Twain).

The chains of literature, humanity's long march, all the grimacing dead, trumpet this:

Encircle the defrauder's camp.

Gargantuan 'root has taken', as Shakespeare put it down, 'the reason prisoner'.

Invoke anti-monopoly laws, bring down legislation if we must.

Volleys to right, volleys to left, ride in the six hundred.

Yes, the writer may occupy, and occupy fully, from zenith of joy to depths of decay, another's skin, a made-up character's self. (Readers, too, blessed be the tribe.) Don't try telling me Tolstoy was not Ivan Ilych, and other citizens in that dramatic terrain as well. Don't tell me Paul Scott did not *stay on* in India with Ibrahim, with Tusker Smalley whose death is stated in line one, as well as with Memsahib Minnie who at the end of *Staying On* (London: Heinemann, 1977) cries: '... [W]hy did you leave me? Why did you leave me here? I am frightened to be alone, Tusker ... but now, until the end, I shall be alone, whatever I am doing, here as I feared, amid the alien corn, waking, sleeping, alone for ever and ever and I cannot bear it ... so with my eyes shut, Tusker, I hold out my hand, and beg you, Tusker, beg, beg you, take it and take me with you. How can you not, Tusker ... how can you make me stay here by myself while you yourself go home?' Her hand is held out to Tusker, yes, but more importantly it is held out to us, to all of us who have known or will come to know love's loss, the reeling planet, the deprivation of solitude; and more yet, for the hand's reach is there in entreatment of and for sake of all the vanished but unsilent dead, and therein does the tale, such tales, encompass, as Irving Howe, in his *Classics of Modern Fiction* (New York: Harcourt Brace Jovanovich, 1972), said of *The Death of Ivan Ilych*, within one range of pages 'the fundamental patterns of human existence'. The writer is (who *else?*) steamy conduit for the world's cruellest and happiest news. The writer may – in the long run *must* – be spoken through – for the Mother of Invention, the Maidens of Imagination – Mercy's own sightless daughters and sons, reside without, reside in shadowy camps beyond the creator's open door (that is their permanent camp). Thus and in no other way does the writer come to know more than the writer knows she/he knows.

Or would we attest, as reads an Edmond Jabès line in *The Book of Dialogue*:

'Others: a fiction.'

How far do we carry this pernicious, aggrandizing load?

Witness the modest expectations of plain, simple folk.

The wonders of spring.

When I was a young reader/writer I wanted in literature encapsulation, directions, conclusions, findings, examples, aphorism, cutting observation, the vivid pie, syngenetic codes, insights capable of drawing blood, spears of meaning that could startle the secret plumbing and ravage the squatter heart. What *is* life about? This arrangement of nations divided by water and mountain, by barbed wire, as, above, the tumbling heavens give approving serenade. What justice through flight of blind stork, birth's accident, geography's giggle? ('How come these weird myths to our shore?') Love, hatred, it is up to what? I'm dumb, dumb, I said, I admit it, but you're the big cheese: there is nothing you don't know, no skin you cannot inhabit, no fiefdom or planet you cannot explore. If the world is round, if knowledge can be contained, you, little book, made it so. I wanted alchemy – and do yet. I wanted what I could not get enough of – and never can. The firmament keepers. Furnace stokers. Change my life, little book, I said. Orient me to the ways of woman to man and (wo)man to the universe, and the universe to – what? And don't, don't, I prayed, let the historian's fumy cyclic theory obtain.

Acquaint me with night and day. Detail the urgent specifics. Inflame me, rapture me, open my flesh with words ('arranged in their proper sequence'). Reveal the unimpeachable truth. Please, I said, and all the better if you can let it sing.

In the rare and sporting book *Talk's Body* (New York: Alfred A. Knopf, 1979), which excavates a theory of creative behaviour by meditation upon the elected objects within his environment – life as improvisation (mind and memory navigating and/or assimilating the turning wheel) – jazz pianist David Sudnow gives this analysis of the phenomena of now: 'When I listen to a Herbie Hancock piano solo, I listen with my hands. I can feel courses of melodies: my palms almost imperceptibly expand and contract, bursts of rapidity and repose make them tighten and relax; the fingers minutely follow the essential shapes and pacing of his improvisations. Most likely' (he continues) 'you do not listen to the jazz piano player that way. There are "parts of you" that do not participate in his movements. If you and I listen to a psychologist or a physiologist talk about hearing, where hearing is reduced to properties of the ear and decoding mechanisms of the brain, the difference between us is ignored. Either scientist might contrast us by saying that memory traces are present in my brain that do not exist in yours, or that habitual skills in pattern recognition are stored somehow in my nervous system but absent in yours, or that perhaps I have an internalized syntax which affords me a greater predictive capacity to hear likely forthcoming notes. In the reduction of the jazz solo to various typical sound-wave sequences and internal coding capabilities, a real communication between Herbie Hancock's hands and my hands goes unnoticed. But this is because the psychologist is not a piano player.' I would risk contemptuousness if I drew attention to the parallels between this and the astute reader with a text. Sudnow defines language as 'improvisationally choreographed courses of movements'. Astute readers are aware that a piece of writing may be revised, and revised again a hundred times; they are largely unaware that, unless it has the air of improvisation – a thing rendered for the first time – it is apt to ring inauthentic and dull; it will have the familiarity of table salt.

Canada's house of (abundant) quality fiction – not so few the rugose gems there – is a noticeably recent addition to the international skyline, but the scaffolding was going up, had of course gone up long before the sixties and seventies when the word-shooters, the text, got hot. It abided there, if not in abundant individual works, in Landolfi's 'chains ... regardless of who forged them'.

Ignes fatui, flickering lights over marsh: one might see it that way. I see flickers, even sometimes outright failures, where ambition was evident and in the absence of any intent to defraud, as inherited wealth.

Begin in bedrock, James Joyce urged.

Be the gods' interpreters, argued Plato.

All our secrets are the same, and that is fiction's – the word's – enterprise. (A phrase minted by Gordon Lish in his *All Our Secrets Are the Same* [New York: W.W. Norton, 1976.])

Words are more than gesture. Play – writing that promulgates the theory of mask – fiction waged with glass swords – idolaters of the I-am-so-amazing 'I'

(– I have a fondness myself for what used to be called the black humorists, but I am compelled to give blackish nod when Cynthia Ozick wickedly asks, Would you consign the planet's governing to them?)

are communing with their primordial cousins, no matter how much you Derrida-it-up. Antics corresponding to, as Denis Donoghue claims in his *The Arts without Mystery* (London: The British Broadcasting Corporation, 1983), 'the speech before the fall into words and the sins of grammar' will earn no seats in heaven. To celebrate literature which is headgame, to banish the heart's journey from the page, to lead into retreat that which Faulkner called Literature's sole concern, the heart in conflict with itself, does not save lives or bring the news or alter by even a syllable a culture's top-40 or next one thousand tunes. Elitism is no friend of Art.

This chouse, this chowse.

It goes without saying that content can be poured into any form whatever.

But previously innocent substances – dilutions of pearl, dollops of ginger, shards of tommyrot – now becloud the dream of hermeneutic, obviotic paradise: writers are no longer what they seem, but what they s-e-a-m. As they p-r-e-e-n, they s-e-a-m. Natural fabrics – cotton, silk, wool, honest sweat – are now synthetic inventions which absorb the sweat, which wash and tumble dry, and are washed and washed again, endlessly and as life-denying as mummy's rune. It is not so much a case, cynicism might say, of literature being so much a 'dead duck' as it is the 'living quack'.

Not me. I did not say that.

The text which *plays* together, in this age, stays together.

But I would not advance this claim.

But ... witness, in their eyes, the modest expectations of plain, simple folk.

Art prospers so long as 'the look' is there.

Shine your shoes, J.D. Salinger had Seymour Glass tell his brothers and sisters, for the Fat Lady, in her rocker on the distant, well-swept porch.

As bees buzz about her head.

Savour excellence for *her*, though she never note your existence in the world. If notice of such undertakings pass her by, all the more crucial then the need.

Virginia Woolf's acrimony towards James Joyce – *Ulysses* as 'ultimately nauseating' text, she records in her diary

– in a wind tunnel you can hear the screech of things

may indeed have as a partial explanation Cynthia Ozick's cure (in her *Art and Ardor* [New York: Alfred A. Knopf, 1983]): '... she (Woolf) knew Joyce to be moving in the same direction as herself; it was a race that, despite her certainty of his faults, he might win. By the time of her death she must have understood that he *had* won. Still,' Ozick amends, 'to be outrun in fame is no martyrdom. And her own fame was and is in no danger, though, unlike Joyce, she is not taken as a fact of nature.'

In Canada there exist competing camps, warring philosophies – throat slasher days come and go – and on the whole, despite the pettiness that accrues and innocent psyches that are wrenched, this is perhaps beneficial stuff. Placid water is made to move and we may thereby question the positioning of face. We shall see in later quieter hours which avatars the tides beach and where the puffery shows.

Innovation in art, though ever necessary and always in traverse of ground as rapid as runaway wheel (else 'tradition' petrify), need not sever the chain that binds a present age to its previously (oh, other) ones; it need not collapse the spirit forged within the chain(s); it need not circumvent the continuity of modest expectations

– look there, in their eyes!

... even and especially the modest expectations of plain, simple folk.

We need not blur humanity's massive shadow from the page.

LITERATURE DOES NOT SIT at the foot of Universal Lamp; it is what installed and best keeps it there. (Not religions, early or late, so much as the stories, the poetry, religions told.)

Ye are of one flesh, though your shoe size be many.

Of what does the single lamp, art's torch, the spirit, the howling bones of inherited time, speak:

Of the marvellous: Baby Jesus, in the new world, rolls her eyes.

Of the pain: I have no home.

Of the love: My swaddling clothes.

Of the hope: Though I be a nasty, bastard child on whom the chaff of this stable clings and though I tell you my future holds for me immersions in boiling oil, my head upon a plate, I shall ...

(– herewith relate, on the whole, a more wholesome tale)

... (I) cite Ozick's tenets next:

'*What literature means is meaning.*'

Good writing is aswim with the idea of redemption: we can change the way we live, the way we breathe. In no way otherwise with salutary domain does the whole of art exist.

'*Literature is for the sake of*' – not itself but – '*humanity.*'

'Of the stories and novels that mean to be literature, one expects a certain corona of moral purpose: not outright in the grain of the fiction itself, but in the form of a faintly incandescent envelope around it.'

I now turn, and end, with the words of a young(*ish*, he would say) Canadian writer with whom I hold the affinity of comradeship. His is the generation at *my* heels, and this is what Keath Fraser, to date the author of one good story collection, *Taking Cover*, and one superb one, *Foreign Affairs* – thinks:

Supreme fiction (1) 'must be autobiographical'. It 'depends first and fundamentally on the thoroughness of its autobiographical voice'. He does not mean the naïve demarcation of first person, or second, or third, or that it must track the inhalations and exhalations of the single personalized breath. He means that the mind must not be apart from its product, that it must be '*engaged in argument with itself*', that the writer must be present in and on the page and in between the lines, that the writing of worthwhile fiction 'is an act inseparable from the mind that conceives it' and is *thus* autobiographical, for imagination is real, and the image that create's one's story birth in Salerno is not for the artist's purpose different from the actual event that took place, in Fraser's case, in Vancouver, B.C. Be one – who was it said? – on whom nothing is lost. Be, as Fraser's characters are, citizens of the world.

(2) 'It must subvert.' It must subvert by seeing that 'true innovation is inseparable from content', 'by overthrowing the predictable', by overturning expectation through 'juxtaposition, nexus, dislocation', by recognition that such fiction 'aspires to an understanding of cultural anorexy' and perceives 'the many ways that our received culture, for all its splendours of cohesion, for all our diplomacy, is suffering from edema of the soul' ... by granting to oneself 'the belief that the great themes are' not now solely 'in the keeping of dissident writers in totalitarian countries, and thereby' not 'to fall into a decadence of technical obsession'. By pinning to the mat not jottings but vision.

Autobiography that takes *notice* of the world.

In a Keath Fraser story, whether told from the point of view of a tortured and dying newswoman in Cambodian incarceration by the Khmer Rouge or from that of an aging heroine in India distributing her hoarded wealth from a restaurant's rooftop perch, Fraser lets fly the names of cities and countries as though to weave a universal flag that would wave over us all, and thus net (and steer) the passions that divide, unite, and/or inflame: Dakar, Nanking, Venezuela, Kingston, Madras, Chunking, Manila ... Guatemala, Leopoldville, Johannesburg, Athens, Lima ... Córdoba, Linz, Barcelona, Santiago,

Asunción ... Brazzaville, Ankara, Mexico City, Hong Kong, Bombay, Melbourne ... Colombo, Sackville, São Paulo, Delhi, Helsinki, Warsaw ... Vatican, Andorra, Buenos Aires, Quito, Moscow. Endless, this calling forth, and what's more, without such roll-calling typical Fraser characters '*would not know where they are!*'

(3) 'It must be wonderful.'

'By what in fiction are we redeemed', writes Fraser, 'if it isn't the writer's love of life, growing out of his awareness of death? ... Our interest in fiction accrues in ratio to the wonder we feel it expressing of the Here and Now as an ideal. The supremacy of fiction resides in its capacity to inhibit Time.... The Other Worldness of great fiction makes everything happen, or so it seems, for the writer's mandate (is) ... to show that within the imagination, capable of evoking the sublime and darkness together, exists a metaphor for ... a benevolent and finally human God....'

Edmond Jabès in *The Book of Dialogue*: 'If you go into the desert, silence no longer envelops you. You become yourself such silence as makes the desert speak.'

Carol Shields

ARRIVING LATE: STARTING OVER

AS A YOUNG WRITER I was not in the least rebellious. Literary genres – the novel, the short story, the essay – seemed to me to be fixed phenomena governed by established definition; a short story, as everyone knew, was a prose narrative that could be read in a single sitting, never mind what that quaint abstraction, 'a single sitting', meant. I could chant such Eng. Lit. absolutes while standing on my head, and for the most part I believed what I was told. A story had to have conflict, it was said. A story consisted of a problem and a solution; I believed that too. A story must contain the kind of characters that the reader can relate to; well, yes, of course. Every detail provided in a short story must contribute to its total effect; well, if Chekhov and Hemingway said so, then it had to be true. The structure of a story could be diagrammed on a blackboard, a gently inclined line representing the rising action, then a sudden escalatory peak, followed by a steep plunge which demonstrated the dénouement and then the resolution. I remember feeling quite worshipful in the presence of that ascending line. Very tidy, very tight, the short story as boxed kit, as scientific demonstration, and furthermore it was teachable.

It wasn't until I had been teaching for several years and found I was passing on these inscribed truths to others that I started to lose faith. The diagram, which I had by then drawn on the blackboard perhaps fifty or sixty times, began one day to look like nothing so much as a bent coat hanger, and yet my students, hunched over the seminar table, were dutifully copying this absurd image into their notes. I stopped talking in mid-sentence and looked around: what was this dead prattle coming out of my mouth? What

First published in *How Stories Mean*.

did I mean anyway by that word 'conflict', and how could I assume the inevitability of a 'resolution'?

Certain familiar critical phrases – chief among them, 'unity of vision' – began to fall on my ear with a remarkably hollow clatter. What had I been babbling about all these years? And wasn't there something infantile about a reader's need to 'relate' to a character in a piece of fiction? I overheard myself one day speaking rather sternly to a student, reminding her that it was aesthetically risky, perhaps even impossible, absolutely forbidden, in fact, to introduce a major character after the first third of the story. She nodded in agreement, *of course, of course*, and I registered her docility with sorrow.

About this time – 1983 – I found myself stuck in the middle of a rather long novel. I knew what I wanted to do, but I couldn't find the structural machinery to bring it about. I had two ideas, one serious, one less so, and I wanted them to mesh like a set of gears, but they wouldn't. I suspected that the trouble might lie in the angle of narration I had chosen, that I had locked myself into too restrictive a voice. Frustrated, I decided to shelve the novel for a year and experiment with other narrative possibilities.

The result was a series of twenty-one short stories called *Various Miracles*. I wrote these stories, one after the other, in a mood of reckless happiness, and I don't think I've ever worked, before or since, with such stirring pleasure. For one thing, I experienced for the first time the curious sensation that I *owned* what I was writing, every word, every comma. The small, chilly upstairs bedroom where I had my desk in those days felt crowded with noisy images. Strange images. Subversive images. Some of them, popping out of my typewriter, frightened me: a reference in 'Mrs. Turner Cutting the Grass' to a baby left at a doorstep and possibly bitten by 'a rabid neighbourhood cat' and another reference in a story called 'Invitations' in which a woman imagines a burglar entering her apartment and carrying off 'her lovely double rope of pearls or a deep slice of her dorsal flesh'. I put these images in, then took them out, then put them back in again – as though I were afflicted with an aesthetic or moral stammer.

Half-way through one story, the idea for the next appeared, and then the next, arriving, it seemed, with a spacy sense of abandon, kindled by the knowledge, I suppose, that these word constructs were no more than an experiment, a way merely of preparing myself to go back to the stalled novel – and so I could do anything I wanted with them.

The first thing I did was jettison the phantom set of rules about what a story should be and how it must be shaped, and before I knew it I found myself not only working around these precepts, but deliberately overturning them. I had, for example, swallowed whole the notion that a writer must never indulge in the artifice of coincidence, even though I had experienced dozens of striking coincidences in my own life and so had everyone I knew. Coincidence, it seemed to me, was one of the strands of existence; synchronicity might even be said to be a sort of force in the world. Why couldn't I write about it, use it? Why couldn't I, in fact, write a story that was nothing more than a tissue of connected coincidences, a fiction that formed a sort of pocket for its own exegesis?

The story, which eventually became the title story of *Various Miracles*, had a few problems. For one thing there was no conflict. There was no strong central sympathetic character. And there was an unsettling mélange of fantasy and realism of the sort that makes reviewers hoist their eyebrows and pronounce in sharply rebuking tones, 'This author doesn't seem to have made up her mind which kind of story she is writing.'

But I *had* made up my mind, or rather I had surrendered that particular sour species of deliberation that once drove me forward. And anyway I was on to the next, a story called 'Home', which also rested on a framework of coincidence. In this story each of a hundred passengers on a transatlantic flight experiences a simultaneous moment of happiness, and the energy generated by their accumulated euphoria causes the walls of the aircraft to become, for a moment, translucent. (I confess I was a little surprised by what was rolling out onto my clean white paper: translucent airplanes? wait a minute – wasn't that the stuff of science fiction? wasn't this out of my territory?)

I thought I knew my territory. I had, after all, written four novels which were generally described, sometimes pejoratively, as being naturalistic. The events revealed in the novels were imaginary, but possible. I had been trying, more and more with each of these four novels, to bring forward a quality of realism that I found missing in so much 'realistic' fiction; I wanted, in short, to make realism more real. Just as it has been observed that people on television sit-coms never watch television, I had been puzzled by the fact that people in novels rarely sat down to read a book. Or to tell each other stories. Nor did they seem to have friends. Or birthdays. Or any semblance of a domestic life, no beds, brooms, wallpaper, cereal bowls, cupboards, cousins, buses, local elections, newspapers, head colds, cramps, or moments when their heads were empty, at ease, happy even. Why had domesticity, the shaggy beast that eats up ninety per cent of our lives, been shoved aside by fiction writers? Because it was too dull? Too insignificant? Too flattened out, too obvious? The inclusion of domestic detail seemed much more to me than just an extra suitcase taken on board to use up my weight allowance. Diurnal surfaces could be observed by a fiction writer with a kind of deliberate squint, a squint that distorts but also sharpens beyond ordinary vision, bringing forward what might be called the subjunctive mode of one's self or others, a world of dreams and possibilities and parallel realities.

I had begun fairly early putting into my fiction the wallpaper and the friends and the birthdays, and had abandoned after my second novel the kind of people-in-crisis set-up that is the engine of much realistic fiction. This meddling with the form, though, had been so gradual and tentative that I had scarcely been aware of it. Now I was. And I felt emboldened enough by the thought, cheeky enough anyway, to allow the stories I was writing to fill up on the natural gas of the quotidian and to find their own shape and form.

Of course writers had been doing this forever: John Cheever, William Gass, Ursula Le Guin, Clark Blaise, Alice Munro, not to mention Nathaniel Hawthorne and Anton Chekhov. Most of the short stories I loved, for that matter, were shaped from their own material, and from the mystery and allusive language that hovered over that material. Literary theory was not, after all, the motor that drove writing forward; theory was no more than an eager young fresh-faced yardworker, intent on raking up the leaves as they fell from the tree, trying to make sense of them, hoping to arrange them in comprehensible piles. (For some reason – my puritan reverence for the written word perhaps, *any* written word – I was rather late in discovering this fact.) We need serious critical analysis, of course, but not the throttling sort of theorizing that proclaims and forbids and ultimately places limits on fiction's possibilities.

Even before I began writing I had been suspicious of the kind of resolutions I stumbled across in stories: the Grail and the Goal; large noble gestures; sudden, blinding awareness; an exaggeration and level of heat which is the equivalent of hurled crockery and slammed doors. Even the word 'resolution' felt false. Difficult situations didn't always resolve themselves, I knew that, and, even when they did, resolution was frequently brought about by silence. I decided that each story I wrote during my experimental year would not take the narration to that comforting downward epiphanic movement, but would spiral upward if it chose or melt into another story, as happens at the end of 'Home' or in 'Mrs. Turner Cutting the Grass'. Or I would fast-forward the final paragraph into the future, something that happens in 'Flitting Behavior', or dive with it into the past, which is the kind of ending that occurs in 'Scenes'. I wanted these endings to hold an aesthetic surprise that spun *off* the narrative, but wasn't necessarily generated *out* of it.

The story 'Scenes' also represents an attempt to dislocate the spine of a traditional story, that holy line of rising action that is supposed to lead somewhere important, somewhere inevitable, modelled perhaps on the orgasmic pattern of tumescence followed by detumescence, an endless predictable circle of desire, fulfilment, and quiescence. I was for some reason drawn to randomness and disorder, not circularity or narrative cohesion. In fact, I had observed how the human longing for disruption was swamped in fiction by an almost mechanical model of aesthetic safety. My story 'Poaching' concerns two travellers who lure hitch-hikers into their car in exchange for the narrative of their separate and unconnected lives. This narrative hunger is assumed rather than explained in this rather slippery little story, though it is acknowledged that randomly gathered stories are often fragmentary, unsatisfying, and even dangerous. 'Behind each of the people we pick up, Dobey believes, there's a deep cave, and in the cave is a trap door and a set of stone steps which we may descend if we wish. I say to Dobey that there may be nothing at the bottom of the stairs, but Dobey says, how will we know if we don't look.'

I had started, around that time, to pay attention to the way in which women, sitting around a table for instance, tell each other stories. I noticed that women tended to deal in the episodic, to suppress what was smoothly linear, to set up digressions, little side stories which were not really digressions at all but integral parts of the story. These parts might contain gathered insights or they might exist for their own expressiveness alone, and they were, to quote from 'Scenes', 'what a life is made of, one fitting against the next like English paving-stones'. As in the stories 'Various Miracles' and 'Flitting Behavior', I wanted 'Scenes' to become a container for what it was talking about – which was the randomness of a human life, its arbitrary and fractured experiences that nevertheless strain toward a kind of wholeness. (I suppose another story, one called 'The Metaphor Is Dead – Pass It On', expresses more directly this melding of form and substance, the story-as-container notion, since its discussion of the richness and the debasement of metaphor is pocketed in a larger, more ironic metaphor which is the story itself, a metaphorical professor giving a metaphor-filled lecture about the death of metaphor.)

The problem-solution story I had grown up with no longer interested me. The form seemed crafted out of the old quest myth in which obstacles were overcome and victory realized. None of this seemed applicable to the lives of women whose stories had more to do with the texture of ordinary life and the spirit of community than with personal battles, goals, and prizes.

There is something else women do when they tell stories: they throw their narrative scraps into a kind of kitty and make of them a larger story. The story 'Dolls, Dolls, Dolls, Dolls' grew out of a discussion I once had with a few of my women friends, each of us producing recollections of dolls we had played with as children. It was true that every anecdote we exchanged had a different structure and feel to it, but afterwards I wondered if they didn't add up to a larger, more complex image, an image that commented in its prismatic way on the nature of women and their ability to care for something beyond themselves, and in their caring create a strategy for survival.

The looseness of structure in 'Dolls' mimics, I hope, the jumble of memory, its contradictions, its tentative linking of experience and awareness. I was anxious to embrace both contradiction and tentativeness, which struck me as more authentic, more real, than the cause/effect hammering of much 'realistic' fiction. As the writer Meershank says in 'Flitting Behavior', 'honesty' is not the only way of coping with the 'truth'.

In the midst of writing a story I often come up against that odd inability of fiction to stare at itself. (In these moments the whole enterprise seems shaky, and I wonder what I'm doing, a grown-up woman, sitting at a type-writer making up stories, *telling* stories.) The question that taunts me, and, in fact, bedevils many of the writers I know, is the problem of who is telling the story. There's something presumptuous, after all, about this act of ven-triloquism, the throwing of the voice, the artful positioning of the narrative stance. Working on *Various Miracles* gave me room to try out different approaches, bringing the voice in close in some of the stories or speaking obliquely in others or from a precisely measured distance. I also experi-mented with a gender-blind narrator in the story 'Poaching', taking pains never to reveal whether the 'I' of the teller is male or female. ('On the way to catch the Portsmouth ferry, Dobey and I stayed overnight in a country hotel in the village of Kingsclere.') Does it matter? I think it does; the story can be one thing or very much another, depending on whether the reader chooses to see the narrator (or Dobey) as a man or woman. The final story in the book, 'Others', represents an attempt to use a double narrator, a husband and wife who take turns telling the history of their twenty-five-year-old marriage. I found the structure wonderfully liberating, for I could use it to demonstrate what I believe to be true of long-lasting relationships, that the two individuals remain, in one sense, strangers one to the other while, at the same time, knowing each other better than they know themselves.

Somewhat similarly, the story entitled 'The Journal' uses a double narra-tive device, a traveller's journal that sets up a muted echo of Sally and Harold, a Canadian couple vacationing in France. 'When Harold and Sally travel, Sally keeps a journal, and in the journal Harold becomes H. She will write down such things as, "H. exclaimed how the cathedral (Reims) is melting away on the outside and eroding into abstract lumps." Has Harold actually *exclaimed* any such thing?' Whose voice can be trusted? – Sally's somewhat posturing journal or the detachment of the omniscient narrator? Both are clearly fictions; each may hold its share of truth.

It was only when I was reading the proofs of *Various Miracles* (for, some-what to my surprise, my year of experimentation did culminate in a book) that I noticed how every story turned on some variable of language, the fail-ure of language, its excess, its preciosity, its precision or distortion, its gaps and silences, its blustering and sometimes accidental ability to arrive at clar-ity or at least to disturb the air with its rhythms and colours, putting a kind of torque on ordinary discourse. The book is far from being what I would want it to be; I know intimately its soft spots and forced conclusions, its unevenness (that odd critical term) and disordered insights.

But its ultimate shape, an inquiry into language held in an envelope of language, amounted to a surprise, something fortuitous and unearned, offering me the kind of permission I needed then: to go on writing, tinkering, looking around, tapping out words, shifting my sentences and paragraphs about, getting the noises in my head onto paper, starting over.

John Metcalf

PUNCTUATION AS SCORE

MANY READERS, if not most, seem to think of punctuation merely as the utilitarian mortar between the blocks. They appreciate the stolid function of the full stop or question mark but when I start to talk of taking pleasure in the more delicate deployment of punctuation, eyes dull like morsels under old aspic. At professorial gatherings where the quicksilver banter is of tenure and mortgage, my recherché enthusiasms seem to be considered the mark of the dandy – or worse. After these brutal encounters, I am left feeling like the Ronald Firbank of Sassoon's account (*Siegfried's Journey, 1916-1920*):

> Anxious to entertain him appropriately, I bought a monumental bunch of grapes, and a glutinous chocolate cake. Powdered, ninetyish, and insuperably shy, he sat with eyes averted from me and my well-meaning repast. His most rational response to my attempts at drawing him out about literature and art was "I adore italics, don't you?" His cup of tea remained untasted, and he quailed when I drew his attention to my large and cosy pile of crumpets. As a gesture of politeness he slowly absorbed a single grape.

In the following notes, I want to suggest that a preoccupation with punctuation is not exclusive to the wildly avant-garde or to the wiltingly effete but is a concern common to all writers who are alive to the possible music of prose.

First published in John Metcalf, *Kicking Against the Pricks* (Downsview, ON: ECW, 1982; 2nd ed. Guelph, ON: Red Kite, 1986). Since the punctuation in this piece is an integral part of the discussion, the publisher has refrained from imposing its house-style rules on the text.

Punctuation both for the fiction and non-fiction writer is primarily punctuation for the eye; the eye translates the symbols into stops and emphases. Yet at the same time, the fiction writer must also write for the ear; he must contend with the problem of dialogue. For many writers of fiction there is a conflict between ear and eye; the conventional symbols do not translate fully all the nuances of the voices that speak on the page.

(As a *further* complication, the fiction writer often has to *suggest* voice even when writing something other than dialogue or monologue. It is sometimes necessary to write in a modified third-person which suggests an accent, an age, an occupation, etc. etc. and punctuation is an integral part of that suggested voice. The differences in voices are, in essence, differences in rhythm; punctuation helps in suggesting and emphasizing those rhythms.)

Standardization of punctuation started early in the nineteenth century and most of this work was carried on by the printers and compositors of the day. Almost as soon as an orthodoxy established itself, fiction writers began to rebel against the tyranny of 'House Rules'. Dickens was one of the first rebels; his is an interesting and extreme example of the conflict between eye and ear. His experiments with punctuation were not so much concerned with dialogue as wholesale with the punctuation of the narrating voice.

The punctuation of *Oliver Twist* when it was first published in serial form (1838-41) conformed to 'House Rules' but by the 1846 book-edition Dickens had worked out a strange system of punctuation which operated as a musical score rather than as an aid to the understanding of syntax; in other words, Dickens had 'scored' his book for recitation.

The following quotation is from the *Standard Oxford Illustrated Dickens*:

He had scarcely washed himself, and made everything tidy, by emptying the basin out of the window, agreeably to the Jew's directions, when the Dodger returned: accompanied by a very sprightly young friend, whom Oliver had seen smoking on the previous night, and who was now formally introduced to him as Charley Bates.

Even this punctuation is somewhat peculiar to the modern eye and would probably not have found favour with Partridge or Fowler.

The 1846 book-edition ran as follows:

He had scarcely washed himself: and made everything tidy, by emptying the basin out of the window, agreeably to the Jew's directions: when the Dodger returned; accompanied by a very sprightly young friend, whom Oliver had seen smoking on the previous night; and who was now formally introduced to him as Charley Bates.

(This quotation is taken from the restored text of *Oliver Twist* edited by Kathleen Tillotson. The Clarendon Dickens. General Editors: John Butt and Kathleen Tillotson. O.U.P. 1966).

The colons and semi-colons in this passage are extreme and irrational stops and suggest that the writing is intended for the boards and the lime-lights. The punctuation is irritating to the eye but less so to the ear; it demands to be read aloud – and read melodramatically. I find this punctuation almost impossible (as did many of Dickens' contemporary critics) because I don't want to sit in my armchair and declaim.

But whatever the obvious difficulties in departing from convention that this passage suggests, the idea of punctuation as 'score' has remained a central concern of many fiction writers. There have been varied experiments in this century which have added useful punctuational devices to the writer's technical stock; works by Joyce, Faulkner, Virginia Woolf, Dorothy Richardson, and e.e. cummings are obvious examples. Yet the experimentation of these writers was so extreme, so much a part of their individual voices, that their experimentation died with them.

No one in his right mind would consider my work 'experimental' but I've been trying for some years now to establish a system of punctuation which is more sensitive to voice than the conventions allow and which, at the same time, is not peculiar to my own individual voice.

I've failed.

And perhaps that's a good thing.

When Byron once criticized Leigh Hunt's style, Hunt said that his style was 'a system'.

"When a man talks of system," Byron said to Moore, "his case is hope-less."

However, an account of my failure might be interesting to readers to illustrate some of the technical preoccupations of writers of fiction. In what follows, I want to examine my use of quotation marks, italic, ellipsis, and paragraphing as ways of conveying *levels of voice*, as 'score'.

The rules for the use of quotation marks are simple. Words spoken are enclosed; words reported are not. Words spoken within spoken words are further enclosed by single or double quotation marks. Most publishing houses use double quotation marks for speech and single quotation marks within them for further speech. If the house uses single initial marks, then further speech is enclosed within double quotation marks.

Italic, where speech is concerned, is generally allowed only as emphasis or for such specialized purposes as indicating foreign words.

(It has been commonly accepted – and reasonably so – that italic should be used sparingly because if a sentence is correctly crafted the desired stress will be produced by the sentence's rhythm. This stricture applies, of course, more to expositional prose than to dialogue. The pepper-pot sprinkling of italic has been seen by Men of Letters as a feminine characteristic – 'feminine' meaning, of course, semi-literate and breathlessly *girlish*.)

And with these rules thus stated, most authorities are content to rest.

Consider the opening of my story "Gentle as Flowers Make the Stones":

Fists, teeth clenched, Jim Haine stood naked and shivering staring at the lighted rectangle. He must have slept through the first knocks, the calling. Even the buzzing of the doorbell had made them nervous; he'd had to wad it up with paper days before. The pounding and shouting continued. The male was beginning to dart through the trails between the *Aponogeton crispus* and the blades of the *Echinodorus martii*.

Above the pounding, words: 'pass-key', 'furniture', 'bailiffs'.

Lackey!

Lickspittle!

The female was losing colour rapidly. She'd shaken off the feeding fry and was diving and pancaking through the weed-trails.

Hour after hour he had watched the two fish cleaning one of the blades of a Sword plant, watched their ritual procession, watched the female dotting the pearly eggs in rows up the length of the leaf, the milt-shedding male following; slow, solemn, seeming to move without motion, like carved galleons or bright painted rocking horses.

The first eggs had turned grey, broken down to flocculent slime; the second hatch, despite copper sulphate and the addition of peat extracts, had simply died.

"I know you're in there, Mr Haine!"

A renewed burst of door-knob rattling.

He had watched the parents fanning the eggs; watched them stand guard. Nightly, during the hatch, he had watched the parents transport the jelly blobs to new hiding places, watched them spitting the blobs onto the underside of leaves to hang glued and wriggling. He had watched the fry become free-swimming, discover the flat sides of their parents, wriggle and feed there from the mucous secretions.

"Tomorrow ... hands of our lawyers!"

The shouting and vibration stopped too late.

The frenzied Discus had turned on the fry, snapping, engulfing, beaking through their brood.

The use of single quotation marks around 'pass-key', 'furniture', and 'bailiffs' where double quotation marks would be considered correct has various effects. First, although they are words spoken *to* Jim Haine, they are not spoken to him directly face to face; a locked door stands between the characters. The "incorrect" use of single quotation marks suggests this distance. Second, Haine's attention is directed elsewhere and these three words are words his mind picks out from what is presumably a tirade. The words 'picks out' in the preceding sentence are important; were the three words in double quotation marks, they would be given greater weight and prominence on the page and this would weaken the intended effect of lack of attention to the harangue. The question of weight (or sheer blackness on the page, if you will) perhaps verges on calligraphy which is related to my third point. Single marks have the appearance on the page of pincers – as if the heard words have been 'picked out' from a flood of other words with tweezers.

The italicized words *Lackey!* and *Lickspittle!* while certainly fulfilling the allowable function of emphasis also do more. Because they lack quotation marks, they are to be understood as words not spoken aloud. But they *are* spoken inside Jim Haine's head to the man beyond the door. Italic hereby becomes interior speech – words formulated but not uttered. This device is now commonly used and commonly understood and has been for years yet it is not described or acknowledged in any of the standard reference works on punctuation.

With the words in conventional double quotation marks ("I know you're in there, Mr Haine!") we are not only hearing the words of the man outside the door but we're also being made aware that Haine is hearing them too, that his agonized attention is being drawn from the tank of fish; he realizes that the noise has gone on too long and that the frantic parents will devour the fry. The double marks here contribute to action and to our awareness of Haine's consciousness.

Such a simple combined use of single and double marks, then, helps to establish the consciousness of the character and adds intensity and *drama* to his immobility and concentration. It also does away with the necessity of saying that he is rapt or staring fixedly or with great concentration. It also does away with having to say that the voice beyond the door was only half-heard or was muffled etc. etc. These effects could not have been achieved so economically and delicately had the conventions been observed.

(It is extremely important to note before going further that the use of single or double marks and italic in ways which differ from the conventional is only effective *because the convention exists and is expected*. The effect is much the same – or should be – as a denial of the ear's expectation in the established rhythm of a poem. The poet's departure from the established rhythm is usually to emphasize a key word or phrase.)

Quotation marks, single or double, have other functions which are widely understood but rarely, if ever, mentioned in books on punctuation such as those by Hart, Fowler, Carey, and Partridge. Most newspaper readers would understand the import of such a sentence as: The Prime Minister stayed at the Lodge with his "niece".

Most Canadian and American restaurants, however, seem ignorant of the dangers of advertising their "famous" this or "delicious" that.

Quotation marks, then, also serve the purpose of irony or the negation of statement.

When I use quotation marks for ironic purposes, I prefer to use single marks for what I suppose I must call calligraphic reasons – the single mark has a lighter, pincer-like, tighter-lipped, more *cruel* look than does the double mark.

The following is a quotation from "Girl in Gingham" where the experiences of a divorced man, Peter, are being recounted:

Subsequently, with a large weariness and a settled habit of sadness, he had become active in the world of those whose world was broken. First it was the single women of his married friends' acquaintance, awkward dinners where he had learned the meaning of 'intelligent', 'interesting', 'creative', and 'kind'.

Single marks here are appropriate to tone and character; I would go so far as to say that they are an aspect of characterization. The irony implied in the single marks would have been too crude had the marks been double; the reader would have been bludgeoned rather than tapped or flicked. And as what I'm writing here is really *modified* third-person (i.e., something suggestive of Peter's voice rather than an omniscient voice) double marks would have been "out of character".

Peter goes upstairs after dinner to kiss his friends' little daughter goodnight and there then occurs the following which is a bridge into a passage of exposition:

As Peter went upstairs, Alan in the kitchen was demanding his apron with the rabbits on it; Nancy's voice; and then he heard the sound of laughter.

'The woman situation'.

Whom, he wondered, had Alan in mind for him?

The woman situation had started again for him some eight months or so after his wife had left him. The woman situation had started at the same time he'd stopped seeing Dr Trevore, when he'd realized that he was boring himself; when he'd realized that his erstwhile wife, his son, and he, had been reduced to characters in a soap opera which was broadcast every two weeks from Trevore's sound-proofed studio.

And which character was he?

He was the man whom ladies helped in laundromats. He was the man who dined on frozen pies. Whose sink was full of dishes. He was the man in the raincoat who wept in late-night bars.

The words in single marks in this extract – 'The woman situation' – are a repetition of his friend's question during dinner: "By the way, nothing new with the woman situation, is there?"

Peter, then, is repeating mentally words spoken earlier. The words could have gone into double quotation marks or into italics.

If I had used double marks, the words would not have been differentiated from *spoken* speech. Double marks in no way suggest mental recall. Double marks would also have recalled more immediately the preceding scene where the words had been spoken when what I need is to move away from that scene and into a situation *interior with Peter.*

The single marks 'echo' Alan's question without repeating it *as speech* and so help to make a more natural bridge or transition into the succeeding passage of exposition.

The exposition begins at the paragraph: The woman situation had started again for him.... The writing here is in the third person but is carefully modified in its repetitions and rhetoric to suggest Peter's speaking voice even though he isn't speaking.

The movement towards the suggested inside of Peter's head is modulated in the following way:

1) The sounds Peter hears from the kitchen which grow fainter.

2) The words in single marks – 'The woman situation' – which recall speech but are not speech.

3) The words 'he wondered' in the next line.

4) The exposition of his past which is performed by the narrating voice taking on the colour and accents of Peter's voice.

This mental movement from exterior to interior is paralleled by his actual physical movements.

Peter is going upstairs. His progress up the stairs and movement away from his friends is marked by semi-colons. Also by Alan's actual heard *words*, Nancy's *voice*, then *sounds*. The external world retreats by means of semi-colons and the decline from *words* to *sounds*, leaving him alone and in silence.

The words 'The woman situation' could also have gone into italic but in this particular situation italic would have seemed too abrupt, too emphatic, too far removed from speech; to have used italic would have been an emphatic announcement almost as vulgar as saying: "I am now bridging into a passage of exposition."

(The line in this extract – Whom, he wondered, had Alan in mind for him? – starts an interesting hare.

The handling of these He wondered... He thought... constructions has exercised writers for years. Convention demands that the words appear:

He thought, "She is the most beautiful girl I've ever seen."

The use of quotation marks in this kind of construction is monstrously unnatural because of the contradiction between *thought* and the implied *said* of the quotation marks.

I have seen writers try the following ways out of this particular horror:

1) He thought, 'She is...
2) He thought: "She is...
3) He thought: She is...
4) He thought, she is...

The colon here is far too heavy a stop and contradicts the essential *speed* of thought.

The most graceful solution I've seen was in a Philip Roth story printed in *The New Yorker* although I'm not sure if it's Roth's invention, *New Yorker* stylesheet, or simply growing American practice.

The construction was:

He thought, She is...

This seems to me a delicate and triumphant solution to the problem and I adopted it the moment I saw it.)

It's always been my aim to make my dialogue as sharp and vibrant as possible by cutting out the use of explanatory adverbs and adverbial phrases – the irritating 'stage directions'. Getting rid of the adverbial mush makes heavier demands on the reader but dialogue should be crisp as a raw carrot and I can't pretend to feel interested in readers equipped with dentures.

Voices whose intonation and intent the reader immediately grasps offer writing a double benefit. The writing moves faster and is more vital but it's also true that the removal of adverbs creates the illusion of the invisibility of the author. The presence of 'stage directions' sets up artificiality within a single line.

"No, I will not!" he said, in angry tone.

Such a line as this offers us the voice of the fictional character but the 'realness' of this imagined voice is immediately countered by the intrusive 'authorial' voice telling us how to hear.

How much better to write: "No, I will *not!*"

And let italic, the exclamation mark, and the reader's intelligence take up the strain.

In the following extract from "Girl in Gingham", Peter and Alan are about to complete an application form for a computer-dating agency:

> "Wait", said Peter. "How's all this nonsense supposed to *work?*"
>
> "You answer all these questions and then it matches you with someone who's given the same kind of answers. And then you end up with a Computer Compatible."
>
> "A 'Computer Compatible'?"

The final line probably fails to capture the voice I want the reader to hear because the single marks are being asked to perform a double function. The single interior marks are used more or less conventionally because Peter repeats Alan's spoken words. At the same time, I wanted the single marks to convey ironic comment in the way I use them in other places. I wanted the single marks to suggest Peter's scorn and unwillingness to cooperate. They enable us to do away with the tedium of: "A Computer Compatible?" said Peter scornfully, in scorn, with distaste, uncooperatively, etc. etc.

It's more than possible that the circuits are overloaded here.

Pity.

THE USE OF ITALIC for other than conventional purposes has never, to my knowledge, been explored in Handbooks and Style Manuals. Apart from its use to indicate words thought but not uttered, it can suggest an amazing variety of voice and circumstance.

Consider the following extract from "Girl in Gingham" where Peter's experiences with a slightly potty psychiatrist are recounted:

> In the centre of Trevore's desk sat a large, misshapen thing. The rim was squashed in four places indicating that it was probably an ashtray. On its side, Trevore's name was spelled out in spastic white slip. Peter had imagined it a grateful gift from the therapy ward of a loony bin.
>
> It presided over their conversations.
>
> *How about exercise? Are you exercising?*

No, not much.

How about squash?

I don't know how to play.

I play myself. Squash. I play on Mondays, Wednesdays, and Fridays. In the evenings.

The words in italic are direct speech and should, according to the rules, go into double quotation marks. I chose to put them into italic for two reasons. First, they are part of a recounting of Peter's *past* experience in a purely narrative setting which otherwise lacks dialogue and to have introduced direct speech at this point would have disrupted the flow of a section of exposition precisely because spoken words (in quotation marks) would have jumped off the page assuming an importance they don't warrant. In contradiction to all authorities, italic here is *less* emphatic than words in quotation marks. Second, the use of italic here suggests the ritual quality of the conversation and somehow reinforces its silliness and sterility.

(A digression. For some years now, I've been playing with ways of producing economical caricatures of minor characters. Dr Trevore rather pleases me. I like the way he is identified with the ashtray, the way he *is* the ashtray. I also like the rhythms of his italicized speech, the *oddness* of the rhythms. Dialogue is the fastest and most deadly way to describe a person. I'd go so far as to say that patterns of speech suggest even physical appearance.)

The following quotation from a shockingly bad story I once wrote called "Playground" uses italic in a similar way but for slightly different reasons. A divorced father has gone to pick up his child at her grandmother's apartment.

As he'd gone into that familiar apartment building a feeling of bitterness almost physical had seemed to tighten his throat, a bitterness like the aftermath of vomit. He'd been surprised again at her grandmother's casualness, a casual amiability which seemed to ignore or even to have forgotten the recent past, the courts of law, the perjury, the pain.

The same scatterbrained flow of statements and the questions which did not wait for answers.

Are you still teaching those kind of people? Granny's bought her new pyjamas.

100% cotton. They're from Hong Kong so wash them before you put them on her. Everything from Hong Kong has Asian germs on it, doesn't it, my little angel? You've lost weight. Hasn't Daddy lost weight? Always buy cotton. So cute in her pretty dress that Granny bought her.

Goodbye.

The suitcase.

Goodbye.

And echoing after them along the corridor,

Buy her Spencer steak. It's the only kind she likes. Just like Granny buys her.

The reason for italic here is, I think, fairly obvious. The grandmother's words are not dignified with quotation marks because her words are sub-speech. Italic suggests better than quotation marks *prattle*. The use of italic, then, again becomes an aspect of characterization.

It seems to be a fact that unbroken italic is intensely uncomfortable to read. The expanse of italic here worried me and I felt compelled to break it up in some way. This led to a new invention – the dispensing with quotation marks around the non-italic Goodbye's.

Goodbye.

The suitcase.

Goodbye.

I was rather pleased with this effect because, calligraphically, it's so *flat* after the italic. And the calligraphic flatness parallels the emotional flatness and hostility. By their very flatness and lack of expected punctuation the words are undifferentiated from the object, the suitcase containing the child's clothes.

(All of this seems to me interesting and technically involving yet I must confess that at the same time this *particular* passage worries me. I'm interested in anything that can help in extending and amplifying the words on the page yet I'm also aware that experimentation with typography can degenerate into eccentricity and preciousness. Take e.e. cummings. Why the lower-case name? What's the *logic*? Sometimes I think his "in Just-/spring" poem is genuinely fresh and that his typographic inventions indeed extend meaning. At other times, I think the poem is pukingly *cute*.

Any departure from convention is treading the high wire.)

The next quotation is from "Private Parts: A Memoir". It suggests another level of voice, a physical level, which italic can command:

The pervert's ritual was unchanging. He would trudge down the path wheeling his bicycle until he was about a hundred yards above us. Then he would prop his bicycle up on its little stand, turn his back, then turn again, mount, and pedal furiously down the steep hill. Just before he was level with us, he would swerve from the track onto the grass at high speed, coming to within five yards of us. By this time he was steering with one hand on the handlebars. In his other hand he gripped his member which he attempted to wave.

Then he would veer back onto the path and wobble down the hill to crash through the bushes at the bottom and debouch onto Gladstone Avenue.

His progress was unsteady and hazardous, rather like the charge of an inept knight whose visor has suddenly obscured vision.

When he neared us, we'd shout,

"Let's have a look at it, then!" and "My sister's is bigger than that!"

And as he careered away from us almost out of control down the bumpy hill, he'd yell, "You bastards!" and then, faintly, *Rotten bastards*, and then the crash as he engaged the bushes.

The words *Rotten bastards*, though spoken and heard, appear in italic here to suggest faintness of sound and distance and to hint at desperate pathos. Again, I think they lack the emphasis that italic is supposed to convey and had I used the "correct" double quotation marks, the effect would have been less funny – and less touching. There's something infinitely pathetic about the idea of a *failed* pervert.

The idea of using italic in this way doubtless came from that marvellous cry in comics as characters fall to their deaths from a great height: *AAaaaaa!*

IF WE CONTINUE thinking of punctuation less as a formal series of stops and more as any devices which help to amplify and clarify the voice and its intent, then it's probably necessary for me to make a few remarks about paragraphing.

In general, paragraphing a line focuses attention on it powerfully.

Paragraphing of non-dialogue within dialogue is particularly useful in *orchestrating* dialogue – in building rhythms, in delaying the beat, in establishing pause and silence, and, by absence, in increasing tempo. Lines of non-dialogue within dialogue, if paragraphed, are not merely pauses and rests in the building of a rhythmic statement but suffer a change into something very close to dialogue itself.

The following passage from *Going Down Slow* is a fairly obvious example:

David sat down at his desk and while the kids found the right place in the book stared at the framed coloured photographs of the Queen and the Duke of Edinburgh.

> "Peter, let's make up for lost time. 'Thou bleeding piece of earth'. Let's start there."

> "I forgot my book in my locker, sir."

> "Mary?"

> "He's bleeding where they stabbed him."

> "Yes, but 'earth'? Umm?"

Norvicki's face disappearing behind a large pink bubble which he deflated and engulfed again.

> "Yes, Marjorie?"

> "He's lying in such a lot of blood it looks like the earth is bleeding."

David shook his head.

> "Support the Work of the Red Cross", said a poster at the back of the room.

> "Yes, Ronnie?"

> "Why couldn't he say what he meant, sir? I mean, if he's so good how come you can't understand him?"

The lines of non-dialogue here retard the pace of the dialogue. The scene is being dragged out because it is seen through the eyes of the teacher, David, for whom the class is an exercise in disappointment and dreariness. Dreariness and futility are the points of the dialogue; the interruptions of the dialogue intensify these feelings. The use of the present participle in 'disappearing' modifies the third-person voice making the perception closer to David and seemed to me to give the line the quality of answer to the preceding question; the expanding pink bubble becomes answer, becomes *speech*.

The following rather rude passage is from the same novel:

David mounted the stand and stood in the middle of the three stalls. He unzipped his trousers. Rubber footsteps squelched in the cloakroom. The swing-door banged open and Hubnichuk came in. They nodded. Hubnichuk was wearing a shabby blue track-suit.

He mounted the stand to David's left. Standing back, he pulled down the elastic front of his trousers. He cradled his organ in the palm of his hand; it was like a three-pound eye-roast. Suddenly, he emitted a tight, high-pitched fart, a sound surprising in so large a man.

Footsteps.

Mr Weinbaum came in.

"So this is where the nobs hang out!" he said.

"Some of them STICK OUT from time to time!" said Hubnichuk.

Their voices echoed.

Mr Weinbaum mounted the stand and stood in front of the stall to David's right.

"If you shake it more than twice," he said, "you're playing with it."

Water from the copper nozzle rilled down the porcelain.

There was a silence.

David studied the manufacturer's ornate cartouche.

The Victory and Sanitation Porcelain Company.

Inside the curlicued scroll, a wreathed allegorical figure.

Victory?

Sanitation?

Mr Weinbaum shifted, sighed.

"I got the best battery in Canada for $18.00", he said.

Again, the lines of what *seem* to be merely simple description are, in fact, mute dialogue. The ritual washroom remarks of the men, the rilling water, the words on the porcelain – all are *the same thing*, comments and statements. The passage also captures, of course, something of the studious silence of a shared washroom.

If I were writing this scene now – some ten years later – I would delete the phrase 'There was a silence.' It's not merely redundant; it is obtrusive. It's interesting to read this passage paragraphed conventionally:

Mr Weinbaum mounted the stand and stood in front of the stall to David's right.

"If you shake it more than twice," he said, "you're playing with it."

Water from the copper nozzle rilled down the porcelain. There was a silence. David studied the manufacturer's ornate cartouche.

The Victory and Sanitation Porcelain Company. Inside the curlicued scroll, a wreathed allegorical figure. Victory? Sanitation?

Mr Weinbaum shifted, sighed. "I got the best battery in Canada for $18.00", he said.

Here, then, is a totally different piece of writing, different in rhythm and different *in meaning*.

(One of the reasons why paragraphed lines of non-dialogue within dialogue approximate speech is purely technical. We are responding to convention. Convention decrees that each new speaker starts his speech on a separate line as a new paragraph. Because we are trained to respond to that convention, we are unconsciously half-prepared to read the lines of non-dialogue as being closely related to direct speech.)

I've so far deliberately chosen examples which are extreme the better to illustrate the idea; the following example from "Girl in Gingham" is more subtle, perhaps, and certainly more typical. The situation is that Peter has gone to the house of a woman he's never met whose name has been supplied by the Computer Dating Agency. The conversation is awkward and nervous.

"Well," she said, "you must tell me about appraising. What does an antique appraiser *do?*"

"Well," said Peter, "furniture's the bread-and-butter side of.."

"That's a dip I make myself", she said, lifting a white limp leather handbag from the floor by the end of the couch and rummaging.

"But porcelain and silver", said Peter, "are my.."

"And I'm sorry about the chips – I was rushed and picked up those awful ones that taste of vinegar by mistake – but the dip's very good. It's very easy in a blender – sour cream and Danish Blue, chives, and a teaspoon of lemon juice."

She found cigarettes at the bottom of the bag.

"Delicious", said Peter. "Absolutely delicious."

And listened to himself crunching.

"Tell me," she said, snapping and snapping the mechanism of the slim gold lighter, "we didn't seem to talk about this, did we? Or did we? I was rather flustered – well, *you* know, and my memory's awful but did you say you *weren't* married? My memory! Sometimes I can't even seem.."

"No", said Peter, leaning across and lighting her cigarette with a match. "No, I'm not."

"You're lucky", she said.

He smiled and sipped.

"Peter," she said, "you listen to me. You pay attention. You're a very lucky man."

Paragraphed lines like, And listened to himself crunching, are intended to work on various levels simultaneously. In that Peter is listening to himself, it implies that the awkward conversation has come to a stop, that there is an equally awkward silence. Peter listens *to himself* – emphasizing his lack of involvement with the woman. 'Crunching' is in itself vaguely funny but with its suggestions of breaking and destroying also painful. The line serves to end, and summarize, a cycle or fit of the conversation. It seems to me that the line almost becomes a comment on the whole situation *by Peter*. While remaining, of course, in the third person.

The following lines from the same extract suggest another way in which speech can be punctuated:

"Tell me," she said, snapping and snapping the mechanism of the slim gold lighter, "we didn't seem to talk about this, did we? Or did we? I was rather flustered – well, *you* know, and my memory's awful but did you say you *weren't* married? My memory! Sometimes I can't even seem..'

"No", said Peter, leaning across and lighting her cigarette with a match. "No, I'm not."

The words which interrupt speech – snapping and snapping the mechanism of the slim gold lighter – serve various functions. First, they halt her question and create, in the smallest way, tension and suspense. Second, they *parallel* her difficulty in asking the question. Third, the word 'snapping' functions in much the same way as did 'crunching' referred to in an earlier instance.

Peter's reply and described action *cut across* her babble both verbally and physically, the described action paralleling the words. Peter's "No", because it is separated from the rest of what he says ("No, I'm not" which *softens* that first "No"), takes on somehow larger significance than an answer to the question. It is a "No" to the whole situation.

I've sometimes listened to actors in CBC studios who have been recording readings of my stories and on various occasions they've wanted to dispense with 'he said' or 'she said', instinctively wishing, perhaps, to turn story dialogue into stage dialogue. The placement of such simple things as a 'he said' or 'she said' can be of vital importance. What *profound* differences there are between "What do you think you're doing?" and "What", he said, "do you think you're doing?"

Prose has its own necessities.

MUCH OF WHAT I'VE SAID so far is too intuitive and personal, relies too heavily on context, to be of *systematic* use to other writers. Systems cannot be expounded when one is constantly forced into using words like "seems", "suggests", and "calligraphy". But there are two unconventional devices I use – minor fragments of the Grand Design – which *could* be used systematically by other writers because neither device depends on context or the writer's sensibility.

The first of these devices is particularly useful in crowd scenes.

Imagine two people talking at a party. The writer wants the words of others to impinge on their central conversation. Such "overheard" conversation might be vital for later plot development, colour, contrast, comedy, or for "fragmented exposition". Yet at the same time, the writer wants the dialogue to remain crisp and uncluttered by such irritating stage directions as: A voice behind me – The fat man to his left –

Convention requires us to use double quotation marks for all speakers. In what follows, A and B represent the "foreground" speakers and C represents the voice "overheard" by A and B.

A: "So what did he do about it?"

B: "Well, by this time, of course, he was crazy with rage and he..."

C: "I know what you mean. I've always felt uneasy about George's appetites."

The words spoken by C *might* have been spoken by A again in response to B. I've deliberately chosen words for C which might be interpreted in this way to illustrate the problem by exaggeration. Two pages like this and most readers would be hopelessly confused and irritated. Stage directions are necessary.

A: "So what did he do about it?"

B: "Well, by this time, of course, he was crazy with rage and he..."

C: "I know what you mean", said the man beside the potted palm. "I've always felt uneasy about George's appetites."

At first glance, there seem to be no great problems with such a construction as this but imagine the annoyance of such identifications as 'the man beside the potted palm' repeated over two pages.

Again, the conversation between A and B, the foreground speakers, might be an intense and passionate conversation. Frequent visual identifications (the man beside the potted palm) might suggest that A and B are constantly looking about them when what the writer wishes to convey is that they are locked visually together. Stage directions force the authorial voice to become obtrusive; the reader is aware of manipulation.

A writer of great power and elegance, Keith Waterhouse, uses what I feel to be a very clumsy device for handling this problem. In the following extract from *Jubb*, two men in a pub have picked up three girls. The five are joined by a third man. The third man (A) is the first speaker. The words in brackets and quotation marks, a mechanically indignant question, are from (C) – one of the girls in the background of the conversation.

A: "No, really," I said, "I must go now."

B: "You're not leaving us to handle three of 'em, are you?"

C: ("Do you mind?")

A: "I'm afraid so."

What is so *very* wrong with Waterhouse's invention is that the weight of the brackets and double marks drags what should be in the background to the foreground.

I was delighted, however, to discover that we are both bothered by the same problem.

My solution is simple and, I think, elegant.

And can be stage-managed over pages if necessary.

Retain double marks for A and B and use single marks for C. A mixing of double and single marks enhances such a scene by suggesting physical distance and lower volume for the words in single marks.

The second device I use in dialogue which might be used by others is the awful ellipsis.

The standard use of the ellipsis in dialogue is to indicate omission.

As in: "I'd like to have a word with you if you..."

Here we understand the uncompleted completion of the sentence to be something like "if you can spare the time" or "if you don't mind". Reading the line and seeing the ellipsis the eye gives the signal to the voice to fall or waffle or "shuffle" forward slightly to suggest continuation.

The ellipsis instructs the voice to extend 'you'.

(Depending on context, the ellipsis can suggest confusion, embarrassment, vagueness – all manner of things.)

What our conventional system of punctuation seems to lack is a mark or a stop which indicates the *interruption* of one speaker by another. Some writers use a dash but a dash has other uses – one of which is to indicate a *pause* – and is therefore possibly confusing.

My invention, if it *is* an invention, is to use a two-point ellipsis instead of a three to indicate interruption. Some such device is important because it scores for the reader the *pacing* of the exchange.

It looks like this:

A: "I haven't the slightest idea", she said, "where they.."

B: "Why? Why haven't you?"

A: "Well, it's all rather..."

A's first line is to be read as if the conclusion of the sentence is coming. In other words, there's a fast breath-check on 'they'. A's second line is to be read with a conventional waffling on the word 'rather'.

Another use of this two-point ellipsis is to indicate the *continuation* of a sentence after an interruption. Imagine three speakers.

Thus:

A: "I've always been very fond of.."

B: "So shall we buy it or not?"

A: "..a nice ham sandwich. I always say that you can't beat.."

C: "Who'll give us a loan?"

A: "..fresh bread and a nice slice of ham."

I think this device is genuinely useful and fills a need. Most of the time I find myself using it for comic purposes.

I wonder why?

My failure to erect a system doesn't really trouble me. I have too much humour in my make-up to join the ranks of Spelling Reformers or Universal Esperanto Speakers. But it would be a mistake, I think, to dismiss these notes as merely eccentric or obsessionally technical. The reader must remember that punctuation is a means to an end. There is nothing odd or silly about the desire to transcribe or create voices in such a way that the reader can immediately grasp their full range and intent.

Voices speaking are the heart of literature.

Punctuation helps us hear.

Keath Fraser

NAZCA

BECAUSE IT'S THE LITERARY EQUIVALENT of the world's long lines, I came to write fiction. Long lines make popular and sometimes useful sense of the world. They give imaginary order to the earth – a frontier, a meridian, the equator – lines telling us where we are, who we are, what time it is, and what brief day tomorrow.

For better or worse I had decided to put my faith in lines of all kinds. The snow line, the horizon. The railway line, the branch line, those winsome bus and spur lines, the lines that carry us to places, even take us somewhere down a phone or cable without our stirring. It was a wealth of lines when I looked at the world that carried me away. *Us* away ... our waste down sewerlines, our gas through pipelines, our opinions and emergencies over hotlines. (Talk about connections.)

Many lines are long because they mark development: the child learning to draw straight with a ruler; the girl listening to a spiel from her date; a reporter awarded his first recognition. It followed, I could see, the man tracing the yearly recession of his hair and the woman her wrinkles ... the pensioner with a fishing pole awaiting his chinook.

I suppose like anybody else I noticed the ordinary lines of labour, love, and death because they ran through mothers hanging out family wash and queues waiting to go to work or buy souvlaki on Greek Day for a friend. They taught me. I already knew there could be no passing on the double line, and I grew to know the fine line between love and hate. When I started writing I couldn't believe, and found it useful to remember, that young Islamic 'volunteers' thought crossing the front line a glorious route to God.

My favourite long lines became those in the desert floor at Nazca. If you

First published in *event* 18.1 (1989).

fly over them in a Cessna they reveal the images of birds, fish, monkeys, drawn by an ancient tribe down hot miles and centuries of Peru. Foreign aliens? Their gifts to posterity remain mysterious.

In fiction, time is everything – a patient study of the length of lines. If you were to trace Relativity's curved line through space, if you were to fly in a straight line around everything, you'd end up at the same place. But it can't be; you wouldn't be. To be sure kings and queens are pleased with such lines as theirs they believe established in nature. Isn't gravity, after all, the weakest force?

Tomorrow and tomorrow and tomorrow is Macbeth's longest line. I think this one made sense when I concluded the present was only an ideal.

Keath Fraser

WHEN IS STYLE MORAL?

IF A WRITER'S STYLE pleases us there's usually something deceptive about its spontaneity. What we know of style suggests that unlike personality, say, it's an act of deliberation, second thought, correction – and not really spontaneous at all. In this way style, I think, is closer to character than to personality: to the shaping of character (the writer's own) but also, in the case of fiction writers, their own imaginary characters. Character is moral in a way personality isn't. You can say that personality is pleasing, for example, but you can't call it moral the way you do character. Character is the quiet blooming of imagination in a room and not the corsage at a ball. Personality is social and occasional; character private and persistent. The one is necessary, the other inevitable. Character accepts revision endlessly without feeling threatened. In this sense it's masochistic but not tortured, working toward the day of its release. Getting knocked about appears to cheer it up, perversely, and instead of losing spontaneity it bit by bit acquires it. This is the paradox of style, the essence of its deception: the surprising lack of bruises. (You can detect writing of personality because there's something specious about its desire to be tough in the company of straw men. It curries acceptance for congenial outspokenness and shuns self-imposed scruple.) Personality is constantly at risk from entropy; but character works against disorder, uniformity, collapse. Something unnatural in character wants to dissent from natural law. It chooses over and over not to fizzle out. Refuses to give in to time, a deadline, above all death. Art is long, we know, and around art as around character the decisions for melioration are endless. Style is moral, you conclude, when it has made of choice a world.

First published in John Metcalf and Leon Rooke, eds., *The Second Macmillan Anthology* (Toronto: Macmillan, 1989).

Keath Fraser

BECOMING COMPLICIT

WHEN I WAS GROWING UP I was refused the world by class, religion, and penury. Or so I believed. In what I was encouraged to think a happy childhood, I felt enjoined by loyalty, Catholicism, and debt to make the best of what I had. What I had was a not unperky time, scarred by doubt and a deep yearning to be of the world. I wanted to travel, be loved, afford new shoes. The size and diversity of my family, just as much as its tenderness for outsiders, held little significance in what to me was my narrow and dutiful place. The heresy that imagination was shaped in such contradictions I would have called traitorous. I was certainly safe from the scoop that I might be cultivating an impostor's talents. Like every other child I could fly in my dreams; wish and I could peer down on earth. It was only natural that I read to escape.

Reflecting on how much felt forbidden to me then, I can see how climbing a neighbour's cedar tree and raising my eyes above the power lines must first have tempted me into voyeurism upon the world. I could gaze all the way to the Sea Island airport. Books themselves, my earliest windows, were few, until I discovered the new neighbourhood library. But even this well-lighted place had its moment of denial, when my father seemed on the cusp of having to refuse my admittance, until I could assure him a card would cost only fifteen cents. My poor well-meaning father. My poor comprehensive Catechism. 'Catholic', as drummed into children of the fifties, meant 'universal', and we parroted answers to encompass the world, anatomizing it from every angle judged necessary to defend the fort. Yet fiction was a way of wandering out through the gates, into forbidden territory, preferably of a frontier variety where tents, lean-tos, and longhouses contained even

---

First published in *Brick: A Journal of Reviews* 40 (1991).

less furniture than we had. This incited my yearning to understand how the past, my city, the larger world could possibly be articulated, in that anatomical sense, to satisfy the child's wonder about everything outside him.

Believe me, everything was outside him. Or so I felt. Magazines, television, lessons, vacations ... I was forbidden to read Dick Tracy in the funnies. I have the feeling yet that the pearly world remains beyond, that a perpetual yearning preys upon my life. It seemed life had prepared me to look at the world with the eyes of someone plagued by an imagination bound in childhood like the feet of a Chinese daughter in pre-revolutionary Nanking. When it began to uncurl, I sensed an invincible need to plant myself firmly upon the earth and, God knows, wander. At university I would sometimes roam the campus at night, peering into buildings, curious about the many paths to the western sea, if only I knew which to choose. It soon dawned that not only would I never know or study what went on in those rooms of that particular faculty, *I would never even enter the building*. This appalled me. How could one learn to live within the limits of one's life, when the frontier instinct, from my grandparents to the first novel I can remember reading with utter absorption, about Pierre Radisson as I entered grade four, had uncovered in me the instincts opposite to limitation, confinement, stricture? The free enterprise of imagination, indeed the entrepreneurial spirit of a family of janitors and carpenters, cabbies and fishermen, shepherds and bus drivers, seemed to disavow the notion of inheriting the earth through doctrinal impoverishment.

I was fortunate in the way I imagine most writers are whose family lives have been too rigorous to turn out well-adjusted members of the body politic. Such an alien body, who could understand it?

In London, where I later went to study for three years, I began to realize that the voyeurism I'd practised as a child was becoming a problem. Now an outsider and foreigner both, still peering into rooms and wondering what went on in these, I began to surmise I was a chronic outsider, either too aloof or too shy to knock and enter the world I was already in. Besides, like a voyeur, I took my pleasure in solitude and imbibed it as I might lady jane (The Stones' drug of choice, and inspiration for that wonderful song of theirs). A mistake if one were preparing, as I was, to offer anatomy lessons to the body politic back home. I'd need to brush up on home, even as I continued to travel farther from my country.

Learning how to read literature, I was also preparing, if I only knew it, to write fiction. But I was circumspect and mistrustful of a vision so voyeuristic as to amount to onanism. What had I to *say*, except that I was here, outside the window, this single cell in the body of a great city? Somebody might call the cops. I was a cop myself, a budding critic, who knew a literary masturbator when I saw one peering in from outside. So a kind of circuitous thinking about writing began to develop. Feeling himself an outsider, the would-be writer yearned to know the inside, to know what went on in there, without wanting to give up his freedom in order to be inside. The same went for a commitment to the Third World, an abiding desire for years. Selfishly now, this dissembler would rather travel in the Third World and be free of commitment to any one country. Ditto for the university teaching he was eventually tenured to back home: needed to get out of that, be free, be outside – deciding that when the Last Day dawned he'd prefer to be judged on how he'd handled his ignorance about writing than how he'd bestowed his knowledge of literature. And so, as these things go, was canonical posturing replaced by imposturing of a decidedly risky nature.

As the oldest child of a large family I must once have felt it expected of me to become something in the world – possibly the priest I answered back in Latin as an altar boy, shaking my head in reverent amazement over the number of years he'd studied to become what he was, the Cadillac among priests, a Jesuit. I had at least aspired to quality. I now sensed that reading fiction had prepared me for nothing so much as a desire to sneak around the world in bare feet.

The smell of summer grass after dark ... how was one to know or understand this, and would anyone else know it in the same way, *want* to know it in the same way? How *did* one know a smell? the configuration of a porch? that woman reading in the lamplight? this texture of squid on my tongue? sunlight on a rocky cliff, back beside the Pacific...? And these poetic impulses of space seemed small in comparison to the narrative impulses of time itself. Fiction, if that's what I was determined to write, was going to be lines in the brow and a pain in the lumbar. How to choose what to write when you discover the entire world is open for your business? More to the point, what *not* to write....

The scope of what he feels himself outside of, I concluded, is a measure of a writer's view of the world, quite apart from his ability to give voice to the spectacle. The more deeply he yearns for imaginative knowledge, then the more various, the more vigorous will be his fictional world. I had to believe that he writes first and foremost because he yearns – and only secondly, thirdly, fourthly, to charm, to draw attention to, to share compassion with ... whatever else seems to explain this initial yearning of one or more senses to understand imaginatively, and hence wholly, the agonizing discreteness of the world. The matter of confidence became my central concern as an impostor.

For the proposition I got wise to is that the fiction writer becomes an impostor to become a voyeur. The confidence man puts on this knowledge (in Yeats's phrase) to satisfy his yearning. Obsession perforce turns him into a woman, a swan, a dead king. What choice has he, what laws could possibly prevent his obsession, when so many choices have to be made? 'Precisely because its variety is infinite,' writes Northrop Frye, 'literature suggests an encyclopaedic range of concern greater than any formulation of concern in religious or political myth can express.' Any formulation of concern of the latter sort is one of those Jesuitical interests I knew wasn't mine.

So unless a writer was obsessed with yearning, no sense of his world could start to approach wholeness. Knowing what his obsession *is*, I thought, was the first step to giving it a metaphorical whole that resists splitting into the partisan politics of form and content. Messianic writing ignores metaphor and has little faith at all in fiction. Conversely – some would say perversely – the voyeur's effort is to train our eyes to the window. He's trying to understand what fiction might be in the context of more than one context, voice, world. The wonder inherent in this multiplicity became my own particular obsession. (*If only*, whines the child, till his poor parents claim that even granted everything he wished for he'd never be satisfied. Feeling shut out of the world, a writer learns to modulate this whine as an impostor whose parents were right.)

My pleasure as a writer began in populating a variegated world of moral dickering. I think we fail to understand ourselves and what's everywhere around us if we neglect to view the local and familiar up against the foreign and exotic: hairpins, lapis lazuli, grief, exuberance, poverty, Club Med, Calcutta.... The net purchase is a refurbished notion of here. Writers hang around windows the way bankers do around interest rates, and panhandlers around coins. I suppose my delight in trying to descry metaphorical models of the imagination was just the agnostic's way of enlarging upon what the nuns used to teach us was important in 'setting an example for others'. It is a terrible presumption, either way you look at it.

But if the writer becomes an impostor to succeed as a voyeur, so does the reader. A word now on how what is forbidden in fiction makes reading a subversive act of complicity.

I LIKE TO FORBID my young son to eat his casserole when I wish he would spoon it down. It's an old trick new parents learn, the delight a child takes in wilful transgression. The trick is in learning how to forbid, convincingly. The child recognizes your enjoinder as a game, yet unless you throw yourself into it with unaffected fabrication, he will refuse to play. 'I don't want to see you –' *scowl*, 'don't let me see you –' *teeth warning him*, 'I forbid you to eat that casserole!' If my performance pleases or impresses him, if he really thinks I mean him not to eat his casserole, even while knowing our engagement is a game, he will reward us both by digging in.

But what happens, say, when I ask a reader *not to imagine* a yellow banana? The result is predictable. It's difficult not to conjure up what is forbidden in direct proportion to its particularity. We know from what psychologists tell us that an attempt to suppress knowledge can lead to obsession about it. If you've ever sat on a trial jury you will know that when the judge instructs you to ignore a particular piece of testimony there's an excellent chance you will do precisely the opposite – not out of perversity but because you can't shoulder it out of your mind. It rewards us to consider this imaginative behaviour carefully, to understand how we read fiction and how its makers have captured our souls.

For even harder than not to imagine a yellow banana is not to imagine a freckled banana, especially if it has just given worms to the neglected little girl of a local judge, whose grocery shopping attests to her slapdashery as a mother. The less generic an invocation (in this case the less yellow the banana) and the more specific the banana's image, then the more likely we are to seize on the forbidden fruit. It's obvious that our purveyor of bananas has a somewhat better chance of creating an indelible effect by selecting the riper, perhaps more beguiling context. Similarly, a race horse in the paddock with a bleeding bruise on its fetlock; or a judge's cheek smooched with lipstick. Given the opportunity as readers to avoid either image in a story by closing the book, we may be tempted to know more of this horse, or at least more of the suicidal character determined to bet on it. And can you imagine having no curiosity about such a judge? She's an interesting study, our judge ... but we are instructed to disregard the stain of this kiss as she holds forth against letting our imaginations wander.

So let me restate the case in another, more obvious way, before moving on to what I think makes reading fiction the act of complicity we know it to be.

Unlike bananas, bruises, and lipstick stains – if I forbid you to think about technology, let us say, you will have little trouble obeying the injunction. Technology is gaseous, an abstraction, akin to Global Village and Testosterone, Environment and Infrastructure. This rhetoric blankets us like smog, especially if it's offered by way of a 'formulation of concern'. Its bewitchery is limited by its reproaches. Incidentally, since rhetoric by definition implores us *to* think about its agenda (having little time for the loucheness of metaphor), it is only natural *not* to think about its agenda and to tell the priest, the activist, or the anarchist to shove it. I exaggerate my case to make the point, Your Honour.

Similarly, what I call the arteologist will wrap himself in the flag of fiction and launch an attack on putative enemies from his pulpit. He despises art and is convinced he knows why. He and no one else is in touch with social reality, which needs be addressed in the language of the soapboxer. He'd kick metaphor in the private parts if he found it lurking in his crowd. He'd like to flush out the corrupt and puny for us, the private and selfish, by separating form from content. He hopes to con the connable, who have forgotten or never read Susan Sontag's seminal essay from a quarter century back: 'In a culture whose already classical dilemma is the hypertrophy of the intellect at the expense of energy and sensual capability, interpretation is the revenge of the intellect upon art. Even more. It is the revenge of the intellect upon the world.' It is, in its Delphic disguise, journalism.

The imagination may be excused if it holds up its old bandages in the crowd to throw at one more priest who thinks he knows the way it ought to be bound. Why so many points, so few views? Rhetoric invites disagreement by its earnestness, and has no understanding of complicity. It addresses a crowd, for one thing. And it addresses it in a recyclable language. I used to enjoy paraphrasing for students Aldous Huxley's reflections on the disposable language of science in *Literature and Science*, countering this with what he mentions of the (ageless) language of art. 'By means of metaphor we can talk about one thing in terms of something else and so, by indirection, express more of life's multiple meanings, subjective and objective, than can be expressed by straightforward speech.' Yeats said he made rhetoric out of his quarrel with others and poetry from the quarrel with himself. This quarrel with self is louche and at odds with upright public utterance. Rhetoric wants to do good, to tell us in turn how to be good: rhetoric as the art of reproach. The arteologist would attempt to engage us in a parody of imposture by refusing to become a voyeur. But complicity in fiction is the art of opening ourselves up to dishonour. It takes courage when we might be ignored; or maybe not ignored and charged with onanism.

Fiction puts us at odds with our social manners. It may be a truth universally acknowledged that a single man in possession of a good fortune is in search of a wife, but that's an affair between him and his own feelings. Isn't it? It may be true that all happy families are alike, but if an unhappy family is unhappy in its own way theirs is a private matter that's none of our business. Agreed? When Miss Emily Grierson dies, aren't we above the gossipy town women who attend her funeral mainly to poke around her house – which no one but a black cook has seen inside in over ten years? The answer to each proposition is, of course, No. The writer has already turned us into voyeurs, has radicalized our polite world of convention, has subverted our expectations by raising them in the context of his own. In a sense, we sin against the privacy of others every time we feel tempted to enter a fictional world. 'Philip has thrown himself across the bed and fallen asleep, his clothes on still, one of his long legs dangling to the floor.' Sinning in this way is our revenge against having the door of the world closed in our face.

Writing fiction and reading it ought to feel illicit. It is, after all, the consummation of the catholic yearning to know ourselves through others. Fiction should somehow convey an illicit desire to keep reading the specific details of its subversive uncovering. In his story 'The End of the Revolution and Other Stories' Leon Rooke opens this way: 'Her windows are always the same. Whether she's out or in I never know. Frustrating, the curtains always drawn.' It isn't enough to stand outside peering in, however. The fiction writer's desire, to turn readers into obsessive readers, will depend on his success in earning our confidence as an impostor. A writer must convince us of his ease within the world of characters and extend himself everywhere as an impostor who enjoys entry. If his characters happen to become impostors themselves, they may try to convince characters within their own spheres to trust them with confidences too. We think of Nabokov's consummate imposturing to become a voyeur in *Lolita*, of those voyeurs within voyeurs in his parody of the *doppelgänger* theme, eclipsing himself with Humbert Humbert and Clare Quilty among others. Becoming a confidence man is akin to turning invisible, every child's fantasy – or every prisoner's, as in John Cheever's *Falconer*, when Farragut finally escapes his penitentiary in a body bag.

The best fiction, it would seem obvious then, begins with and trades in the voyeuristic. It attracts us by what is seemingly forbidden and unseemingly revealed. This imaginative world speaks to *me*. How could anyone else possibly know it as I know it? Privacy is all. But this isn't onanism, but rather the coupling of writer with reader, writer with character, character with character. The writer, the character, the reader become complicitous in the secret knowledge of the world. Hear Don DeLillo, as a character he's impersonating in *Libra*: 'You wear a uniform, it makes all the difference. Look at me. I put on my captain's jacket, all this bleary shit just falls away. I become a captain for Eastern. I talk like a captain. I instill confidence in anxious travelers. I actually fly the goddamn plane.' His novel is full of voyeuristic ways of penetrating the unknown myths surrounding the public event of President Kennedy's assassination. And as Alberto Moravia claims in his novel *The Voyeur*, 'The voyeur spies not only on what is forbidden, but also on what is unknown. In other words, voyeurism implies a need to discover the unknown.'

When we read fiction, we need to ask what is forbidden me in this work, what is unknown that I would like to know. If nothing is forbidden, if nothing is unknown, little is being asked and therefore risked, no matter how much the trappings of textual monkeying may want me to think otherwise. How strong is my addiction to know the heart of this narrative? A work of literature ought not lead us to suppose that we can know more than it's able to forbid. A work of literature that isn't ineffable, that can be spoken of in other terms and so induce paraphrase, has at best a facile obsession and at worst an interested position. The more prolix the paraphrase the less sophisticated the art. It can be disagreed with – it may even invite this. Yet the essence of art is that it can't be contradicted (let alone recycled). This audacity surprises us.

I would submit, Your Honour, that fiction writers create a responsible and necessary game called complicity. They become impostors, their readers scheme. Our complicit pleasure is urgent and subversive. Fiction is a private attempt to enter the imagination when the world has somehow failed to deliver. Fiction is popular anatomy of no less than the world. We would know it to its bones.

I HAVE OFTEN WONDERED whose is the shadowy, epicene face in that famous photograph of Auden and Isherwood leaving London for China in 1938, gazing out the window over Auden's left shoulder, past the Smoking sign of the coach, to the press camera on Victoria station platform. Isherwood would have wanted to know, since he claimed to be a camera. Auden too. 'Private faces in public places are wiser and nicer than public faces in private places', as he wrote in *The Orators*. That face inside the coach is a private face.

If I had to shape a story around this photograph, what not to write about would be as important as what to. Choosing not to write about two public writers, I would be choosing instead to enter an imagined world of the anonymous, nonhistorical character, whose unexpected brush with greatness might also be ours. As a fiction writer I am, along with another voyeur who once rode by train from Richmond to Waterloo, rejecting the influence of famous writers to concentrate on rendering the anonymous 'Mrs Brown' as truthfully as I can. 'I believe that all novels begin with an old lady in the corner opposite', wrote Virginia Woolf. And later in that essay: 'But do not expect just at present a complete and satisfactory presentment of her. Tolerate the spasmodic, the obscure, the fragmentary, the failure.' Woolf was preparing to publish that great voyeuristic novel of London, *Mrs Dalloway*, and clearing critical ground for its acceptance. She of all writers was the most persistent of outsiders, peering in and shut out, in constant wonder at the profusion of her city's unaccounted-for inhabitants. It is history like hers we remember, when the rhetoric of an age has receded. Private history in public places is truer and wiser than public history in public places. 'She parted the curtains; she looked. Oh, but how surprising! – in the room opposite the old lady stared straight at her! She was going to bed.' As Wyndham Lewis (not a Woolf admirer) wrote, 'Truth or Beauty are as much public concerns as the water supply.'

I sense the nature of metaphorical writing is that it articulates, in this anatomical sense, a body politic, by resetting the bones of our private dislocations and so outflanking the politic. It isn't limited, in other words, by the historical. It fuses the private and the public, not by design of hindsight, but as if by chance. Metaphor contains the wonder, the uncanniness, the strange simultaneity of coincidence. I sometimes think coincidence is the essence of metaphor, the unexpected fusion of memory with memory in a circle inside a circle whose concentric point, long since vanished, was the Big Bang or Creation itself.

The design of the world is mirrored in images aspiring to such unity, yet images rippling out from one another in the narrative deployment of imagined time. The mind that would hold together this expanding world is necessarily a metaphorical one, and the larger the mind the more singular and lasting its world. To this extent the mind of God would view the entire universe as a coincidence, a metaphor. And we would no more think of refuting the universe than we would the world in a grain of sand. We may not care for the size of either, and consider both presumptuous, but this hindsight is irrelevant to art. So the language of history remains outside the body of fiction. In fiction, the private experience of the world can never be too small or unimportant if it's haunted by time and the struggle against death. Inevitably, rhetorical formulations of concern about time seem either incomplete or non-existent.

In becoming complicit with time *now* the fiction writer conjoins not what's received, but what has until now been outside meaning – forbidden us by the absence of a voyeur who can hook us a fish through the chance discovery of a ram's testicles. In time it gathers its meaning for the future. It is a louche meaning, at odds with the straightforward and circumscribed time of history. The language of metaphor seeks to offer an ineffable truth about the body of the world. This ambition may be off-putting, difficult to reconcile with the diversion of an evening. Yet without metaphor fiction is simply narrative. Story *qua* story bores us by the predictability of its telling, since telling a story isn't the same thing as observing the world. Without metaphor we can't remake the world, which is what fiction does in its own image and grand obsession. Fiction without metaphor lacks unity, a reason for being, a coming together in integrity. As such it lacks itself.

But not as happy families lack themselves, whose particular lack may strike the outsider as resident solely in a child, who, it turned out, enjoyed being forced up against the window of the world. I certainly looked to writers to bring me the news from China, of bound feet, and I was as interested in the dogs of Jack London as in that pair of *coureurs de bois*, Radisson and Groseilliers, who rose above their anonymity to become famous among the Iroquois. Yet it was the friendship of my grandmother for an old Indian woman – I shall call her Mrs Brown – in the Musqueam reservation not far from the house my grandparents had carved for themselves out of the Dunbar forest, that brought home to my young attention the craft of anonymous design. This had to do with social responsibility for those less fortunate than us. Not that my grandmother's generosity went unreciprocated; I inherited from her a cedar basket, woven by Mrs Brown, which sits to this day on my mantel.

May I be forgiven for lifting a glass to the cedar tree and the way it sustains my vocation even yet? As I write I'm propped up by a cedar beam on Bowen Island, a few hundred yards along the beach from where Lowry, Birney, and others came forty years and more ago to write their fiction as guests in a house since burned to the ground. Years later, as if by chance, I came to own a cabin here. If this coincidence sounds contrived, it pales sadly in comparison to the news just in from Italy of Alberto Moravia, who died two days ago, the day I was typing out his words above. This sceptered isle, this profession of voyeurs beachcombing the world for patterns.

BUT I WAS PROPOSING to reflect on anatomy. I have little doubt that the urge writers feel to articulate the world originates in the bodies of their families. My earliest anatomy lesson came at the kitchen table of my grandparents' home where we all lived for the first five years of my life. The carcass was supplied by my maternal grandfather. At night he worked as a janitor at a junior high school in Kerrisdale. (My grandmother was janitor at the Catholic school we later attended in the parish of Immaculate Conception. Oddly, she never ever spoke to her husband, who slept in the basement.) By day my grandfather ran a shipyard from a chaotic office at the foot of Blenheim Street, in a slough off the north arm of the Fraser River, and pedalled himself by bicycle all over the south slope, until a stroke killed him one night pumping home.

He had no bookkeeping savvy, and my mother, with some secretarial skills, would sometimes 'go down to the river' to help her father create order in the lean-to he called his office. He rarely made a dime from the fishboats he welcomed into dry dock, but when he did soon squandered it, to my grandmother's dismay, by giving it away. His young visitors would wander through the amazing smells of marine paint and planer shavings, creosote and drying gillnets, to get down to a float where we fished for bullheads. Useless fuckers – yet vital food for the growing imagination. Living by water, my grandfather must have appreciated how it soon gave him more ways to drift through life than when he used to drive horses from Montana into Alberta to sell to the North West Mounted Police. I've never heard of anyone else who regularly swam a horse and wagon across the fast-flowing Second Narrows to save ferry fare, before the first bridge connected his family's mudflat shack to Vancouver.

He also raised sheep on Iona Island and as an old man would row us across the river at dusk to check on his rams and ewes. The island wasn't his, but the sheep were, and I can remember mutton carcasses at home being sawn up on the kitchen table, fat and suety, lean and bloody, my own parents pitching in with knives and cleavers, together with a young uncle in the same house, who liked to spank me hard after dark, and otherwise torment his pimples with a boiling kettle, by enshrouding his head under towels to pen in the steam.

From the sheep came wool-carding on rainy Saturdays and the spreading of an apparatus across the big bedroom upstairs, where, as I later calculated, I was conceived – not in this apparatus used for quilting, under which we crawled to play, but in the bedroom during an Air Force furlough of my father's. Iona Island now houses Vancouver's sewage treatment centre, so the bucolic oasis squatted on by my grandfather has vanished along with his Y-handlebar bike. He had no talent for legacy. Fishermen stole his tools, seldom paid him what they owed; and at his death B.C. Packers, from whom he rented the spit of land for his shipyard, appropriated everything, including machines that belonged to us. We were a faceless family who worked hard and did not question authority.

No wonder an articulation of injustice became important to the – . Or, do I mean, No wonder a nascent writer might eventually turn his back on all authority and – ? Etc. And so on. I'm suddenly defeated by my distaste for trying to get such transitions right....

Hindsights of history may seem as contrived in fiction, but here they lack irrefutableness. Is memoir writing circumscribed by the very memory that can be contradicted tomorrow in the realization that such generalizations were never really *seen?* Articulations of my blanket sort are never seen. Fashionably, we've come to accept this kind of writing as another form of fiction, in the same way we have history – seductive for those of us who believe that all good writing is autobiographical. Yet is this a good enough reason to forget that language not grounded in what it's looking at can be refuted? To *see* ... is the voyeur's first and abiding desire.

I am not suggesting that something like the shape of my family as recalled in these fragments as accurately as I can wasn't responsible for my becoming a writer. An articulated quilt may have shape. But we like to know what's under the covers. Ideas are blankets with certain imaginative con-tours; but imaginative truth requires the voyeurism of wrinkles and those dyed red lines wrapped around flannelette sheets like ribbons. Metaphorical language isn't the blanket language of expository prose. It requires the illicit every line of the way. Absence of the illicit is probably a more accurate rea-son for my quitting teaching than was any growing up of mine to reject authority out of hand.

I've long had this thing about touching and smelling the world. It's no more possible for me to read a book without habitually raising it to my nose than it would be to make love to my wife without smelling her hair. I set aside the more obvious analogies of roses, roast pork, orange peel.... As an incorrigible voyeur I am, I trust, typically human in my deviance. I also worry about time and how it might scar me, unless it's watched closely, taken into my confidence, made love to. Writers of fiction want badly to make metaphors of the lines that time makes in us all.

I think the complicity required to do this is the same for writer and reader alike. We want to see the whole body of what in historical writing must necessarily be limited to a leg up or a shoulder to the wheel. I must sound as if I am impugning historians, Your Honour, but my intention is really to argue the case for the integrity of fiction by analogy. Imagination is the ability to see what we have never seen, by particularizing and generalizing from what we *have* seen, and may only dimly remember. To write successful imaginative literature, I suspect, one must see more vividly with the eyes shut than one ever does with them open. This is why the very best stories possess a dream-like essence, and why the finest novels possess irrefutable memory.

In a way, though not necessarily, the short story mediates – meditates, even – between the denser texture of the lyric poem and the attenuated narrative of the novel. It is a meeting ground for another use of language, though not a different kind. This kind of language is moral to its bones in opposing 'evil' – defined by Sartre as 'the systematic substitution of abstraction for the concrete'. I think of the story and novella as spiritually restorative forms, in the way a summer cabin is, where solitude winnows worry, and where the first deep breath puts us in touch again with the natural world. Meanwhile, a house in the city may be filling up with refugees, whose stories demand attention in the novel, with no less urgency and no fewer skeletons.

The windows of the world are innumerable. Which to trust our luck at, which to choose? I became an impostor to see into character, enter worlds not my own, entice others with the illicit I would make moral. But I can only write about home, no matter where I may set my stories. 'Here' is the exotic location of every narrative, grounded in these senses. Or so I believe. Home is nowhere but the imagination, a world you finally re-enter, this house my father built with *his* father, crowned with chimney bricks from the old Hotel Vancouver, that year I learned to read, 1950. How can we know anything worth knowing until the anonymous soul of our home meets history? Here, as I imagine, will it still stand as fiction when all the hotels have fallen down.

George Bowering

STAINED GLASS

I CAN READ fiction that acts like a window on the world once in a while, at bedtime perhaps, as a kind of relaxation something like crime thrillers on television. But I dont anymore want to write it, and I dont want to find it in prose that purports to be serious and contemporary.

Prose is no longer interesting just because it offers a slice of life. If you want to see what a South Chicago street looks like, take a 747 to Chicago. I dont want to look through a novel at it. If I find some fiction I want it to look like fiction. If it is a window, let it be a stained-glass window. You dont look through a stained-glass window. It has to be interesting itself.

Of course a stained-glass window looks better when there is some outside light coming through. But the glass uses that light for its own purpose. And the eye inside is a careful reader, not a passive customer of the wares 'outside'.

First published in George Bowering, *Craft Slices* (Ottawa: Oberon, 1985).

Hugh Hood

PRACTICAL FORMALISM: MINING THE SENTENCE

MEDDLE WITH THE SYLLOGISM, said Maritain, and you do damage to
human nature. He was right. The syllogism embodies the capacity to make
inferences, upon which human civilization rests. It is not the only form of
inference, but it was the form first described accurately by logicians, and its
history is intertwined with the history of thought itself. I would go a step
further than M Maritain and say that we mustn't meddle with the sentence.
Tamper with the sentence and you may damage very gravely our human
capacity to think and speak. If the syllogism is the prior form of inference,
the sentence is the prior form of thought and speech. Everything we can
take in, our sensations, imaginings, fantasies, recollections, everything that
we judge by instinct or taste, our concepts, is fed to us by ourselves, in articulated segments which take the form of sentences. Our unconscious life is
probably fed to us in sentences rather than in a messy indeterminate mani-
fold. We can only communicate with ourselves, in the recesses of our
natures, in sentences, the original unit of experience. The sentence cannot
be left to the fumblings of transformational grammarians or linguistics, spe-
cialists or logicians. It is the common property of humankind, which we
must be on our guard to preserve against those who deny it or try to dissolve
it into dubious atoms.

Consider the sad example of the athletes, and especially the politicians,
who appear on televised interviews, trying to communicate their ideas or
imaginings. Very seldom indeed do they show any mastery of the sentence;
their conversation is peppered with interjected single words or grunts such
as 'well', 'like', 'uh', or short phrases like 'y'know?'. This last phrase has for

---

First published in Hugh Hood, *Unsupported Assertions* (Concord, ON: House of
Anansi, 1991).

some speakers become a verbal tic; we often hear speakers on radio or television who repeat it every five or six words, adjusting the position of their heads and necks as they utter it, as though there were some close physical connection between their use of the meaningless words and their nervous systems, as no doubt there is. A curious turning of the head to one side and involuntary bobbing or ducking accompanies the 'y'know?' suggesting an achieved mental emptiness.

The person who can speak in sentences as well as write them has an ascendancy over her fellows. Eliminate the 'like' and the 'y'know?' and the 'uh' (shuffle shuffle of embarrassed feet) from your conversation and you will rise high in society, a progress which is still, I trust, a reasonable object of woman's or man's ambition. Nothing promotes personal success like clear plain thought, speech and writing. 'Why should I sell your wheat?' 'Just watch me!' Sentences which we may disagree with, uttered by Pierre Elliott Trudeau at different moments in his political career. 'The universe is unfolding as it should.' 'The state has no place in the bedrooms of the nation.' You won't forget them.

But now let's see you quote another Canadian political figure.

Writing, utterance, thought are vested in the sentence and can't be carried on without it. Below and behind what we write and speak our inner experience is given to us sequentially and in due form. Our mental life is almost entirely, so far as it can be grasped or fixed at all, a continuing address to ourselves. We are at once speaker and listener in our inner lives. The stability, purposiveness and coherence of our selves, whether awake or asleep, whether fully conscious, half-conscious or unconscious, is given in the form of address, *speech-to*. Reading is obviously a variation on this process; we examine the written or printed or video-projected word, or the painting or motion picture, and we hear it inwardly as speech. Many of us move our lips silently while scanning, looking or reading, as though we are speaking a text to ourselves. Jacques Derrida is perfectly correct to state that writing precedes speech, in this sense, that our experience is received by us as something to be read, deciphered, a series of sentences. Listening to, apprehending, sentence structures is the fundamental activity of the existing mind. Think of the people who speak to you in dreams. What pithy, gnomic sentences they employ!

'Arise and take ship for Basra! There go to the bazaar and accost the first jeweller you see. Buy the lamp he offers you!'

Consider the information proffered by the words in those little boxes at the edge of comic-strip panels, or in balloons, or simply in obtrusive lettering. 'Midnight, Gotham City'. 'Later'. 'The Bat-cave'. 'Next morning'. 'Commissioner Gordon's office'. And so on until the final 'Whap' or 'Biff'. All these signals deliver themselves as segments of experience, units of thought, sentences.

We were taught as children that 'a sentence is a unit of expression that conveys a complete thought or action'. Despite the attacks of grammarians or linguists upon this classical statement, it remains largely correct and useful, and far less limiting than the alternative definitions sometimes proposed. It tells us that the minimum requirement for a sentence is exactly that it is the expression of somebody's experience. The sentence must first of all be *framed*. And once framed it must portray the action of its *subject*, who performs or undergoes the mental activity or physical action (or both) which is described. The framer of the sentence tells us that somebody does something. Take away its utterer and the sentence doesn't take place. Take away the subject of the sentence, or the action described, and likewise there is no sentence. Even the brief words which deliver exclamations imply both a framer and a subject (who are often identical). 'Holy cow!' 'Golly!' 'Who?' 'When?' 'Drat!'

'Drat!' in the words of the immortal Bill Fields embodied not just a subject and an action, but a great world of feeling, a context. Noel Coward's 'Very flat, Norfolk!' is the biggest laugh line in *Private Lives*, signalling to actors and audience the rich comic implications of a superb first act.

'The cat sat on the mat.' Subject: the cat. Verb: sat. Predicate: indirect object, locative, on the mat. Easy. Simple! Many brief utterances appear extremely economical, perhaps even devoid of a visible subject-verb-predicate structure. In these cases we customarily say that the missing elements are 'understood' by the writer and his readers or hearers. But this device is purely fictive and probably unnecessary. All that we need to understand is that the primordial element of the sentence is its utterer or framer. Utterances made in sleep, or as automatic reflex responses to shock or surprise, groans, moans, pantings, don't count as sentences because they are involuntary. Sometimes it's hard to tell a deliberate exclamation from an involuntary reflex action, one 'Drat!' from another. And words delivered by subjects under hypnosis or in drug treatment are probably not sentences, though this is debatable. The freely experiencing utterer or framer is, however, the *sine qua non* of the sentence, which can therefore be seen to be intimately connected to the actuality of human psychology. Parrots and chimpanzees and some other creatures can produce lifelike imitations of the sound of the human voice, but they do not produce sentences properly so-called and they produce no literature. 'Want a cracker!' doesn't *mean* 'Want a cracker!' It doesn't mean anything, and we tease ourselves by pretending that it does. The only beings that make sentences are humans; we should put aside cant notions which deny this. We honour our humanity in reserving the sentence for our own use.

It is the vehicle of one of the greatest and most humane arts. In the sentence lie immense possibilities of artistic refinement, of imaginative and fantastic play, of purely verbal sport, of drama, fiction, poetry. Don't let parrots and chimpanzees mess about with it!

I should stress once more that the *framer* of the sentence is not invariably or necessarily its grammatical subject. I can perfectly well say, 'She went to the grocery store', where the subject of the sentence is a person distinct from myself. Nevertheless the framer of the sentence invariably encloses it within the limits of his experience. In this sense, every sentence has a form like 'I say that she went to the grocery store.' The purely grammatical distinction among first, second and third persons dissolves under scrutiny. Every sentence testifies to the witness of its framer and is intimately connected with her moral life. To a great extent our lives *are* what we assert them to be. Our truthfulness embeds our being.

Chaucer's Clerk of Oxenford, 'ful of hy sentence', was one who habitually spoke in elevated, grave, generally received moral maxims; he had a standard of perfection constantly in his mouth. Chaucer does not treat him as a hypocrite like the Pardoner, but as a dignified and honourable speaker, very familiar with the gems of European moralism. Nowadays when we describe someone as a sententious person, we seem to imply a certain sanctimonious hypocrisy in her attitudes and speech. That isn't how Chaucer thought of sententiousness; perhaps his view of it was more just than our own.

The connection of the beautiful forms of the sentence to the various forms which the culture of the West has taken is very clear. The classical languages and especially Latin possessed a cluster of sentence forms of which we have retained the names, though we may no longer understand or employ the grammar and syntax which they named. Clause, mood, indicative, imperative, subjunctive, the names of grammar, are almost all of Latin derivation. We have only recently, within the memories of many now living, begun to divest ourselves of the trappings of Latinate grammar, in education and in our personal expression. We are coincidentally becoming less and less a people of the letter. We read progressively less and less and we write almost nothing. The fax machine may help to correct this trend, allowing as it does the almost instantaneous transmission of our lightest thoughts. I wouldn't bet money on it.

Expression is the dress of thought, and still
Appears more decent, as more suitable.   (Pope)

As our grammar and syntax change form, our thoughts and our capacity to verbalize them change too. Probably the most important shift in the culture of the English-speaking peoples in this century has been our pronounced turning-away from the Latinate model of sentence construction towards one which does away with more and more of the syntactical underpinnings of expression. I thought of calling this essay 'From Syntaxis to Parataxis, or, Who Cares?' but reflected that my choice of words was certainly derivative and might appear captious. I used to think all the time of the different classifications of sentences: simple, compound, complex, compound-complex. I enjoyed thinking about them, saw in them the richest resources of narrative and poetry, and began my adventures as a writer by playing with sentence forms the way other kids played with balls and bats.

'I gave the bottle to the baby.' SIMPLE

'I gave the bottle to the baby and she knew what to do with it.' COMPOUND

'I gave the bottle, which was full of milk, to the baby.' COMPLEX

'I gave the bottle, which was full of milk, to the baby and she, without having had the benefit of a training course or educational manual, or anything like that, knew at once and with amazing aptitude, which can only have been instinctual, what to do with it.' COMPOUND-COMPLEX

Here we arrive at the frontiers of literature. The thing begins not with the word but with the sentence. In my novel *You Cant Get There From Here* (no apostrophe in *Cant*, please) I deliberately inserted an enormously long sentence, which takes up half a page of closely printed type. The text is presented as a revolutionary declaration of insurgency and independence, broadcast by a cruel, illegitimate, racist junta. It begins typically, 'Mindful of griefs too weighty to be borne, and in the expectation of eventual justification ...', and continues in the customary self-serving tone of the interested activist. I won't give the entire passage, but I will just note that even the characters in the novel notice the event.

General Abdelazar said to Mr Zogliu, 'What a sentence!'
'Two hundred and twenty words. It will sound even more impressive in French', said Zogliu.

The rhetoric and style of mob insurgency of course originated in France in 1789 and thereafter. Mr Zogliu is quite correct to notice that this rhetoric and tone are best delivered by the French tongue. The barricades, *Madame la guillotine* and the rest of the apparatus of revolutionism should only be described in demotic French because that is where it comes from. In this way, the forms of sentences approved by a culture illustrate better than anything else the beliefs, politics, ethics and moral style of that culture. If this seems to empower and enshrine literature as the chief interpreter of social meaning, the most pragmatically expressive of the arts – even more than music or painting – then let the claim stand, for there may be truth in it.

The great writers of our age have characterized themselves and the societies that give them birth in their employment of sentence form. Dickens, Henry James, Proust, Conrad, Faulkner, Evelyn Waugh, P.G. Wodehouse (an unrivalled master of sentence form) and above all Ernest Hemingway have all exhibited their art for us in the way they form those segmented distinct utterances. All of these writers seem available for parody. Perhaps serious imitation of their writing is the best way to understand and then to love them. Most of them favour the long, syntactically complex sentence as their principal means of expression, but there are invariably exceptions to these observations. One of Dickens' richest and most *directing* sentences consists of the single word 'London'.

I was so impressed by this little sentence that I virtually plagiarized it for the opening sentence of *Around the Mountain*, which consists of the single word 'Snow'. Both words are followed by extended passages of scenic descriptions, of particular cities in specific moods; both suggest a prevailing moral climate. *Bleak House* is a much greater work of fiction than *Around the Mountain*, containing and giving birth to the later work in the way peculiar to literature.

We find no one-word sentences in Henry James, and a prevailing comic use of the comma to order the long leisurely periods, rivalled by Proust but by nobody else.

'It was with a, for him, careless regard to appearance, that our poor serious gentleman ...' The commas which enclose 'for him' are James's commas, nobody else's. The hesitant qualificatory tone, and the nuanced judgement, are made possible by the commas.

Proust again achieves miracles by his distinctive use of enclosed clauses and other syntactical divagations which owe much to Saint-Simon and to Ruskin, but more to *le petit Marcel* himself. His marvellous parody of the syntax of the brothers Goncourt allows us a view of the salon of M et Mme Verdurin obtainable in no other way.

These matters have a special interest of their own but more than that, the great changes in an entire society's understanding of the sentence sometimes signal world-shaking events. Western society's understanding of itself and its history has altered so radically since the time of James, Conrad, Proust, that it cannot rejoin itself as it was then: the insistence on the simple sentence helps to make our century the century of genocide. When I wrote *You Cant Get There From Here* I had in mind Sinclair Lewis's beautiful title *It Can't Happen Here.*

But it can and it does. You can and you do.

The best way to grasp the magnitude of this evolution is to look briefly at sentences which are long and others which are short. I shall provide only two examples and in considering them will argue that our entire world, manners, morals, science, ethical standards, philosophy, religion, use of language, education, changed as sentence forms changed.

By a really extraordinary coincidence these two men attended the same English public school, Dulwich College in South London, at almost the same moment. P.G. Wodehouse was at Dulwich in the very last years of the nineteenth century. Raymond Chandler was there in the very first years of the twentieth century. Wodehouse was born in 1881, Chandler in 1888. Despite this close connection a whole world of thought and expression divides them. It is terrifyingly illuminating to recall that although he was seven years older than his colleague, Wodehouse outlived Chandler by fifteen years. Chandler died in 1959, Wodehouse in 1974. Their great achievements (they are the two writers in English whom I admire most) are *enclosed* within one another's voices and works, in a way which outgoes individual consciousness. They are the turning voice of the English-speaking world from the beginning of the century until the present time.

Here's Wodehouse at his ripest:

And half an hour later I was toddling up the steps of her residence and being admitted by old Seppings, her butler. Little knowing, as I crossed that threshold, that in about two shakes of a duck's tail I was to become involved in an imbroglio that would test the Wooster soul as it had seldom been tested before. I allude to the sinister affair of Gussie Fink-Nottle, Madeline Bassett, old Pop Bassett, Stiffy Byng, the Rev. H.P. ('Stinker') Pinker, the eighteenth-century cow-creamer and the small brown leather-covered notebook.

Look at the way he leaves out the commas in 'small brown leather-covered notebook' to allow the sentence to accelerate at the close. The whole passage is a writer's dream, so overwhelming in its effects that I leave it to you for leisured contemplation.

Now here's Ray Chandler at the top of his form:

He turned and walked across the floor and out. I watched the door close. I listened to his steps going away down the imitation marble corridor. After a while they got faint, then they got silent. I kept on listening anyway. What for?

These two great writers went to the same school and received a classical education within a year of one another, and see what lies between them!

To get from Totleigh Towers to Marlowe's office in Hollywood, you go from Gussie Fink-Nottle and Madeline Bassett through Hemingway and

Hammett to Moose Malloy and Carmen Sternwood and Eddie Mars, and as you travel the human world turns and changes. The footsteps are silent now. We keep on listening anyway. What for?

John Metcalf

THAT DAMN CLOCK AGAIN

IN 1982, I EDITED an anthology called *Making It New* which represented those I considered the most accomplished story writers in Canada. The book was not ecstatically received; many reviewers grumbled about stories set in France, the U.S.A., Hungary, and England; the general feeling seemed to be that the book wasn't 'Canadian'. R.V. Cassill, the American editor of *The Norton Anthology of Short Fiction*, wrote to me:

> The best thing I can say is to mention the impact of the volume as a whole. Clearly this is world-class writing. *It is not altogether distinct from the best that is being done in the* U.S. *and England. How could it be, or why should it be?* And yet, by virtue of subject matter and those mysterious nuances that link subject with craft, the whole book speaks brilliantly for Canada. [emphasis added]

You may be baffled by my insistence on the obvious but the obvious is not obvious to literary critics in Canada. Bear in mind that the most widely circulated anthology of Canadian stories – *The Penguin Book of Canadian Short Stories* – attempts to link Canadian stories with a tradition of Letters to the Editor of *The Pioneer Times and Daily Stump-Remover*. There are few critics in CanLit circles who could write perceptively on the texture of the stories of Hemingway, Lardner, Eudora Welty, Caroline Gordon, or Flannery O'Connor – and it is precisely these writers who are our influences. If some of you think my opinions of CanLit extreme, it is just as well that I haven't the time to talk at length of CanCrit.

First delivered to the German Association of Canadian Studies at Grainau, Bavaria. Excerpted from 'The Curate's Egg' in *Essays on Canadian Writing* 30 (1984-85).

Many of our academics *still* show little understanding of technique and style and *still* expend their energies on such high-school abstractions as 'plot' and 'theme'. Although there are signs that a few critics are learning how to read, many more still have twigs in their hair from beating about the bush in pursuit of the whimsicalities propounded in Margaret Atwood's *Survival.*

There has been little critical writing on our better writers and what little there has been is largely inept. It does not surprise me that Simone Vauthier of Strasbourg is the *first* critic to write seriously on Norman Levine; it does cause me some fleeting sense of shame to say that her essay is one of the best I have read on *any* Canadian writer.

The first collection of stories which exhibited a command of modern technique was Hugh Hood's *Flying a Red Kite* which was published in 1962. This is an *extraordinary* statement and should occasion questions. How had Canada remained unaffected by the revolutionary changes in prose which had been sweeping the English-speaking world since the early twenties? I suggested an answer in my essay 'Editing the Best'.[1]

> It seems that Canada was isolated from the rest of the world by some inex-
> plicable time-lag.... A partial explanation may be a ponderous conservatism
> and the total lack of an informed audience. I haven't read enough to *know*
> but I have a suspicion that literature in Canada up until, say, 1950 was so
> largely crappy because it was a narrow class preserve. Audience *and* writers,
> I suspect, were part of an Establishment which was characterized by ghastly
> good taste, gentility, and doctorates – an Anglican world of pianoforte and
> good posture with attachments to Empire and 'Beauty'.

I would now like to digress for a few minutes to say something of Morley Callaghan and to explain why I think his story collections of 1929 and 1936 were less modern than the Hood collection of 1962. Callaghan is a central figure in CanLit and it is received opinion that he is a great, if neglected, writer; it is further stated that his major achievement is his stories. These

---

1 First published in John Metcalf, *Kicking Against the Pricks* (Downsview, ON: ECW, 1982; 2nd ed. Guelph, ON: Red Kite, 1986). Republished in *How Stories Mean.*

claims are agreed to by all – if only by silence. George Woodcock, who is usually sensible and lucid but who is not always sound on short fiction, tempers the general estimation of Callaghan in an entry on him in *The Oxford Companion to Canadian Literature* but still writes of the 'laconic sureness of the early short stories'.

Callaghan certainly knew the *shape* of what is now the classic 'modern' story but his sensibilities were not characteristic of 'modern' short story writing; the story tends to be tentative, exploratory, tremulous even; it tends to be intensely visual and sensuous; it tends – in brief – towards lyric poetry. Callaghan's major impulse was moralistic and didactic, and these qualities are constantly at war within his work with what artistry he had. Which wasn't much.

He has spoken of being influenced by Hemingway but I can see little evidence that he ever understood what Hemingway was doing. In *That Summer in Paris*, Callaghan talks of his desire to pare down his prose and rid it of simile and metaphor, and I must assume from the evidence of his stories that he thought the essence of Hemingway's style was simplification. If this were the case, he was, of course, wildly mistaken because Hemingway's 'simplicity' was positively baroque.

Here are two not unrepresentative quotations.

They were closing the drugstore, and Alfred Higgins, who had just taken off his white jacket, was putting on his coat and getting ready to go home. The little gray-haired man, Sam Carr, who owned the drugstore, was bending down behind the cash register, and when Alfred Higgins passed him, he looked up and said softly, 'Just a moment, Alfred. One moment before you go.'

The soft, confident, quiet way in which Sam Carr spoke made Alfred start to button his coat nervously. He felt sure his face was white. Sam Carr usually said, 'Good night', brusquely, without looking up. In the six months he had been working in the drugstore Alfred had never heard his employer speak softly like that. His heart began to beat so loud it was hard for him to get his breath. 'What is it, Mr Carr?' he asked.

That was from Callaghan's 'All the Years of Her Life', chosen at random, the first two paragraphs of the first story in his collected stories.

And now consider the opening two sentences from Hemingway's *A Farewell to Arms*.

> In the late summer of that year we lived in a house in a village that looked across the river and the plain to the mountains. In the bed of the river there were pebbles and boulders, dry and white in the sun, and the water was clear and swiftly moving and blue in the channels.

Quite apart from anything else – and there is *much* else – notice that Callaghan's syntax and punctuation could have been used by the young Dickens; Hemingway's syntax and punctuation are highly original and are being employed to further his artistic purpose. When Hemingway employs commas to set off the phrase 'dry and white in the sun' it is not for some conventional syntactical purpose but to make those pebbles and boulders more visible, to raise them above the flow of the water, to check the flow of our reading as the water checks around their base. The commas help to change our *focus* from house, village, river, plain, and mountains to pebbles and boulders, from noun to adjective, holding the sentence before releasing it to flow with its 'ands'. Notice, too, the lovely way the released sentence rests for a moment on the word 'blue' slowing the rhythm to suggest depth.

It was a measure of Hemingway's genius that he did not punctuate the first sentence at all; consider the havoc we would wreak by sprinkling commas.

This prose *was* modern; it remains magical.

Many of Callaghan's stories are mawkish and read like the earnest effusions of a muscular vicar who puts in his time at a Boys' Club embarrassing the disadvantaged, but this is not their major flaw. Nor is it the condescending tone which I find repellent and which is typical of those who write about the trials and tribulations of 'little' people. The major flaw is the prose itself – flat, conventional, plodding, clumsy, *dogged* – prose which continues to be hailed because Edmund Wilson on an off-day once made extravagant claims for Callaghan, and Canadians always accept the imprimatur of a foreign expert rather than trust their own eyes and ears.

Callaghan – and this is the essence of his 'non-modernity' – can never leave the reader alone to *experience* the story; he *presides* over the story, interpreting, explaining, enforcing, pointing the moral.

The following brief quotations from 'A Cap for Steve' are not much worse than his earlier work and illustrate precisely the lack of artistry I find typical of all his work.

'It's a lot of money', Dave said finally. When Steve didn't answer him, he added angrily, 'I turned to you, Steve. I asked you, didn't I?'

'That man knew how much his boy wanted that cap', Steve said.

'Sure. But he recognized how much it was worth to us.'

'No, you let him take it away from us', Steve blurted.

'That's unfair', Dave said. 'Don't dare say that to me.'

'I don't want to be like you', Steve muttered, and he darted across the road and walked along on the other side of the street.

'It's unfair', Dave said angrily, only now he didn't mean that Steve was unfair, he meant that what had happened in the prosperous Hudson home was unfair, and he didn't know quite why. He had been trapped, not just by Mr Hudson, but by his own life.

The story concludes:

Finally, he got up and went into Steve's room. The room was in darkness, but he could see the outline of Steve's body on the bed, and he sat down beside him and whispered, 'Look, Son, it was a mistake. I know why. People like us – in circumstances where money can scare us. No, no', he said, feeling ashamed and shaking his head apologetically; he was taking the wrong way of showing the boy they were together; he was covering up his own failure. For the failure had been his, and it had come out of being so separated from his son that he had been blind to what was beyond the price in a boy's life. He longed now to show Steve he could be with him from day to day.

Dialogue wooden, authorial intrusion massively offensive, prose boring, impact bathetic – it would be difficult to imagine prose more *Reader's Digest*-ish, yet Robert Weaver in an entry on 'Short Stories in English' in *The Oxford Companion to Canadian Literature* describes Callaghan as 'the most influential figure in the development of the modern short story in Canada'. Far from being influential in the development of the modern story, he was rather the very figure of that unspeakable badness of Canadian writing which held sway until the sixties. My contention is that Callaghan never *was* a 'modern' writer and never understood wherein 'modernity' lay.

The dust-jacket of the 1959 issue of *Morley Callaghan's Stories* bears a tribute from Wyndham Lewis which time has rendered ironically comic: 'These are tales very full of human sympathy ... this book is beautifully replete with a message of human tolerance and love ... the plot, however tragic, is not some diabolic and meaningless phantasy, in other words – which is the fatal conclusion that we are required to draw from the perusal of a story, say of Mr Hemingway's.'

What, then, *was* the nature of the revolution in prose which took place in the sixties? Obviously, as I have been hammering home with blows far harder than necessary, it was characterized by nothing peculiarly Canadian; it *could* not have been. The changes were precisely the *same* changes that had been taking place in prose in the U.S.A., and elsewhere, since 1923.

I would like to quote what I wrote on the subject in 1982 in my essay 'Editing the Best'.

Where twenty years ago Canadian stories stressed content – what a story was *about* – the main emphasis now is on the story as verbal and rhetorical *performance*. Our best writers are concerned with the story as *thing to be experienced* rather than as *thing to be understood*. This more than anything else is what seems to baffle some readers – and not a few critics; it is difficult for those of us writing stories to understand why this is so since these concerns have been dominant since about 1920.

In an essay that Alice Munro wrote for me this year for a book I was editing, she said:

I will start by explaining how I read stories written by other people. For one thing, I can start reading them anywhere; from beginning to end, from end to beginning, from any point in between in either direction. So obviously I don't take up a story and follow it as if it were a road, taking me somewhere, with views and neat diversions along the way. I go into it, and move back and forth and settle here and there, and stay in it for a while. It's more like a house. Everybody knows what a house does, how it encloses space and makes connections between one enclosed space and another and presents what is outside in a new way. This is the nearest I can come to explaining what a story does for me, and what I want my stories to do for other people.

The implications of this paragraph alone should be enough to give pause to those who consider Alice Munro a simple 'realist'. What she says here is very like some notes for school children I wrote in 1980 for a junior high-school text called *New Worlds*:

The 'What does it mean?' approach to the story could be compared with the package-tour traveller who 'does' Europe or Africa in four-teen days. I suggest settling down in a place, learning the language, observing the ways of the inhabitants until you begin to understand their world.

It's probably a very dangerous analogy to make because painting and writing really cannot be compared, but the changes in the short story in Canada over the last twenty years are not wildly unlike the changes in painting at a slightly earlier period. I'd suggest that the story pre-1962 could be compared with traditional representative painting and that the changes since have moved the story closer to an equivalent of abstraction. Though it's precisely there that the analogy collapses – for words have meanings. I don't mean to suggest by 'abstraction' that the modern story lacks immediate reference to the external world. Obviously not. I mean rather that formal concerns are becoming increasingly important.

What did I *mean* by the story as 'performance', by the story as 'thing to be experienced'?

I am going to be entirely presumptuous now and speak for other writers too. Good writers would refuse to allow that that beloved CanLit abstrac-tion 'theme' was an element which was in any way abstractable. To be plonk-ingly boring, *how* something is written *is* what is written. The quest for 'theme' – what the story is 'about' – is arid and doomed to failure. The American poet John Ciardi put this succinctly when he advised readers of poetry not to ask 'What does this poem mean?' but rather '*How* does this poem mean?'

This sounds simple but is not.

Although writers usually know what a story is 'about' before they start writing, stories for them are a process of discovery. A story's general 'theme' is so basic – and uninteresting – that it's taken for granted. What does *that* mean? As Degas grew older, he no longer had much interest in painting in facial detail; heads became shapes. Was he painting and drawing dancers and nudes in bathtubs or was he drawing *lines?*

It means something like that.

What is being discovered as the writing and rewriting progresses is the fascination of the theme's ramifications, variations, and *embodiment*. The writer is fascinated by the embodiment of the theme in the physical world of the story (texture) and fascinated by the literary and rhetorical devices necessary to capture and suggest that world.

Sometimes writers do *not* know what a story is 'about'; the language itself reveals to them new directions, new dimensions as it unfolds. This is true for all writers to some degree or another; language is alive under their hands as clay is for a potter. Sometimes it has its own shape and insistence.

I chose the word 'embodiment' carefully but it is, I realize, quite the *wrong* word. It seems to imply that a preconceived idea is given concrete form. I mean exactly the reverse. Stories do not begin with an idea; usually they begin with a detail, a sound, a voice.

The writer's special kind of attention is first caught by, let us say, a woman's dress. This image stays in his mind. He does not know why. Later, he might find himself seeing this woman in this dress standing in a particular room. In this room on the mantelpiece is a large ormolu clock. The process of accretion continues. Soon the writer knows that here is the world of a story. By the time that this world is ready to be written about, the accumulation of details and images in the writer's mind will have suggested the nature they have in common; the general thematic aspect of the story will have emerged and clarified itself through particularities.

Yes, *yes*.

But what grips the writer is that marvellous *clock*. Victorian. Black. Cold to the touch. Its ornamental pillars. Its architrave and pediment. Its massive weight. The remorseless swing of its brass pendulum visible through its glass door. It is a clock like a house.

Can you feel this story growing?

Of course you can. Difficult to say exactly, though, what it is 'about'. Though you can already *sense* something.

Let us now add a pipe. Put it on the mantelpiece. A meerschaum pipe, its bowl with a heavy patina like old ivory. It is lying across its black leather case which is open and lined with red felt.

The *kind* of pipe, its relationship to the clock, the care taken of the pipe – all these things lead us on into a world.

But.

This is *not* a story of a woman oppressed by a stifling marriage; it is *not* a statement that marriage is oppressive. Those are lifeless reductions. It is a story about a particular woman in a particular room which is furnished with a *very* particular clock.

Forgive me this insistence on the elementary.

Until you see and feel that clock in all its massive physicality, you will not be reading the story the writer has written.

Clark Blaise, Alice Munro, Hugh Hood, Ray Smith, Norman Levine, Mavis Gallant, Audrey Thomas, myself – we have all been consistently mis-read and misunderstood for twenty years and more because readers have balked at the 'clockness' of that clock.

Well-written stories tend to be organic; that is, *they grow into a whole*. Readers, in turn, must *grow* into an understanding. Stories are a complex totality of feeling and meaning and can only be experienced by immersing oneself in the world they create; this 'immersing' can only be achieved by giving oneself to the *process* of the story, to the story as verbal performance, to its rhetoric, for the story's world lives only in language.

'Theme' is implied in every connotation and nuance, in the very rhythm of every sentence, in every pause and silence. It lives in every bright detail. It is sculpted by every punctuation mark.

The desired final purpose of stories is to move the reader emotionally, to extend the boundaries of his emotional world. Stories are not puzzles to be solved. Nor do they convey simple moral messages. They are not sermons; they are not propaganda for *any* cause. Their primary purpose, I must insist, is emotional. But that emotional impact will not be felt until the reader has responded with great skill and knowledge to all the nuances of a highly complex performance. *Reading a story is a purely literary activity.*

The reader's final emotional response, however, is *not* literary but it can only be felt by someone with a refined knowledge of and honed skill in the rules of the game. There is a paradox here. Certainly not a new paradox and not a profound one. I think I'm trying to say in my unfortunately unintellectual way that genuine *depth* of emotional response can only be achieved by those willing and able to immerse themselves in amazing artificiality – in language, in literary device, in rhetoric. The 'real', in other words, is only available to us through an embrace of the unreal and artificial.

I have always assumed that this applies to all the arts.

If there is any validity to this assertion, then the implications are considerable. It implies that all those books which offer us in the blurb such words as 'raw', 'brutal', 'shocking', and 'searing' will be offering us not art but raw data; data will not move us. It implies that those books which are touted as 'speaking directly to us' are not speaking at all; the books of the Beat movement spring instantly to mind. It implies that the 'relevant' will be irrelevant. It implies that such books as *Last Exit to Brooklyn* will move us to a sympathetic understanding of homosexuality *less* than such eggshell frailties as Ronald Firbank's *Concerning the Eccentricities of Cardinal Pirelli*. It implies that the ineffable artistry of Naipaul's *In a Free State* will move us more deeply than all the earnest and overtly political scribblings of Third World writers who despise Naipaul as effete and uncommitted.

And, finally, it implies that any critical approaches which seek to quarry 'ideas' or derive fashionable patterns – be they biographical, sociological, political, or mythological – are a misunderstanding of the game's purpose and rules before play has even started.

The activities of a Northrop Frye, for example, strike me as being of about the same level of fascination and usefulness as the contrivance of giant-size crossword puzzles.

Most of the best writing in English hasn't one idea to rub together with another; most writers in English are distrustful of ideas. What fascinates them is that ormolu clock; they're quite happy to leave to the French such topics as Time.

I usually like to pretend that writing is purely a matter of sober craftsmanship. I'm always a little embarrassed at being thought in any way 'artistic'; it seems somehow pretentious. Berets and dark glasses. Writing, I like to think, is simply what I do. I sit on my behind, I say to people who ask, and write things. But this *is* a pose. For I am forced to admit that writing *is* touched by magic.

Sometimes there are in our stories things which we ourselves do not fully understand, things irreducible in their 'thingness', things that demand to be there, luminous things.

That damn clock again.

Or it might be juxtapositions.

Or language itself.

We should all have the humility to admit, even if people *do* think us rather odd, that the workings of language *are* magical and often beyond the reach of analysis. I do not speak here merely of the vatic; I mean that there is in *all* successfully employed literary language a core of the inexplicable, the mysterious.

For years, I have been haunted by this line from an Elizabethan lyric: 'Time hath my golden locks to silver turned.'

It is a simple line; it contains no great Empsonian ambiguities; yet it is a line whose perfection is ultimately mysterious.

I am urging on you, then, the idea that sometimes there is profound wisdom in *not* understanding; as readers and critics you should never be afraid of being tentative, of being passive in the face of the experience of the story.

Everything that I have been saying so far about contemporary stories has been meandering down towards this point: good contemporary stories should be read with the same care that would be given to the reading of poems; they should also be read in the same spirit.

I am suggesting that all the resources of poetry – imagery, sound, weight, alliteration, assonance – the most subtle reaches of the poetic – are now fully and consciously employed in story writing. The very organization of stories is poetic in that they usually develop through a series of images. I stress this because it has been proven more than once that our own critics are blind and deaf to what is before them; Frank Davey, professor of English, proponent of the post-modern, editor of a recondite literary journal, author of a critical guide to Canadian literature, and himself a much-published poet, once delivered a paper at my invitation on the stories of Clark Blaise wherein he described Blaise's style as *journalistic*.

If a *poet* is capable of such monumentally grotesque misreading, from what sad inadequacies might mere intellectuals suffer?

But I am not drawing attention simply to that which is *obviously* poetic, to the gorgeous, painterly textures of, say, Alice Munro. There are different kinds of poetry. Poetry of voice. Poetry of line. There is a marvellously chaste and austere poetry in the dialogue of P.G. Wodehouse. Monet and Bonnard were great painters but there is poetry, too, in the line of Daumier or Georg Grosz.

Even that statement is not particularly radical.

I want to go much further.

Because prose *isn't* poetry, it has been forced to adapt and modify its borrowed techniques. I believe that over the last sixty years the story form, because of its complexity, has been forced to invent what for want of critical terminology I will call 'new verse forms'.

What do I mean by this?

I'm not quite sure.

Let me approach my point by looking at a piece of writing with you; this tiny piece must stand for much else; I'll use something of mine simply because it's recently finished and therefore much in my mind. It is an extract from a novella called 'Polly Ongle'.

The scene describes a middle-aged man in a bar with a beautiful young girl. They have sought shelter from a torrential summer downpour. The man is the owner of an art gallery. The girl is his employee. He is restless with his life, dissatisfied, and his obscure longings for that elusive 'more' have centred themselves on this girl. At the same time, he realizes that his undeclared passion for her is slightly ludicrous because she is so young and so difficult to talk to.

The opening of this section of the story reads like this:

'*Tabarouette*!' said the waitress, depositing on their table a bowl of potato chips. 'Me, I'm scared of lightning!'

Turning the glass vase-thing upside down, she lighted the candle inside.

'Cider?' she repeated.

'No?' said Paul.

'Oh, well,' said Norma, 'I'll have what-do-you-call-it that goes cloudy.'

'Pernod', said Paul. 'And a Scotch, please.'

'Ice?'

'They feel squishy', said Norma, stretching out her leg.

'Umm?'

'My sandals.'

He looked down at her foot.

It was the Happy Hour in the bar on the main floor of the Château Laurier. People drifting in were pantomiming distress and amazement as they eased out of sodden raincoats or used the edge of their hands to wipe rain from eyebrows and foreheads. Men were seating themselves gingerly and loosening from their knees the cling of damp cloth; women were being casually dangerous with umbrellas. Necks were being mopped with handkerchiefs; spectacles were being polished with bar napkins.

I'm very pleased with this passage. As I recall, it took me three long days to write. Criticism in Canada describes me as a traditional and conventional writer but this writing is very far from what my critics think they mean by 'conventional'.

How to describe what it does?

The first thing to say about it is that it is concerned with more than the ordering of drinks.

This is the first time we have met the girl, Norma, outside Paul Denton's thoughts and picturings of her and so this brief passage is concerned with characterization. The characterization is traditional enough though economical in its compression. What do we learn about her?

We learn that she asks – presumably through Paul – for cider, a drink not normally available in most bars and definitely not available in the bars of large hotels. We learn that she doesn't know the name Pernod. The hyphenating of 'what-do-you-call-it' and the awkwardness of 'that goes cloudy' suggest a slightly childish quality. Her use of the word 'squishy' and her stretching out of her leg to show him the squishiness reinforce this suggestion.

Now let's look at the same lines from a different point of view. Their arrangement is meant to convey something of the rush to shelter they've made from the downpour; they're still a little breathless, perhaps. The *movement* of the lines is slightly confused and intentionally so. In the line ' "Cider?" she repeated.' the speaker *must* be the waitress responding to the question that does not appear in the text but I intended a fraction of confusion. The 'she repeated' is intended to suggest the waitress's surprise at the request. The speaker of the line ' "Ice?" ' is intentionally not identified or answered.

These tiny ambiguities also serve the function of drawing the reader more actively into the dialogue.

After the line 'He looked down at her foot.' the writing changes focus. If the first twelve lines were in close-up, the camera, as it were, now draws back into a longer shot which more thoroughly establishes locale. But notice the camera movement from people, men, women, down to necks and spectacles. It is a sequence that starts wide and then moves into a series of cuts which are much closer up. This is because the next line of the story moves back into the close-up of dialogue between Norma and Paul.

Notice in passing, he said modestly, the felicity of 'loosening from their knees the cling of damp cloth'; it is the *sound* to which I wish to draw your attention.

Everything about the writing that I've so far mentioned is traditional enough. Only its extreme compression is a departure.

But now I want to draw your attention to what is my central point.

The first twelve lines are certainly concerned with the ordering of drinks, and with characterization and with setting, but at the same time the *essence* of the lines is the *awkwardness* which exists between Norma and Paul. Although most of the lines are *speech*, they are, essentially, a mapping of *silences*. There is an *emotional* movement in these lines. They wind down to silence. They are stopped by the line 'He looked down at her foot.' This is a 'heavy' line, a 'plonking' line, a line, if you'll notice, of successive heavy stresses; it captures, I feel, something central in the scene and in the relationship.

These lines are what I meant by 'new verse forms'.

By using the word 'new', I am making no claims to originality. Hemingway structured a whole story on the device – 'Hills Like White Elephants' – and frequently used some non-dialogue variation of the basic device in other stories. But the device was not original with him. The love-scenes in P.G. Wodehouse must offer more than one example; the device feels as if it might well have derived from comedy or farce. I'm sure that a little thought would turn up dozens of examples with many variants and many purposes.

So 'new' the device isn't, but what does one *call* this general kind of trope?

Until things are *named*, they do not, in a sense, fully *exist*. If we had a term for what I just demonstrated to you (let us call it an x), we could then say: 'Metcalf suggests the relationship by means of an x.' We could *then* go on to the far more interesting question of whether it was a good x or a bad x.

But, of course, before we could even talk about an x, we would have to have identified it and collected numerous examples. Such work seems to me vitally necessary but I have neither the time nor the temperament.

Let us say, for the sake of argument, that there are fifty such 'new verse forms', fifty such rhetorical devices, in common use by contemporary writers, and that not one of them has a commonly agreed–upon name. Doesn't this argue that criticism is positively condemned to imprecision and vain groping? To inevitable misunderstanding?

Because we lack the critical terminology, much of what goes on in stories remains misunderstood or undervalued or, worst of all, invisible. I have never seen any criticism anywhere which has the terminology to describe the technical achievements of a story by, say, Eudora Welty. Or, come to that, even of Hemingway. Criticism, it seems to me, lags light years behind the techniques which we are always extending and refining; no critical language exists to chart our explorations.

Very little critical work has been done to identify the typical forms of beginnings, developments, or endings. There exists no real critical vocabulary to describe the shape even of the classical 'epiphany' story. Existing critical descriptions of point of view tend to suffer from hardening of the arteries; they're inadequate to catch the quicksilver movements and shadings in contemporary work.

I am suggesting, then, as humbly as I can, that the contemporary story is vitally rich and fiendishly subtle and that it is, for critics, *terra* which is close to *incognita*.

Ray Smith

TRUST ME – HAVE I EVER TOLD YOU A FICTION BEFORE?

TRUST: Of course we judge books by their covers: a panic-stricken damsel fleeing a ghostly mansion promises a gothic romance; an open medical bag with a bottle of cyanide prominently displayed indicates a detective story in the tradition of Agatha Christie; while a tasteful print from the Tate suggests a Penguin or Oxford classic.

Titles are also usually indicative: *Velvet Moonlight, The Murder of Roger Ackroyd, Vanity Fair.*

But these external clues are not merely informative: they calibrate the judgements we expect to apply. The mystery must have its poisons right, but is excused wooden characters; the romance must touch the right emotional keys, but can fudge on period architecture or politics; the classic we measure against more stringent standards.

With genre works, the relationship is fairly simple because the experience we are looking for is essentially a repeated one: a Christie for Christmas must be the same as last year's, just as the tree, the carols, and the plum pudding must be the same. We trust that if she has changed anything substantial she will warn us: *A Caribbean Mystery, Evil under the Sun*, or *Murder on the Orient Express* clearly do not take place in St. Mary Mead. We trust that P.D. James's Inspector Dalgleish will not pistol-whip a suspect, that Mike Hammer will not turn gay.

How we trust a work of literature is altogether more complex. If, as literate adults, we approach a classic such as *Emma* or *War and Peace*, we do so with the knowledge that generations of critical readers of sundry predilections have judged them to be masterpieces, although a minority demur.

First published in *How Stories Mean.*

However, the books and their authors are likely to have our trust as a ground. What arguments we do have – that Jane Austen is prissy or bourgeois, that *War and Peace* is flawed by the didactic sections – are perhaps matters of taste, or objections in detail; but we are likely to concede that the works and their authors are not to be dismissed lightly.

A first collection or novel by an unknown is in a different position. When they first appeared, *Dance of the Happy Shades* and *Catch-22* had to make their own ways with little help. Yet both books soon established themselves as works to be taken seriously: both earned trust.

I must digress. I was amazed recently when a classroom discussion evoked heated argument on critical authority. The students argued over the relative merits of judgement by generations of readers, mass sales, a select group of critics, adoption into the canon, individual taste, and other such categories as have from time to time been advanced as authoritative. Had these been regular students taking a compulsory English course I would have taken the incident as a serendipitous outbreak of philosophical enquiry by teenage mutant ninja derridas. But they were some of the best students I have ever encountered; they had all read a wide variety of literature and had studied logic and the history of philosophy; they have alert and enquiring minds. Yet they did not see at once that most questions of aesthetic judgement must be fuzzy. The problem is that aesthetics is a sloppy business, and the philosophers have not recently updated the field manuals for us; on the literary battlefield, alas, the high ground these days is occupied by the modern critical theorists, hunkered down behind their barbed wire jargon, holed up in mazes of paradox and conundrum. I am not the one to smoke them out, so I shall ignore them, and content myself with a few rough premises and categories:

- most works in the minor genres (mysteries, romances, thrillers) are not to be taken seriously, nor do their authors expect them to be taken seriously;
- some genre works (Eric Ambler's thrillers, for example) are quite good;
- most works which aspire to literature are boring, pompous, self-indulgent, or derivative, but their authors ask that they be taken seriously, and so they should be in praise or condemnation;
- the canon of the great works of literature in English is probably close to

the mark up to about the First World War, but it is not perfect because it cannot be;

- the distinction between first-ranked and second-ranked works will always be unfair: while *Hard Times* is canonical, *North and South* is not, yet I doubt the first is superior to the second in a degree proportionate to the difference in numbers of readers or in critical attention;
- I have used the terms 'classic', 'work of literature', and 'works to be taken seriously' in seemingly casual senses; a classic is a work which has been taken seriously for perhaps a century or more, while the other terms seem obvious enough; I am being about as rigorous as I can be and readers searching for attempts at definitions in such areas must look elsewhere;
- while I understand that *The Stones of Venice* or *The Decline and Fall of the Roman Empire* may well be great works of literature, dealing with them or with poetry or drama or other variants complicates the job too much and needs too much definition; I am here concerned with questions about fine prose fiction, especially the novel.

No doubt all this seems commonsensical. But I wanted to establish some distinctions before getting to some points which are perhaps not so obvious:

- the trusted writer can take chances;
- interesting writing is only accessible through trust;
- what is innovation and originality in a trusted master seems self-indulgence or impertinence in an untrusted unknown.

Here I should distinguish the various sorts of trust I am discussing: the writer must trust himself to be able to solve the problems; he must trust that the reader is willing to follow him to his solutions; the reader must trust that the writer knows his job and will play fair; and the reader must trust himself to distinguish the real from the bogus, the blithe from the facile, the profound from the dense.

The genre writer gains the least from trust. Because the reader wants a repeated experience, the writer tampers at his peril with the elements he has established in his previous works. The detective writer Nicolas Freeling is an interesting case in point. His Van der Valk ('From/of the Falcon') novels were quickly recognized by aficionados as wonderfully subtle and sophisticated works; glowing reviews, enthusiastic word of mouth, and green Penguin covers swelled his readership. Critics tried to reassure the doubtful that the books are related to the Simenon tradition of the psychological mystery: 'They're not *that* different.' In fact, with their playful rococo progresses, they are very different from Simenon's austere fables. And Simenon could repeat his Maigrets seemingly endlessly; Freeling clearly loathed repetition, and tried a number of innovations to keep his own interest alive. But after fewer than a dozen books, he killed off Van der Valk, moved on to a new detective, the Frenchman Henri Castang, and tried some regular novels. I doubt he has since achieved the same sales, but I expect he is a happier man and probably a better writer than he would have been were he now slogging through his twenty-seventh Van der Valk.

In regard to serious literature, we must distinguish several categories of work and categories of trust. Among works by dead authors, there are the classics which were written when the author was already acclaimed – *Emma*, *War and Peace*, or *Bleak House* – and the classics which were written when the author was unknown or obscure – *Pride and Prejudice* or *Wuthering Heights*. There are the contemporary works by authors who are respected, acclaimed, or even loved – Alice Munro's work after about 1980 – and those – Alice Munro's work before about 1970; or *Catch-22* – by unknown or obscure writers.

Two qualifications. First, I use *Dance of the Happy Shades* and *Catch-22* because, although they are not strictly contemporary with this investigation, they have been widely accepted for a long enough time that they are at least candidates for canonization, and are recent enough that many of my readers may recall their publication. Second, I realize that works by unknowns in the past faced problems at publication similar to those faced by contemporary meteors, but I distinguish the two because *our* relations with, for example, *Wuthering Heights* are very different from those of its first readers.

To begin with the case of a classic by an acknowledged master. Someone, perhaps Granville-Barker or Dover Wilson, made the point that it is impossible to find a literate English speaker for whom *Hamlet* is a fresh, surprising theatrical experience. In various jurisdictions throughout the English-speaking world, school children still read *Great Expectations* or *A Tale of Two*

Cities. Whether this is a fruitful pedagogical experience, I'll leave to others; in any case, everyone knows that Dickens is an acknowledged master and he still has a great many adult readers outside of the classroom. What is the nature of the trust between this writer and these readers? An extremely complex one.

Let me use *Bleak House* as an example. A hypothetical non-academic fan of Dickens enters the work expecting eccentric characters, suspense, amusing scenes, heart-wrenching death or illness, and a certain amount of social criticism. He will be prepared for Dickens' elaborate descriptions, his coincidences, his stereotypes, especially his stereotypical young women. And he will not be disappointed, for *Bleak House* is a masterwork and it is pure Dickens. But how would such a reader describe the book?

Well, it's about a court case that never ends ...

But the case in itself is not really very important, surely?

And about various people searching out the relationship between the proud Lady Dedlock and her natural child, Esther Summerson ...

But there is so much else going on along the way.

Oh, certainly: there are orphans and abandoned children of one sort and another, and there are people who work for charity, but neglect their own families ...

But finally the plots and themes shimmer before us.

Well, one remembers the weather – a lot of fog and rain and some snow storms ...

Why?

Well, the fog symbolizes the insanity of Chancery Court where nothing is decided and no one knows what is happening, and the rain, usually in Lincolnshire, symbolizes the gloom which hangs over the childless Dedlock family, and the snow storms seem to come when reality arrives with some nasty truths ...

Come, come, only an academic reads for symbolism!

True, but finally, of course, it is that great cast of characters that you remember. John Jarndyce the Guardian, Harold Skimpole the child, Miss Flite, Krook, Nemo, the man from Shropshire, Esther, proud Lady Dedlock, little Jo the sweep, the Pardiggles and Jellybys, Caddy Jellyby, Mr Turveydrop and his Deportment, Mr Guppy, Mr Tulkinghorn, the Smallweeds, the Snagsbys, Mr George and Phil Squod, the Bagnets – and many more, any number of others – all so marvellous ...

Dickens repays this reader's trust; this ability to satisfy the generality of people earned him many readers during his lifetime, and continues to please many today. This is interesting because *Bleak House* is in many ways a very curious book. How did Dickens hold it together in his head? What did he think it was about? Is it really about any one thing? Any three things? What does 'about' mean? For those who don't know it, *Bleak House* is a great sprawling work: far more than *War and Peace*, it is, in Henry James's phrase, a 'large loose baggy monster' which often must seem (as *War and Peace* never does) beyond the author's control. Yet I contend, but cannot prove, that Dickens was so confident that during composition, and despite the detailed plan he made, he could allow the book to explode in any number of directions. It was also published serially during composition, and was written at Dickens' usual furious pace. He could do this because he trusted himself to pull it off, he trusted the material and the form to expand without fatal danger, and he trusted his readers to follow him. Even leaving aside the fast writing and serial publication, a previously unpublished writer could only take this sort of chance if he were wilful or supremely self-confident, but would most likely proceed with more bravado than bravery. Among the few who might have pulled off such an audacious feat, it seems to me, is Emily Brontë; in a sense, the various extremities of *Wuthering Heights* are at least as strange as the extensions of *Bleak House*.

Emily Brontë was not quite a 'previously unpublished writer': the collection of poems by her and her sisters appeared while she was writing her novel, but it only sold two copies. Nor was she strictly a novice writer, for she and her siblings had been writing almost non-stop since childhood. Nor was she quite as isolated as we sometimes think her: she spent a year at school in Brussels and had access to current journals such as *Blackwood's Magazine*. Despite all this, we can fairly contrast the virtually unknown and reclusive woman writing *Wuthering Heights* with the famous and gregarious big city buster writing *Bleak House* four or five years later. In terms of the trust they could expect, what a different experience it must have been for them.

And yet she managed it. If we probe down into the text with the receptors of the sensitive reader, we can, I think, see through the screens of words and scenes and see her at work: Emily Brontë didn't so much trust us as dare us to trust her. We can sense her sitting in the shadows and murmuring: 'Follow this if you will!' Looked at with a cool eye, Catherine Earnshaw is the most selfish, temperamental, and insufferable main character, male or female, in the English novel. Heathcliff is a monster, and, for our purposes, more interesting. He helps Hindley Earnshaw to his destruction then brutalizes Hindley's son, Hareton; tricks Isabella into marriage only so he can get revenge and a hold on her money; kidnaps Cathy Linton and forces her to marry his beastly son, Linton Heathcliff, whom he then virtually murders; bribes a lawyer so that Edgar Linton cannot change his will; and twice digs up Catherine's body, the second time sixteen years after her death. Yet, when we read carefully, Heathcliff is sympathetic. The book is a stunning achievement, one that even her sister Charlotte found dangerous. Modern judgements on Emily generally agree on her audacity, and the following remarks by F.R. Leavis are typical. Consider the various sorts of trust implied:

> The genius [of the Brontës], of course, was Emily. I have said nothing about *Wuthering Heights* because that astonishing work seems to me a kind of sport. ... [S]he broke completely, and in the most challenging way, both with the Scott tradition that imposed on the novelist a romantic resolution of his themes, and with the tradition coming down from the eighteenth century that demanded a plane-mirror reflection of the surface of 'real' life.[1]

But perhaps the most interesting aspect of trust is the moment the reader agrees to grant it. As I have said, it could well happen before the reader opens the covers, or it might not happen until a third reading, but when it does happen it entirely changes the aspect in which the reader takes every interesting element of the book. Once we accept that Dickens, for example, is not just bumbling along, but that he *knows what he is doing, where he is going, and why*, then we can relax and enjoy the adventure; and Dickens, sure of our trust, can fly.

It is the failure to trust which makes reviewers criticize a book for not being another book.

---

1 F.R. Leavis, *The Great Tradition* (Harmondsworth: Penguin, 1972) 39.

It is the failure to trust which favours conservative taste.

It is the failure to gain trust which drives young writers to suicide ... or to the insurance business.

I cannot tell readers when to trust – readers must trust their own instincts – but part of developing our taste as readers involves learning to trust that writers know what they are doing, that they are doing it on purpose, that (usually) they have thought through (though not necessarily planned) everything from the whole architecture of the book down to the placing of that particular comma.

The first work I read by Leon Rooke was *Shakespeare's Dog*. It had won the Governor General's medal, but I'm no more likely than the next person to be impressed by awards, so I entered the book without bestowing trust automatically. The tale, told by the title character, is ripe with an earthy archaic and invented vocabulary, a voluptuous scatology. But a few pages into it I came upon a word which would have been unknown in Elizabethan times: a mistake? Perhaps, because the book has the feel (as does most of Leon's work) of being written at speed, in a concentrated state, almost a trance. But when I found a second anachronism a few pages later I knew Leon was deliberately allowing them. At that moment I gave him my trust. I was relieved, but knowing his reputation I was not surprised. The next time I saw Leon, I put this question to him:

'A moment must have come when you had to decide whether or not you were going to use anachronistic vocabulary: how did you feel when you made the decision?'

Long pause.

'A great ... emetic release.'

Readers of the book will understand.

LISTS AND PARTICULARITY: Several years ago I wrote a piece[2] suggesting, among other things, that the vocabulary we use to talk about fiction is not satisfactory to writers or readers because it was developed by and for critics. I wanted to give names to the things I could see on the page as I

---

2 'A Refusal To Mourn ...', *Carry On Bumping*, ed. John Metcalf (Toronto: ECW, 1988).

wrote, or as I read the works of others. I knew other writers shared my problem, for they are always searching for words to describe their work. I offered some alternative words, and suggested writers might profitably change or enlarge my list. It would be redundant to republish the relevant section here, but I think readers might find some use in an expanded exploration of two of the terms, LISTS and PARTICULARITY.

For most critics, a LIST is simply an anti-artistic jumble, a refugee from the social sciences, barely better than a table of statistics, a piece of business the writer was too lazy to make pretty. But for the writer, a list is a complex selection from the tumble of people, of things, of the *stuff* of the world. The selection of things, how the selection is made, what is left out, how it is ordered: all these tell much about the world being created, of its relation to, or fit with, or penetration of the actual world. A list is a particularly concentrated distillation, and therefore a writer is making himself vulnerable or obvious in his lists.

Consider this list: Ypres, Vimy Ridge, Dieppe. Important or obscure on the great stage of human history, these names should explode in the Canadian consciousness with technicolor fireworks. For Australians, the equivalent list is perhaps Gallipoli, Singapore, Tobruk. The names are so powerful that they do not even need a context such as, 'Members of her family had fought at ...' Lists such as this should not be used lightly, lest they become devalued. Consider the sacrilege when the six million Jews who perished in the Holocaust are invoked in a trivial argument: I once heard this happen during a procedural squabble in a college departmental meeting.

Some lists are more subtle. Elizabeth Barrett Browning asks the question: 'How do I love thee?' and answers with a list: 'Let me count the ways.' Shakespeare's 'Shall I compare thee to a summer's day' is a similar list, as is 'My mistress' eyes are nothing like the sun'. In these three we are perhaps not immediately aware that we are reading a list. By contrast, Sonnet 66 is unmistakable:

Tired with all these, for restful death I cry:
As, to behold desert a beggar born,
And needy nothing trimmed in jollity,
And purest faith unhappily forsworn,
And gilded honor shamefully misplaced,

And maiden virtue rudely strumpeted,
And right perfection wrongfully disgraced,
And strength by limping sway disablèd,
And art made tongue-tied by authority,
And folly (doctor-like) controlling skill,
And simple truth miscalled simplicity,
And captive good attending captain ill.
   Tired with all these, from these would I be gone,
   Save that, to die, I leave my love alone.

The repeated *and* foregrounds the list, as if daring the reader to object. A much more subtle list appears in Sonnet 129:

Th' expense of spirit in a waste of shame
Is lust in action; and, till action, lust
Is perjured, murd'rous, bloody, full of blame,
Savage, extreme, rude, cruel, not to trust;
Enjoyed no sooner but despisèd straight;
Past reason hunted, and no sooner had,
Past reason hated as a swallowed bait
On purpose laid to make the taker mad:
Mad in pursuit, and in possession so;
Had, having, and in quest to have, extreme;
A bliss in proof, and proved, a very woe;
Before, a joy proposed; behind, a dream.
   All this the world well knows; yet none knows well
   To shun the heaven that leads men to this hell.

The items in lines three and four are unexpected and shocking, coming down like hammer blows, rhythmic repetitions, the rhythms combined with the power of the words to make this list an incantation. The complexity of the relations between the later items is clearly enough indicated by the end-of-line punctuation[3] between lines four and twelve: one non-end-

---

3 The Pelican edition, ed. Douglas Bush and Alfred Harbage.

stopped, one full-stopped, one with a colon, one with a comma, and five with semi-colons, with a sixth semi-colon within a line. The punctuation (admittedly quirky in this edition) only suggests the more interesting complexity of sound and sense. This complexity (whatever the punctuation) shows us a writer pirouetting audaciously, stretching the form, working with an apparently crude device, yet crafting from it one of his finest sonnets.

A more mechanical use of a list is common in the detective novel: when Hercule Poirot examines the body in the library, we are given a list of items in the corpse's pocket. More evocative, more sensual at least for male readers, is that other list, the contents of a woman's handbag. It is a most dreadful rule of etiquette that a man must never go through a woman's handbag, for there she carries the talismans of her sexuality. When the detective empties the handbag for our examination, we may find the telltale ticket stub, the book of matches from an intimate café, the key to the back-street hotel. More likely we will have listed for us her lipstick, her cologne, her mascara. Perhaps we shall even find a spare package of pantyhose, that ghostly skin she wears from toe to waist. A body-in-the-library mystery will no doubt include a small bottle of pills: tranquillizers because she feels guilt; birth control pills because she is having an affair with another suspect; or poison. In harsher modern fiction, we are liable to find even more revealing devices: drug paraphernalia, a booklet on venereal disease, a packet of menstrual tampons.

Lists can be as obtrusive as those in Rabelais or as subtle as those in Jane Austen. This bracketing is suggestive. Rabelais is at the far end of a scale, inhabiting an edifice of self-conscious constructs, a building with the plumbing and such not hidden behind the plasterboard, but on the outside of the building: a Pompidou Centre of words. At the other end, Jane Austen almost entirely eschews lists of things. In this rare example, one of two from *Pride and Prejudice*, she is getting through the business of moving Elizabeth Bennet from her home to Darcy's estate in Derbyshire:

> It is not the object of this work to give a description of Derbyshire, nor of any of the remarkable places through which their route thither lay; Oxford, Blenheim, Warwick, Kenelworth, Birmingham, &c. are sufficiently known.

This list is so obtrusive that most critics would prefer to ignore it; this is not real Jane Austen. Of course they are right, but the novel was still a rude and unruly form, and Jane Austen herself was in the process of cleaning up most of its crudities. I rather enjoy it as proof that she could be completely ruthless when she saw the need to get her heroine from one place to the other. And in three recent readings of *Emma*, I noticed no list such as this one, because by the time she wrote that mature masterwork she had learned better ways of doing things.

But if Jane Austen largely avoids lists of objects, she is a genius with lists of attributes. For even a pair of adjectives make a list, and putting together such lists is an inescapable part of the writer's day. The following immortal example (which concludes the opening chapter of *Pride and Prejudice*) should serve to make the case:

> Mr Bennet was so odd a mixture of quick parts, sarcastic humour, reserve, and caprice, that the experience of three and twenty years had been insufficient to make his wife understand his character. *Her* mind was less difficult to develope. She was a woman of mean understanding, little information, and uncertain temper. When she was discontented she fancied herself nervous. The business of her life was to get her daughters married; its solace was visiting and news.

I would go so far as to suggest that all creative writing students be made to study this paragraph for a month or two. They would progress to other writers only when they had mastered the variations, the rhythms, the sheer brio of: the four attributes, two with adjectives, of Mr Bennet; the perfect triplet of Mrs Bennet; her little doubled 'discontented' sentence; the efficient semi-coloned conclusion. It is in such passages that we begin to learn to read the music of prose, so much more subtle, self-effacing, and beguiling than the heated music of poetry.

I should add two points about the lists I myself have constructed in presenting lists. First, I generally used groups of three items – 'her lipstick, her cologne, her mascara' or 'subtle, self-effacing, and beguiling' – because groups of three have the feel of rationality: two hardly seem a group, while four or five are long-winded. Second, the list which is most evocative is the one given in greatest detail: the items in the handbag. Surely many male readers felt a slight, secret voyeuristic thrill as they imagined sniffing the cologne, or testing the texture of the pantyhose between finger and thumb. And surely many female readers felt a surrogate violation as each item was held up for examination: 'Put those tampons back, you pig!'

Of course, this is exactly what the writer wants – to get past our eyes, past our defences, past our literary judgement and back through our senses to the secret lusts and fears of our souls, for it is here that much of art operates. (Those who doubt that Jane Austen stirs secret terrors need only consider the implications in Elizabeth Bennet's refusal of Mr Collins' proposal; or, in *Mansfield Park*, the angry lecture Fanny Price receives from Sir Thomas Bertram when she refuses to marry Henry Crawford.) A writer can evoke these lusts or fears with any number of strategies, and a list is only one of them. The quality which gives a list the power to move us is contained in the individual items in the list, a quality I call PARTICULARITY.

Flaubert sought *le seul mot juste*, and Orwell fought the lies which lurk in the dead words of politicians and their flacks. Particularity is an expression of these impulses, of course, and there is no point my repeating them. But I should like to touch on two implications.

Particularity often appears as a negative, as an absence of, for example, unnecessary detail. It seems to me natural that writers are more liable to notice this than are readers. They are more aware, I think, of the infinite number of choices which another writer had to make. Is that a cat sleeping by the hearth? A kitty by the grate? A tabby by the mantelpiece? A feline by the fender? Is it a Manx cat with no tail or a pussy which is a piece of tail? Is the cat called Geoffrey? Hodge? Old Possum? Andrew Lloyd Webber? Is it innocent white, sinister black, or homey tortoise-shell? Or:

> The other day upon the stair
> I met a cat who wasn't there;
> He wasn't there again today,
> O, how I wish he'd go away!

That is, perhaps the cat was too sentimental, too much the cliché cat, and like the Cheshire cat just disappeared – somewhere around the fourth draft. Modern critical theorists are fond of deriving logical cats which are not there: by turning the work upside-down or inside-out to find the unintended other cats. Although my philosopher friends assure me that literary theorists are simply wild cats, philosophically untamed, the notion of the absent other cats is entirely valid, and fiction writers were investigating their nine lives long before the critics tried swinging them in their tiny rooms. You sense the absent cat after you have lived in every room in the house and have found no unnecessary cats, dogs, people, conversations, descriptions, adjectives: when, in short, you have read two or three novels by Jane Austen and have gradually realized that everything is necessary, nothing is unnecessary, all is in its proper place. There are no named cats in Jane Austen (and only one named animal, a dog) and I do not recall any unnamed cats; if there are any, they strut and fret no hour upon the stage, but slip catlike from the room. What remains are all the particulars Jane Austen needed to craft her fine novels. This negative particularity is chastity, restraint, discretion. It is, of course, a classical trait, a mark of the gregarious person; or, as Casper Gutman put it to Sam Spade:

> 'I distrust a close-mouthed man. He generally picks the wrong time to talk and says the wrong things. Talking's something you can't do judiciously unless you keep in practice.'

The Canadian writer most skilled at choosing the perfect particularity – and of perfect discretion in her writing – is cheerful, chatty, and classical Alice Munro.

The other implication of particularity I wish to note is by no means discreet; indeed, it draws attention to itself and therefore must also be used with exquisite restraint. This is the choice of a particular detail which is, let us say, exotic. In my earlier remarks about particularity, I mentioned with admiration *The Victory and Sanitary Porcelain Company*, a detail from John Metcalf's *Going Down Slow*. The setting is a men's toilet; here is the relevant passage:

> David mounted the stand and stood in the middle of the three stalls. He unzipped his trousers. Rubber footsteps squelched in the cloakroom. The swing-door banged open and Hubnichuk came in. They nodded. Hubnichuk was wearing a shabby blue track-suit.
>
> He mounted the stand to David's left. Standing back, he pulled down

the elastic front of his trousers. He cradled his organ in the palm of his hand; it was like a three-pound eye-roast. Suddenly, he emitted a tight, high-pitched fart, a sound surprising in so large a man.

Footsteps.

Mr Weinbaum came in.

'So this is where the nobs hang out!' he said.

'Some of them STICK OUT from time to time!' said Hubnichuk.

Their voices echoed.

Mr Weinbaum mounted the stand and stood in front of the stall to David's right.

'If you shake it more than twice,' he said, 'you're playing with it.'

Water from the copper nozzle rilled down the porcelain.

There was a silence.

David studied the manufacturer's ornate cartouche.

The Victory and Sanitary Porcelain Company.

Inside the curlicued scroll, a wreathed allegorical figure.

Victory?

Sanitation?

Mr Weinbaum shifted, sighed.

'I got the best battery in Canada for $18.00', he said.

Apart from the otiose 'There was a silence' the passage is a gem of compression, rhythm, and implication. Several details are worth noting – 'eye-roast' and 'rilled' are very good, and the punch line is unsurpassable – but what raises the episode above the common is the ornate cartouche, the name, the figure, the queries. Each little touch is brought into high relief and made unforgettable by the paragraphing and especially the italics, so that the experience of reading the novel is slowed down and concentrated on the urinal's emblem. Such a detail is so powerful, so obtrusive, so memorable that it must be perfect. Had the company had only one name, had the two names been wrong, had there been two wreathed allegorical figures, had the identity of the figure been clear, had any of these or a dozen other things been wrong, the passage would have failed and endangered the entire book.

(I might also note in passing that this incident is a fine example of FOCAL LENGTH, another term I suggested in my earlier piece. *Going Down Slow* is about spiritual poverty and moral betrayal in an ugly world. Naturally, these questions are discussed from time to time, albeit briefly, and the action puts the characters through a number of significant dilemmas. Yet in this scene, following the character's eyes and consciousness, the reader's attention is gradually pulled in from the washroom with its three stalls and outer cloak-room, to the urinal with its copper nozzle and rilling water, then to extreme close-up on the cartouche, its motto, and wreathed figure. I'll content myself with drawing attention to the point; *why* Metcalf does it is an issue for another context.)

Here, from his collection *Leaping Up Sliding Away*, is one of Kent Thompson's postcard stories:

SPIEL DER WELLEN

This is serious business. Betty has disappeared. She was performing in a *tableau vivant* at Madame Essen's – only for old friends, of course – and went rowing on the river with an old man reputed to be a millionaire. Was there a frolic? Can you imagine the sublime Betty surface-diving under a lily-pad? But she has not been seen since, and beyond the shallows that river opens up into the sea. Maddi is gone too – which is less surprising – she can be replaced easily enough in the theatricals – but unfortunately the horse has disappeared as well.

One of the main attractions of the postcard story form is the extreme compression, the use of implication, and the well-placed detail. Here we can luxuriate in the perfection of *tableau vivant*, 'reputed to be a millionaire', the river opening up into the sea, and the fact that Maddi can be replaced.

But the horse!

To appreciate the perfect particularity, the danger of this exotic choice, try substituting any of a dozen or so alternatives: dog, cat, rabbit, pig, ferret, chicken, duck, pigeon, turtle, peacock, snake, trained flea, lion, ocelot, cheetah.

It is sometimes pointed out that many intellectual pursuits such as philosophy and history aspire to the general, but that art aims to capture the particular. From my experience talking about writing with writers over a quarter of a century, I can assure my readers that lists and the particular are more important and more interesting than the critics realize. It's true; trust me.

Alice Munro

WHAT IS REAL?

WHENEVER PEOPLE get an opportunity to ask me questions about my writing, I can be sure that some of the questions asked will be these:

'Do you write about real people?'

'Did those things really happen?'

'When you write about a small town are you really writing about Wingham?' (Wingham is the small town in Ontario where I was born and grew up, and it has often been assumed, by people who should know better, that I have simply 'fictionalized' this place in my work. Indeed, the local newspaper has taken me to task for making it the 'butt of a soured and cruel introspection'.)

The usual thing, for writers, is to regard these either as very naïve questions, asked by people who really don't understand the difference between autobiography and fiction, who can't recognize the device of the first-person narrator, or else as catch-you-out questions posed by journalists who hope to stir up exactly the sort of dreary (and to outsiders, slightly comic) indignation voiced by my home-town paper. Writers answer such questions patiently or crossly according to temperament and the mood they're in. They say, no, you must understand, my characters are composites; no, those things didn't happen the way I wrote about them; no, of course not, that isn't Wingham (or whatever other place it may be that has had the queer unsought-after distinction of hatching a writer). Or the writer may, riskily, ask the questioners what is real, anyway? None of this seems to be very satisfactory. People go on asking these same questions because the subject really does interest and bewilder them. It would seem to be quite true that they don't actually know what fiction is.

First published in John Metcalf, ed., *Making It New: Contemporary Canadian Stories* (Toronto: Methuen, 1982).

And how could they know, when what it is, is changing all the time, and we differ among ourselves, and we don't really try to explain because it is too difficult?

What I would like to do here is what I can't do in two or three sentences at the end of a reading. I won't try to explain what fiction is, and what short stories are (assuming, which we can't, that there is any fixed thing that it is and they are), but what short stories are to me, and how I write them, and how I use things that are 'real'. I will start by explaining how I read stories written by other people. For one thing, I can start reading them anywhere; from beginning to end, from end to beginning, from any point in between in either direction. So obviously I don't take up a story and follow it as if it were a road, taking me somewhere, with views and neat diversions along the way. I go into it, and move back and forth and settle here and there, and stay in it for a while. It's more like a house. Everybody knows what a house does, how it encloses space and makes connections between one enclosed space and another and presents what is outside in a new way. This is the nearest I can come to explaining what a story does for me, and what I want my stories to do for other people.

So when I write a story I want to make a certain kind of structure, and I know the feeling I want to get from being inside that structure. This is the hard part of the explanation, where I have to use a word like 'feeling', which is not very precise, because if I attempt to be more intellectually respectable I will have to be dishonest. 'Feeling' will have to do.

There is no blueprint for the structure. It's not a question of, 'I'll make this kind of house because if I do it right it will have this effect.' I've got to make, I've got to build up, a house, a story, to fit around the indescribable 'feeling' that is like the soul of the story, and which I must insist upon in a dogged, embarrassed way, as being no more definable than that. And I don't know where it comes from. It seems to be already there, and some unlikely clue, such as a shop window or a bit of conversation, makes me aware of it. Then I start accumulating the material and putting it together. Some of the material I may have lying around already, in memories and observations, and some I invent, and some I have to go diligently looking for (factual details), while some is dumped in my lap (anecdotes, bits of speech). I see how this material might go together to make the shape I need, and I try it. I keep trying and seeing where I went wrong and trying again.

I suppose this is the place where I should talk about technical problems and how I solve them. The main reason I can't is that I'm never sure I do solve anything. Even when I say that I see where I went wrong, I'm being misleading. I never figure out how I'm going to change things, I never say to myself, 'That page is heavy going, that paragraph's clumsy, I need some dialogue and shorter sentences.' I feel a part that's wrong, like a soggy weight; then I pay attention to the story, as if it were really happening somewhere, not just in my head, and in its own way, not mine. As a result, the sentences may indeed get shorter, there may be more dialogue, and so on. But though I've tried to pay attention to the story, I may not have got it right; those shorter sentences may be an evasion, a mistake. Every final draft, every published story, is still only an attempt, an approach, to the story.

I did promise to talk about using reality. 'Why, if Jubilee isn't Wingham, has it got Shuter Street in it?' people want to know. Why have I described somebody's real ceramic elephant sitting on the mantelpiece? I could say I get momentum from doing things like this. The fictional room, town, world, needs a bit of starter dough from the real world. It's a device to help the writer – at least it helps me – but it arouses a certain baulked fury in the people who really do live on Shuter Street and the lady who owns the ceramic elephant. 'Why do you put in something true and then go and tell lies?' they say, and anybody who has been on the receiving end of this kind of thing knows how they feel.

'I do it for the sake of my art and to make this structure that encloses the soul of my story, which I've been telling you about', says the writer. 'That is more important than anything.'

Not to everybody, it isn't.

So I can see there might be a case, once you've written the story and got the momentum, for going back and changing the elephant to a camel (though there's always a chance the lady might complain that you made a nasty camel out of a beautiful elephant), and changing Shuter Street to Blank Street. But what about the big chunks of reality, without which your story can't exist? In the story 'Royal Beatings', I use a big chunk of reality: the story of the butcher, and of the young men who may have been egged on to 'get' him. This is a story out of an old newspaper; it really did happen in a town I know. There is no legal difficulty about using it because it has been printed in a newspaper, and besides, the people who figure in it are all long dead. But there is a difficulty about offending people in that town who would feel that use of this story is a deliberate exposure, taunt, and insult. Other people who have no connection with the real happening would say, 'Why write about anything so hideous?' And lest you think that such an objection could only be raised by simple folk who read nothing but Harlequin Romances, let me tell you that one of the questions most frequently asked at universities is, 'Why do you write about things that are so depressing?' People can accept almost any amount of ugliness if it is contained in a familiar formula, as it is on television, but when they come closer to their own place, their own lives, they are much offended by a lack of editing.

There are ways I can defend myself against such objections. I can say, 'I do it in the interests of historical reality. That is what the old days were really like.' Or, 'I do it to show the dark side of human nature, the beast let loose, the evil we can run up against in communities and families.' In certain countries I could say, 'I do it to show how bad things were under the old system when there were prosperous butchers and young fellows hanging around livery stables and nobody thought about building a new society.' But the fact is, the minute I say *to show* I am telling a lie. I don't do it to show anything. I put this story at the heart of my story because I need it there and it belongs there. It is the black room at the centre of the house with all other rooms leading to and away from it. That is all. A strange defence. Who told me to write this story? Who feels any need of it before it is written? I do. I do, so that I might grab off this piece of horrid reality and install it where I see fit, even if Hat Nettleton and his friends were still around to make me sorry.

The answer seems to be as confusing as ever. Lots of true answers are. Yes and no. Yes, I use bits of what is real, in the sense of being really there and really happening, in the world, as most people see it, and I transform it into something that is really there and really happening, in my story. No, I am not concerned with using what is real to make any sort of record or prove any sort of point, and I am not concerned with any methods of selection but my own, which I can't fully explain. This is quite presumptuous, and if writers are not allowed to be so – and quite often, in many places, they are not – I see no point in the writing of fiction.

Kent Thompson

READING & WRITING

ON THE ADVICE OF CHARLES RITCHIE (given in the Foreword to the second volume of his diaries, *The Siren Years*), I have been reading Elizabeth Bowen's *The Heat of the Day*. Haven't finished it yet. But it's a good book – although it is both its virtue and its failing that it is very much of its time. It was published in 1949; it is set in the middle of the Second World War in Britain and Ireland. It is perceptive and unsettling – both, to my mind, very good qualities in a novel.

But it also demonstrates a good deal about the literary and historical era in which it was written – the intellectual and historical circumstances of the kind demonstrated ingeniously by Bruce Duffy's *The World As I Found It* – a novel about Bertrand Russell, G.E. Moore, and Ludwig Wittgenstein, deduced and imagined from their writings and the facts available about them. *The World As I Found It* is a novel about philosophers in the contexts of their minds and their worlds.

All of which is to say that every creative writer finds himself or herself born into a certain method of thinking, a certain literary tradition/scene, and certain events (personal, national, historical) which cannot be avoided.

For Elizabeth Bowen this seems to have meant that her literary world – her literary thinking, her literary methods, even her *sentences* – were written as they were because she was born into a world usually represented by Virginia Woolf. *The Heat of the Day* is compared (favourably) to the fiction of Virginia Woolf in a quotation from a review used as a blurb on the back of the Penguin edition of Bowen's novel – and the similarities are not difficult to see.

For example, in Bowen's novel we are faced with the effect of a war on

---

First published in *How Stories Mean*.

sensibility and morality. I thought of Septimus Smith in *Mrs. Dalloway* when I encountered Elizabeth Bowen's odd man, one Harrison (no first name given; as featureless as Smith might have been without Septimus), who insinuates himself into the life of Stella Rodney. He seems to be some sort of intelligence agent, probably from that era's version of MI5. He tells her that her lover is suspected of selling information to the enemy, and he, Harrison, will hush it up if she will become his mistress. Grubby enough. Blackmail of feelings. (Impossible not to think of Graham Greene here.)

And there is, moreover, a woman who refuses to face the world outside her room and therefore lives in a room in a house for 'uncertified mental patients' (lovely term, that – and impossible not to think of Virginia Woolf) and there is, of course, an estate. We are in that time, in that place. The estate is smallish (only one servant left – with his wife and two daughters), and in Ireland. (Henry Green, too, is cited in a blurb on the back of Bowen's book.)

Furthermore, there is a neat little set piece about a factory girl and her chum who are devoted to the popular press, which tells them what to think. Of course I am interested in this: I live in Fredericton, which is full of monuments to Lord Beaverbrook, a popular-press baron (to use the old term) in Britain in the first half of this century.

The set piece about the working class is perceptive – but of course seen from the outside, despite the attempt to write in Voice. That is, the ideas about the working-class girl are almost certainly accurate, but Bowen would never for a moment consider giving her any nuance of feeling.

No, nuance of feeling is the province of the educated middle class. And how good they are at it! The sentences revise themselves in mid-stream to reach for ever more particular distinctions.

She came to a stop; he pushed against a door showing a dimmed sign, OPEN. Inside, light came up stone stairs which he took her down; at the foot he held open another door and she walked ahead of him into a bar or grill which had no air of having existed before tonight. She stared first at a row of backviews of eaters perched, packed elbow-to-elbow, along a counter. A zip fastener all the way down one back made one woman seem to have a tin spine. A dye-green lettuce leaf had fallen on to the mottled rubber floor; a man in a pin-stripe suit was enough in profile to show a smudge of face powder on one shoulder. A dog sitting scratching itself under one bar stool slowly, with each methodical convulsion, worked its collar round so that the brass studs which had been under its ear vanished one by one, being replaced in view by a brass nameplate she could just not read. Wherever she turned her eyes detail took on an uncanny salience – she marked the taut grimace with which a man carrying two full glasses to a table kept a cigarette down to its last inch between his lips. Not a person did not betray, by one or another glaring peculiarity, the fact of being human: her intimidating sensation of being crowded must have been due to this, for there were not so very many people here. The phenomenon was the lighting, more powerful even than could be accounted for by the bald white globes screwed aching to the low white ceiling – there survived in here not one shadow: every one had been ferreted out and killed.

This is of course very fine writing of a kind. It is the kind of sentence you would expect from Henry James, with some of the same intentions, as well as from Virginia Woolf. It is the linguistic attitude to the refinement of sensibility which is evident in the Cambridge philosophers of Duffy's book: exquisite sensibility; exquisite attention to language – just because language is so tricky, so ready to change and escape intention and meaning.

It is a problem which in fact the factory girl, Louie, recognizes: 'It's the taking and taking up of me on the part of everyone when I have no words. Often you say the advantage I should be at if I could speak grammar; but it's not only that. Look the trouble there is when I have to only say what I *can* say, and so cannot ever say what it is really. Inside me it's like being crowded to death....'

But Elizabeth Bowen's problem is also pretty clear: she cannot write from a factory girl's perspective without using a middle-class English which is heavily influenced by written English: look at her use of the semi-colon in the speech of a factory girl. For Bowen, language is a problem for her characters and for herself as well. The only voice she has is her own auctorial voice – and it is a voice which owes too much (sometimes) to her predecessors. At a key point in *The Heat of the Day* she writes one of the worst lines ever: 'In the street below, not so much a step as the semi-stumble of someone after long standing shifting his position could be, for the first time by her, heard.'

But I am being unfair. She is writing in the language of her time, and if we no longer use language in that way it is because our minds in prose now *work differently* than theirs. Which is why the frauds who enter literary contests with old Hemingway stories are so pitiful. They think that excellence once achieved is merely repeated in subsequent years. Of course – that view is not unusual in university English departments, either.

SO WHAT IS the World as I've Found It? It is a world which, when I began writing, was modern – as modern as a car, full of cause and effect. A world of physics and mechanics. Care for language was demonstrated by Hemingway, Fitzgerald, and George Orwell. It was, of course, Orwell who pointed out that bad writing reinforces bad thinking.

But it is a world which has shifted itself radically. In Eastern Europe an ideology which has killed countless people has fallen before Shopping. Consumerism, McDonald's hamburgers, leather jackets have defeated the Secret Police. The victory is that of Bob Newhart's television employee, Steffie. It is astonishing, and *I* certainly didn't predict it. It is amazingly absurd. We live in an absurd world.

And certain metaphors (we sometimes call them theories, and even sometimes Truth and now and then Reality) have been shoved aside: Freudianism, Marxism, New Criticism. Once upon a time there were excitable people called Leavisites. Where have they gone?

In short, we are now post-modernists (I write this on a post-modern computer instead of the modern typewriter which is still beside me), like it or not. Cause and effect have given way to connections, to linguistic anthropology. We court absurdity. We live in a Disneyland of Scholarly Exhibits. To those of us who grew up in Modern Times, the Post-Modern world is an Oddity.

But not without interest. And the *most* interesting book (so far as I'm concerned) is Steve McCaffery's *The Black Debt*. You have probably not heard of it. There is in fact probably only one review of it published. I wrote the review; it appeared in *The Fiddlehead* (No. 163).

The Black Debt is an art object as demonstration. You can't read it, nor are you expected to. Each page is almost entirely given over to phrases between commas. They mean nothing. But on every page there are some numbers (in word form) and, out of nowhere, bits of word play: a pun, a palindrome.

What McCaffery wishes to demonstrate is that the World as We've Found It is a linguistic chaos *except* that there is the possibility (nothing more) for order – indicated by the numbers – and the play of the mind with language, indicated by the puns and palindromes. This is the world where we begin to create; this is (perhaps) the creation of our world.

So this is in fact a very exciting time to be a writer – possibly because there are fewer and fewer people who can read. We are starting over again, with a new audience. But it is a time of infinite possibilities. Old forms are worn out; there are no accepted conventions. And no, I have no idea where literature is headed next.

But I do of course have some idea where I am in my scribbling and arrangement of words on paper. I know that I have a passion for brevity and on-going suggestion. And, after serving on the notorious jury for the 1989 Governor General's Award for Fiction, I have some idea of my priorities: what I value first, second, and third in fiction. I know what I want as a reader.

What seems to me the best indication of good writing is linguistic play. Not only in the narrow sense of word play (which is common to Steve McCaffery, Elizabeth Bowen – in her horrible sentence – and country music) but creative play with syntax, phrase, and balance: writing which, by its rhythms, alters the consciousness of the reader. Here are two deservedly well-known examples:

1) Call me Ishmael.
2) It is a truth universally acknowledged, that a single man in possession of a good fortune, must be in want of a wife.

In both cases we are flung into the fiction by the power of odd suggestion. Ishmael! Universally acknowledged? *Want?* Two quite different novels about two quite different worlds (almost contemporary with one another, mind) – but superb writing.

By which you may take it that I have no truck with those who insist that it is the story that counts, not the writing. You are right. Those people who believe that it is the story, or the idea for the story, which makes it work are unsuccessful Hollywood producers who make the 'sequels' to commercially successful films; or publishers who want last year's whale book (or whatever) repeated; or academics who want books which fit into their pet categories. No, the story is important and remembered because a good writer put his or her linguistic abilities to work on it. In itself it is just another story, neither more important, nor less, than the talk around the Tim Horton's counter.

But this is *not* to say that subject matter or the material world does not exist, that only language, tricky and evasive as it is, is 'Real'. It is that kind of solipsistic thinking which has post-modernists talking to themselves – which is one of their problems. And indeed, post-modernism is best demonstrated by its wickedly comic practitioners. Don DeLillo, in *White Noise*, has great fun with the idea of the signifier and the signified. (A drug dealer who offers an escape from the fear of death takes his own product. The product has a side-effect: he cannot distinguish between signifier and signified. So the protagonist shouts 'Gunfire!' and the drug dealer dives for the floor.) And Julian Barnes's mockery of deconstructionism becomes a quite touching comedy in *Flaubert's Parrot*. Deconstructionism (wretched word) as a method of understanding is only as good as its practitioner. Writers like Barnes (or D.H. Lawrence) do it well; scholars frequently do it badly.

My point is that the material world as well as literary tradition exists. There is matter as well as idea; stuff as well as word. Nobody is less fond of that pompous old fart Dr Johnson than I am, but when he kicked the stone for the lady who believed that only thought exists he demonstrated – as surely as did Albert Einstein in his great poem, $E=MC^2$ – that matter matters. And so does event in that material world. Especially for writers. Things happen – and as soon as they have happened, disappear – unless of course the writer preserves a form of them in (printed) words. So, almost exactly 100 years ago (August 1890), Joseph Conrad, sailing as a first mate, went up the Congo River and returned – broken in health and perhaps in spirit; certainly changed. In 1898 he wrote 'Heart of Darkness'. Conrad's experience was the material for the story. It was his experience which has his narrator, Marlow, see that savagery is at the heart of human life, whether we call it 'civilized' or not. There are heads on stakes in the Congo (and in

Vietnam in *Apocalypse Now*) and on London Bridge during the reign of Elizabeth I. But why did Kurtz go into the jungle and become an evident savage? Because he wanted to get rich and marry the beautiful girl.

It was a story which F. Scott Fitzgerald admired immensely. He borrowed the narrative technique of the peripheral narrator for *The Great Gatsby* and even the idea of moral failure for the sake of the beautiful girl. Kurtz betrayed civilization's professed ideals by turning savage; Gatsby betrays American dreams by helping the man who fixed the 1919 World Series – all for the love of Daisy, who owes something to Henry James's figure of the same name, although a good deal more to Fitzgerald's wife, Zelda. Literature and experience.

Some twenty-five years after Fitzgerald, Arthur Miller, writing about the jungle of American business (which he knew first-hand; his father was an immigrant who fulfilled the American dream by becoming rich – and then went bankrupt in the Depression), has a character named Uncle Ben in *Death of a Salesman* who owes a great deal to Conrad's story about the Congo. Willie Loman, failed salesman, asks Uncle Ben how to get rich. Ben demonstrates (he trips Biff and points the ferrule of his umbrella at Biff's eye and says, 'Never fight fair with a stranger, boy') and then explains that he made his fortune in Africa: 'William, when I walked into the jungle, I was seventeen. When I walked out I was twenty-one. And, by God, I was rich!'

My point is: both Fitzgerald and Miller drew on the story which Conrad wrote out of his experience, but both used their own experience as well.

And again, it is the *writing* which makes their works great – not their lives, not their debt to Conrad. (Fitzgerald was always quick to point out his admiration for Conrad's writing; but it is probable that Miller had forgotten he'd ever read 'Heart of Darkness' when he wrote *Death of a Salesman*. Ben appears in Act I, and Act I was apparently written in a rush of hours – after Miller had built a studio/shed to write it in; Miller, like Willie, was good with his hands.)

So emulating the life of the great writer is, alas, a useless exercise – although every writer I know has tried it at one point or another. Because of Fitzgerald and Hemingway, I believed I had to go to Paris, at least to have a look at it, before I was twenty-one, and did. But I knew enough not to become an alcoholic just because Fitzgerald was an alcoholic (and insisted it helped his writing) and Faulkner as well. Some young writers fall for that delusion, and understandably. It's easier to become an alcoholic than it is to become a writer.

Mind you, I think I understand the temptation. Good writing seems to come almost in a trance: it has that inevitability of those strange stories which flit through one's mind sometimes just before one falls asleep – a state which is very much indeed like that moment in drinking just before you've had too much.

But it is the writing which we must evaluate – not the lives of the authors, not their reading. What makes us read the fiction is its language, not its sources. Look back at those opening lines to *Moby-Dick* and *Pride and Prejudice*.

Now look at one of the most perfect stories ever written. Here it is in its entirety:

They shot the six cabinet ministers at half-past six in the morning against the wall of a hospital. There were pools of water in the courtyard. There were wet dead leaves on the paving of the courtyard. It rained hard. All the shutters of the hospital were nailed shut. One of the ministers was sick with typhoid. Two soldiers carried him downstairs and out into the rain. They tried to hold him up against the wall but he sat down in a puddle of water. The other five stood very quietly against the wall. Finally the officer told the soldiers it was no good trying to make him stand up. When they fired the first volley he was sitting down in the water with his head on his knees.

Of course I *would* think that's a great story, wouldn't I – given my passion for the very short story and my practice of it. But its virtues are plain: look at his use of numbers; look at the way he saves the word *puddle* for the most effective moment. But most of all, consider the image. Perhaps you can walk away from it and forget it. I could not. It has stayed in my mind for forty years – *because of the writing*, although I didn't know that when I first read it.

And while we're at it, consider the fact that it's an *unclosed* story, too – which may well be why it is so memorable. If Hemingway had continued the story to tell us who won the war, or if he had made an epiphany story out of the image, would the story continue in the reader's mind, at least in my mind, for forty years? Not likely.

But it is a story of My World as I Found It. Its existence might well explain my passion for the very short story. But not, I suspect, without other parts of the world of my youth like *Reader's Digest*, which was for years the only magazine in our house. (Oh, all right, there were two others: *Country Gentleman*, because my father was a high-school teacher only because the family farm failed, and sometimes *Life*. Like Susan Sontag, I was stunned by the pictures in *Life* of the liberation of the Nazi death camps.)

So perhaps my practice of the postcard story form was inevitable – as it was (I discovered, when I began putting together the anthology *Open Windows*) for so many others who also seemed to have grown up with brief forms of writing exemplified by both *Reader's Digest* and Ernest Hemingway.

But of course the World as I Found It did not stay as I found it. It became absurd, surreal. The past and present fused. So 'Uncle Harry's Truck' owes much to my grandfather, who was a country storyteller, and 'NASA' owes something to Gus Grissom – the early astronaut (killed in a training exercise) who once, to the consternation of ground-control, took a peanut-butter sandwich into space. 'Why are you eating a peanut-butter sandwich?' asked ground-control. 'Because I'm hungry', replied Grissom. He grew up twenty miles from me. And appearance and reality have always interested me, which may be why my B.A. is in Philosophy as well as English. I would today probably be a Professor of Philosophy instead of English if I hadn't been given a big grant to study English Literature. I had the best and worst of justifications: I needed the money.

Here are three of my very short stories to demonstrate some of the things I've been talking about.

UNCLE HARRY'S TRUCK

Uncle Harry came out of the Legion to find two naked girls sitting in his pick-up truck. He was surprised. He went back into the Legion to collect his wits and have another beer. You might think he'd already had one too many, but no, he says, they were still there when he came out again. He thought they might be getting cold so he gave them the keys to the truck so they could run the heater, then went back into the Legion for another beer, but got worried about the muffler on the truck and the girls dying of monoxide poisoning so he went back out again and they were gone. He said he wasn't going to call the police. They were real good-looking. He never saw the pick-up truck again. They were one blonde and one brunette, he says, and he could say more but not in mixed company. What he's decided is that they were country and western singers on their way to Texas to get a start, and he's sticking to that. Sometimes you hear a girl duet on the radio, and there, says Uncle Harry, those are the girls who stole my truck.

NASA

Walter walked in the back door big as you please after being gone god knows how long and sat down to supper. Where had he been? NASA. SECRET MISSION. Dark of the Moon. He was having a pee when Buzz and Jack Armstrong took off and left him. They never liked him because he was average. He hadn't changed a bit. Natural, he said. Time is an illusion caused by change. He has the same supper every night: two fried pork chops, two scoops of mashed potatoes, peas & carrots, coconut cream pie for dessert. Two fried pork chops, two scoops of mashed potatoes with gravy, peas & carrots, coconut cream pie for dessert.

UNREELING

Helen has left me and moved back to 1930. She is singing in a log-cabin Roadhouse out on old Highway 42. Almost nobody travels out that way anymore. She wears an ivory coloured evening gown and has marcelled her hair. Her lover is the owner who sometimes gives ballroom-dancing exhibitions with her. The patrons are kids who stare in wonder – not, as Helen and her lover believe, at the grace of the old ballroom dances or the sweetness of the lachrymose songs – but at the audacity of the two of them, daring to live outside their allotted time. I sometimes go there and contribute to the decor by sitting at a table wearing a fedora. But I think I am slipping out of her memory, and will disappear as soon as I am forgotten.

It is the sentence which is the fiction writer's chief tool. It is the sentence which catches the reader's mind in the material. When I wrote 'Uncle Harry's Truck' (for Erika Ritter's *Dayshift* CBC radio programme), I believed I had a good story underway when in the first line I had two – not one –

naked girls in the pick-up truck, but I was even happier when I discovered the imperative rhythms of the second sentence: *He was surprised.* It is impossible to read that line without equal stresses on the four syllables. If the line is funny (and it seems to get laughs), it is because of that rhythm. And where does it come from? From the country storyteller's laconic comment, of course – played in understatement against the outrageous opening image. But it also comes from the same use of that rhythm for a quite different purpose: Keats's refrain from 'La Belle Dame Sans Merci': *And no birds sang.* I was probably reminded of it by Farley Mowat's book title.

But there is much else in the world behind that story. The fact that I'm one of the radio generation, for example. (See Woody Allen's film *Radio Days.* He and I are the same age.) In its golden age, radio created verbal pictures (you can put a naked girl on radio, but not on TV) and used sequence very carefully. The print writer knows that readers can and do read chunks of material at a glance. But you cannot skip over sequence in radio, nor can you go back, so sequence is extraordinarily important. So radio comedy, for example, depended upon a sequence of pictures tossed into the imagination one after the other, each with a surprise. Each revised its predecessor.

The English periodic sentence does much the same thing. It relies on sequence, word order, for its effect. It is the purpose of the periodic sentence to put its power at the end. The grammarian James Sledd demonstrates its power in *A Short Introduction to English Grammar* by citing two sentences dealing with a very similar topic. The first is from an eighteenth-century traveller in Scotland: 'When we were taken upstairs, a dirty fellow bounced out of the bed on which one of us was to lie.' The second is from the much-damned Samuel Johnson: 'Out of one of the beds on which we were to repose started up, at our entrance, a man black as Cyclops from the forge.' Sledd much prefers the second, and so do I. The effective sentence saves the power until the last.

Sledd avers that the periodic sentence is found chiefly in written form, and not much recently, and I suppose he is right – although it was common in radio comedy and can be heard today in any of Dave Broadfoot's Sgt Renfrew sketches for the Royal Canadian Air Farce. But to see it used badly, look again at that sentence from Elizabeth Bowen's novel: 'In the street below, not so much a step as the semi-stumble of someone after long standing shifting his position could be, for the first time by her, heard.'

Length of sentence is almost as important as sequence. Another book I've just opened is Richard Ford's *The Sportswriter*, and it seems to me his sentences are one phrase longer than usual, which may give them their gravity – in the same way that iambic pentameter is one foot longer (I think) than the habitual English statement. But length is part of Ford's style in the same way that the parenthesis (see above, and here) is part of mine. I am not sure that the use of the parenthesis is a virtue.

But another legacy of the radio generation is the incorporation of voice into the sentence in what I call 'indirect dialogue'. It is also common to the country storyteller who will say: *What he's decided is that they were country and western singers on their way to Texas to get a start, and he's sticking to that.* The storyteller incorporates the voice of the original speaker, but the key is the use of *that*. By incorporating the voice of the speaker into his own voice, the storyteller *evaluates* the speaker. Here the evaluation is found in the storyteller's use of the speaker's word *decided*.

Here's a paragraph from 'Mrs. Turner Cutting the Grass', by my college classmate Carol Shields. There is not a quotation mark in it, but I count three distinct voices.

High-school girls on their way home in the afternoon see Mrs. Turner cutting her grass and are mildly, momentarily repelled by the lapped, striated flesh on her upper thighs. At her age. Doesn't she realize? Every last one of them is intimate with the vocabulary of skin care and knows that what has claimed Mrs. Turner's thighs is the enemy called cellulite, but they can't understand why she doesn't take the trouble to hide it. It makes them queasy; it makes them fear for the future.

But the use of voice raises the problem of punctuation. It amazes me that what I am about to say is not a commonplace, but it isn't. That is: there are different punctuation systems for fiction and non-fiction. Moreover, each writer develops his or her own punctuation system.

For some reason, this obvious truth is largely ignored, especially in the academies where generations of schoolchildren are taught that comma splices are WRONG even as they are reading Alice Munro's fine stories, which are full of them. This puzzles and confuses the schoolchild who is reading Alice Munro's stories because they are examples of good writing, and yet when the child uses a comma splice in an essay, the paper is MARKED DOWN in Scornful Red.

The point is, of course, that Non-Fiction (Expository) practice is to agree on a certain number of conventions (called rules) so that what is written can be understood in a hundred years, a thousand miles away, by a person for whom English is a second language. Rules help.

But Fiction has quite different purposes – one of which is to get the spoken word onto the page – and therefore will use, *must use*, different punctuation systems. So Elizabeth Bowen makes a terrible error when she drops that semi-colon into Louie's speech.

Amazingly, however, this different punctuation of fiction is addressed by only two essays that I know of: John Metcalf's essay in *Kicking Against the Pricks* (republished in *How Stories Mean*), and Vladimir Nabokov's essay on *Madame Bovary*, which Doug Glover cites in his 1989 essay on fiction in *Quarry* (Vol. 38, No. 3).

Here's the opening of my novel *playing in the dark*, in which I try to work with fragments and suggestion (as in the postcard story) and many different voices. In fact, I think *I* am the speaker of this opening section (I will use a semi-colon), but I am imagining myself in the line at the back behind Stringy, who is going to rob the bank. The comma splices are used to deny connections.

> You could smell the drink on him when he entered the bank, he was dirty, his clothes were dirty. We left a space around him; we didn't want to look at him. His face was grimy, his long fair hair was greasy, one arm was smeared with a blue tattoo, he was wearing dirty yellow gloves, he was still drunk. It was a snake tattoo.

Purpose? For me, the writing of the English sentence is first of all the search for character, to look beneath the surface, to make the reader think twice, three times, four times. But this is not at all post-modernist. The post-modernist is interested chiefly in surfaces – or so suggests Annie Dillard in *Living by Fiction*, and I think I agree with her. She says that contemporary art

> is the art of surfaces. It no longer seeks a technique which dissolves invisibly

'down' into the depths of things. It seeks instead what might be called a new perspective, the careful flattening of forms on the surface in such a way that the depths of things float 'up' into technique. Characters' role in this fiction is formal and structural. Their claim on us is not emotional but intellectual. They are no longer fiction's center.

Yep. I think she's right. And Borges bores the ass off me. Words without a foot in the material world seem to me as memorable as whistling.

I want to look behind the story in the newspapers and on TV to the private story (which is what *playing in the dark* does, I hope); people are to me more challenging than ideas. I am the least autobiographical writer I know, but I know, too, that much of what I write is grounded in one way or another in both my experience and my reading.

Here is a draft piece from the novel I am working on these days:

Debts. He had always wanted to be a natty dresser and thought he could be somebody if he brought Italian men's fashions to Enfield, population 8700. He was a slim fellow although since his marriage he had put on weight and once Wanda his wife yelled at him, 'You're blaming me because your shoe size has gone up a half? You're blaming me for your *fat feet?*'

He was spending the money of the Booster's Club, of which he was the Entertainment Officer, to pay his shirt-supplier, and when the man in the police uniform walked into Brian's store there was a terrible moment when he wanted to confess all. Also he had done something nifty with his taxes. When he saw the man in the State Trooper's uniform he saw himself being led away in handcuffs, and everybody on Main Street came out to watch and felt sorry for him. That would be a good moment to end his life.

For what it's worth: I worked in a clothing store afternoons after school when I was a boy. The owner of a competing store had been a locally famous athlete who had become quite fat. When I was living in Toronto a couple of years ago and working for the radio programme *Later the Same Day*, I attended a Trade Show of men's clothing. I was once a government investigator and had a drunken man, left in charge of the business by his mother while she was out of town, confess to me that he cheated on his taxes. This incident obviously made a great impression on me. I used it in a very short story 'Corn Flakes', which I sent on a postcard to Carol Shields. In that story I also borrow something from *Death of a Salesman*. I acted in a production of that play when I was a graduate student. I played Uncle Ben – badly. The word *nifty* in the draft above comes from one of the Everett Coogler poems by my friend Bill Bauer. Other influences of his poetry can be found in the third story of mine quoted earlier, 'Unreeling'. Wanda's retort to her husband owes much to Hemingway's line (somewhere) that a character 'had that fat married look'. Recently I heard (somewhere) of a man whose shoe size had gone up a half size in his middle years.

But at the heart of the postcard story – at the heart of all fiction – is the Event. Something happens. In fact, when you stop to think about it, it is the Event which is the link between human consciousness and the material world. The Event is best caught by the art of fiction, not least of all because only the art of fiction can say 'he thought; she felt'.

The best example of the importance of art might be seen in the Event we call *battle*. Once a battle has ended, it has disappeared. Its only existence is in the accounts of it; and when we think of a battle – Waterloo, for example – we are in fact thinking about the accounts of it.

But, as John Keegan has pointed out so brilliantly in *The Face of Battle*, we can demonstrate that the accounts frequently (in fact, usually) cannot be squared with the material world. That is, we can see from the terrain that the battle could not have happened as the official account says it did.

Where then can we turn for an understanding of this term? Only to art – if only because the fiction writer has a range of tools available to him or her which the historian does not. So to understand this abstraction, *battle*, we have to read *The Red Badge of Courage*.

PART II: THE SHORT PART. Time passes. Between the first draft and this draft of this essay I have (not surprisingly) finished reading Elizabeth Bowen's *The Heat of the Day*. If I have given the impression that I think it is a bad novel because it has some bad lines in it, I have given a false impression. I think it is a good novel – with at least one terrible line in it. But lots of works of successful art have bad lines. The worst lines in literature are Shelley's 'I fall upon the thorns of life, I bleed' and Wordsworth's 'Nature never did betray the heart that loved her' – which sets my students in New Brunswick into howls of laughter, and rightly. It is a fatuous statement. It

will not hold up to experience or the material world. You believe that statement and you can drown – which his brother did. Surprised William. What
an idiot. But not a bad poet at times.

Between the first draft and now I have also been travelling abroad (Den-
mark) and reading. I am different than I was. I cycled up to Fyns Hoved and
met a dog who behaved much like me: running in mad circles for the sheer
delight of running.

The world shifted yet again. No sooner was the Cold War ended than the
military world hustled into the Persian Gulf. Events are taking place and
disappearing, ready to emerge again in accounts and fiction.

Travelling, I read Stanley Middleton's *Two Brothers*, Milan Kundera's
Life Is Elsewhere, Germaine Greer's *Daddy, We Hardly Knew You*, and am
now in the final pages of Paul Theroux's *My Secret History*. Theroux, it
turns out, is a great admirer of Conrad. Theroux made the decision early in
his life to go to Africa. It is a good book. Why? Because he went to Africa?
No. Because it is very well written.

Which leads me to a last consideration. I won't dignify it by using a
grander term. Nor will I say that it is in any way a conclusion.

That's because I'm increasingly wary of *conclusions* of any kind. Novels
which wrap up their loose ends become *closed books* and thereby fail. In
Theroux's *My Secret History* (which echoes the nineteenth-century porn
work, *My Secret Life*, of course), the narrator's wife condemns his writerly
practice of completing stories. Life isn't like that, she suggests. It goes on;
it's messy.

She has a point worth considering. It may well be that wrapping up novels is a mistake. I deliberately left *playing in the dark* open-ended because I
wanted it – as with the postcard stories – to continue on in the reader's mind
after the book was put back on the shelf. I wanted that unclosed quality
which I admire so much in Hemingway's very short story.

A closed story is forgettable. A story which can be *solved* is a failed story.
More often than not, the reader of an epiphany story believes that an understanding of art and the recognition of a point are the same thing. No. (This
is an old hobbyhorse of mine. I don't want the reader to escape. I don't want
anyone to walk away unscathed.) Too often, moreover, the recognition of the
epiphany erases the characters from the reader's mind. They slip away from

our memories in the intellectual procedure of recognition. We tuck them away in history.

My students despair. 'Isn't the point the point?' they ask.

No.

Next question.

Biographical Notes

MARGARET ATWOOD is the author of numerous works of fiction, poetry, and criticism. Her collections of short fiction include *Dancing Girls and Other Stories* (1977), *Bluebeard's Egg* (1983), *Murder in the Dark* (1983), *Wilderness Tips* (1991), and *Good Bones* (1992). Among her several longer fictions are *The Handmaid's Tale* (1985) and *Cat's Eye* (1988). She has edited *The New Oxford Book of Canadian Verse in English* (1982), has co-edited *The Oxford Book of Canadian Short Stories in English* (1986) and has guest-edited *The Best American Short Stories 1989*.

CLARK BLAISE is the author of several collections of short fiction, including *A North American Education* (1973), *Tribal Justice* (1974), *Resident Alien* (1986), and *Man and His World* (1992). He has written two novels, *Lunar Attractions* (1979) and *Lusts* (1983), has co-authored two books of non-fiction, and is the author of an autobiographical work, *I Had A Father* (1993). He has co-edited several anthologies.

GEORGE BOWERING is the author of numerous works of fiction, poetry, and criticism. His collections of short fiction include *Flycatcher & Other Stories* (1974), *Protective Footwear* (1978), and *A Place To Die* (1983). Among his several longer fictions are *A Short Sad Book* (1977), *Burning Water* (1980), *Caprice* (1987), and *Harry's Fragments* (1990). He has edited or co-edited a variety of anthologies.

KEATH FRASER is the author of two collections of short fiction, *Taking Cover* (1982) and *Foreign Affairs* (1985). He has edited an anthology of travel writing, *Bad Trips* (1991).

MAVIS GALLANT is the author of many collections of short fiction, including *The Other Paris* (1956), *My Heart Is Broken* (1964), *The Pegnitz Junction* (1973), *From the Fifteenth District* (1979), *Home Truths: Selected Canadian Stories* (1981), and *Overhead in a Balloon: Stories of Paris* (1985). She has written two novels, *Green Water, Green Sky* (1959) and *A Fairly Good Time* (1970), a play, and a book of non-fiction.

JACK HODGINS is the author of two collections of short fiction, *Spit Delaney's Island* (1976) and *The Barclay Family Theatre* (1981). He has written several novels, including *The Invention of the World* (1977), *The Resurrection of Joseph Bourne* (1979), *The Honorary Patron* (1987), and *Innocent Cities* (1990), and an autobiographical work, *Over 40 in Broken Hill* (1992). He has edited or co-edited several anthologies or textbooks.

HUGH HOOD is the author of numerous works of fiction, including several early novels as well as *The Swing in the Garden* (1975), *A New Athens* (1977), and subsequent novels in his epic series *The New Age / Le Nouveau Siècle*. His first collection of short stories, *Flying a Red Kite* (1962), has been republished as the first volume in his *The Collected Stories*. Among his many other books of short fiction are *The Fruit Man, The Meat Man & The Manager* (1971), *None Genuine Without This Signature* (1980), and *You'll Catch Your Death* (1992). He has published three essay collections.

NORMAN LEVINE is the author of several collections of short fiction, including *One Way Ticket* (1961), *I Don't Want To Know Anyone Too Well and Other Stories* (1971), *Selected Stories* (1975), *Thin Ice* (1979), *Why Do You Live So Far Away?* (1984), *Champagne Barn* (1984), and *Something Happened Here* (1991). He has published three collections of poetry, two novels, *The Angled Road* (1952) and *From a Seaside Town* (1970), and an autobiographical work, *Canada Made Me* (1958).

JOHN METCALF is the author of several collections of short fiction, including *The Lady Who Sold Furniture* (1970), *The Teeth of My Father* (1975), *Girl in Gingham* (1978), *Selected Stories* (1982), and *Adult Entertainment* (1986). He has published two novels, *Going Down Slow* (1972) and *General Ludd* (1980), various works of criticism, including *Kicking Against the Pricks* (1982) and *What Is A Canadian Literature?* (1988), and numerous anthologies and textbooks, including *Writers in Aspic* (1988), *The New Story Writers* (1992), *Canadian Classics* (1993), and *How Stories Mean* (1993). He has acted as senior editor for The Porcupine's Quill since 1988.

ALICE MUNRO is the author of several collections of short stories, including *Dance of the Happy Shades* (1968), *Something I've Been Meaning To Tell You* (1974), *The Moons of Jupiter* (1982), *The Progress of Love* (1986), and *Friend of My Youth* (1990). She has written a novel, *Lives of Girls and Women* (1971), and a collection of linked stories, *Who Do You Think You Are?* (1978).

LEON ROOKE is the author of many collections of short fiction, including *Last One Home Sleeps in the Yellow Bed* (1968), *The Love Parlour* (1977), *Cry Evil* (1980), *Death Suite* (1981), *The Birth Control King of the Upper Volta* (1982), *A Bolt of White Cloth* (1984), *How I Saved The Province* (1989), *The Happiness of Others* (1991), and *Who Do You Love?* (1992). He has written several longer fictions, including *Fat Woman* (1980), *The Magician in Love* (1981), *Shakespeare's Dog* (1983), and *A Good Baby* (1989), as well as several plays. He has co-edited a number of anthologies.

CAROL SHIELDS is the author of various works of fiction, poetry, drama, and criticism. In addition to several novels, including *Small Ceremonies* (1976), *The Box Garden* (1977), *Happenstance* (1980), *A Fairly Conventional Woman* (1982), *Swann: A Mystery* (1987), and *The Republic of Love* (1992), she has published two collections of short fiction, *Various Miracles* (1985) and *The Orange Fish* (1989).

RAY SMITH is the author of the short fiction collection *Cape Breton is the Thought-Control Centre of Canada* (1969) and of three longer fictions, *Lord Nelson Tavern* (1974), *Century* (1986), and *A Night at the Opera* (1992). He has published a number of essays on the art of fiction.

J. R. (TIM) STRUTHERS has won wide recognition for his efforts as a bibliographer, interviewer, critic, editor, and publisher. He is the general editor of the Critical Directions series published by The Porcupine's Quill and the editor and publisher of several titles issued by Red Kite Press. He has edited three individual collections of criticism: *Before the Flood* (1979), on Hugh Hood, *The Montreal Story Tellers* (1985), and *New Directions from Old* (1991), on Canadian short fiction. He has prepared the two-volume anthology *The Possibilities of Story* (1992) and, with John Metcalf, the collections *Canadian Classics* (1993) and *How Stories Mean* (1993).

AUDREY THOMAS is the author of several collections of short fiction, including *Ten Green Bottles* (1967), *Munchmeyer and Prospero on The Island* (1971), *Ladies & Escorts* (1977), *Real Mothers* (1981), *Two in the Bush and Other Stories* (1982), *Goodbye Harold, Good Luck* (1986), and *The Wild Blue Yonder* (1990). She has written a number of novels, including *Songs My Mother Taught Me* (1973), *Blown Figures* (1974), *Latakia* (1979), *Intertidal Life* (1984), and *Graven Images* (1993).

KENT THOMPSON is the author of a variety of works of fiction, several radio plays, and two collections of poetry. In addition to several longer fictions, including *The Tenants Were Corrie and Tennie* (1973), *Across from the Floral Park* (1974), *Shacking Up* (1980), *Married Love: A Vulgar Entertainment* (1988), and *Playing in the Dark* (1990), he has published three collections of short fiction, *Shotgun and Other Stories* (1979), *A Local Hanging and Other Stories* (1984), and *Leaping Up Sliding Away* (1986). He has edited or co-edited several anthologies.

BASS

PRINTED IN CANADA